UNDERSTANDING
T h e   A n a t o m y   o f

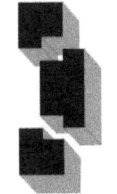
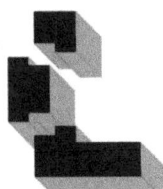

Lies, Deception

Demonization, Destruction

Coercion, Censorship

Political Correctness

Perversion, Persecution

Rebellion against Authority

Sexual Liberation, Licentiousness

Parasitic Politics, Inverse Incentives

Calling Good Evil and Evil Good

Racism, Rioting

Majoring in Minors

Circles of Corruption

William Nitardy

D. James Kennedy, "Why I believe in the Bible," Why I Believe, (Nashville: Word Publishing, 1999), p. 4-7, http://www.harpercollinschristian.com/

Scripture taken from the New King James Version®. Copyright © 1982 by Thomas Nelson. Used by permission. All rights reserved.

Appendix E Symbolic Biblical History Diagram by author
Appendix E Serpent's Head for Diagram by Lloyd Rogoski

The opinions expressed in this manuscript are solely the opinions of the author and do not represent the opinions or thoughts of the publisher. The author has represented and warranted full ownership and/or legal right to publish all the materials in this book.

Understanding The Anatomy of Evil
All Rights Reserved.
Copyright © 2016 William Nitardy
V4.0

Cover Photo © 2016 William Nitardy. All rights reserved - used with permission.

This book may not be reproduced, transmitted, or stored in whole or in part by any means, including graphic, electronic, or mechanical without the express written consent of the publisher except in the case of brief quotations embodied in critical articles and reviews.

Outskirts Press, Inc.
http://www.outskirtspress.com

ISBN: 978-1-4787-7018-3

Outskirts Press and the "OP" logo are trademarks belonging to Outskirts Press, Inc.

PRINTED IN THE UNITED STATES OF AMERICA

Acknowledgments

First I need to acknowledge my wife Diane for putting up with my absence during all those hours that were spent writing this book. Also, her proofreading that identified and corrected many clerical and other errors was invaluable.

I also want to acknowledge the many authors and publishers that gave me permission to quote liberally from their works.

I also want to acknowledge Lloyd Rogoski who created the serpent's head on the "Symbolic Biblical History Diagram" in appendix E and put up with me changing my mind on needed artwork for both the cover and diagram.

Dedication

I want to dedicate this book to all those who currently do not believe in the truth. It doesn't matter if they have come to believe false doctrines and evil philosophies through an indoctrination of false foundations that have been established in our culture or are prevented from accepting and believing the truth by the unrighteousness in their lives. The dichotomy between their unrighteous behavior and the knowledge of what their behavior should be based upon true biblical principles would haunt them if they didn't suppress the truth in their mind. We hope for those that have been deceived by the false foundations that have been established in our culture that this book makes the picture so clear between good and evil that the intellectual argument would be convincing enough for them to realize that the bible has the answer to spiritual, cultural, political and physical behavioral truth. For those that have had to rationalize away the truth because of unrighteousness in their lives we hope that the truth is clear enough to overcome the emotional attachment to the false beliefs and behavior. The bible explains this in Romans 1:18 which states:

> [18] For the wrath of God is revealed from heaven against all ungodliness and unrighteousness of men, who suppress the truth in unrighteousness, . .

Beyond the above general dedication I want to specifically dedicate this book to the people closest to me including my family, friends, acquaintances and in addition all fellow Americans that do not believe and have their faith in the truth. It is also my hope that even Christians will gain a clearer picture of the good and evil in our world that would encourage them to be better Christians and make the world a better place.

Disclaimer

When we discuss evil and condemn it, we want to be extremely clear that we are not condemning people. We write about evil because we love people and do not want to see them deceived and receive negative effects for themselves and for other people close to them, as a result of following false doctrines and philosophies. The bible teaches that we all are sinners because we have evil thoughts and do evil things. Romans 3:23 states:

[23] for all have sinned and fall short of the glory of God, . .

We are not saying that God doesn't condemn anybody. In fact, He has, He does, and He will. However, the bible also teaches that God doesn't want to condemn people. He only does it as a last resort since there is no way to justifiably reconcile them to God's holiness because of their rebellion. It is not our intent to condemn people in this book! Additionally, we are not implying that some of us are good and superior and the rest of us are evil or inferior. We are saying that none of us have any great merit in God's eyes. However, we are saying that any of us can be forgiven and given the righteousness of Jesus Christ. It is only as a result of that relationship with Jesus that our selfish, evil desires can be minimized.

The reader may be aware that some homosexual activists do not give us the freedom to separate their behaviors from their personhood. We do believe in separating beliefs and behavior from personhood since we need to condemn some beliefs and behaviors but we do not want to condemn personhoods. We look at people like computer hardware that runs software. They can choose to run good software or choose to run bad software and they always have the choice to switch from one to the other whether that is from good to bad or from bad to good. Based upon this view, condemning people wouldn't make sense except perhaps condemning our or their choices.

The goal of this book is to condemn evil and encourage people to resist it and expose it, not to condemn people that are created in the image of God.

Table of Contents

Introduction i

Part 1: Getting the true picture of evil

Chapter 1: What is the source of evil?..2

Chapter 2: How prevalent is evil? 7

Chapter 3: Attributes of Satan and God...9

Chapter 4: Concepts relating to evil...16

Part 2: How can we recognize evil?

Chapter 5: How can we recognize evil based upon what the bible says? 26

Chapter 6: How can we recognize evil based upon modus operandi?...............29

Chapter 7: How we can recognize evil by seeing "Majoring in minors"? 31

Chapter 8: How can we recognize evil based upon effects? 37

Chapter 9: How can we recognize evil based upon our conscience? 38

Part 3: How do we recognize evil based upon beliefs diametrically opposite to biblical beliefs?

Chapter 10: From cultural and political positions...43

Chapter 11: From humanism philosophies...64

Chapter 12: By comparing the Anti-Christ with the Mahdi 74

Chapter 13: By corroborating that Allah is Satan and
             that Mohamad was demon possessed 78

Part 4: Establishment of false secular foundations

Chapter 14: The false foundation of uniformitarianism and biological macro evolution 90

Chapter 15: The false foundation of relative truth vs. absolute truth 108

Chapter 16: The false foundation of the basic goodness and perfectibility of man 110

Chapter 17: The false foundation of global warming 111

Chapter 18: The false foundation of The New Tolerance and Outrage Based Coerced Conscience 113

Chapter 19: The false foundation of political correctness 115

Chapter 20: The false foundation of case law 120

Chapter 21: The false foundation of the separation of church and state 121

Part 5: Why haven't religions effectively resisted the evil progressing rapidly in America?

Chapter 22: Apostasy and heresy in christian churches 126

Chapter 23: Accepting new age and other false religions 150

Part 6: Why has evil progressed so rapidly in America?

Chapter 24: Stealth evils 156

Chapter 25: Source of diametrically opposite worldviews and control of America 193

Chapter 26: Convincing us that America is evil and should be diminished and destroyed 221

Chapter 27: America is beyond the tipping point 235

Part 7: Where is America headed politically?

Chapter 28: Hillary and the Clinton crime family 261

Chapter 29: Conservative candidates 274

Part 8: What can we do?

Chapter 30: To resist and defeat evil 280

Chapter 31: Study to strengthen our confidence in the truth of God's existence and the bible 285

Appendix A: Appeal to pastors 302

Appendix B: Letters to the editor 310

Appendix C: Why does the world hate Israel? 330

Appendix D: "From slimy goo, came me and you" 333

About the author 335

Endnotes 336

Introduction

The bible teaches that in the beginning a transcendent God created the universe including the heavens and the earth and everything in them. He created light and all matter including the design of matter with subatomic particles, forces including gravity, the physics and chemistry parameters and the level of each fixed constant.

In heaven He created angelic beings, principalities and powers. On earth He created all plant life and animal life. He created mankind in the image of God and mankind (Adam and Eve) lived in the presence of God and talked to Him.

After the creation of heaven and earth, "God saw everything that He had made," and said "indeed it was very good." Consequently, at the beginning, the harmony both in heaven and on earth was perfect. However, the bible teaches that at some point Lucifer, the anointed cherub and some of the other angels, rebelled against their creator and His legitimate authority because he or they wanted to be like God. At some time later Lucifer was not content that it was only himself and some of the angels in rebellion against God the Creator.

The bible tells the story of how Lucifer seduced Eve, and subsequently Adam through Eve, to join him in rebellion against the Creator God, the legitimate authority. Until the time that Lucifer rebelled there was no imperfection or disharmony in heaven. That was the origin of evil in heaven. Until Lucifer seduced Eve to also rebel against God by disobeying Him everything was perfect on earth with no disharmony, death or suffering. That was the origin of evil and sin in heaven and on the earth.

The bible tells the story that Lucifer (Satan) and his fallen angels have no path to redemption and are doomed ultimately to eternal punishment. However, this is not so for us (mankind) even though we were also created in the image of fallen man. Genesis 5:1-3 states:

> This is the book of the genealogy of Adam. In the day that God created man, He made him in the likeness of God. 2 He created them male and female, and blessed them and called them Mankind in the day they were created. 3 And Adam lived one hundred and thirty years, and begot a son in **his own likeness, after his image**, and named him Seth.

God has provided a path to redemption through His Son Jesus Christ for us. However, that path requires us to cease rebelling against Him. In the same way, evil will not end and we will not have peace on the earth until those who insist on rebellion against God are taken out of the way.

To understand the anatomy of evil we need to understand that all evil is based upon rebellion against God and His principles. The bible also teaches that we are the focal point of a battle between God and Satan. The battle centers around a debate of whether Satan was justified in rebelling against God and then trying to justify his rebellion. One way for him to accomplish that would be for him to influence mankind to rebel against God. Certainly, that was the case with Job. And certainly most if not all of the evil in our world revolves around Satan and the powers of darkness trying to physically and spiritually destroy mankind and the plan of God. The bible documents historically how Satan has consistently tried to destroy God's plan in many ways. Today, evil in our world is growing rapidly just like it did in the days of Noah before the flood.

Dr. David Reagan documented a plethora of various evils that are skyrocketing in America and in our world today on a Christ in Prophecy television program.[1] He points out the skyrocketing of evil in America and identifies the cause of those evils as our nation turns against God and Christianity; basically the fact that we have become a secular and Pagan nation. His comments are paraphrased below:

- Since 1973 we have murdered 4000 unborn babies per day for a total of about 60 million
- We are consuming about half the illegal drugs and are only 5% of the world population
- We are spending about 2.8 billion dollars on pornography per year out of 4.9 billion spent worldwide
- Cohabitation has increased 10 fold since 1960 with 12,000,000 cohabiting today
- Our divorce rate is the highest in the world
- 40% of children are born to unmarried women
- We spend 100 billion per year on gambling
- We have about 17.6 million adult alcoholics or have alcohol problems
- Our nation has become a debt junkie and are addicted to both government and personal debt
- We continually blaspheme God's name or His Son's name on TV and in movies
- We have forsaken Israel and demand her to surrender her heartland and divide Jerusalem, her capital city
- We are calling evil good and good evil and we are paying the price
- Our schools have become arenas of deadly violence
- Our prisoner population has increased exponentially, going from 500,000 in 1980 to 2,500,000 today
- We have 7,200,000 who are under correctional supervision

- We have 1,500,000 women reported victims of domestic violence with most not being reported
- We are currently averaging over 3,000,000 child abuse cases each year involving 6,000,000 children
- We have experienced more than 12,000,000 crimes per year more than any other nation
- Teen violence has increased exponentially, with youngsters being killed over tennis shoes
- Gangs are terrorizing our cities and even the nicest of our neighborhoods are not even safe requiring us to protect our homes with security systems and weapons
- Our money is becoming become increasing worthless
- Our economy is being choked to death by a pile of debt that is beyond comprehension
- Our major corporations and labor unions are in bondage to greed
- Our society has become deeply divided, splintered among competing groups defined by racial, religious and economic factors
- Our families are being destroyed by an epidemic of divorce
- Our entertainment industry consists of barbarians amusing barbarians
- One of our fastest growing businesses is the Pagan practice of tattooing and body piercing
- Our universities and media outlets are controlled by radical leftists who hold God in contempt
- Our federal government has become top heavy with bureaucrats that have become insensitive to taxpayers
- Our politicians have become more concerned with power than service
- All levels of government have become increasingly oppressive seeking to regulate every aspect of our lives
- Taxation has become confiscatory in nature
- Our legal system has been hijacked by activists who desire to impose their will on the people regardless of what the people desire
- Our freedom of speech has been threatened by hate crime legislation
- Our forums of sports are becoming increasing violent, reminiscent of the gladiators of ancient Rome
- Our society has become "star struck" more interested in celebrities than people of integrity
- Our churches have been caught up in an epidemic of apostasy as they set aside the word of God in an effort to cozy up to the world and gain its approval

- We are experiencing one major natural disaster after another in unprecedented volume and ferocity
- We have become afflicted with a plague of sexual perversion producing an army of hard core militant homosexuals

All of these skyrocketing evils in America have been occurring at the same time that God and Christianity have become increasingly less popular and where our culture is increasingly hostile toward God and Christianity. Dr. Reagan recounts the story of Jim Garlow, a Nazarene minister, who pastors the Skyline Church in La Mesa California in the same program. Pastor Garlow presented the following table to the National Religious Broadcasters. He is considered to be an expert on Church history. The Quoted table documented below shows the change in which the culture has viewed God and Christianity:

1607-1833	The Establishment (236 years)
1833-1918	The predominant Force (85 years)
1918-1968	The sub-dominant Force (50 years)
1968-1988	A sub-culture (20 years)
1988-1998	A Counter Culture (10 years)
1998-2008	An Antithetical Culture (10 years)
2008- Present	A persecuted Culture (7+ years)[2]

This illustrates that when we rebel against God and suppress biblical truth, evil thrives and the promoters of truth become the persecuted class.

Satan has many deceptions that he uses to keep us in rebellion against God. One way Satan attempts to destroy us is by making self-destructive behaviors attractive when the actual effect is to destroy us. Some of these allurements include promiscuous and perverted sexual behaviors and mind altering drugs. These allurements are particularly effective since they are addictive and ensnare us, consequently they prevent us from coming to God to repent and getting our life changed. Satan has so many other ways of keeping us from accepting the legitimate God and keeping us in rebellion against Him. Some of these involve pleasure, distractions and various idols.

In this book we seek to examine the anatomy of evil from different perspectives. In Part 1 we look more at the source of evil, realize the prevalence of evil, examine the attributes of Satan and learn some additional concepts of evil. In Part 2 we identify the ways of recognizing evil. In Part 3 we learn how diametrically opposite beliefs can essentially prove the existence of God and the truth of the bible. In Part 4 we will learn of the false foundations that have been built and accepted to support false cultural and political positions and philosophies. In Part 5 we will learn about the church's complete failure to teach the whole council of God to expose the false cultural and political beliefs and to produce bible based Christians. In Part 6 we will learn why evil has progressed so rapidly from additional causes beyond the failure in our churches. In Part 7 we will ask where America is politically, coming into the 2016 elections. In Part 8 we will ask what we can do to resist and defeat evil from within.

The only answer is for America to recognize its rebellion against God and to repent and change its ways. Without that dramatic change, America is in a tenuous position and awaiting the judgement of a holy and righteous God. Also in Part 8 we document information that will give those who do not have confidence in the truth of the bible reasons to give them confidence. I sincerely hope from reading this book that you will develop a new insight into evil, how you can avoid it and most importantly what you can do to expose evil and promote God and biblical truth.

Part 1

Getting the true picture of evil

CHAPTER 1
What is the source of evil?

Saul Alinsky, through his book, "Rules for Radicals," through his philosophy, and with his life, set the stage perfectly to support the thrust of this book. Saul Alinsky believed that Lucifer's rebellion against God was a good thing. He stated the following in the introduction to his book, "Rules for Radicals":

> Lest we forget at least an over-the-shoulder acknowledgment to the very first radical: from all our legends, mythology, and history (and who is to know where mythology leaves off and history begins—or which is which), the first radical known to man who rebelled against the establishment and did it so effectively that he at least won his own kingdom—Lucifer.[3]

Surprisingly, the bible agrees with Alinsky except for a few caveats. The main caveat being that Lucifer's rebellion was not a good thing for Lucifer, Alinsky or the rest of us in the world even though Alinsky sees it that way! Also the bible clarifies that it is history, not legend. However, the bible does agree that Lucifer's actions as a result of his rebellion did win him his own kingdom at least for a period of time. The fact that Alinsky is aligned with the satanic rebellion is also verified by a 1972 interview with "Playboy." In it he said, "If there is an afterlife, and I have anything to say about it, I will unreservedly choose to go to hell." When the interviewer asked why, Alinsky said, "Hell would be heaven for me. Once I get into hell, I'll start organizing the have-nots over there. They're my kind of people."[4] We will discuss the biblical support for the existence of Satan and the ongoing battle between God and Satan further throughout this book.

The word rebellion and the concept of a rebel is both interesting and revealing. Rebellion means to resist and disobey authority whether against God, parents or government. It usually has the connotation of rebelling against a legitimate authority. Certainly Lucifer rebelled against a legitimate authority. God being the creator of all things including Lucifer, principalities and powers, certainly was a legitimate authority. That makes rebellion unjust since it is against a legitimate authority. Consequently, rebellion against an illegitimate authority is not rebellion but a just cause. Police action against a crime syndicate is an example of a just cause, not rebellion. When Alinsky sees what Lucifer did as a good thing, he admits that he is a fellow rebel and a partner in crime. This can be shown not only from this biblical analogy, but from showing that his cause is illegitimate, based upon both biblical principles and real world evidence. When others accept Alinsky's rebellion, philosophy and beliefs they are just continuing the chain of rebellion and false beliefs that started with Lucifer and are supporting the evil in our world today.

By definition, those rebelling against an authority, adopt exactly the diametrically opposite worldview beliefs that the legitimate authority holds up as truth. If they agreed with the authority on important worldview beliefs, they would not be resisting and rebelling against the authority. Consequently, Alinsky and all of us that are in rebellion against authority have diametrically opposite worldview beliefs than the authority, which, being legitimate, is the true belief that has desirable long term effects. Consequently, Alinsky and all of us agree that important diametrically opposite worldview beliefs have a profound significance. When we see them we can be assured that if one side is right, true and just the other side is wrong, false and unjust. It is just that Alinsky believes that rebellion against the legitimate authority is just. Later in the book we will show that his rebellion is not just (as in justified) based upon evidence and rationale.

Unfortunately, those groups and individuals pushing wrong, false and unjust philosophies and positions on issues are legion. They include academia, media, entertainment, politics, economics, and religions. The modus operandi for selling these wrong, false and unjust beliefs are the same ones that Lucifer used in the Garden of Eden and what the bible documents as Satan's modus operandi. The primary ways that the evil forces have been able to convince us to accept essentially a completely false worldview that is diametrically opposite from a biblical worldview is by establishing a false foundation to build upon and by seducing us to into fleshly, sinful behaviors that create a conflict of interest within us that makes us susceptible to rationalizing away and suppressing the truth.

We will also show that the diametric opposition of worldviews we see in our world is no accident, but results from a guiding force ensuring opposition on every issue. After establishing that concept we will expose the manifestation of these evils on multiple fronts. However, before we go there, we need to better understand the biblical story and biblical concepts in this chapter.

CREATION STORY

Most people know the story well. After God created Adam and Eve in the image of God and placed them in a perfect creation with only one thing that they (or at least Adam) were instructed not to do. Genesis 2:16-17 states:

> [16] And the LORD God commanded the man, saying, "Of every tree of the garden you may freely eat; [17] but of the tree of the knowledge of good and evil you shall not eat, for in the day that you eat of it you shall surely die."

The story continues in Chapter 3 verses 1-6 where the serpent, indwelt by Lucifer, tempted Eve through questioning God's motives and credibility and got her to eat the forbidden fruit.

> Now the serpent was more cunning than any beast of the field which the LORD God had made. And he said to the woman, "Has God indeed said, 'You shall not eat of every tree of the garden'?" [2] And the woman said to the serpent, "We may eat the fruit of the trees of the garden; [3] but of the fruit of the tree which is in the midst of the garden, God has said, 'You shall not eat it, nor shall you touch it, lest you die.'" [4] Then the serpent said to the woman, "You will not surely die. [5] For God knows that in the day you eat of it your eyes will be opened, and you will be like God, knowing good and evil." [6] So when the woman saw that the tree was good for food, that it was pleasant to the eyes, and a tree desirable to make one wise, she took of its fruit and ate. She also gave to her husband with her, and he ate.

The story continues with God cursing the serpent in Genesis 3:14:

> So the LORD God said to the serpent:
> "Because you have done this, You are cursed more than all cattle,
> And more than every beast of the field; On your belly you shall go,
> And you shall eat dust All the days of your life.

The story continues with the first prophecy in the bible in Genesis 3:15:

> And I will put enmity
> Between you and the woman,
> And between your seed and her Seed;
> He shall bruise your head,
> And you shall bruise His heel."

This prophecy is in reference to Jesus, being born of woman, and that He will bruise (some versions say crush) Lucifer's or Satan's head but in the process Satan will bruise Jesus' heel. This is in reference to Jesus, the creator of the universe, leaving His heavenly domain, being born of the Virgin Mary, living a sinless life and being Crucified on a Roman cross to become sin so we can take on his rightness and be saved from what we deserve. John 19:30 states Jesus' last words were "it is finished:"

> [30] So when Jesus had received the sour wine, He said, "It is finished!" And bowing His head, He gave up His spirit.

What did Jesus mean by "it is finished?" One website stated:

> Of the last sayings of Christ on the cross, none is more important or more poignant than, "It is finished." Found only in the Gospel of John, the Greek word translated "it is finished" is *tetelestai*, an accounting term that means "paid in full." When Jesus uttered those words, He was declaring the debt owed to His Father was wiped away completely and forever.

Also completed was the fulfillment of all Old Testament prophecies, symbols, and foreshadowings of the coming Messiah. From Genesis to Malachi, there are over 300 specific prophecies detailing the coming of the Anointed One, all fulfilled by Jesus. From the "seed" who would crush the serpent's head (Genesis 3:15), to the Suffering Servant of Isaiah 53, . . [5]

Another website stated that:

He was declaring victory over the enemy—Satan, sin and death.[6]

Although Satan no longer had a claim on legal grounds to condemn us to death for our sins, he still has that power if we let him by not accepting Jesus' atonement for our sins. The cure is fully paid for, but we must lay a claim to it. His power to even tempt mankind will be suspended for a 1000 years during the millennial reign (Revelation 20:1-3), but his physical defeat will not be completed until after the millennium (Revelation 20:10).

The story continues in Chapter 3:16 where God curses the woman.

> To the woman He said: "I will greatly multiply your sorrow and your conception;
> In pain you shall bring forth children;
> Your desire shall be for your husband,
> And he shall rule over you."

The story continues with God cursing the man in Genesis 3:17-19.

> [17] Then to Adam He said, "Because you have heeded the voice of your wife, and have eaten from the tree of which I commanded you, saying, 'You shall not eat of it': "Cursed is the ground for your sake; In toil you shall eat of it All the days of your life. [18] Both thorns and thistles it shall bring forth for you, And you shall eat the herb of the field. [19] In the sweat of your face you shall eat bread Till you return to the ground, For out of it you were taken; For dust you are, And to dust you shall return."

The final result was that death entered our world and the serpent, Satan, woman, man and the earth were cursed. The rest of the universe may have been cursed as well. From then on man was not made only in the image of God, but in the fallen image of man also. Genesis 5:1-3 states:

> This is the book of the genealogy of Adam. In the day that God created man, He made him in the likeness of God. [2] He created them male and female, and blessed them and called them Mankind in the day they were created. [3] And Adam lived one hundred and thirty years, and begot a son in his own likeness, after his image, and named him Seth.

It is interesting to notice that God did not curse the institution of marriage and make what He had already created obsolete. Genesis 2:18, 22-24 states:

> [18] And the LORD God said, "It is not good that man should be alone; I will make him a helper comparable to him."

> ²² Then the rib which the Lord God had taken from man He made into a woman, and He brought her to the man. ²³ And Adam said: "This is now bone of my bones And flesh of my flesh;
> She shall be called Woman, Because she was taken out of Man." ²⁴ Therefore a man shall leave his father and mother and be joined to his wife, and they shall become one flesh.

Previously God stated in Genesis 1:27-28:

> ²⁷ So God created man in His own image; in the image of God He created him; male and female He created them. ²⁸ Then God blessed them, and God said to them, "Be fruitful and multiply; fill the earth and subdue it; have dominion over the fish of the sea, over the birds of the air, and over every living thing that moves on the earth."

Although God gave man dominion over the remainder of his creation, He also expected us to care for the creation. Genesis 2:15 states:

> ¹⁵ Then the Lord God took the man and put him in the Garden of Eden to tend and keep it.

Although most of readers know about Lucifer and the Garden of Eden, familiarity with the whole story is not as common. The remainder of the story about Satan will be completed in Chapter 3. In the next chapter we will discuss the prevalence of evil. The remainder of Part 1 will identify concepts relating to evil.

CHAPTER 2
How prevalent is evil?

For most of us, evil is something that is unusual and far removed from us. When we think of evil people we think of people like Hitler, Mao Zedong or Pol Pot that murdered millions of people. We don't normally think of evil ideas, evil behaviors or evil people with which we are familiar. We think that our world is made up of primarily normal people that are neither evil nor saints. We think of evil people and saints as very rare. However, the bible paints a very different picture.

WHAT IS THE BIBLICAL VIEW OF EVIL?

The bible is certainly the most identified book that addresses good and evil and is believed to be the only book to adequately address this issue. We need to understand the basic biblical principles that relate to good and evil before we can understand evil in a proper perspective. The bible teaches not only that God is good, but that He is the source of all good. It also teaches that although God did not create evil, he allowed the potential for it by giving created beings free will to be in sync with Him or rebel against Him.

Above we suggested that the way we look at evil beliefs and actions is that they are rare and distant like Hitler etc. Next we will cover biblical concepts that dispel this false belief and bring evil much closer to home.

BIBLICAL SUPPORT FOR "NO NEUTRAL GROUND" BETWEEN GOOD AND EVIL

Revisiting the fact that we view evil and saintly behavior as rare and consider most human ideas, behaviors and our morality as neutral, we need to rethink that perspective in light of biblical principles. Although some previously identified texts may give some hint that no neutral ground exists, the texts below will confirm that no neutral ground exists between good and evil. Consequently, in the realm of philosophies, behaviors, cultural beliefs and political positions and even pseudo-science, if it is not good, it is evil.

Jesus stated in Matthew 12:30:

> [30] He who is not with Me is against Me, and he who does not gather with Me scatters abroad.

We are either with Him or against Him. Matthew 7:13-14 states:

> [13] "Enter by the narrow gate; for wide is the gate and broad is the way that leads to destruction, and there are many who go in by it. [14] Be-

cause narrow is the gate and difficult is the way which leads to life, and there are few who find it.

No third gate exists. John 3:19-21 states:

[19] And this is the condemnation, that the light has come into the world, and men loved darkness rather than light, because their deeds were evil. [20] For everyone practicing evil hates the light and does not come to the light, lest his deeds should be exposed. [21] But he who does the truth comes to the light, that his deeds may be clearly seen, that they have been done in God."

First, a third neutral realm between light and darkness does not exist. Secondly, men are not seeking a neutral ground between light and darkness.

Isaiah 5:20 states:

[20] Woe to those who call evil good, and good evil;
Who put darkness for light, and light for darkness;
Who put bitter for sweet, and sweet for bitter!

Nothing is said about calling things neutral. Only the two realms exist.

Matthew 25:31-34 & 46 states:

[31] "When the Son of Man comes in His glory, and all the holy angels with Him, then He will sit on the throne of His glory. [32] All the nations will be gathered before Him, and He will separate them one from another, as a shepherd divides his sheep from the goats. [33] And He will set the sheep on His right hand, but the goats on the left. [34] Then the King will say to those on His right hand, 'Come, you blessed of My Father, inherit the kingdom prepared for you from the foundation of the world: [46] And these will go away into everlasting punishment, but the righteous into eternal life."

No third category exists between the sheep and the goats (saints and the dammed).

Next we will see what happened when God gave his angels free will, what Lucifer transformed into and learn more concepts of evil.

CHAPTER 3
Attributes of Satan and God

LUCIFER'S INITIAL ATTRIBUTES AND REBELLION

Lucifer was not created as a monster or a rebel. Ezekiel 28:12-19 tells the story of Lucifer's attributes when he was created:

> [12] "Son of man, take up a lamentation for the king of Tyre, and say to him, 'Thus says the Lord GOD:
> "You were the seal of perfection,
> Full of wisdom and perfect in beauty.
> [13] You were in Eden, the garden of God;
> Every precious stone *was* your covering:
> The sardius, topaz, and diamond,
> Beryl, onyx, and jasper,
> Sapphire, turquoise, and emerald with gold.
> The workmanship of your timbrels and pipes
> Was prepared for you on the day you were created.
> [14] "You were the anointed cherub who covers;
> I established you;
> You were on the holy mountain of God;
> You walked back and forth in the midst of fiery stones.
> [15] You were perfect in your ways from the day you were created,
> Till iniquity was found in you.
> [16] "By the abundance of your trading
> You became filled with violence within,
> And you sinned;
> Therefore I cast you as a profane thing
> Out of the mountain of God;
> And I destroyed you, O covering cherub,
> From the midst of the fiery stones.
> [17] "Your heart was lifted up because of your beauty;
> You corrupted your wisdom for the sake of your splendor;
> I cast you to the ground,
> I laid you before kings,
> That they might gaze at you.

In addition to Lucifer's attributes when he was created the passage covers Lucifer's rebellion against God and the reason for his rebellion. Today the reasons cited for rebellion and victimhood are being poor or disadvantaged. This is in diametric opposition to the reason the bible gives for Lucifer's rebellion.

One line stands out with a profound message. It states, "You corrupted your wisdom for the sake of your splendor;" In one word, "pride." This is one of the major reasons why evil can prosper. Our pride in ourselves (even though usually unjustified) blinds us to the truth of who God is and how we compare with God and what our relationship should be with Him. Our pride even makes us believe that God doesn't exist.

A similar passage found in Isaiah 14:12-17 expands on Lucifer's rebellion:

> [12] "How you are fallen from heaven,
> O Lucifer, son of the morning!
> How you are cut down to the ground,
> You who weakened the nations!
> [13] For you have said in your heart:
> 'I will ascend into heaven,
> I will exalt my throne above the stars of God;
> I will also sit on the mount of the congregation
> On the farthest sides of the north;
> [14] I will ascend above the heights of the clouds,
> I will be like the Most High.'
> [15] Yet you shall be brought down to Sheol,
> To the lowest depths of the Pit.
> [16] "Those who see you will gaze at you,
> And consider you, saying:
> 'Is this the man who made the earth tremble,
> Who shook kingdoms,
> [17] Who made the world as a wilderness
> And destroyed its cities,
> Who did not open the house of his prisoners?'

ATTRIBUTES OF SATAN

As a result of man's fall, God's perfect creation was corrupted and cursed, and Satan was given a degree of dominion over the earth for a time.

Ephesians 2:1-3 states:

> And you He made alive, who were dead in trespasses and sins, [2] in which you once walked according to the course of this world, according to the prince of the power of the air, the spirit who now works in the sons of disobedience, [3] among whom also we all once conducted ourselves in the lusts of our flesh, fulfilling the desires of the flesh and of the mind, and were by nature children of wrath, just as the others.

This text confirms that Satan is the "prince of the power of the air" and has been given a level of dominion over our world and that dominion is associated with everything in this world including the lusts of our flesh, fulfilling the desires of the flesh and the mind. It also implies that by nature we are under the wrath of God with rebellion in our hearts just like Satan. That associates many of the things we do with our basic evil nature. Jeremiah 17:9 states:

"The heart is deceitful above all things,
And desperately wicked;
Who can know it?

Isaiah 64:6 states:

But we are all like an unclean thing,
And all our righteousnesses are like filthy rags;

These texts confirm our basic nature. Satan confirms his dominion over the earth in the temptation of Jesus as documented in Matthew 4:8-10:

[8] Again, the devil took Him up on an exceedingly high mountain, and showed Him all the kingdoms of the world and their glory. [9] And he said to Him, "All these things I will give You if You will fall down and worship me." [10] Then Jesus said to him, "Away with you, Satan! For it is written, 'You shall worship the LORD your God, and Him only you shall serve.'"

Satan was even bold enough to tempt Jesus, the son of God. Certainly, he doesn't hesitate to tempt us. The other thing we can glean from this text as indicated above is that Satan had been given dominion over the earth. Otherwise, Jesus would have told him that the kingdoms of the earth were not his to give.

John 8:44 states:

You are of your father the devil, and the desires of your father you want to do. He was a murderer from the beginning, and does not stand in the truth, because there is no truth in him. When he speaks a lie, he speaks from his own resources, for he is a liar and the father of it.

Revelation 12:9 states:

[9] So the great dragon was cast out, that serpent of old, called the Devil and Satan, who deceives the whole world; he was cast to the earth, and his angels were cast out with him.

These verses state that Satan is a murderer, a deceiver and a liar and that the lying and deceiving is his Modus Operandi for getting us to do what he wants us to do. That is what he did to Eve. When we look carefully at the faces of evil, we will see temptation, lies, deception, demonization and destruction. Consequently, when we see those things happening we know that we are looking at evil.

1 Peter 5:8 states:

[8] Be sober, be vigilant; because your adversary the devil walks about like a roaring lion, seeking whom he may devour.

This states that we must be careful because Satan wants to devour us. If not physically he wants to destroy us mentally, spiritually, emotionally and certainly destroy our eternal soul. One method we see active in our world is to demonize people that are Christians or have conservative biblical beliefs. Alinsky certainly recommends this as a tactic in his book.

> His fifth rule is that "ridicule is man's most potent weapon." His thirteenth rule is "pick the target, freeze it, personalize it and polarize it."[7]

Consequently, the bible teaches that Satan's attributes are diametrically opposed to God's attributes as we will see below and later as biblical principles. This means that Satan's actions are evil. In addition, when we see people having a worldview that is diametrically opposed to the biblical worldview, they also are acting on the side of evil.

GOD'S ATTRIBUTES

A great synopsis of God's attributes is found in A. W. Tozer's book "The Knowledge of the Holy" and on the internet. They are quoted below with permission:

> **Wisdom:** "Wisdom is the ability to devise perfect ends and to achieve these ends by the most perfect means." In other words, God makes no mistakes. He is the Father who truly knows best, as Paul explains in Romans 11:33: "Oh, how great are God's riches and wisdom and knowledge! How impossible it is for us to understand His decisions and His ways!"
>
> **Infinitude:** God knows no boundaries. He is without measure. This attribute by definition impacts all of the others. Since God is infinite, everything else about Him must also be infinite.
>
> **Sovereignty:** This is "the attribute by which He rules His entire creation." It is the application of His other attributes of being all-knowing and all-powerful. It makes Him absolutely free to do what He knows to be best. God is in control of everything that happens. Man still has a free will, and is responsible for his choices in life.
>
> **Holiness:** This is the attribute that sets God apart from all created beings. It refers to His majesty and His perfect moral purity. There is absolutely no sin or evil thought in God at all. His holiness is the definition of that which is pure and righteous in all the universe. Wherever God has appeared, such as to Moses at the burning bush, that place becomes holy just for God having been there.
>
> **Trinity:** Though the actual word is not used in the Bible, the truth of God revealing Himself in three persons is included. The Father, Son, and Holy Spirit are all called God, given worship as God, exist eternally, and are involved in doing things only God could do. Although, God reveals Himself in three persons, God is One and cannot be divided. All are involved completely whenever One of the Three is active.
>
> **Omniscience:** "God possesses perfect knowledge and therefore has no need to learn. God has never learned and cannot learn." Omniscience

means all-knowing. God knows everything, and His knowledge is infinite. It is impossible to hide anything from God.

Faithfulness: Everything that God has promised will come to pass. His faithfulness guarantees this fact. He does not lie. What He has said in the Bible about Himself is true. Jesus even said that He is the Truth. This is extremely important for the followers of Jesus because it is on His faithfulness that our hope of eternal life rests. He will honor His promise that our sins will be forgiven and that we will live forever with Him.

Love: Love is such an important part of God's character that the apostle John wrote, "God is love." This means that God holds the well-being of others as His primary concern. For a full definition of love, read 1 Corinthians 13. To see love in action, study the life of Jesus. His sacrifice on the cross for the sins of others is the ultimate act of love. God's love is not a love of emotion but of action. His love gives freely to the object of its affection, those who choose to follow His son Jesus.

Omnipotence: Literally this word means all-powerful. Since God is infinite and since He possesses power, He possesses infinite power. He does allow His creatures to have some power, but this in no way diminishes His own. "He expends no energy that must be replenished." When the Bible says God rested on the seventh day, it was to set an example for us and our need for rest, not because He was tired.

Self-existence: When Moses asked who he was talking to in the burning bush, God said, "I AM THE ONE WHO ALWAYS IS." God has no beginning or end. He just exists. Nothing else in all the universe is self-caused. Only God. In fact, if anything else had created Him, that thing would be God. This is a difficult concept for our minds since everything else we will ever encounter comes from something other than itself. The Bible says, "In the beginning, God." He was already there.

Self-sufficiency: The Bible says that God has life in Himself (see John 5:26). All other life in the universe is a gift from God. He has no needs and there is no way He can improve. To God, nothing else is necessary. He does not need our help with anything, but because of His grace and love, He allows us to be a part of advancing His plan on earth and being a blessing to others. We are the ones who change, but never God. He is self-sufficient.

Justice: The Bible says that God is just, but it is His character that defines what being just really is. He does not conform to some outside criteria. Being just brings moral equity to everyone. When there are evil acts, justice demands there be a penalty. Since God is perfect and has never done evil, no penalty would ever be necessary; however, because of His love, God paid the penalty for our evil deeds by going to the cross Himself. His justice needed to be satisfied, but He took care of it for all who will believe in Jesus.

Immutability: This simply means that God never changes. It is why the Bible says, "Jesus Christ is the same yesterday, today, and forever."

Mercy: "Mercy is the attribute of God which disposes Him to be actively compassionate." Since God's justice is satisfied in Jesus, He is free to show mercy to all those who have chosen to follow Him. It will never end since it is a part of God's nature. Mercy is the way He desires to relate to mankind, and He does so unless the person chooses to despise or ignore God at which time His justice becomes the prominent attribute.

Eternal: In some ways, this fact about God is similar to His self-existence. God always has been and will forever be, because God dwells in eternity. Time is His creation. It is why God can see the end from the beginning, and why He is never surprised by anything. If He were not eternal, God's promise of eternal life for those who follow Jesus would have little value.

Goodness: "The goodness of God is that which disposes Him to be kind, cordial, benevolent, and full of good will toward men." This attribute of God is why He bestows all the blessing He does on His followers. God's actions define what goodness is, and we can easily see it in the way Jesus related to the people around Him.

Gracious: God enjoys giving great gifts to those who love Him, even when they do not deserve it. Grace is the way we describe that inclination. Jesus Christ is the channel through which His grace moves. The Bible says, "The law was given by Moses, but grace and truth came by Jesus Christ."

Omnipresence: This theological term means "always present." Since God is infinite, His being knows no boundaries. So, clearly He is everywhere. This truth is taught throughout the Bible as the phrase "I am with you always" is repeated 22 times in both the Old and New Testaments. These were even Jesus' words of assurance just after giving the challenge to His disciples to take His message to the entire world. This is certainly a comforting truth for all who follow Jesus.[8]

There is one more attribute of God that should be highlighted. It is probably a subset of his other attributes. God is impartial and he wants us to be impartial. The following texts are a few of many in scripture:

Leviticus 19:15 states:

[15] 'You shall do no injustice in judgment. You shall not be partial to the poor, nor honor the person of the mighty. In righteousness you shall judge your neighbor.

Deuteronomy 1:17 states:

[17] You shall not show partiality in judgment; you shall hear the small as well as the great; you shall not be afraid in any man's presence, for the judgment is God's. The case that is too hard for you, bring to me, and I will hear it.'

Job 34:19 states:
> [19] Yet He is not partial to princes,
> Nor does He regard the rich more than the poor;
> For they are all the work of His hands.

Romans 2:11 states:
> [11] For there is no partiality with God.

Certainly God's attributes documented above are diametrically opposed to Satan's attributes as can be seen in the chart below: Scripture also states that God has a diametrically opposite worldview than Satan. This is what results in the polar opposite worldviews we see in our society.

Satan's attribute	Scripture Reference	God's Opposite Attribute	Above Characteristic that contains God's Attribute
Lies & Deception	John 8:44 & Rev. 12:9	Truth	Faithfulness & Justice
Murder & Destroyer	John 8:44 & 1 Pet. 5:8	Wants what is best for us	Love & Goodness

In the next chapter we will take a closer look at additional concepts relating to evil.

CHAPTER 4
Concepts relating to evil

When the serpent asked Eve in the Garden of Eden "Has God indeed said, 'You shall not eat of every tree of the garden'?" what was his purpose? Was he seeking whether God had actually made that statement so he could make sure that those that possibly could have inadvertently eaten the fruit would be alerted and avoid eating the fruit? Or alternatively, was he questioning God as the first step in denigrating God's motives when in response to Eve he stated "You should not surly die (calling God a liar). For God knows that in the day you eat of it your eyes will be opened, and you will be like God, knowing good and evil." That whole statement sounded good to Eve. Who doesn't want to have their eyes opened and be like God and know the difference between good and evil! That is what Eve's ears heard. The truth was that she would lose her innocence, seeing and experiencing evil and aligning herself with Satan while rejecting God her creator. What sounded good turned out to be very bad and evil. Satan knew exactly how to use innuendo, lies and half-truths to seduce Eve to join him in rebellion against God.

That is exactly what is happening in our world today to promote evil and get people to rebel against the God that loves them and desires to save them from their sins. When we see denigration, innuendo, lies and half-truths our evil detector should go up and reject whatever and whoever is promoting anything with this Modus Operandi. A few more things can be added to this list of concerns. Some of these include censorship, coercion, heavy top-down control, promoting special interests, corruption, using other people's money for charity or spending other people's money to buy power and votes.

Certainly Satan was not seeking truthful information so he could make the world a better place. Today, we have similar questions which would be great if they are asked for the purpose of getting truthful information. However, it seems they are usually asked for the purpose of denigrating God, His Word and His character. The primary questions asked are: What is the origin of suffering sickness and death? Why do the good as well as the bad suffer? Why do earthquakes, famine and tornadoes cause so much suffering and death? Who is behind violence and war? Rarely are these questions asked with the purpose of exonerating God from blame, but by skeptics with the purpose of promoting skepticism. Let's answer each of these questions based upon what the bible teaches to clarify that God is not to blame even though he is in complete control of everything.

WHAT IS THE ORIGIN OF SUFFERING, SICKNESS AND DEATH?

On one level this was answered in Genesis 3 when God included suffering during childbirth for women and death for mankind in the curses. I believe the remaining question is, were these curses justified? Does anyone believe that if God just blinked at sin and rebellion against Him that man should not have had any punishment for disobedience and rebellion? Does anyone think that criminals should not have any punishment for crimes against humanity? I don't believe that anybody believes either one of those scenarios. God's perfect justice requires that sin, crime and rebellion be punished. If that perfect justice required that God needed to have His Son tortured and killed just to pay for our sins so we can be reconciled to a holy God, certainly our punishment for our rebellion is justified! Why should God continue to let us live in a perfect world? God basically had two choices when he created the angels and mankind. He either could have created robots or he could have created beings with free will. He choose the latter. This meant that he took the risk that created beings had an option to rebel against Him. You have heard the expression that "all's well that ends well." The bible teaches that all ends well for those that accept Jesus' sacrifice and align themselves with Him.

Matthew 10:22 states:

> [22] And you will be hated by all for My name's sake. But he who endures to the end will be saved.

Either way we are slaves to something; if not a slave to God and righteousness then a slave to Satan and to sin leading to death.

Romans 6:16 states:

> [16] Do you not know that to whom you present yourselves slaves to obey, you are that one's slaves whom you obey, whether of sin leading to death, or of obedience leading to righteousness?

The bible teaches that people that are against God not only will die, but, like Alinsky, love the death that they will receive.

Proverbs 8:35-36 states:

> For whoever finds me finds life,
> And obtains favor from the LORD;
> [36] But he who sins against me wrongs his own soul;
> All those who hate me love death."

WHY DO THE GOOD AS WELL AS THE BAD SUFFER?

First the bible agrees that the good as well as those that are bad suffer. i.e. if we can call anybody good.

Matthew 19:17 states:

> [17] So He said to him, "Why do you call Me good? No one is good but One, that is, God. But if you want to enter into life, keep the commandments."

Luke 13:2-5 states:
> There were present at that season some who told Him about the Galileans whose blood Pilate had mingled with their sacrifices. [2] And Jesus answered and said to them, "Do you suppose that these Galileans were worse sinners than all other Galileans, because they suffered such things? [3] I tell you, no; but unless you repent you will all likewise perish. [4] Or those eighteen on whom the tower in Siloam fell and killed them, do you think that they were worse sinners than all other men who dwelt in Jerusalem? [5] I tell you, no; but unless you repent you will all likewise perish."

Both of these texts (verse 1-3 and 4-5) teach that punishment for rebellion and unrighteous living will be after death, not in this life. Consequently, the curse on our world is the same regardless how you respect God.

Matthew 5:45 states:
> [45] that you may be sons of your Father in heaven; for He makes His sun rise on the evil and on the good, and sends rain on the just and on the unjust.

WHY DO EARTHQUAKES, FAMINE AND TORNADOES CAUSE SO MUCH SUFFERING AND DEATH?

When God cursed woman and man, He also cursed nature while bringing death and suffering into our world. He mentioned the ground will require hard work to produce crops and thorns and thistle weeds were created to compete with crops. As mentioned earlier, we didn't deserve a perfect world anymore and consequently had to endure suffering and death.

Romans 8:18-23 states:
> [18] For I consider that the sufferings of this present time are not worthy to be compared with the glory which shall be revealed in us. [19] For the earnest expectation of the creation eagerly waits for the revealing of the sons of God. [20] For the creation was subjected to futility, not willingly, but because of Him who subjected it in hope; [21] because the creation itself also will be delivered from the bondage of corruption into the glorious liberty of the children of God. [22] For we know that the whole creation groans and labors with birth pangs together until now. [23] Not only that, but we also who have the firstfruits of the Spirit, even we ourselves groan within ourselves, eagerly waiting for the adoption, the redemption of our body.

WHO IS BEHIND VIOLENCE AND WAR?

In one sense God is behind violence and war. When two forces are diametrically opposed to each other, violence and war are inevitable. The difference is that God wants only what is true, just and good for all created beings. He knows that two diametrically opposite worldview beliefs cannot coexist. His whole plan is based upon victory for truth, justice and goodness. That is exactly what will result in the end. We always blame the environment, poverty or injustice as our excuse for our sin and rebellion. The bible teaches that after the church age and his second coming that Jesus will set up a 1000 year millennium reign on earth where He will rule the nations with a rod of iron with perfect justice.

Revelation 19:15 states:
> [15] Now out of His mouth goes a sharp sword, that with it He should strike the nations. And He Himself will rule them with a rod of iron. He Himself treads the winepress of the fierceness and wrath of Almighty God.

Revelation 20:1-3 states:
> Then I saw an angel coming down from heaven, having the key to the bottomless pit and a great chain in his hand. [2] He laid hold of the dragon, that serpent of old, who is the Devil and Satan, and bound him for a thousand years; [3] and he cast him into the bottomless pit, and shut him up, and set a seal on him, so that he should deceive the nations no more till the thousand years were finished. But after these things he must be released for a little while.

Revelation 20:7-10 states:
> [7] Now when the thousand years have expired, Satan will be released from his prison [8] and will go out to deceive the nations which are in the four corners of the earth, Gog and Magog, to gather them together to battle, whose number is as the sand of the sea. [9] They went up on the breadth of the earth and surrounded the camp of the saints and the beloved city. And fire came down from God out of heaven and devoured them. [10] The devil, who deceived them, was cast into the lake of fire and brimstone where the beast and the false prophet are. And they will be tormented day and night forever and ever.

I truly believe that God's purpose for the a 1000 year period with perfect environment and perfect justice where rebellion still flourished is to demonstrate that the environment, poverty and injustice are not the cause of rebellion!

This completes the answers to those questions typically asked by skeptics to discredit God, His Word and His justice. Hopefully, this will remove some of those haunting doubts that will cloud your understanding and acceptance of the truths presented in this book.

In the remainder of this chapter we continue to expose additional false concepts or beliefs that prevent us from believing the truth to be presented in the next chapter and the rest of the book.

RELATIVE TRUTH

Our postmodern culture has somehow embraced a philosophy of relative truth that denies absolute truth exists. In Chapter 15 we will identify the belief in relative truth as a false foundation. One aspect of this evil is promoting a false construct in a belief that, if examined, could be readily falsified! If one believes in relative truth that means they hold that belief up as an absolute truth. Consequently, those that believe in relative truth believe in absolute truth. If that sounds like an oxymoron, that is because it is. Beyond that, denying absolute truth is unbelievably naive. If someone doesn't believe in gravity, that doesn't mean that gravity is not an absolute truth. The other aspect of relative truth is that it changes truth from something universal and true anyplace and anytime to the idea that truth is just something that an individual believes in. i.e. What is true for you may not be truth for me.

Consequently, with this belief things are only true to the extent that we embrace a specific truth. This contradicts the fact that absolute truths are inherently true. This causes great confusion and this confusion prevents us from recognizing evil and consequently excuses many evils. In case this confusion is not completely clear several examples are listed below. Let's clarify the difference between choices and preferences and opposite worldview beliefs.

CLARIFYING THE DIFFERENCES BETWEEN BELIEFS, CHOICES AND ABSOLUTE TRUTH

Below we attempt to list all possible types of opposite individual beliefs or choices and delineate them from true facts:
1. To like or choose something or to not like or choose it.
2. To believe that a historical event happened or not believe it.
3. To believe that a future event will occur or not believe it.
4. To believe in a philosophy, concept or doctrine or not believe it.
5. To believe in a specific philosophy, concept or doctrine as opposed to believing in another philosophy, concept or doctrine that is essentially parallel and the diametric opposite.

Examples and explanations:
1. Example: To like or choose a vegetarian diet or not to like it or choose it. Even though one of these opposite likes or choices may be better based upon statistical outcome effects than the opposite like or choice and

therefore may be more-true than the other, no general truth statement can be made or associated with our likes or choices that are not related to a philosophy, concept or doctrine. However, we find in our relativistic, politically correct culture that such likes or choices are likened to what is true for you or what is true for me. This confounds likes and choices with truth, thus reduces the meaning of truth from something that is absolute at all times and in all places to a meaningless relativistic term. We need to recognize this as a deception that establishes a foothold in a false foundation to build a false worldview.

2. Example: To believe that the German Holocaust existed where they exterminated millions of Jews or not believe it. It is either true or it is false! It is not anecdotal and is not based upon likes, choices or tastes. It is based upon verifiable facts. In spite of this, many deniers of the Holocaust are vocal about their opinion that is based upon a conflict of interest. They don't want it to be true. This type of thinking is prevalent in our culture. Two examples in the field of pseudoscience are macro-evolution and man caused global warming. This is backward science where desiring a conclusion is the first step and then they hunt for real or imagined data to support their conclusion while censoring all conflicting evidence. Real science begins with the facts and draws conclusions based upon where the facts lead.

3. Example: To believe that we are headed toward a utopia produced by mankind or not believe it. Although we can speculate whether that is true or not, the truth will not be known until some future time. It does relate to absolute truth rather than likes and choices, but we don't know the truth yet.

4. Example: To believe that what we will reap will be related to what we sow or not believe it. To establish the truth or falsehood of this statement or similar philosophies, concepts or doctrines, we need to examine empirical evidence and make a judgment solely on the evidence and not upon what we want it to be. The truth of the specific question above is important since the answer will greatly affect our behavior for better or worse. Philosophies, concepts and doctrines relate to absolute truth both in respect to reality and to the effects of believing and following such a philosophy, concept or doctrine. What we believe affects our behavior and our behavior affects our world.

5. Example: To believe in capitalism vs. socialism is to believe in essentially two diametrically opposite beliefs. If one is true the other is false. Which is which, depends upon our criteria of success. If I am poor, destitute and lazy, socialism may be better for me than capitalism since the gov-

ernment will take care of me and doesn't expect anything from me except my vote. However, since others will have to sacrifice for my benefit, there is a downside for others. If we draw a larger circle to evaluate the success of capitalism or socialism, we find that rather than a redistribution scheme from a shrinking unproductive base caused by inverse incentives, we have a system that generates wealth so that potentially more resources will be available to all including those in need. Consequently, if our success criteria is benefiting the general interest as opposed to special interests and we want justice to be served, capitalism is the one that is good, true, just and with good general effects. If our focus is what is best for a special interest group, it is always a benefit for a special interest group at the expense of the general interest. The benefiting of a special interest group is only just and fair when the ones financially supporting the special interest group agree that they deserve special benefits. Legitimate examples of this might include military personnel, handicapped or sickly people etc. However, this type of charity supported by government should be highly restricted to prevent abuse. In general, government should stay out of the charity game because they have a conflict of interest wanting to buy votes. Even if the government charity would be considered justified, they are incapable of doing it effectively and efficiently. Look at the horrible job the government has done with Veterans Hospitals and medical service. Even with unlimited resources they fail miserably.

This 5th category of parallel and essentially diametrically opposite beliefs, concepts or doctrines is what we want to examine to determine its significance. Are there any profound conclusions that can be drawn? Can we show that our current cultural, economic and political philosophies being promoted are in perfect opposition to a documented standard? If so, what is the significance of this opposition? What could possibly be the source of these diametrically opposite beliefs? Does the bible identify any sources of this opposition? Is rebellion a source of diametric opposition? Can you think of any other reasons for diametric opposition in what should be an intellectual realm? Before we go where the above paragraph is leading us we need to expose more false beliefs so your mind will more readily accept the truth.

DEFINING RELIGIOUS AND SECULAR

Before we continue in that direction we need to delineate between religious beliefs based upon a supernatural God and non-supernatural religious beliefs. The Merriam-Webster dictionary has basically five definitions for "religion." They are:

1. The service and worship of God or the supernatural
2. A commitment or devotion to religious faith or observance
3. A personal set or institutionalized system of religious attitudes, beliefs, and practices
4. Scrupulous conformity
5. A cause, principle, or system of beliefs held to with ardor and faith

Only the first one is specific about service and worship to a God or the supernatural. The other four basically relate to the secular realm. Let's call these later beliefs "religious secular" beliefs. I know that sounds like an oxymoron, but that is only because we have been programmed to only relate religious beliefs to the supernatural. By doing this the "religious secular" realm can exempt themselves from all the restrictions and condemnation they place on religions that worship a supernatural God. This deception along with "Case Law" replacing "Constitutional Law" has provided a basis for the whole false "separation of church and state" doctrine. This will be covered later in Part 4 concerning false foundations. In a similar way the adamant progressive / liberal positions on global warming and macro-evolution are religious secular positions masquerading as scientific positions. They also will be discussed in Part 4, Chapters 14 & 17.

We need to make one more distinction. The secular realm includes the truly secular realm in addition to the "religious secular" realm. The truly secular realm includes things like your favorite color, sports, homemaking, traveling, hobbies etc. Everyone knows about this truly secular realm. Things in the truly secular realm are never disputed or cause polarization. The problem is that we have been programmed to combine the "religious secular" realm with the normal secular realm in our thinking. The normal secular realm does not cause polarizing debates in culture, politics and religion. By not distinguishing between "religious secular" and purely secular realms the whole atheistic or Secular Humanist religious beliefs or positions get transferred into the secular realm of facts, truth and science rather than being recognized as a religious belief similar to God based religions. At that point they can accuse biblical Christianity of being based upon pure faith and their opposing view being based upon facts, truth and science! Wow, what a scam! Consequently, when we speak of secular issues in this book we are addressing "religious secular" issues.

THE RELIGIOUS REALM

In addition to being programmed not to believe in the two secular realms ("religious secular" and purely secular) we have also been programmed to believe only in one religious realm. This belief is exemplified with expressions like "all roads lead to God" or "all religions are the same" or "good and evil don't exist." Another example is the absence of the words "true" and "false." Religions are all put in the same basket and then denigrated by the bad things that one or more religions (or possibly specific denominations of a doctrinal religion) have done. We need to look at various religions (doctrinal as opposed to denominational) and compare their beliefs with biblical doctrines and principles and then make a judgment on whether they are good or bad or true or false. This is also true for denominations within doctrinal religions. A legitimate concern is whether the bible is true or not. Although some evidence supporting biblical truth will be presented throughout this book, that issue will be addressed specifically in Chapter 31. The probability science we cover in Chapter 10 is certainly one huge pillar supporting the truth of the bible.

CONCLUSION

So far we have explained that evil is something that is more prevalent and closer to home than we would normally think. Things that are not godly or biblical are evil with no neutral ground between good and evil. We have identified Satan as the source of evil and shown how he has corrupted God's perfect creation. We explained how Satan not only corrupted himself, but mankind. We learned how man's fall resulted in God cursing Satan, man, women, the earth and nature itself. We learned about the origin of suffering, sickness and death, relative truth, delineating true worldview facts from choices, defining religious and secular and the religious realm.

This completes Part 1, "Getting the true picture of evil." We proceed to answer the question of "How can we recognize evil?" in Part 2.

Part 2

How can we recognize evil?

CHAPTER 5
How can we recognize evil based upon what the bible says?

The following table lists various attributes of evil that we can use to recognize as evil based upon the bible. It lists the supporting texts that support the evil attribute.

Attribute	Text Reference	Biblical Text
Demonization	Matthew 5:11	[11] "Blessed are you when they revile and persecute you, and say all kinds of evil against you falsely for My sake.
Bad Thoughts	Matthew 9:4	[4] But Jesus, knowing their thoughts, said, "Why do you think evil in your hearts?
Bad Actions	Matthew 12:35b	an evil man out of the evil treasure brings forth evil things.
	Matthew 15:19	[19] For out of the heart proceed evil thoughts, murders, adulteries, fornications, thefts, false witness, blasphemies. . .
Jealous	Matthew 20:15	[15] Is it not lawful for me to do what I wish with my own things? Or is your eye evil because I am good?'
	Job 5:2	Surely vexation kills the fool, and jealousy slays the simple.
	Proverbs 27:4	Wrath is cruel, anger is overwhelming, but who is able to stand before jealousy?
Evil Spirits	Luke 7:21	[21] And that very hour He cured many of infirmities, afflictions, and evil spirits; and to many blind He gave sight
Love of Darkness	John 3:19	[19] And this is the condemnation, that the light has come into the world, and men loved darkness rather than light, because their deeds were evil.
Hating Truth and Light	John 3:20	[20] For everyone practicing evil hates the light and does not come to the light, lest his deeds should be exposed.

*Censorship – Suppressing the truth – Conflict of Interest	Romans 1:18	[18] For the wrath of God is revealed from heaven against all ungodliness and unrighteousness of men, who suppress the truth in unrighteousness,
*Agnosticism	2 Peter 3:3-5	[3] knowing this first: that scoffers will come in the last days, walking according to their own lusts, [4] and saying, "Where is the promise of His coming? For since the fathers fell asleep, all things continue as they were from the beginning of creation." [5] For this they willfully forget: that by the word of God the heavens were of old. . .
Hating Jesus, Christians and Jews	John 7:7	[7] The world cannot hate you, but it hates Me because I testify of it that its works are evil.
Self-seeking	Romans 2:8-9	[8] but to those who are self-seeking and do not obey the truth, but obey unrighteousness—indignation and wrath, [9] tribulation and anguish, on every soul of man who does evil, of the Jew first and also of the Greek;
Following Lusts	1 Cor. 15-33	[6] Now these things became our examples, to the intent that we should not lust after evil things as they also lusted.
Love of Money and Power	1 Timothy 6:10	[10] For the love of money is a root of all kinds of evil, for which some have strayed from the faith in their greediness, and pierced themselves through with many sorrows.
Deception	2 Timothy 3:13	[13] But evil men and impostors will grow worse and worse, deceiving and being deceived.
Boasting and Arrogance	James 4:16	[16] But now you boast in your arrogance. All such boasting is evil.
Coercion	See Chapter 6 & 10	See Chapter 6 & 10
Impartiality	See Chapter 3	See end of Chapter 3

*Censorship and agnosticism go together since agnosticism is just a special case or a special way to censor the truth. This probably is not obvious if your understanding of the word is similar to my Merriam-Webster Dictionary since it identifies the Greek source word for agnostic as "agnostos" which simply means unknown or unknowable. There is no object of application associated with the source word. Although that is the meaning of the base word, its usual application is in conjunction with a specific application. This application is identified in the internet Merriam-Webster dictionary that defines the application typically associated with the word agnostic as "a person who holds the view that any ultimate reality (as God) is unknown and probably unknowable; *broadly*: one who is not committed to believing in either the existence or the nonexistence of God or a god."[9]

This definition is the normal claim of agnostics. It is strange that they apply it to both of two diametrically opposite possibilities!

The question I have "is the real concern of agnostics that they do not want to be associated with support for or a belief in something when they cannot know for sure that it is real or true?" That should be the fundamental concern of an agnostic. The question is, is that the case or is something else going on? First, it is interesting that the only area of application that agnostics relate their agnosticism to is the existence of God or His lack of existence. Why is that? Why don't they question the wisdom of driving their car since they cannot be certain that they will arrive safely? Why don't they question the food they eat? They cannot know for sure that it doesn't contain poison? Why aren't they frozen in space by the uncertainly of the unknown. Why don't they fret over all the decisions made by the courts since we can't be certain they are correct?

However, even more revealing is the fact when they do focus their agnosticism on the uncertainty of knowing whether God exists or not, 100% of them either question the existence of God rather than questioning the lack of existence of God or they apply their agnosticism to both. That is not a trivial question. For someone that is concerned about being associated with the support for or a belief in something when they cannot know for sure that it is real or true, the logical choice would be to choose the one that by definition can never be known rather than the one that could have abundant evidence to support its truth. It is a logical fact that a universal negative cannot be proven or even known. i.e. we should all be agnostics on this side of being uncertain of the lack of existence of God since that is a very safe position and you can never be proven wrong! In spite of this fact 100% of the agnostics base their agnosticism on either the diametric opposite concern, that of the existence of God or apply it to both opposite assertions. Consequently, rather than agnosticism being a concern of wanting to be certain before supporting or believing in something, it is simply another way to deny or censor the existence of God while claiming to be on the intellectual high ground.

This completes how we can recognize evil based upon the bible. In the next chapter we will see how we can recognize evil through opposite Modus Operandi.

CHAPTER 6
How can we recognize evil based upon modus operandi?

SATAN'S MODUS OPERANDI

The bible teaches that Satan is the true antichrist and that he is in rebellion against God and wants to thwart all God's plans and destroy His creation. This means that Satan will use his authority to undermine God, truth, Christians, biblical symbols, spreading of the gospel, the Jews (God's chosen people) and America that was based upon biblical principles. The tools Satan uses to accomplish this are lies, coercion, deception, demonization, destruction and hate.

The primary evil modus operandi examples of great deception in our society today include "Political Correctness," "The New Tolerance" and a new right not to be offended which results in violating other people's conscience by forcing them to think and do things against their conscience. We will say more about these things under false foundations in Part 4. "Political Correctness," is actually "cultural Marxism (see Chapter 19)." Karl Marx's primary two goals were dethroning God and destroying capitalism. Consequently, political correctness is all about dethroning God and destroying capitalism. There is nothing correct about it!

"The New Tolerance" was coined by Josh McDowell in his book by the same title where any debate concerning the truth is censored and the messengers of truth are demonized to make them look evil in the process. The current coercion that is destroying people and their businesses that will not go against their own conscience and accept homosexuality and homosexual marriage is based upon a false foundation that people have a right not to be offended. Let's coin this new evil coercion as "Outraged Based Coerced Conscience." If our culture was not practicing "Political Correctness" and "The New Tolerance," so a discussion on homosexuality would not be censored, the discussion would identify what they are pushing as an evil depravity that benefits nobody. The primary difference between "The New Tolerance" and "Outrage Based Coerced Conscience" is that the later extends the demonization into destruction by getting the evil codified into law.

Although the right to not being offended is a negative right that our constitution generally supports, it is completely contrary to the first amendment of free speech. The type of speech being objected to is not the kind that would have serious consequences like yelling fire in a crowded theater. It is not even initiated speech where someone is offended by something they say. It is demanding them to take a position against their conscience and what they believe.

The whole offensive speech issue started with racial issues where certain speech was offensive to black people. Although highly offensive, the speech was not coercive in any way. Similarly people's actions like refusing to bake a cake for a homosexual wedding or refusing to photograph a homosexual wedding have been demonized and legal action has been taken against them. When it comes to crimes and evil actions, offensive speech without coercion is one of the least serious crimes (not really a crime). See the next chapter titled "Majoring in minors" for a fuller explanation.

People that are currently being persecuted for speech and action crimes are simply speaking and acting in support of their own beliefs which normally are biblical. The result of this is that unbiblical beliefs are able to trump biblical beliefs by being coercive (a much higher crime – See Chapter 7). This is simply false religion trumping true religion.

So the primary Modus Operandi to look for as a flags for identifying evils are as follows:
- Censorship
- Coercion
- Deception
- Political correctness
- The New Tolerance
- Outrage Based Coerced Conscience
- Majoring in minors

Next we will cover "Majoring in minors" as a way to censor the critical and important issues.

CHAPTER 7
How we can recognize evil by seeing "Majoring in minors"?

When it comes to biblical Christians addressing and trying to mitigate evil, the emphasis, if not censored completely, usually seems to be on somewhat minor issues rather than major ones. Generally, even Christian activists that are trying to address various evil philosophies and beliefs usually attack the bad fruit that keeps reappearing on the bad tree rather than attack the trunk or roots that support the tree (more on this in Part 4). This majoring in minors is also valid for what is highlighted and covered by the media when they censor the entire major concern. To be able to delineate between major and minor issues and anywhere in between, we need a method of ranking issues, false beliefs, evils etc. One way to do this is to establish indices. Reliability engineers use a Failure Mode and Effects Analysis (FMEA) to classify or categorize potential defects or hazards so the most critical ones can be addressed. i.e. major in majors. They take several critical parameters like "likelihood of occurrence," "severity of the failure" and "chance of detection" and estimate an index number from one to five or six for each and multiply them together to estimate the relative criticality. Let's do a similar thing here, except let's use bigger numbers because it is practical to use the number of people affected as one of the parameters and we want the other indices to be roughly the same order of magnitude.

The three parameters would include an action that is evil, the number of people affected and the motivation behind the action. Since the number of people can be hundreds of millions, severity line items of the other parameters can be increased by a factor of 10, 100 or 1000 above the lesser line item just below it (slightly less critical) depending upon how much more critical the action or motivation is.

Again, the purpose of these indices is to give a relative geometric weighting to issues, actions or attacks that will facilitate comparing the various ones to put them in the proper perspective to prevent us from majoring in minors and minoring in majors and to recognize evil when this is happening. Nothing is more tragic than concern, time and money spent on relatively minor things and having no concern over the major issues or attacks that are extremely destructive to ourselves, our families and our country. The numbers in the table below are somewhat arbitrary based upon what is viewed as the relative seriousness of the action. In this type of statistic, accuracy is not critical since differences are not critically important unless they have "orders of magnitude" differences.

ACTION SEVERITY INDEX

1.	Missing Heaven	1,000,000,000
2.	Murder of a child or unborn baby	1,000,000
3.	Murder of an adult	100,000
4.	Big lie that supports other evil actions	10,000
5.	Assault or injury	1,000
6.	Arson	500
7.	Identity theft	100
8.	Robbery	50
9.	Coercion	20
10.	Lying or deceiving	10
11.	Harassment or bulling	5
12.	Offending or causing stress	2

Notice how minor the offense of causing stress is compared with the far more serious actions. Several of these probably need some explanation to justify the numbers selected. These include missing heaven, murder of children or aborting unborn babies. The murder of children was set at 10 times higher than murdering an adult. This is supported below based upon biblical principles. Certainly, a child's murder should have a higher index than the murder of an adult. Abortion has been given the same index as murder of a child. I know that many may not agree with that, but the biblical principles quoted below support the value and potential viability of an unborn baby as equal to that of a child. The "missing heaven" index of just a 1000 times higher than murdering a child is very conservative based upon the infinitely longer time that we will exist in heaven (right here on earth) than our current time here on earth. Again, although most people believe in heaven, those that don't may take issue with using such an index. For those, please read Chapter 31 to increase your confidence in the truth of the bible.

The reason we have chosen to have the statistical weighting of murdering children higher than that of adults is based upon what Jesus said.

Matthew 18:6 states:

> [6] "Whoever causes one of these little ones who believe in Me to sin, it would be better for him if a millstone were hung around his neck, and he were drowned in the depth of the sea.

If God feels that way about just getting them to sin, how would He feel about killing them! Obviously He would see it as a great evil!

The bible reveals the great value of unborn children and their design and viability in two additional texts.

Exodus 21:22:23 states:

> [22] "If men fight, and hurt a woman with child, so that she gives birth prematurely, yet no harm follows, he shall surely be punished accordingly as the woman's husband imposes on him; and he shall pay as the judges determine. [23] But if any harm follows, then you shall give life for life,

This shows how valuable unborn babies are to God. Even the inadvertent killing of an unborn baby justifies death to those responsible, how much more will He hold us accountable that kill unborn babies intentionally!

Psalm 139:13-16 states:

> [13] For You formed my inward parts;
> You covered me in my mother's womb.
> [14] I will praise You, for I am fearfully and wonderfully made;
> Marvelous are Your works,
> And that my soul knows very well.
> [15] My frame was not hidden from You,
> When I was made in secret,
> And skillfully wrought in the lowest parts of the earth.
> [16] Your eyes saw my substance, being yet unformed.
> And in Your book they all were written,
> The days fashioned for me,
> When as yet there were none of them.

EXTENT OF THE EFFECTS OF EVIL INDEX

Regarding statistical parameters for the extent of the effects of an evil action, we could just use the estimated number of people affected or potentially affected. For one person the parameter index would simply be 1 and for a country of 300,000,000 people affected it could be 300,000,000.

MOTIVATION OF EVIL INDEX

In our criminal justice laws we differentiate between various motivations in determining the severity of the crime and the punishment. Premeditated (first degree) murder is considered more serious than second degree murder. Second degree murder is considered more serious than manslaughter etc. Now we have hate crimes that are more serious than crimes where hate was not the motivation (as if that was possible). With this in mind the following relative motivation index of evil is proposed.

EVIL MOTIVATION INDEX TABLE

1. Conspiring to control the whole world — 1,000,000,000
2. Conspiring to control a country — 10,000,000
3. Systematic teaching of hate to a population — 1,000,000
4. Conspire against a group — 100,000
5. Hate toward a group by an individual — 10,000
6. Conspire against an individual — 5,000
7. Hate toward individual by an individual — 1,000
8. Disregard for others rights — 100
9. Demonization and denigration of others — 10
10. Ambivalence toward others — 3
11. Love others — 0.1

TOTAL INDEX OF EVIL STATISTIC

The relative total effect would be the product of the action severity index, the extent index and the evil motivation index. For example if a person in an office was harassing or bulling 10 people in the office just for fun the total index of evil would be 5 (harassment) X 10 (number affected) X 3 (ambivalence) = 150. The use of a weapon of mass destruction where a population was systematically taught to hate the victim population of 100,000 people where 10,000 adults were killed and 10,000 children were killed and 80,000 wounded would be 10,000 X 100,000 X 1,000,000 + 10,000 X 1,000,000 X 1,000,000 + 80,000 X 1,000 X 1,000,000 = 1,000,000,000,000,000 + 10,000,000,000,000,000 + 80,000,000,000,000 = 11,080,000,000,000,000. All statistics should be rounded to not only one significant digit, but only using 1's as opposed to 2 through 9's. Doing this, the harassment statistic of 150 would be 100 or 10^2 and the weapon of mass destruction statistic of 11,080,000,000,000,000 would be 10,000,000,000,000,000 or 10^{16}. Usually an attack or evil philosophy with high index numbers can be simplified by only including the most severe action and those affected by it and worst motivational reason. The statistic was calculated for an action that actually took place. Alternatively, such statistics could be calculated for a potential attack or action. For the potential statistic, the extent would be the total target population.

These statistic numbers get so big that we need to convert them into numbers that we can better understand. To do this we simply use the base 10 log of the number to compress the statistic. Then, the statistic for the harassment is 2 and the statistic for a weapon of mass destruction is 16. We must keep in mind that for each increase of one the statistic is actually ten times more critical.

ADDITIONAL STATISTIC WHEN TAX DOLLARS PROMOTE EVIL ACTIONS

Typically when our government is promoting some evil philosophy or action they spend tax dollars to promote it. One great example of this is the promotion of macroevolution. The government spends money on grants to promote evolution. All the textbooks and time spent by teachers promoting a false evil religious philosophy is not only wasted, but used to support other evils. A statistic on this evil action would be as follows:

Action Index for big lie that supports other evil actions	=10,000
Extent index of affected population	= 300,000,000
Motivation index for disregard for others rights	=100
Dollars spent (in millions) to promote evil	=$1,000
Total index	= 3×10^{17} or a compressed statistic of 17.

TYPICAL MEDIA REPORTING

Typically the media does not make it clear who is on the side of evil and who is not. Sometimes when they do, they have it backwards. They typically have an ideology to promote. Before we can even identify something as evil we need to be able to delineate between good and evil. As we will show in Chapter 10, sometimes we need special instruments to identify evil. Other times we need to be able to see through the lies to recognize who are the good guys and who the bad guys are. One great example of this is the conflict in the middle-east between Israel and their Arab, Muslim neighbors. The UN basically views Israel as the bad guy. Europe views Israel as the bad guy. Now with President Obama we view Israel also as the bad guy. Almost any commentary or article about Israel either views Israel in a negative light or in a neutral light. Most of the world has a negative view of Israel in spite of all that the facts that make it extremely clear that Israel is not the bad guy. Charles Krauthammer wrote an article in the Washington Post that was published in the St. Paul Pioneer Press on July 19th or 20th, 2014. The title was "Moral clarity in Gaza" and it made it extremely clear that Israel was not the bad guy. It is amazing how the whole world can be duped into believing the good guys are the bad guys and the bad guys are the good guys. Krauthammer stated:

> "Here is the difference between us," explains the Israeli prime minister. "We're using missile defense to protect our civilians and they're using their civilians to protect their missiles." Rarely does international politics present a moment of such moral clarity. Yet we routinely hear this Israel-Gaza fighting described as a morally equivalent "cycle of violence."[10]

Also, Appendix C has an article written by my Sunday school teacher Bob Barlow showing how the Jews should be given high recognition for what they have done both based upon humanitarian efforts and technical successes.

A lot more could be stated here in defense of Israel, but these facts should be sufficient to clarify who is good or bad.

Basically all the attention by the media in the daily news is for low total indices of non-stealth evils that have a relatively low total index of evil. This is primarily because they affect either one person or very few even though the severity of an action may be high. Typically when the media reports on terrorist actions or war, it doesn't clearly delineate between good and evil. Sometimes when it identifies one side as more evil, it is the wrong one. My biggest concern is the existence of stealth evils. These evils are not recognized as evils and are typically thought of as something that is good. All of the things listed as false foundations in Part 4 are stealth evils as well as others cited. Everyone thinks of them as based upon science or as post-modern enlightenment. One that is being pushed today includes man made global warming. Stealth evils will be covered in Chapter 24. It is our misfortune that these evils are stealth, thus invisible.

Next we will cover the effects of evil.

CHAPTER 8
Recognizing evil based upon effects

EFFECTS OF FOLLOWING THE FLESH VS. FOLLOWING GOD

Galatians 5:19-21 states:

[19] Now the works of the flesh are evident, which are: adultery, fornication, uncleanness, lewdness, [20] idolatry, sorcery, hatred, contentions, jealousies, outbursts of wrath, selfish ambitions, dissensions, heresies, [21] envy, murders, drunkenness, revelries, and the like; of which I tell you beforehand, just as I also told you in time past, that those who practice such things will not inherit the kingdom of God.

This text connects our fleshly desires with ungodly behaviors and in line with what Satan wants us to do. These are the effects that would be expected from a people, group or country that is not following God and the bible. Those things are exactly what we are seeing in our country.

Galatians 5:22-23 states:

[22] But the fruit of the Spirit is love, joy, peace, longsuffering, kindness, goodness, faithfulness, [23] gentleness, self-control. Against such there is no law.

Based upon the above bible texts evil has many bad effects whereas the effects of a life that has been transformed by God has good effects. The same is true of nations that recognize God and give Him the allegiance He deserves or nations that "thumb their noses" at God. Certainly, that is exactly what we see in our world. Although as we learned earlier, we as individuals are punished for our sins in the afterlife. However this is not so with countries and nations.

I fear for our national health and survival for "thumbing our nose" at God. Additionally, I fear for our country because of the way we have treated and are treating Israel. Genesis 12:3 states:

I will bless those who bless you, And I will curse him who curses you; .

William R. Koenig, a presidential reporter, wrote a book titled "Eye to Eye." In his book he showed how our country was consistently devastated by some storm or flood within 24 hours of when we tried to force Israel to trade land for peace.

Next we will cover how we can recognize evil based upon our conscience.

CHAPTER 9
How can we recognize evil based upon our conscience?

The following article on our conscience shows that our conscience does recognize evil. This excerpt from Orthodox America is quoted with permission.

The Action of Conscience in Man

One woman, by reason of poverty, took something from a store and carried it away surreptitiously. No one saw her. But from that moment a certain unpleasant feeling gave her no peace. She had to go back to the store and return what she had taken. Having done this, she came home with a feeling of relief. Such cases, in which people are forced to act contrary to their advantage or their pleasure, are impossible to enumerate.

Each individual is acquainted with his inner voice which at times reproaches and persecutes him as it were, and at other times encourages and gladdens him. This refined, innate moral feeling is called conscience. Conscience--it is a kind of spiritual instinct which differentiates between good and evil more quickly and more clearly than the mind. He who follows his conscience will not regret his actions.

In the Holy Scriptures the conscience is also called the heart. In the Sermon on the Mount the Lord Jesus Christ likens the conscience to the eye, by means of which a person sees his moral state (Matt. 6:22). He also likens it to an adversary with whom a man must make peace before he appears before the Judge (Matt. 5:25). This last comparison reveals the distinguishing characteristic of the conscience: to oppose our bad actions and intentions.

Our personal experience likewise proves that this inner voice, called the conscience, is located outside our control and expresses itself independently, quite apart from our desire. Just as we cannot convince ourselves that we are full when we are hungry, or that we are rested when we are tired, so, too, we cannot convince ourselves that we have done something good when our conscience tells us that we have done something bad.

Some see in Christ's words concerning the "worm that dieth not", which will torment sinners in the life to come, a reference to the gnawing of the conscience (Mark 9:44). Similar torments of the conscience were expressively and colorfully described by A. S. Pushkin in his dramatic work, "The Avaricious Knight":

"Conscience -

A clawed beast, scraping the heart; conscience is An uninvited guest, a tiresome interlocutor, A churlish creditor; it is---a witch, Before whom the moon and the tombs grow dim."

And further the knight with terror recalls the pleading and the tears of all those whom he pitilessly robbed.

A Common Natural Law

The presence of the conscience gives evidence that indeed, just as the Bible relates, in the very process of creating man, God placed within the depths of his soul His image and likeness (Gen. 1:26). For this reason it is customary to call the conscience the voice of God in man. As a moral law written directly on man's heart, it acts in all people, independent of age, race, upbringing and level of development.

Anthropologists who study the morals and customs of various underdeveloped and primitive peoples testify that to this day they have yet to find, even among the wildest savages, a people lacking some form of an understanding of good and evil. Furthermore, many tribes not only place a high value on good and despise evil, but for the most part their views agree on the essence of the one and the other. Many even primitive tribes stand just as high in their understanding of good and evil as many cultured peoples. Even among those tribes which place a positive value on certain deeds which are unacceptable according to prevailing opinion, there is in general a marked consensus in the moral consciousnesses of all people.

In the first chapter of his epistle to the Romans, the holy, Apostle Paul writes in some detail concerning the actions of the inner moral law in man. The Apostle reproaches the Jews who, knowing the written law of God, often transgress it, whereas the pagans, which have not the [written] law, do by nature the things contained in the law....Which [thereby] shew the work of the law written in their hearts, their conscience also bearing witness, and their thoughts the meanwhile accusing or else excusing one another (Rom. 2:14-15). Here, too, Apostle Paul explains how this law of conscience sometimes rewards and at other times punishes a man. Each person, therefore, no matter who he may be, Jew or Gentile, has a feeling of uneasiness, of distress and oppression, when he does something wrong or indulges in licentiousness; an inner feeling gives him to know that such actions will incur God's punishment (Rom. 1:32). At the coming Dread Judgment God will judge people not only according to their faith, but also according to the witness of their conscience. For this reason, as the Apostle Paul teaches, even pagans can attain salvation if their consciences bear witness before God of a life of good deeds.

The conscience has a highly refined sense of good and evil. If man were not marred by sin, he would have no need of the written law. His conscience could rightly guide all his actions. The need for a written law arose after the Fall, when man, darkened by passions, ceased to hear clearly the voice of his conscience. But in essence, both the written law and the inner law of the conscience speak about the same thing: Whatsoever ye would that men should do to you, do ye even so to them: for this is the law and the prophets (Matt. 7:12).

In our daily relations with people we subconsciously place greater trust in a man's conscience than in written laws and rules. After all, one cannot track down every violation, and even the law "something drew a breath, you turn around, it's gone". Whereas the conscience contains in itself the eternal and immutable law of God. And because of this, normal relations between people are possible only as long as people have not lost within themselves the voice of conscience.[11]

Next we will go to Part 3, "How do we recognize evil based upon beliefs diametrically opposite to biblical beliefs?"

Part 3

How do we recognize evil based upon beliefs diametrically opposite to biblical beliefs?

The following poem purported to be written by a Minnesota high school student on how America's worldview has been turned around 180 degrees is in sync with the concept of Part 3. Everything that used to be good is now bad and everything that used to be bad is now good! Source unknown.

NEW School Prayer:
~~~~~~~~~~~~~~~~~~

Now I sit me down in school
Where praying is against the rule
For this great nation under God
Finds mention of Him very odd.

If scripture now the class recites,
It violates the Bill of Rights.
And anytime my head I bow
Becomes a Federal matter now.

Our hair can be purple, orange or green,
That's no offense; it's a freedom scene..
The law is specific, the law is precise.
Prayers spoken aloud are a serious vice.

For praying in a public hall
Might offend someone with no faith at all..
In silence alone we must meditate,
God's name is prohibited by the State..

We're allowed to cuss and dress like freaks,
And pierce our noses, tongues and cheeks...
They've outlawed guns, but FIRST the Bible.
To quote the Good Book makes me liable.

We can elect a pregnant Senior Queen,
And the 'unwed daddy,' our Senior King.
It's 'inappropriate' to teach right from wrong,
We're taught that such 'judgments' do not belong..

We can get our condoms and birth controls,
Study witchcraft, vampires and totem poles...
But the Ten Commandments are not allowed,
No word of God must reach this crowd.

It's scary here I must confess,
When chaos reigns the school's a mess.
So, Lord, this silent plea I make:
Should I be shot; My soul please take!
Amen

CHAPTER 10
From cultural and political positions

Now that we have established a biblical understanding of the significance of evil in our world, we are about ready to dive into the heart of the issue. However, first let's cover what the bible says about the difficulty in receiving and accepting the truth.

Jesus tells the disciples why He speaks in parables in Matthew 13:13-15:

> [13] Therefore I speak to them in parables, because seeing they do not see, and hearing they do not hear, nor do they understand. [14] And in them the prophecy of Isaiah is fulfilled, which says: 'Hearing you will hear and shall not understand, And seeing you will see and not perceive; [15] For the hearts of this people have grown dull. Their ears are hard of hearing, And their eyes they have closed, Lest they should see with their eyes and hear with their ears, Lest they should understand with their hearts and turn, So that I should heal them.'

Obviously God would have no trouble if He wanted to force us to understand and accept what we at times refuse to understand. However, that is not His plan. If we are willing to blind ourselves and not see His truth, He is willing to let us to continue in darkness. Romans 1:18 & 25 states:

> [18] For the wrath of God is revealed from heaven against all ungodliness and unrighteousness of men, who suppress the truth in unrighteousness, . .
>
> [25] who exchanged the truth of God for the lie, and worshiped and served the creature rather than the Creator, who is blessed forever. Amen.

One requirement needed to understand the truth is to want to know the truth. Evil certainly cannot thrive with the light of truth shining on it and perhaps can't even exist in the presence of light. Perhaps it is appropriate here to quote John 3:19-21 again. It states:

> [19] And this is the condemnation, that the light has come into the world, and men loved darkness rather than light, because their deeds were evil. [20] For everyone practicing evil hates the light and does not come to the light, lest his deeds should be exposed. [21] But he who does the truth comes to the light, that his deeds may be clearly seen, that they have been done in God."

TOOLS NEEDED TO SEE EVIL

In addition to the above texts explaining the blindness that allows evil to thrive, it also supports the concept expressed earlier that good and evil have a dual (diametric opposite) nature with no neutral ground between good and evil. However, just trying to see evil and how it appears in our world is not always sufficient for it to be readily identified. Sometimes we also need appropriate tools or instruments to be able to identify evil. I am sure that the reader is familiar with our inability to see the electromagnetic spectrum beyond the visible range and hear the audio spectrum beyond our hearing range. However, with appropriate instruments we can see and hear the complete spectrums. One tool that will help us see the evil in our world that is not normally perceived is simple probability science.

PROBABILITY SCIENCE

One way this tool can help us see evil is by recognizing that our cultural, political, economic and religious issues are basically only two sided. We believe in abortion or we don't. We believe in homosexual marriage or we don't. We believe in either socialism or capitalism. Consequently, if we can find two different philosophies, political parties, beliefs or specific religions etc. that are basically diametrically opposed to each other in every respect, we can draw some statistical conclusions that some rational cause is behind the diametric opposition rather than random chance. If one of those philosophies or religious beliefs could be viewed or considered a standard of some type like the bible that is fixed and doesn't change, the conclusions could be quite profound since the standard would either have to be completely true or completely false and the same would be true for the other philosophy, political party or religion etc. We would only need to identify which was which!

POLITICAL POSITIONS

A wonderful, scholarly source for this type of information is a 600 page book titled "Politics According to the Bible," By Dr. Wayne Grudem. In Section 2 of the book he covered 62 specific political issues. It is my interpretation of his overall conclusion that the progressive, liberal or secular positions are all diametrically opposed to explicit or implicit biblical principles or violate factual knowledge. If these issues were "cherry picked" just to show the diametric opposition, any statistical analysis would be invalid. However, Grudem picked all popular current issues under the following categories: The Protection of Life, Marriage, The Family, Economics, The Environment, National Defense, Foreign Policy, Freedom of Speech, Freedom of Religion and Special Groups. From a biblical perspective that means that those progressive, liberal or secular positions are all wrong! However, we must also keep an open mind that the bible has it all wrong and that basically the Democrats have it all right. I used Democrats here in place of progressives, liberals and secularists because they are the same. However, I do not believe that Republicans are basically conservatives since Republican moderates are very similar to Democrats since they are for big government and everything that goes with that that philosophy. Consequently, when we contrast opposite political positions on issues it should be against true conservatives not Republicans.

My interpretation of Dr. Grudem's book is supported by the following quotes and conclusions that he draws. Quotes from his book are made with permission.

In his introduction he begins with laying a foundation of the Christian worldview to make sure that biblical texts are not out taken of context. He states:

> Before turning to specific issues, I attempt . . . to lay a foundation concerning the main components of a Christian worldview: What does the bible say about God as Creator, about the earth He created, about us as men and women created in His image, about sin, and about God's purpose for putting human beings on the earth in the first place? I lay this broad foundation so as to avoid a common mistake of using bible verses out of context to support nearly any position on current political disputes.[12]

He continues immediately to put this in perspective and explains where he is going in the rest of the book:

> This foundation of a Christian worldview is necessary in order to "see the parts in light of the whole" and thus to understand individual verses correctly from within the overall framework of the Bible's primary teachings. I put this material at the beginning of the book because basic worldview differences have profound implications for many matters of government policy. In fact, differences over worldview questions explain many of the disagreements between "liberals" and "conservatives" in politics today.
>
> In the rest of the book I examine about sixty specific current issues. I attempt to analyze them from the standpoint of that biblical understanding of civil government and that biblical worldview and also with reference to specific teachings of the bible that pertain to that issue.[13]

He goes on to explain his three level basis for analysis:

> On some issues I think the overall teaching of the bible is clear, direct and decisive, . . There is a second set of issues where I depend on arguments from broader principles. . . Then I have a third type of argument: an appeal to facts in the world.[14]

The 62 item list below is basically a list of the political issues that Dr. Grudem compared to biblical teaching in his book as part of the Table of Contents that he refers to as simply "Contents:"[15] This list is slightly different because all items were not really political issues and some were split into two separate political issues.

Category	No.	Issue
The Protection of Life	1	Abortion
The Protection of Life	2	Euthanasia
The Protection of Life	3	Capital punishment
The Protection of Life	4	Gun ownership and self-defense
Marriage	5	Marriage between one and one woman
Marriage	6	Adultery, homosexuality and incest
Marriage	7	Polygamy
Marriage	8	Divorce
Marriage	9	Definition of marriage and family
Marriage	10	Pornography
Family	11	Bearing children vs. population control
Family	12	Parents having primary control over children vs. government
Family	13	School voucher system
Family	14	Discipline of children and spanking
Economics	15	Private property
Economics	16	Economic development
Economics	17	The money supply
Economics	18	Free markets
Economics	19	Regulation
Economics	20	The rich and the poor
Economics	21	Government and business
Economics	22	Taxes
Economics	23	Social security
Economics	24	Health care
Economics	25	The cure for recession
Environment	27	The current state of the earth's resources
Environment	28	Energy resources and energy uses
Environment	29	Global warming
Environment	30	Carbon fuels
Environment	31	CAFÉ standards for automobile millage
Environment	32	Cap and trade
National Defense	33	Pacifism
National Defense	34	Defense policy in the US
National Defense	35	Islamic jihadism
National Defense	36	Nuclear weapons

National Defense	37	The CIA
National Defense	38	Coercive interrogation of prisoners
National Defense	39	Homosexuals in the military
National Defense	40	Women in combat
Foreign Policy	41	The United Nations
Foreign Policy	42	Foreign aid
Foreign Policy	43	Israel
Foreign Policy	44	Immigration
Freedom of Speech	45	The United States Constitution
Freedom of Speech	46	Restrictions on freedoms of speech
Freedom of Speech	47	Campaign finance restrictions
Freedom of Speech	48	Hate Speech
Freedom of Speech	49	The "Fairness Doctrine" and talk radio
Freedom of Religion	50	Religious expression in the public square
Freedom of Religion	51	Faith-based programs
Freedom of Religion	52	Political advocacy by churches
Special Groups	53	Regulators: invisible bureaucrats who regulate people's lives
Special Groups	54	Earmarks
Special Groups	55	Affirmative action
Special Groups	56	Gender based quotas
Special Groups	57	Farm subsidies
Special Groups	58	Tariffs
Special Groups	59	Trial lawyers, medical malpractice awards and reform of tort law
Special Groups	60	The National Education Foundation
Special Groups	61	Native Americans
Special Groups	62	Gambling

In Part 2, Specific Issues, the book explains why each progressive, liberal or secular position on these issues is opposed to the biblical position or relevant facts in the world today. Here we will not take the time to go into detail on how all the progressive positions are opposed to the biblical position; they are covered in Dr. Grudem's book. However, we will cover some of these in a later chapter.

At this point we need to consider what possibilities can explain how progressive, liberal or secular positions and the bible can be in diametric opposition on all of a large number of independent two sided positions. If it came about by accident without a foundational reason like an authority and rebellion against the authority or good vs. evil or truth vs. falsehood etc., we can calculate the probability of that happening by random chance using probability science. It is the same probability as flipping a coin and getting heads each and every time with the number of flips equaling the number of issues. The formula is simple and it is 2^n where "n" is the number of flips or issues. Don't let the mathematics scare you. It simply means you multiply two times itself "n" times. For n=2 it is just 2 x 2 or 4. For n=3 it is 2 x 2 x 2 = 8. On your calculator it is y^x where "y" is 2 and "x" is "n." For an "n" of 62 it is 4.6 x 10^{18} or 4,600,000,000,000,000,000 or 4.6 quintillion. Consequently, the chances of perfect opposition between 62 liberal progressive independent sequential or random positions (not "cherry picked") and the biblical position is one in 4.6 quintillion unless some underling foundation or force is the cause. The fact that those chances are so slim means that some foundational reason or forces like those suggested above exists to explain that complete opposition. However, what remains to be explained is which is right and which is wrong. Building on what we just learned, we can establish that one of the following tables is correct and one is false and we need to decide which is which:

Proposed scenario:

Bible correct	Progressives wrong
Right	Wrong
God as authority	Satan and progressives as rebels
Good	Evil
True	False
Desirable effects	Undesirable effects
Good fruit	Bad fruit

Alternate scenario:

Progressives correct	Bible wrong
Right	Wrong
Satan as authority	God as the rebel
Good	Evil
True	False
Desirable effects	undesirable effects
Good fruit	Bad fruit

I don't believe that anyone has ever proposed the alternative scenario as the correct one. However, we need to either eliminate it as a possibility or accept it as a possibility. Lucifer or Satan has never claimed that he created God; only that he wanted to be like the Most High. God never said that he wanted to be like Satan or wanted to have Satan's power and position. Also, if the alternative scenario is true all the biblical precepts, commandments etc. would be bad. I never have heard anybody claim that if people followed the commandments it would result in a bad and evil society. The complaints about the commandments include that they are too difficult to keep, they prevent us from fulfilling our desires and secondly when we do fulfill our desires, they make us feel guilty.

Let's carry this one step further to help us understand the full implications of this diametric opposition. Another way of helping us understand this profound anomaly is to have you pretend that you are a school teacher. You give your students a 50 question true and false test. The answers to half of the test questions are true and half false. You randomize the order of the questions so the next question would have an equal chance of being true or false. Several of your students got all the questions right. The rest of the student's test results were as expected except for one student. That student got all the answers wrong. The question is, what would you conclude about that student? Would you conclude he just didn't know the material? Would that explain the result? Definitely not! If he knew nothing about the material he would get about half of the answers correct by random chance. So how would you explain getting all wrong answers? The only possible explanation is that either the student basically knew all the right answers and intentionally gave the wrong answers or someone trained the student in a 100% diametric opposite way to what was right. How else could you explain this test result? You can bet that no student ever got all the questions wrong on a 50 question true and false test because of ignorance or lack of knowledge; it is statistically impossible. The fact that in our culture and politics we get it all wrong based upon the bible is so profound that it should shake us to our core! It screams that some outside influence has affected our culture and our politics. We already rejected the possibility that perhaps our culture has it right and the bible has it all wrong. Consequently, as the bible teaches, it is Satan that knows what is right, yet does and teaches everything that is wrong. Rebellion against God, the bible and the good and truthful authority is the only reasonable explanation.

CULTURAL, POLITICALLY CORRECT POSITIONS

In a similar way that the progressive / liberal political positions are in diametric opposition to biblical positions, we can show that cultural, politically correct positions are also diametrically opposed to biblical principles and consequently also verify the evil in the culture and the truth of the bible. First let's demonstrate that concept just based upon the first several chapters in Genesis and then based upon the overall contrast between the beliefs of our politically correct culture and biblical principles.

EARLY GENESIS CONCEPTS

We covered an overview of some of the fundamental concepts documented in the first few chapters in Genesis in Chapter 1. Here we would like to go into more detail on these concepts and show how our politically correct culture is 100% diametrically opposed to each biblical concept. The purpose of this is to add more support to our assertion that something more than chance is behind the cause of the diametric opposition.

THE CHRISTIAN WORLDVIEW RADIO PROGRAM – DAVID WHEATON HOST

The concepts and comments below are based upon a syndicated radio program called "The Christian Worldview" hosted by David Wheaton. The specific program that relates to this issue was titled "So What's New in the World? Well, Actually Nothing." That program was aired on October 27, 2015. Quotes, paraphrases and concepts are documented here with permission. We start with David's introductory quote and continue with paraphrases.

> Many people, including Christians, watch what is taking place around the world and find it hard to understand. It seems that everything is changing and that we have entered a "brave new world."
> For example, why is public life in America (education, government, business, etc.) expunging anything Christian as fast as possible? Why has marriage been redefined to include homosexual unions? Why is there perpetual turmoil in the world, especially in the Middle East? Why is man-made climate change alarmism a constant refrain? Why don't the recent abortion videos cause taxpayer funding to be withdrawn?
> Why is there a push for global unity, global government. A world without borders. In Europe, historically Christian countries are now secular, welcoming Muslim emigrants into their countries that don't want the values of their countries."

He continues:

With all these questions we need to look at the very early chapters of the first book of the bible, Genesis, to understand that what is taking place today actually started at the very beginning. He stated, we could answer all those questions listed above with the following explanation.

The explanation for everything that is taking place on the world is this:

1. What God has established or said man rejects! That is the operating principle of the world. Why does he do this? What is the motivation behind this rejection or rebellion against God? Because God gave man free will and his or her chosen desire is to be like God, not under God's authority.

2. How does man go about rejecting God and accomplishing this? Man either has to make up and believe a lie about what God has said and/or established or pretend that God doesn't exist.

As we look across all the various events in the world, those events can be confusing and seem convoluted. But what is helpful is to look across history and realize that God has a metanarrative of history with a really big story above the little stories going on and connecting the dots between them. God's really big story has four components. Creation, the fall of man (corruption), redemption and restoration. This is a very helpful way of understanding the trajectory of where God is taking human history. Behind this is a heavenly conflict taking place where Satan is the inspiration and instigator of man's rejection and rebellion against God. God meanwhile is the gracious and merciful instigator of man's redemption. I am going to read a couple short portions of Genesis from the first three or four chapters. Genesis 1:1-5.

Genesis Chapter 1

In the beginning God created the heavens and the earth. [2] The earth was without form, and void; and darkness was on the face of the deep. And the Spirit of God was hovering over the face of the waters. [3] Then God said, "Let there be light"; and there was light. [4] And God saw the light, that it was good; and God divided the light from the darkness. [5] God called the light Day, and the darkness He called Night. So the evening and the morning were the first day.

There are a few takeaways we can get from these verses based upon our premise of the day: What God had established, man rejects. It not only explains that God exists, but that he preexists. So how does man reject that? Man rejects that by becoming atheistic or secularistic by trying to basically eliminate God from even existing. The very first verse God doesn't give an apologetic as to why he exists. The phrase, "In the beginning God," is a presupposition. God is there and exists. Man rejects that. Point 2 is that God's word is powerful and authoritative. God just speaks things into existence and they happen. The power there is authoritative and man's rejection is not to take God's wisdom as the authority but takes his own human wisdom. We don't look to God's word for truth and wisdom on how to live our lives and please God but use our own human wisdom instead. Man turns, twists, rejects and rebels against what God says. The third thing is that the supernatural or the miraculous exists. In other words God spoke these things into existence. Out of nothing the things existed. This is miraculous. We cannot do this in a scientific lab. Man rejects this today by being naturalistic. Only what is natural exists. There is nothing beyond what we can taste, feel and touch and create with our own hands. There is nothing beyond the natural world. That is the worldview of our day. In the very first five verses of the bible our premise: What God has established or said, man rejects. You can see that from the very first verse. Now skipping down to later in the chapter to verse 26. We are in the creative part of that metanarrative; that first stage.

> [26] Then God said, "Let Us make man in Our image, according to Our likeness; let them have dominion over the fish of the sea, over the birds of the air, and over the cattle, over all the earth and over every creeping thing that creeps on the earth." [27] So God created man in His own image; in the image of God He created him; male and female He created them. [28] Then God blessed them, and God said to them, "Be fruitful and multiply; fill the earth and subdue it; have dominion over the fish of the sea, over the birds of the air, and over every living thing that moves on the earth. . ."
>
> [31] Then God saw everything that He had made, and indeed it was very good. So the evening and the morning were the sixth day.

Now we skip to the final day of creation. There are so many things that can be pulled out of those first five verses. First of all, let's make man in our image. God is a Trinitarian God. He is speaking about Himself and his son and his spirit. That completely repudiates the god of Islam, Allah, who is not the same god. Many evangelicals somehow believe that Allah and the biblical God are the same God. That is absolutely false. That is a heresy. Allah has no son and no spirit. The God of the bible has a father, son and a spirit: A gigantic difference. Also you see that man is made in God's image distinct from animals. That man is not another animal. Of course man rejects that this is what God has established by saying that we are just part of the animal kingdom, perhaps a more intelligent animal, but just part of the animal kingdom. You see how man rejects that. The third thing is that God creates two sexes, male and female. Distinctly one or the other. How does man reject this today? We see man in America where you can choose your own gender. If you are a boy and want to be a girl you can make that so. Another thing is that man and women were called to procreate and raise children. Today man rejects that by maybe getting married or perhaps not getting married. Children are optional and pretty much a problem to have. It puts us out to have children. Many countries in the world are not having enough children to replace their population. They are actually dying demographically because they are not reproducing enough. Not so in the Islamic world. Another thing from this short passage is that man has stewardship and dominion over creation. We know very well with the modern environmental movement, man-made climate change, how that has been rejected by man. Man overprotects the earth, he worships the earth. He overprotects the earth to his own detriment. What the poor need in the world is safe and clean uses of energy. Not to be told that they can't have energy so they can develop. It is just the opposite. And then finally we learn that what God creates is very good. However, we will soon find out in the next stage how man will corrupt it. Creation, fall, redemption and restoration and the guiding principle is that what God established man rejects.

Genesis Chapter 2

In Genesis 2 we see more parts of God's initial perfect creation. He establishes and says things that are good and right. We see how man didn't reject them right away but soon did reject them and that is the story that has been taking place ever since. So, in Genesis 2:1-3 by the 7th day "God completed his work that he had done. And he rested on the 7th day from all of the work that he had done. Then God blessed the 7th day and sanctified it because in it he rested from all the work he created and made." God sets an example for us to rest from our work. He rested from his work even though He didn't need to rest. He and the trinity are working constantly upholding, restraining the universe. He doesn't need rest but he sets an example for us that we would need rest. The modern day example of this is that there is a complete "workaholism" in corporate America in this country today. If you work 12-16 hours days that is exemplary, that's how you climb the corporate ladder. It is interesting that Chick Fillet, which is a Christian owned business that does incredibly well, closes its stores on Sunday so their employees can have some rest. So, man rejects what God says to take rest. So only a few follow God's command that we rest from our work one day of the week. Now it is interesting how God establishes this idea of rest from our work, but in the very same chapter he says we are to work and sustain things (Genesis 2:15). And today we see man's rejection of this example of rest from our work. But, we are to work and sustain things. And of course today, we see man's rejection of this. Man doesn't want to work. We have 95 million people of working ability and working age who are out of work in this country. Not all of them don't want to work. But certainly a government industry has been established that incentivizes not working. You can get benefits from government you can get all of these things even if you don't even need them. Even if you could work it's almost beneficial for you not to work so you get government benefits. Certainly there should be a safety net for those who just cannot support themselves and sustain themselves and the church should be involved in that. But there is a whole worldview with the focus of "I will do as little as I can." Maybe even no work if possible so I can do what I want to do in life. This is a complete rejection of God's command. Work is a good thing. It's a divine institution. That's where we will spend most of our life. That's how we sustain families and so forth. We also see as a side note that we often think that God is restrictive and has a lot of rules. Notice how he says you can eat from any tree in the garden you may eat freely. That's not very restrictive. It was very wide latitude within that boundary. And the boundary for man is good by the way. It is not that he wanted to set it to lord it over man. For the day you shall eat of it you shall die. If you eat it you will die. So don't eat from it; eat from every other tree in the garden (Verses 18-25). This is the end of Genesis 2, the end of the stage of perfection. And we see what God has established in this perfect stage. He creates the helper for the man. He established the roles between men and women for today. Now fast forward to today. How does man reject what God has established or said? The feminist movement believes that man and women should be coequals. They should have the exact same roles. They are coequals certainly in value. But their roles are distinct from one another. Not one more important than the other, but serve distinct roles. The bible teaches that a man needs to love his wife and the wife should be in submission to her husband in a beautiful relationship. This is a picture of how God loves his church. This concept has been completely rejected. This is an explanation for so much of how the family has broken down today. The second thing that is key is that God establishes heterosexual marriage. Not a polygamist marriage, not a homosexual marriage but a man marrying a woman. We know how that has been completely rejected by man today and redefined. Homosexuality has been around since the very early days of creation. But codifying it by government into law and recognizing it as legitimate marriage is new. I don't believe that has ever been done in human history before. I don't think America was the first country to do it, but certainly this is relatively new to mankind.

Genesis Chapter 3

Somewhere between the creation and where man falls, Satan fell himself. He chose to be like God. He took a third of the angels with him and he created this adversarial relationship between God and himself. Satan as the instigator did and will continue to try to get man to do the same against God.

There is so much in that passage that is relevant. Here is the adversarial relationship between God and Satan. Satan enters with one key weapon; the lie. There is always a twisting of what God says. What God has said or established man rebelled against. Man has to eliminate God or twist what He says. He must believe or make up a lie about what was said by God. All sin comes from believing a lie. What God has established man rejects.

So what's new in the world? According to the first chapters of Genesis really nothing is new in the world. Just a perpetuation of more sin and more fallenness and man's rebellion against God.

In the things that God has established we see an explanation of everything going on in the world today such as Middle East tensions, secularism, expunging of anything Christian, global unity and global warming. All this is explained in the early chapters of Genesis. We were going over the key passage in Genesis 3 where the serpent tempts Eve and this absolutely changed everything in the world. It goes against what we are told about man today. We are told that man is inherently good. Man is good. And with enough education and financial resources he'll act civilized. This is not the case. Unlike God who is infallible. Man is fallible. Man is not basically good. Man chooses to worship himself instead of God. Man doesn't want to be under God's authority but wants to be his own god and authority. The eyes of Adam and Eve were opened. God has given man a conscious to know right from wrong. Man has a conscious. There is a conscience that says this is wrong. You can sear that conscience so there is no conscience, but initially we have a God-given warning system. So we can know how to please him.

We read in Genesis 3:8-13 how they were hiding from God. We can see the Lord God had a daily pattern of walking and relating to Adam and Eve. That is the purpose for all of our lives. To be in relationship with God. Not to just know He exists but God's intention for every one of us is to have a right relationship with Him. And relate to Him intimately. That is the purpose of life. To be in a relationship with Christ. We can enter this relationship because God gives us forgiveness and reconciliation and restores the relationship that we break. Adam and Eve sinned and that broke the relationship with God and causes them to hide from God. Man always shifts blame for his sins.

Immediately after the fall we see God in his grace and mercy immediately moves on to the stage of redemption. The fall still impacts everything through this stage of redemption. But now the fall and redemption occur concurrently. The wages of sin is death (Romans 3:23). Sin explains why you have cancer or people die and terrible things happen. There are murders and wars. It is all because of sin. It is the overall explanation for everything that happens. Immediately God begins his plan of redemption. Genesis 3:15 states what God will do to Satan: "Shall bruise you on the head." That was first mention of redemption and a redeemer and a conflict between Satan and God. Right away, there is a redemption. God immediately knows man will die and be judged and sentenced to Hell but he will graciously redeem some out of this. There will be a conflict in marriage. There will be a rejection of the roles. The wife is going to desire to rule over her husband. And her husband will sinfully lord it over his wife. This a great explanation for all of the divorce. Sin brings forth death. In Genesis 3:20 Eve was called the "mother of all the living" and it stated that the "Lord God made skins and clothed them." This is a picture of the substitute for our sin. Blood shed for their sins. Without shedding of blood there is no redemption from sin. Penal substitutionary atonement is necessary. God provided a substitute so we can be atoned with God. Substitutionary atonement through Christ.

God drove the man out of the Garden of Eden. He stationed a cherubim to guard the way to the tree of life. Man may have sinned but now in the stage of redemption, God has put a restraint on our desire to want to be like God. God knew for our own good that He would cast Adam and Eve out of the garden or they would continue to corrupt themselves. That is why the world has not imploded. Not now, but God will allow it to implode at some point. Until then there is a restraint that has taken over. If it wasn't there, our world would be far worse than what we are experiencing now.

Genesis Chapter 4

The sacrifices that Cain and Abel brought to the Lord represented the Beginning of false religion. God must have told them to bring an animal sacrifice; a blood sacrifice. That's what Abel did. Cain must have brought an agriculture sacrifice. But, Cain brought a sacrifice to God that was not commanded by God. This was the beginning of false spirituality or false religion. Man made up his own way to worship God. What did Cain do when God rejected his sacrifice? He got revenge by murdering Abel. Why was Christ persecuted and crucified? It is because Satan hates God, His chosen people, His followers and the righteous. This is the end of the summary of the radio program.

This concludes the paraphrase of the radio program.

Summarizing and conclusion of program concepts

God's plan is right on track. Christ will return and bring restoration. It showed for every concept or principle that God ordained, man rejected it and believed or did the diametric opposite. Let's summarize all to those opposing concepts below:

God's ordained principle or concept	Man's diametrically opposite belief
God exists	Denies God's existence
God's authority	Man rejects God's authority
God's wisdom	Man reject God's wisdom and asserts man's wisdom
God's supernatural creation and miracles	Man denies the possibility of miracles, holds to naturalism
Man is made in God's image	Man is simply an intelligent animal
God distinctly created male and female	You can chose your own gender
Men and women are called to	Children are optional and approve of gay

procreate	sexual partners
Stewardship and dominion over creation	Man individually pollutes the earth
Stewardship and dominion over creation	Politically man overprotects the earth
Stewardship and dominion over creation	Spiritually man worships the earth not the creator of it
God instructed man do not eat of one tree	Man did eat of the fruit of that tree
God instructed us to rest one day per week	Business men and other men work seven days per week
Other than the 7th day we are taught to work	We have a large entitlement class that refuse to work
Different roles established for men and women	Feminist movement, roles should be the same
God ordained heterosexual marriage	Man legitimatizes gay marriage and polygamy
Man is deceitful and wicked	Man is basically good and perfectible
God has placed a conscience in man that knows good from evil	Man is the measure of all things and can create his own morality
Our purpose is to have a relationship with God	Our purpose is pragmatic seeking self-pleasure
Sin explains all evil and misery in the world	Evil doesn't exist and misery is from nature or random happenings
God provided a redemption to cure the effects of sin with His Son	Man rejects God and belittles his redemption plan
God commanded that we should not worship other gods or worship idols	Man worships many other gods including God's creation and places many idols above God

This list of God's ordained concepts and principles at the beginning of Genesis includes more than 20 items. Again the probability of this happening by random chance is less that one chance in a million.

OVERALL CONTRAST BETWEEN THE BELIEFS OF OUR POLITICALLY CORRECT CULTURE AND BIBLICAL PRINCIPLES

The following table of diametric opposite cultural or progressive, liberal or secular beliefs adds additional support to our conclusion that a force behind the scenes is guiding our culture and politics:

Biblical Theism Position	Biblical References	Cultural or Liberal, Progressive or Secular Belief
God exists	Gen. 1:1; Rev. 1:8; John 1:1-3	Man is god
Bible is true	John 17:17; 2 Tim. 3:16; Psalm 119:160	Deny biblical truth
Absolute truth	Malachi 3:6; John 14:6	Relative truth
Special creation	Gen. 1 & 2; Exodus 20:11	Macro-evolution
Man made in image of God	Gen. 1:26-27; Gen. 5:1	Man is just an animal
Man is wicked	Jeremiah 17:9; Isaiah 64:6	Man is good and perfectible
Principled	Psalm 111:7; 119:4, 40, 45, 69, 93, 100	Pragmatic
Truth	John 14:6; 17:17; 18:37	Lies & deceit
Objective	Lev. 19:36; Deut. 10:17; 2 Chron. 19:7; Isaiah 1:23; Amos 5:12	Lies & deceit
Open debate	*	Censorship
Free choice	**	Coercion
Government of the people	1 Sam. Ch. 8 – Warns against having a king with top down control	Top down control
Limited government	Genesis Ch. 11 – God prevented a one world government and scattered people by tribe by confounding their language.	Big government
Capitalism / Equal Opportunity	***	Socialism and other ism's / Equal Outcome
Serving others	Matthew 23:11-12; Mark 9:35	Serving self
General interest	****	Special interests
Life	Deut. 30:15-16; Prov. 11:19; Rom. 8:6	Death

Healthy behaviors	1 Cor. 6:19; Gal. 6:7-8; Gal. 5:16-24; Rom. 1:28-32	Self-destructive behaviors
Austrian Economics	Deut. 15:6; Rom. 13:8	Keynesian economics
Content with possessions	Luke 3:14; Phil. 4:11; 1 Tim. 6:6-10; Heb. 13::5	Forever seeking more money, fame and power
Individual responsibility	1 Thess. 5:6; 1 Tim. 3:2; Titus 2:6-8; Titus 2:12; Prov. 10:4-5	Victimhood
Multiply and fill the earth	Gen. 1:26-28	Population control
Worship the Creator	Rom. 1:18-25	Worship the creation

*Open Debate vs. Censorship -- The bible addresses this issue both directly and indirectly.
Romans 1:18 states:
> [18] For the wrath of God is revealed from heaven against all ungodliness and unrighteousness of men, who suppress the truth in unrighteousness, ..

This text really nails the reason evil people censor the truth that is in diametric opposition to the positions they are promoting. They have a conflict of interest!
John 3:19-21 states:
> [19] And this is the condemnation, that the light has come into the world, and men loved darkness rather than light, because their deeds were evil. [20] For everyone practicing evil hates the light and does not come to the light, lest his deeds should be exposed. [21] But he who does the truth comes to the light, that his deeds may be clearly seen, that they have been done in God."

Verse 21 states "but he who does the truth comes to the light, that his deeds may be clearly seen." If we believe, follow and promote the truth we have no need to censor the truth since we are trying to promote truth. Alternatively, based upon verses 19 & 20, those that love the darkness rather than light (truth) have every reason to censor the truth or try to cover it up so their evil beliefs and deeds will not be exposed.

The Pharisees were always trying to trap Jesus so they could condemn Him. He never failed to answer their question even knowing the questions were not legitimate. He never side-stepped the question to censor it. He always exposed their hypocrisy and evil intents.

Also, the bible has so many examples that are very embarrassing and incriminating. These things would normally be censored if the writers were trying to promote an image. In addition there are many details that would certainly be left out if God wanted to hide bad stuff to protect His image and that of Christianity. No evidence of censorship exists to protect anything.

**Free Choice vs. Coercion – Jesus said in Revelation 3:20:

> [20] Behold, I stand at the door and knock. If anyone hears My voice and opens the door, I will come in to him and dine with him, and he with Me.

The Sermon on the Mount in Matthew 5:39-44 states the exact opposite of coercion:

> [39] But I tell you not to resist an evil person. But whoever slaps you on your right cheek, turn the other to him also. [40] If anyone wants to sue you and take away your tunic, let him have *your* cloak also. [41] And whoever compels you to go one mile, go with him two. [42] Give to him who asks you, and from him who wants to borrow from you do not turn away. [43] "You have heard that it was said, 'You shall love your neighbor[a] and hate your enemy.' [44] But I say to you, love your enemies, bless those who curse you, do good to those who hate you, and pray for those who spitefully use you and persecute you, . .

2 Corinthians 3:17 states:

> [17] Now the Lord is the Spirit; and where the Spirit of the Lord is, there is liberty.

Luke 3:14 states:

> Likewise the soldiers asked him, saying, "And what shall we do?" So he said to them, "Do not intimidate anyone or accuse falsely, and be content with your wages."

Here John is instructing soldiers not to intimidate people. Coercion is foreign to Christianity and biblical teaching.

Matthew 13:10-13 states:

> [10] And the disciples came and said to Him, "Why do You speak to them in parables?" [11] He answered and said to them, "Because it has been given to you to know the mysteries of the kingdom of heaven, but to them it has not been given. [12] For whoever has, to him more will be given, and he will have abundance; but whoever does not have, even what he has will be taken away from him. [13] Therefore I speak to them in parables, because seeing they do not see, and hearing they do not hear, nor do they understand.

Not only does Jesus not believe in coercion, but he doesn't even believe in compelling people to understand the truth if they are not really searching for truth.

*** Capitalism / Equal Opportunity vs. Socialism and other ism's / Equal Outcome -- The bible addresses this directly in several ways. Matthew 13:11-12 states:

¹¹ He answered and said to them, "Because it has been given to you to know the mysteries of the kingdom of heaven, but to them it has not been given. ¹² For whoever has, to him more will be given, and he will have abundance; but whoever does not have, even what he has will be taken away from him.

That certainly does not teach equal outcome. Also in Matthew 25:15-29 the parable of the talents is presented:

¹⁵ And to one he gave five talents, to another two, and to another one, to each according to his own ability; and immediately he went on a journey. ¹⁶ Then he who had received the five talents went and traded with them, and made another five talents. ¹⁷ And likewise he who had received two gained two more also. ¹⁸ But he who had received one went and dug in the ground, and hid his lord's money. ¹⁹ After a long time the lord of those servants came and settled accounts with them. ²⁰ "So he who had received five talents came and brought five other talents, saying, 'Lord, you delivered to me five talents; look, I have gained five more talents besides them.' ²¹ His lord said to him, 'Well done, good and faithful servant; you were faithful over a few things, I will make you ruler over many things. Enter into the joy of your lord.' ²² He also who had received two talents came and said, 'Lord, you delivered to me two talents; look, I have gained two more talents besides them.' ²³ His lord said to him, 'Well done, good and faithful servant; you have been faithful over a few things, I will make you ruler over many things. Enter into the joy of your lord.' ²⁴ "Then he who had received the one talent came and said, 'Lord, I knew you to be a hard man, reaping where you have not sown, and gathering where you have not scattered seed. ²⁵ And I was afraid, and went and hid your talent in the ground. Look, there you have what is yours.'
²⁶ "But his lord answered and said to him, 'You wicked and lazy servant, you knew that I reap where I have not sown, and gather where I have not scattered seed. ²⁷ So you ought to have deposited my money with the bankers, and at my coming I would have received back my own with interest. ²⁸ Therefore take the talent from him, and give it to him who has ten talents. ²⁹ 'For to everyone who has, more will be given, and he will have abundance; but from him who does not have, even what he has will be taken away.

In Matthew 26:11 states:

¹¹ For you have the poor with you always, but Me you do not have always.

Jesus definitely did not teach equal outcome. The rationale for socialism is the lack of acceptance of unequal outcome. This worldview is diametrically opposite to what the bible teaches. He also was not trying to eradicate poverty.

Many believe that government sponsored entitlements are justified because of unequal outcome. Jesus didn't even believe in private entitlements. His goal was not to give entitlements to people. This was demonstrated in John Chapter 6. The day after Jesus fed the 5000 they followed him to the other side of the Sea of Galilee and spoke to Jesus. The story unfolds in verses 25-27:

> [25] And when they found Him on the other side of the sea, they said to Him, "Rabbi, when did You come here?" [26] Jesus answered them and said, "Most assuredly, I say to you, you seek Me, not because you saw the signs, but because you ate of the loaves and were filled. [27] Do not labor for the food which perishes, but for the food which endures to everlasting life, which the Son of Man will give you, because God the Father has set His seal on Him."

Jesus could have easily fed them again if the social gospel was His mission. He made it clear that that was not his primary mission. Many people use Acts 4:32-37 as biblical support for socialism where the apostles were at the center of a communal financial and food distribution plan. That was not a government coerced wealth redistribution scheme. It was a private charity organization not much different than current religious charities. This will be addressed specifically in Chapter 24 under Social Justice.

**** General Interest vs. Special Interest – To understand how the bible relates to this issue we need to realize that the primary difference is how large a circle we draw or how large a group we include in our consideration. When our government includes everyone in our country in a special group that is what we mean by general interest. When the group is a segment of the whole it is a special interest group. What happens in our government is that political parties have constituencies that they favor at the expense of the remainder of the population. What is promoted is the benefit to a constituent group with no consideration or highlighting the detriment to the others. All the special interest groups are promised monetary benefits, laws that favor them for the purpose of financial gains, legitimatizing their previously illegitimate status or some kind of influence or power position. All of this can be thought of as starting with a pie and deciding how much more each special interest gets than their fair share of the pie. In some cases the process of a bigger share to special interest groups actually shrinks the pie so that if it was split equally everyone would get less. This is the case for wealth redistribution where those that have to sacrifice so others can have more have less incentive to be more productive. With proper government incentives, productive people actually multiply wealth so the pie expands and on average there is more for everyone.

So at least in the financial area, the government promotes envy and covetousness amongst those with less toward those that have more. This is the diametric opposite of the biblical teaching in the 10th Commandment that you shall not covet. Then the government taxes those with more than their fair share and redistributes the money to those with less. That includes coercion and theft. We covered above that coercion is in opposition to biblical principles. Theft is also in diametric opposition to the 8th Commandment stating that you shall not steal.

The bible also states that God is not partial and we should not be partial toward any special interest group. Deut. 10:17 states:

> ^{17} For the LORD your God is God of gods and Lord of lords, the great God, mighty and awesome, who shows no partiality nor takes a bribe.

2 Chronicles 19:7 states:

> ^{7} Now therefore, let the fear of the LORD be upon you; take care and do it, for there is no iniquity with the LORD our God, no partiality, nor taking of bribes."

Job 34:19 states:

> ^{19} Yet He is not partial to princes, Nor does He regard the rich more than the poor;
> For they are all the work of His hands.

CONCLUSION

These cultural progressive, liberal or secular beliefs that have been shown to be diametrically opposed to the biblical position include 23 more items (in the above table) that seem to be independent (not redundant) from the 62 items that Wayne Grudem listed in his book "Politics According to the Bible" and the cultural list we made from David Wheaton's presentation. If we treat this last table separately the random probably of them all being opposed without a causal agent is 2^{23} or about one chance in 8,000,000. However, if we include these oppositions to the 62 political items and the 22 cultural items we cited earlier, it would be 2^{107} or one in 128,000,000,000,000,000,000,000,000,000,000 chances. With Satan being the "prince of the power of the air" we certainly can see his influence using probability science. Without this tool we are oblivious to what is going on in our world. We need to look through the probability science lens and see Satan's clear image! I am sure that some skeptics are going to try to illegitimatize this analysis and conclusion by saying that not all of the issues are independent. I agree that they may not all be independent. However, even if half of them were related and thus not independent, the conclusion of the analysis would still be valid!

In the next chapter we will cover Secular Humanism which also is diametrically opposed to biblical principles.

CHAPTER 11
From humanism philosophies

The best description of the liberal / progressive religion that we have been exposing that is diametrically opposed to biblical principles is Secular Humanism. This chapter will expand on Secular Humanism. However, first we need to make it clear that there is more than one way to be diametrically opposed to biblical principles. One other way to oppose biblical Christianity is through promoting false religions or corrupting Christian religions through denominations or less organized religions like "New Age." That topic will be covered later in Part 5.

A definition of "Secular Humanism" from Wikipedia states:

> The philosophy of life stance secular humanism (alternatively known by adherents as Humanism, specifically with a capital H to distinguish it from other forms of humanism) embraces human reason, ethics, social justice, philosophical naturalism, while specifically rejecting religious dogma, supernaturalism, pseudoscience or superstition as the basis of morality and decision-making.[16]

Wikipedia also documented the following under "Torcaso v. Watkins Case Law:"

> The phrase "Secular Humanism" became prominent after it was used in the United States Supreme Court case *Torcaso v. Watkins*. In the 1961 decision, Justice Hugo Black commented in a footnote, "Among religions in this country which do not teach what would generally be considered a belief in the existence of God are Buddhism, Taoism, Ethical Culture, Secular Humanism, and others."[17]

Wikipedia also documented the following under "Conclusion:"

> Some religious groups argue that secular humanism—and, by association, secularism—in government and in the schools constitutes state favoritism towards a particular religion (namely, the denial of theism), and a double standard is used in granting protections to these groups. The U.S. courts, however, have consistently rejected this interpretation [to our dismay].
>
> Decisions about tax status have been based on whether an organization functions like a church. On the other hand, Establishment Clause cases turn on whether the ideas or symbols involved are inherently religious. An organization can function like a church while advocating beliefs that are not necessarily inherently religious.[18]

That last sentence would be more to the point if it stated, an organization can be a religion even though it doesn't function like a church or believe in God.

The court's view of the Establishment Clause documented above is based upon defining the word "religious" to exclude "religious secular" beliefs. This limits the meaning of religions to include only those based upon a God or belief in the supernatural. This is contrary to the dictionary, the Supreme Court decision, to secularist's quotes and to 100 years of secular humanist's admissions. This is a sleight of hand that allows the censorship of the true religion in the public square. This not only doesn't prevent the opposite false religious belief from being allowed, but it is sponsored and promoted with tax money. This has only been possible by the legal system jettisoning Constitutional Law and replacing it with Case Law! We made this important distinction earlier and will be specifically addressed again in Chapter 20 and 21. We reiterate the concepts below here again since they are so important to understand:

DEFINING RELIGIOUS AND SECULAR

However, before we continue in that direction we need to delineate between religious beliefs based upon a supernatural God and non-supernatural religious beliefs. The Merriam-Webster dictionary has basically five definitions for "religion." They are:
1. The service and worship of God or the supernatural
2. A commitment or devotion to religious faith or observance
3. A personal set or institutionalized system of religious attitudes, beliefs, and practices
4. Scrupulous conformity
5. A cause, principle, or system of beliefs held to with ardor and faith

Only the first one is specific about service and worship to a God or the supernatural. The other four basically relate to the secular realm. Let's call these later beliefs "religious secular" beliefs. I know that sounds like an oxymoron, but that is only because we have been programmed to only relate religious beliefs to the supernatural. By doing this the religious secular realm can exempt themselves from all the restrictions and condemnation they place on religions that worship a supernatural God. This deception along with "Case Law" replacing "Constitutional Law" has provided a basis for the whole false "separation of church and state" doctrine.

Dictionary.com defines the word "coup" as follows:
> a highly successful, unexpected stroke, act, or move; a clever action or accomplishment.[19]

This pretty well describes how secular humanism has basically eliminated biblical Christianity in education in the public square and has replaced it with their diametrically opposite belief system! They have accomplished this under the radar with virtually no opposition and no outrage! The saddest, most tragic thing is that the churches are completely silent on this issue!

MORE EVIDENCE THAT SECULAR HUMANISM IS A RELIGION

It was mentioned above that in the Torcaso v. Watkins legal case Justice Hugo Black considered secular humanism to be a religion. We also explained that dictionaries define secular humanism as a religion. The following information and quotes add additional support to the claim that secular humanism is a religion.

> Secular humanist John Dewey described Humanism as our "common faith." Julian Huxley called it "Religion without Revelation." Many other humanists could be cited who have acknowledged that humanism is a religion. In fact, claiming that humanism was "the new religion" was trendy for at least 100 years.[20]

EVIDENCE THAT SECULAR HUMANISM IS DIAMETRICALLY OPPOSED TO BIBLICAL CHRISTIANITY

John Dunphy, a secular humanist, wrote in the *Humanist* magazine,
> I am convinced that the battlefield for humankind's future must be waged and won in the public school classroom. . The classroom must and will become an arena of conflict between the old and the new – the rotting corpse of Christianity, together with all its evils and misery, and the new faith of humanism. . .[21]

This certainly shows the humanists modus operandi and that their beliefs are parallel and opposite of Christian theism. So consequently what has happened in our schools and in our culture under the guise of replacing religion with secularism is that we have replaced a true religion with a false religion.

HUMANIST MANIFESTO # 1

Let's examine the first humanist manifesto documented in 1933 and show how it is in is 100% diametric opposition to biblical Christianity. Quotes of the Humanist Manifesto are with permission. Our author comments are all in *italic*.

> The time has come for widespread recognition of the radical changes in religious beliefs throughout the modern world. The time is past for mere revision of traditional attitudes. Science and economic change have disrupted the old beliefs. Religions the world over are under the necessity of coming to terms with new conditions created by a vastly increased knowledge and experience. In every field of human activity, the vital movement is now in the direction of a candid and explicit humanism. In order that religious humanism may be better under-

stood we, the undersigned, desire to make certain affirmations which we believe the facts of our contemporary life demonstrate.[22]

First it is obvious that the Humanists want to replace traditional religions and their beliefs with something completely different. They are assuming that no true religion exists and they are all basically rituals, myths and superstition. They state that vastly increased science, knowledge and experience show we need to essentially replace traditional religions with their new religion of humanism which they confirm is a religion.

> There is great danger of a final, and we believe fatal, identification of the word religion with doctrines and methods which have lost their significance and which are powerless to solve the problem of human living in the Twentieth Century. Religions have always been means for realizing the highest values of life. Their end has been accomplished through the interpretation of the total environing situation (theology or world view), the sense of values resulting there from (goal or ideal), and the technique (cult), established for realizing the satisfactory life. A change in any of these factors results in alteration of the outward forms of religion. This fact explains the changefulness of religions through the centuries. But through all changes religion itself remains constant in its quest for abiding values, an inseparable feature of human life.[23]

They are saying that the word "religion" needs to be associated with their new religion and disassociated with the traditional religions that it is normally associated with. At least if they are referencing the one true religion based upon the bible, they are wrong on the "changefulness" of that religion. However, if their reference is to all the man-made denominational changes of man-made religions they are correct.

> Today man's larger understanding of the universe, his scientific achievements, and deeper appreciation of brotherhood, have created a situation which requires a new statement of the means and purposes of religion.[24]

By referencing understanding the universe and scientific achievements we believe they mean Biological macroevolution and the evolution of cultural and societal values that necessarily follows. We will show that the biological evolution foundation for their assumption to be false below under the Biological Macroevolution section in Chapter 14.

> Such a vital, fearless, and frank religion capable of furnishing adequate social goals and personal satisfactions may appear to many people as a complete break with the past.[25]

It is a complete break from the past at least in regard to traditional biblical Christianity. The religion they are proposing is 100% diametric opposition to biblical Christianity.

68 | PART 3: HOW DO WE RECOGNIZE EVIL BASED UPON BELIEFS DIAMETRICALLY OPPOSITE TO BIBLICAL BELIEFS?

While this age does owe a vast debt to the traditional religions,[26]

When the traditional biblical religion was the accepted worldview in our country; before these Secular Humanist ideas took hold, our culture and our society was much better in every respect.

is none the less obvious that any religion that can hope to be a synthesizing and dynamic force for today must be shaped for the needs of this age.[27]

To see how they shaped it, check the daily newspaper or watch the evening news – they have made our world a very broken place

To establish such a religion is a major necessity of the present. It is a responsibility which rests upon this generation. We therefore affirm the following:[28]

FIRST: Religious humanists regard the universe as self-existing and not created.[29]

This is diametrically opposite to the creation story stated in the bible.

SECOND: Humanism believes that man is a part of nature and that he has emerged as a result of a continuous process.[30]

This is diametrically opposite to the creation story stated in the bible.

THIRD: Holding an organic view of life, humanists find that the traditional dualism of mind and body must be rejected.[31]

This is diametrically opposite to the creation story stated in the bible.

FOURTH: Humanism recognizes that man's religious culture and civilization, as clearly depicted by anthropology and history, are the product of a gradual development due to his interaction with his natural environment and with his social heritage. The individual born into a particular culture is largely molded by that culture.[32]

Here they are denying the truth of biblical Christianity and thus promoting pluralism and evolution which are both false based upon the bible. If we eliminate the creation story and the effect of people following the absolute truths of the bible, what they say is basically true.

FIFTH: Humanism asserts that the nature of the universe depicted by modern science makes unacceptable any supernatural or cosmic guarantees of human values.[33]

They are assuming that the Creation story is false and that macro biological evolution is true. See Chapter 14 & 31 that refute those assumptions. Based upon those assumptions they have changed the definition of science to exclude a search for truth, evidence of God or the supernatural to a study of natural phenomenon – consequently their false assumptions makes their statement true by definition.

Obviously humanism does not deny the possibility of realities as yet undiscovered, but it does insist that the way to determine the existence and value of any and all realities is by means of intelligent inquiry and by the assessment of their relations to human needs. Religion must formulate its hopes and plans in the light of the scientific spirit and method.[34]

When they say intelligent inquiry and scientific spirit and method they mean evolution. This is diametrically opposed to the Creation story stated in the bible and current scientific facts.

SIXTH: We are convinced that the time has passed for theism, deism, modernism, and the several varieties of "new thought".[35]

They are denying the existence of God again. This is diametrically opposed to the God of creation as stated in the bible.

SEVENTH: Religion consists of those actions, purposes, and experiences which are humanly significant. Nothing human is alien to the religious. It includes labor, art, science, philosophy, love, friendship, recreation--all that is in its degree expressive of intelligently satisfying human living. The distinction between the sacred and the secular can no longer be maintained.[36]

They are implying that if we eliminate the sacred we no longer need to distinguish between the sacred and the secular. They are denying the existence of God and replacing the true religion with a false one. This is diametrically opposed to the bible.

EIGHTH: Religious Humanism considers the complete realization of human personality to be the end of man's life and seeks its development and fulfillment in the here and now. This is the explanation of the humanist's social passion.[37]

They are making man the object of everything with the exclusion of God. They use a slogan that states, "Man is the Measure of all Things." They also discount the afterlife and the need for redemption of mankind. This is diametrically opposed to biblical teaching.

NINTH: In the place of the old attitudes involved in worship and prayer the humanist finds his religious emotions expressed in a heightened sense of personal life and in a cooperative effort to promote social well-being.[38]

They are invalidating the need for worship and prayer. This is obviously based upon their rejection of God and making "Man is the Measure of all Things." This is diametrically opposed to the bible.

TENTH: It follows that there will be no uniquely religious emotions and attitudes of the kind hitherto associated with belief in the supernatural.[39]

They are denying the existence of man's soul and Spirit and God. This is diametrically opposed to the bible.

ELEVENTH: Man will learn to face the crises of life in terms of his knowledge of their naturalness and probability. Reasonable and manly attitudes will be fostered by education and supported by custom. We assume that humanism will take the path of social and mental hygiene and discourage sentimental and unreal hopes and wishful thinking.[40]

They are denying the existence of God. They are expressing their desire to eliminate "our blessed hope" and even sentimental emotions through their control of education. In addition to being against the biblical existence of God, they are exposing their modus operandi of coercion and repression of religious liberty. This is all anti-biblical.

TWELFTH: Believing that religion must work increasingly for joy in living, religious humanists aim to foster the creative in man and to encourage achievements that add to the satisfactions of life.[41]

The bible teaches that joy is a result or effect of a proper relationship with God not an objective in life. The bible teaches that we were created to be creative and the fact that almost all scientific achievements have been discovered and developed by Christian and Jewish scientists refutes their thinking. The bible teaches that our primary goals should be to be a servant and to love both God and our fellow man rather than being completely self-serving.

THIRTEENTH: Religious humanism maintains that all associations and institutions exist for the fulfillment of human life. The intelligent evaluation, transformation, control, and direction of such associations and institutions with a view to the enhancement of human life is the purpose and program of humanism. Certainly religious institutions, their ritualistic forms, ecclesiastical methods, and communal activities must be reconstituted as rapidly as experience allows, in order to function effectively in the modern world.[42]

Again, their focus is completely on individual human fulfillment with the exclusion of God. Also, they are exposing their coercive modus operandi again when they speak of control and direction. They want to adopt the symbols of religion like ritualistic forms and ecclesiastical methods into their new religion ASAP. They want religiosity without God, salvation or morality. Again, all of these are unbiblical.

FOURTEENTH: The humanists are firmly convinced that existing acquisitive and profit-motivated society has shown itself to be inadequate and that a radical change in methods, controls, and motives must be instituted. A socialized and cooperative economic order must be established to the end that the equitable distribution of the means of life be possible. The goal of humanism is a free and universal society in which people voluntarily and intelligently cooperate for the common good. Humanists demand a shared life in a shared world.[43]

To understand what they are saying here we need to understand Communism and Keynesian economics which are closely associated. Karl Marx's goal was to dethrone God and destroy capitalism! Even Marx knew that capitalism and God were connected. They are saying that they are going to promote communist ideology and Keynesian economics in our classrooms. They have certainly accomplished that objective. They are promoting wealth redistribution through a social justice philosophy (see Chapter 24) and through inflating currency as another way to redistribute wealth. Again, they used the word "control" to show their modus operandi. In this book we will refer to controlling people as coercion. All this is in diametric opposition to the bible.

> **FIFTEENTH AND LAST**: We assert that humanism will: (a) affirm life rather than deny it; (b) seek to elicit the possibilities of life, not flee from them; and (c) endeavor to establish the conditions of a satisfactory life for all, not merely for the few. By this positive morale and intention humanism will be guided, and from this perspective and alignment the techniques and efforts of humanism will flow.[44]

a – if they affirmed life they would not be for abortions!

b – by saying "elicit the possibilities of life" they mean license to break God's laws and do as they please.

c – by this they mean socialism or communism and reject capitalism.

All of this is in diametric opposition to the bible.

> So stand the theses of religious humanism. Though we consider the religious forms and ideas of our fathers no longer adequate, the quest for the good life is still the central task for mankind. Man is at last becoming aware that he alone is responsible for the realization of the world of his dreams, that he has within himself the power for its achievement. He must set intelligence and will to the task.[45]

In the application of communism in the USSR and in the application of socialism or communism and the move toward a "One World Government" in our world today, the rhetoric sounds like it is for the common man, but it really is to empower the elites to control society by using the wealth of those who earned it, by giving it to a voting bloc that didn't earn it. This is simply buying votes or power. They always make their devious schemes sound good and use euphemisms like Free Inquiry, critical thinking etc.

ADDITIONAL COMMENTS ON THE HUMANIST MANIFESTO

Although the above commentary helps the reader to understand the problem with secular humanism it raises additional questions and needed clarifications. First we need to clarify that secular humanism and humanism are basically equivalents. As is obvious by reading it, the original Humanist Manifesto touts their philosophy as a religion. The main difference is that they have tried to cover up or mask that humanism is a religion by calling it secular humanism! Paul Kurtz, who is the father of secular humanism, was a signer of the original Humanist Manifesto.

ARE HUMANIST MANIFESTO POSITIONS IN OPPOSITION TO BIBLICAL POSITIONS?

We need to confirm that the secular humanist positions we refuted are diametrically opposed to biblical principles. The secular humanist motto is: Man is the measure of all things

Matthew 22:37 states:
> "You shall love the LORD your God with all your heart, with all your soul, and with all your mind."

Psalm 8:4 states:
> What is man that You are mindful of him, And the son of man that You visit him?

Matthew 20:26-28 states:
> "Yet it shall not be so among you; but whoever desires to become great among you, let him be your servant. And whoever desires to be first among you, let him be your slave— just as the Son of Man did not come to be served, but to serve, and to give His life a ransom for many."

SEEK JOY THROUGH HUMANIST RELIGION INCLUDING ACHIEVEMENTS ETC.

John 15:11 states:
> These things I have spoken to you, that My joy may remain in you, and *that* your joy may be full.

John 16:24 states:
> Until now you have asked nothing in My name. Ask, and you will receive, that your joy may be full.

PROMOTING PLURALISM

John 14:6 states:
> Jesus said to him, "I am the way, the truth, and the life. No one comes to the Father except through Me."

DISCREDITING PRAYER AND WORSHIP

Matthew 4:10 states:
> Then Jesus said to him, "Away with you, Satan! For it is written, 'You shall worship the LORD your God, and Him only you shall serve.' "

Matthew 22:37 states:
> Jesus said to him, " 'You shall love the LORD your God with all your heart, with all your soul, and with all your mind.' "

1 Thessalonians 5:16-18 states:

Rejoice always, pray without ceasing, in everything give thanks; for this is the will of God in Christ Jesus for you.

PROMOTING CONTROL AND COERCION

Revelation 3:20 states:
Behold, I stand at the door and knock. *(He doesn't knock the door down!)* If anyone hears My voice and opens the door, I will come in to him and dine with him, and he with Me.

Matthew 11:29:
Take My yoke upon you and learn from Me, for I am gentle and lowly in heart, and you will find rest for your souls.

Luke 10:3 states:
Go your way; behold, I send you out as lambs among wolves.

2 Corinthians 3:17 states:
Now the Lord is the Spirit; and where the Spirit of the Lord is, there is liberty.

SUMMARY

Secular humanism is in diametric opposition to God and biblical principles. The progressive liberal positions taken on issues listed in chapter 10 are a direct result of the influence of secular humanism and their "sleight of hand" with the words "secular" and "religion" in the separation of church and state debate. Secular humanism has driven our culture, the main stream media, and liberal political positions for more than 50 years. Liberal politicians have also been in complete control of Detroit for the last 50+ years. Detroit and secular humanist progressive liberal beliefs are the poster children for the downward spiral taking Detroit and other cities from thriving, wealthy cities to poverty-stricken "hell holes."

In the next chapter we will show how we can recognize evil based upon very similar beliefs between the Islamic savior and the Christian Anti-Christ who of course have very opposite roles or purposes.

CHAPTER 12
By comparing the Anti-Christ with the Mahdi

One purpose of this book is to show the significance of diametrically opposite worldview positions wherever they are encountered. In this chapter and the next we will show that Islam is in diametric opposition to the bible and Christianity. Islam's god, Allah, has diametrically opposite views and beliefs than the Christian God, Jehovah. The Islamic Jesus (Isa) is completely different than the Christian Jesus. Islam also has exactly the opposite modus operandi to Christianity. The historic and current catastrophic effects of Islam are diametrically opposite to the peace they claim to represent. Most readers may not know that Islam is a "Jonny come lately" religion on the world scene. It was born in about 600 AD and claims to be the last revelation from God and claims that the bible is completely corrupted. Our purpose is primarily to cover how Islam is diametrically opposite to the Christian worldview for the purpose of demonstrating the truth of the bible and how Islam's god, Allah, is in diametric opposition to our God, Jehovah and His plan.

Most of the information covered in this chapter and the next is from a book titled, "God's War on Terror" by Walid Shoebat and Joel Richardson. Shoebat was an Islamist terrorist born in the middle-east who found the truth through reading the bible. Consequently, he has intimate knowledge of Islam and what is going on in the middle-east. He has compared Christianity and Islam and Biblical prophecy with Islamic "end times" beliefs. He understands that Biblical prophecy explains exactly what has transpired in the middle-east and found that the "end times" beliefs between Islam and the Bible are strangely similar, yet opposite so everything fits together like a glove.

We emphasized earlier that diametric opposites have profound significance. The same is true for a large number of similarities that run in parallel. It is also profoundly significant when similarities occur sequentially throughout history. The pre-Islamic history, the history of Mohammed, the subsequent history of Islam and the future prophecies of both Islam and the Bible include many correlations that cannot be explained by random chance or coincidence.

Much of the opposition or similar correlation involves the relationship between God, Satan, Allah, Jesus, Isa, the Mahdi, the antichrist, the Bible and the Quran.

Shoebat sees the beliefs about and the relationships between these entities as follows:

Name	Identity according to Shoebat	Identity according to Islam
Jehovah	God	Not God
Jesus	Son of God, fully God, Fully man	Isa, not God, just a prophet
Lucifer	Satan, Devil, Deceiver	Not identified
Allah	Satan, Devil, Deceiver	God
Mahdi	Antichrist	Type of Christ, savior, deliverer

Perhaps some of these facts are completely new to you. You may also find the facts in the table shocking and difficult to believe. Shoebat presents a very comprehensive case that is a very compelling argument that Islam is a false and demonic religion that has deceived 1.3 billion people.

In this chapter we will only cover Shoebat's comparison between the biblical Christian Antichrist with the Islamic Mahdi. In the next chapter we will cover the rest of the story that corroborates that Allah is Satan, Islam is diametrically opposite to biblical Christianity and that Mohamad was demon possessed.

SIMILAR ATTRIBUTES BETWEEN THE MAHDI AND THE ANTICHRIST

The list below identifies strikingly and profoundly similar attributes between the Mahdi, the Islamic savior and the Christian Antichrist. Although this list comes from Shoebat's book, "God's War on Terror," it is based upon a series of chapters that discuss each item on the list. However, besides the Mahdi and the Antichrist, when appropriate, these attributes can and do also include those ascribed to Allah and Satan. With the Antichrist being Satan's surrogate and the Mahdi being Allah's surrogate, this isn't surprising.

ATTRIBUTES FOR BOTH THE MAHDI AND THE ANTICHRIST

- Both deny the trinity and the cross
- Both deny the Father and the Son
- Both are Blasphemous
- Both are called deceiver
- Both attempt to deceive Christians and Jews
- Both practice deception through Kitman and Taqiyya
- Both claim to be Messiah
- Both kingdoms suffer a head wound
- Both work false miracles
- Both ride a white horse
- Both attempt to change the law

- Both deny women's rights
- Both rule over ten entities
- Both are source of death and war
- Both use military force
- Both honor their god with Gold and Silver
- Both honor a god of war and advance his glory through war
- Both condone rape
- Both usher in a seven year peace treaty
- Both deceive and destroy by peace
- Both break treaties
- Both love war for booty
- Both desire world domination
- Both lead a Turkish-Iranian invasion
- Both exalted as god
- Both ascent to heaven
- Both are described as a Beautiful and wise bird
- Both are beings of light
- Both are pride-filled
- Both are lords of this world and the underworld
- Both are called the "Son of the dawn"
- Both are afflicters
- Both are cast out of heaven
- Both are the lord of demons
- Both are possessed
- Both practice beheading
- Both desire Israel's destruction
- Both occupy the temple mount
- Our Messiah is their Antichrist and their Antichrist is our Messiah
- Both stop the rain
- Both enjoy desecrating bodies

The above attributes total 40 plus. In Chapter 10 we considered the probability of 60 plus two sided progressive positions and concluded that the random chance of occurrence was less than one in a quintillion. That analysis was based upon each one being in opposition to the biblical position and being exclusively a two sided position. The above 40 plus attributes are similar rather than opposed and some have a potential to be more than two sided. For opposition analysis, a more than two sided opposition cannot be done. However, with an analysis of similar attributes, possible multiple positions actually make the similar concurrence even less likely. The probability of 40 two sided occurrences would be one in a trillion or even less likely.

In the next chapter we will be corroborating that Allah is Satan and that Mohamad was demon possessed.

CHAPTER 13
By Corroborating that Allah is Satan and that Mohamad was Demon Possessed

PRE ISLAMIC HISTORY

Shoebat connects pre Islamic history with Allah as follows:
> Before Mohammad encountered the angel of light in the cave of Hira, he was engaged in what was known in Arabia as Tahannuth (religious devotion to pagan idols). "The Apostle would pray in seclusion on Hira every year for a month to practice Tahannuth as was the custom of the Quraysh in the heathen days. After praying in seclusion, he would walk around the Ka'ba seven times."[46] In other words, Mohammad was a heathen and the Islamic Pillar that requires fasting during the month of Ramadan was a purely pagan tradition, as was going around the Black Stone.
> Today, Islam still practices Tahannuth and with it self-justification and meditation during the pagan holy month of Ramadan.[47] There is nothing new; but instead of calling it Thannuth, now they just call it Hajj. There is an array of evidence that black stones were commonly worshipped in the Arab world. In 190 A.D., Clement of Alexandria mentioned, "The Arabs worshipped stone." He was alluding to the black stone of Dusares at Petra. In the 2nd century, Maximus Tyrius wrote, "The Arabians pay homage to what god I know not, which they represent by a quadrangular stone." Maximus was speaking of the Ka'ba (the cube) that contains the Black Stone."[48] Even the ancient worship of Cybele pronounced Hybele is interestingly the same word Muslims use for the direction of prayer towards the Black Stone called the Qibleh. The stone associated with Cybele's worship likely originated at Pessinus, Pergamum or on Mount Ida, "a small dark sacred stone not formed into any iconographic image that had fallen to the shrine of Pessinous from the sky."[49]
> Alongside Isis, Cybele retained prominence in the heart of the Roman Empire until the fifth century when the stone was lost. Her cult prospered throughout the empire and it is said that every town or village remained true to the worship of Cybele.[50]
> Islam began as a heretical Arab Christian cult focused on Aphrodite and the Morning Star. This was confirmed during that era by John of Damascus (676-749), who called Islam a "superstition among the Ishmaelites that is the forerunner of Antichrist." According to John, Muslims were, "idolaters [who] reverenced the morning star and

Aphrodite, who they indeed named Akbar."[51] Today they call this idol Allah, but the same satanic spirit that was worshiped then is still worshiped today.[52]

Shoebat continues on pre-Islamic history:

In Judges 8:21, the word used for crescent is saharon, which literally means 'crescent moon'. It comes from the root word sahar, which is literally used for the name of Satan in Isaiah 14 as Hilal ben Sahar. Hilal, or heylal, is the word that the King James Bible translates as Lucifer. The full phrase actually means "morning star/ crescent moon," which is the very symbol of Islam. In other words, the symbol of Islam and the name of Satan are one and the same. This is significant and a very clear hint into the spiritual origins of Islam and the Antichrist.

So we see that the ancient enemies of Israel worshiped a God that was symbolized by the image of the crescent moon. To this day, this has not changed. In fact, all evidence points to the fact that Allah is simply another name for Bel or Baal, which simply means "lord" and is also the title of reverence to the Babylonian moon-god. The Romans had the same god, and so did the Greeks, who worshiped the Gog (Gygez), a war deity called Men. This is also the god that Abraham left behind for Jehovah, the one true God. It comes as no surprise then that Jesus referred to Satan as Beelzebub (Ball Thubab, Arabic) (Matthew 12:24-27). The Hastings Encyclopedia of Religion and Ethics confirms the fact that the Arab name "Allah" correlates to Bel: "Allah is a pre-Islamic name…corresponding to the Babylonian god known as Bel."[53]

Gideon was named as "Jerub-Ba'al", the one who contends with Ba'al, the moon god. Gideon was a type of the warring Messiah because he fought Ba'al. Likewise Christ, the ultimate Jerub-ba'al will fight Ba'al in the flesh, and bruise his head, completing what was promised in Genesis 3:15.

Dr. Arthur Jeffrey, professor of Islamic and Middle East studies at Colombia University and one of the world's foremost scholars on Islam, wrote that the name "Allah" and its feminine form "Allat," were well known in pre-Islamic Arabia and were found in inscriptions uncovered in North Africa. According to Jeffrey, "Allah, "is a proper name applicable only to their peculiar god. He adds, "Allah is a pre-Islamic name corresponding to the Babylonian god known as Bel."[54] Bel simply means 'lord' and this is a title of reverence to the moon-god Sin."[55]

But maybe you have not seen the significance of all of this. Perhaps Isaiah can add the convincing final piece to complete the puzzle on why this is the moon-god of Islam. Isaiah gives us a powerful picture of what Bel (a.k.a. Allah) will do at the end of the age. Most Westerners miss the hint in the famous passage: "I have sworn by myself, the word is gone out of my mouth in righteousness and shall not return, That unto me every knee shall bow, every tongue shall swear" (Isaiah

45:23). This verse is later echoed in the New Testament: "every knee shall bow, every tongue shall confess...that Jesus Christ is Lord" (Philippians 2:10-11). A few years later, Isaiah also tells of one being in particular who is among them: "Bel bows down, Nebo stoops; Their idols were on the beasts and on the cattle" (Isaiah 46:1). Bel will now bow down before God. This is none other than the image of Allah-Satan, the crescent moon.

In the purest form of poetic justice, the demonic god of Islam will bow low before Jesus, the Mighty One of Israel which the beasts wore on their necks: "Their idols were on the beasts and on the cattle"—the very symbol that Gideon removed—the crescent moon in Judges 8:21.[56]

Shoebat continues:

In Isaiah 14, we find the story of sin and the fall of Satan. What we will discover when we analyze the passage a bit closer are some very telling points. The passage reads as follows: "How art thou fallen from heaven, O Lucifer, Son of the Morning! How are thou cut down to the ground, which didst weaken the nations! For thou hast said in thine heart, I will ascend into heaven, I will exalt my throne above the stars of God: I will sit also upon the mount of the congregation, in the sides of the North: I will ascend above the heights of the clouds; I will be like the most High" (Isaiah 14:12-14).

In this passage we are given the name Lucifer, which has, through the ages, come to signify Satan. In truth, the passage doesn't so much give us a proper name as it provides us with a description of who Satan really is. In Hebrew, the name for Lucifer is three words: *Heylal Ben Shahar*. Translated fully, this means "Shining One of the Morning Star," or "the Shinning Brilliant One." Etymologically, Hebrew Helel corresponds to the *Ugaritic hll* which occurs in the following expression: *bnt hll snnt*, Daughters of Brightness, swallows, or perhaps 'Shinning Ones' and *bnt hll b'l gml*, 'Daughters of Brightness, Lord of the Crescent moon."[57]

Hilal is an Arabic word that means 'Crescent Moon."[58] When we put the whole phrase together, *Heylal Ben Shachar* simply means, "Crescent Moon, Son of the Morning Star" (or the Dawn)—or in simpler terms, a crescent moon with a star lingering over it. Of course, this is the very symbol and image of Islam. . .

Nearly every mosque displays this symbol on the pinnacle on its dome and/or its minarets. Consider the implication of this, Islam applies to itself the very description that the bible uses to describe Satan. When it comes to Islam, everything is upside down. But what makes it so damning to Islam is that Hilal was the very name of the Lord of the Ka'ba, according to Muhammad's biographer, Ibn Hisham. He admits that the pagan Kinanah tribe and Quraysh (Muhammad's tribe) called the supervising god of the *Kaaba* IHLAL. They called the Kaaba "*Beit-Allah*," the house of Allah![59] [60]

This should be convincing evidence that the Islamic god, Allah, is actually Lucifer or Satan with all of his attributes. Next let's examine Mohammed's experience receiving the Quran and Islamic doctrine.

MOHAMMED EXPERIENCE -- ENLIGHTENED OR POSSESSED

Shoebat stated the following:
> The Qur'an was not inspired—inspiration is conveying God's thoughts and words, not dictating them. Each individual author of the books of the Bible was entirely conscious and brought to the scriptures his own individual style and personality. God used the human agents as His vessels, but He did not literally override them. The Qur'an was dictated to Mohammed; however, this is not inspiration—rather it is known as possession. All Muslims claim that, "The Prophet was purely passive—indeed unconscious: the book was in no sense his, neither its thought, nor language, nor style: all was of Allah, and the Prophet was merely a recording pen."[61]

It is no wonder Karen Armstrong became an apologist for Islam. Armstrong, a former nun who had experiences similar to Mohammed, with seizure-like religious hallucinations, gives an account quite reminiscent of Mohammed's initial encounter with the angel in the cave of Hira:
> "Mohammed was torn from his sleep in his mountain cave and felt himself overwhelmed by a devastating divine presence. Later he explained this ineffable experienced by saying that an angel had enveloped him in a terrifying embrace so that it felt as though the breath was being forced from his body. The angel gave him a curt command: 'iqra!' 'Recite!" Mohammed protested that he could not recite; he was not a kahin, one of the ecstatic prophets of Arabia. But, he said, the angel simply embraced him again until, just as he thought he had reached the end of his endurance, he found the divinely inspired words of a new scripture pouring forth from his mouth."[62] Alfred Guillaume however, in *The Life of Mohammed*, mentions that it was not actually until the third time that the "angel" had strangled Mohammed, demanding that he recite, that he finally did so."[63]

True divine encounters in the Bible always begin with "Do not be afraid" (Genesis 15:1, 26:24, 46:3, Daniel 8:15-19, 10:12, 19, Matthew 28:5, Luke 1:13; 26-31, 2:10, Revelation 1:17). Even Mohammed himself believed that he was demon possessed and became distraught, even suicidal: So I [Mohammed] read it, and he [jibril] departed from me. And I awoke from my sleep, and it was as though these words were written on my heart...I thought, 'Woe is me poet or possessed...I will go to the top of the mountain and throw myself down that I may kill myself and gain rest.' So I went forth to do so and then when I was midway up the mountain, I heard a voice from heaven saying, "O Mohammed! Thou are the apostle of God and I am Gabriel."[64] The reference to "poet or possessed" comes from Mohammed's belief that poets created their poetry under the inspiration of demons. At-Tabari, Islam's renowned historian explains: "The pre-Islamic Arabs believed in the demon of poetry, and they thought that a great poet was directly inspired by demons..."[65]

After the terrible experience, Mohammed returned home to his wife Khadija. Terribly disturbed, he: "returned with the inspiration, his neck muscles twitching with terror till he entered upon Khadija and said 'Cover me! Cover me!' They covered him till his fear was over and he said, 'O Khadija, what is wrong with me?' He told her everything that happened and said, 'I fear that something may happen to me.'"[66]

It was not only Mohammed who suspected a demonic source behind his revelations. Many of Mohammed's contemporaries also believed that his revelatory experiences were demonically inspired. The Qur'an records the following accusations that were leveled against Mohammed: "Yet they turn away from him and say: 'Tutored by others, a man possessed!'" (Qur'an 44:14) "What! Shall we give up our gods for the sake of a Poet possessed" (Qur'an 37:36)? The accusations became so bad that Allah even had to come to Mohammed's defense: "It (the Qur'an) is no poet's speech: scant is your faith! It is no soothsayer's divination: how little you reflect! It is revelation from the Lord of the Universe (Qur'an 69:41, 42). "No your compatriot (Mohammed) is not mad. He saw him (Jibril) on the clear horizon. He does not grudge the secrets of the unseen, nor is this the utterance of an accursed devil" (Qur'an 81:22-25).[67]

This certainly is convincing evidence that Mohammed received the Islamic doctrine through a demon (Satan) and not from God or Gabriel as claimed.

THE BLACK STONE AND APHRODITE

Shoebat includes comments about the Antichrist in this segment. We are not trying to emphasize the Antichrist at this point, but Shoebat believes the Islamic Mahdi is the Antichrist. See table in the previous chapter. He states:

> Both Antichrist's followers and Muslims bow to an image. The great idol of Islam, the Black Stone and its veneration has been around since time immemorial. Yet despite the very clear correlations, few prophecy Analysts have ever linked this to what has already been spoken of in the book of Acts: "Everybody knows that Ephesus is the official guardian of the temple of the great Artemis, whose image fell down to us from heaven" (Acts 19:35). The image of Artemis is strikingly similar to

the meteorite stone image in Mecca which Allah commands 1.3 billion Muslims to literally bow down and prostrate themselves toward at least seventeen times during their five day prayers.

John of Damascus (676-749) who lived at the advent of Islam and served in the court of the Caliph, and was thoroughly familiar with Islam from its inception, writes in his work, Concerning Hersey, "So then, these were idolaters and reverenced the morning star and Aphrodite, who they indeed named Akbar in their own language, which means 'great'".[68] The Islamic connection to Aphrodite is evident in the Muslim cry "Allah Akbar" (Allah is Great). Aphrodite is actually Allat, the feminine root of the name "Allah". Even the Greek historian Herodotus, writing in the 5th century B.C., considers Allat the equivalent of Aphrodite: The Assyrians call Aphrodite Mylitta, the Arabians Alilat."[69] According to the book of idols (Kitab al-Asnam) by Hiham b. al-Kalbi, the pre-Islamic Arabs believed Allat resided in the Ka'aba and also had an idol for her inside the sanctuary: "The Quraysh, as well as all the Arabs, were wont to venerate Allat. They also used to name their children after her, calling them Zayd-Allat and Taym-Allat."[70]

Even the Bible confirms this style of naming. The name Sanballat (Nehemiah 2:19) is a derivative of two words; Sin (the Moon-god), and Allat (Aphrodite), the feminine of Allah and one of his three daughters. Such names existed long before Mohammad, whose father's name, Abd-Allah, means "slave of Allah", the Moon-god. Sanballat was known to have harassed Israel as they were attempting to build the Temple, alongside with Tobiah the Amonite and Geshem the Arab. Nothing has changed. Today these same people with an evolved form of the same religion still harasses Israel and are the main obstacle to the rebuilding of the Temple.[71]

THE BLACK STONE AS SATAN STAR AND IMAGE

Shoebat continues relating the Black Stone to Satan's star and image:
> What is this whole thing about venerating an asteroid? What is this whole image about? Does the Bible warn of this? The Bible is very clear in exposing this issue. Jehovah simply wants us to dig deeper. Lucifer's image is depicted in Revelation 8 and 9, showing Satan wanting to be worshipped. He is a star that fell from heaven: "And the fifth angel sounded, and I saw a star fall from heaven unto the earth: and to him was given the key to the bottomless pit" (Revelation 9:1). This "him" cannot be an object, but rather Satan himself, a living being (him) cast out of heaven as described in Isaiah 14 and Revelation 8:10. The most important verse in the Qur'an that describes Allah is perfectly mirrored in Isaiah 14, it is Satan or Lucifer that is described as the Bearer of Light, and in the Qur'an it is Allah that is depicted as a lamp

(light, torch). In the chapter of the Star, we read: "Allah is the light of the heavens and the earth; a likeness of His light is as a niche in which is a lamp, the lamp is a glass, (and) the glass is as it were a brightly shining star" (Qur'an 24:35-36). Compare this with Revelation 8:10: "And the third angel sounded, and there fell a great star from heaven, burning as it were a lamp and it fell upon the third part of the rivers and upon the fountains of waters."

Take note of the fact that the death of one-third of the earth's population during the rise of the eighth empire, which will be an Islamic empire. Satan, who is the falling star, and destroyer who is unleashed, will precede the "mountain" empire that will cause one third of mankind to die. The Black Stone of Mecca owes its reputation to the tradition that it fell from the "heavens." Like the Black Stone Aphrodite, the Black Stone of Mecca is also clearly an "image" of Satan. Yet this Satanic image that is created by the beast in Revelation 13:15 which can speak and cause all who do not worship it to be killed, is mentioned as a holy thing by Mohammad. In an Islamic tradition authenticated by At-Tirmidhi, Al-Abani notes, "Allah will raise up the Stone [the Black Stone] on the Day of Judgment, and it will have two eyes with which it will see and a tongue which it talks with, and it will give witness in favor of everyone who touched it in truth." According to Muslim traditions, the Black Stone is even a redeemer of Muslims. Al-Tirmidhi notes that many years ago, the Black Stone was, "whiter than milk; it was only later that it became black as it absorbed the sins of those who touched it."

The blasphemy doesn't stop here. The Black Rock, the image of Satan, the Fallen Star, which attempts to take the place of Christ the Great Redeemer is called by Mohammad, the son of perdition Yameen Allah. This means that it is "the right hand of Allah" with which "he touches his servants."[72] It is the visible right hand of the invisible Allah.[73] It is even the Shekina Glory, which dwells in all believers. Venerating it and rotating seven times around it will cleanse the Muslim of all prior sins.

The veneration of Satan through this act of rotating around an idol image is even alluded to in the Bible and rarely understood by Western Analysis. Ezekiel 31:3 declares "Behold, the Assyrian (the Antichrist, Satan in the Flesh) was a cedar in Lebanon with fair branches, and with a shadowing shroud, and of high stature; his top was among thick boughs. The waters made him great, the deep set him on high with her rivers running around about his plants, and sent out her little rivers unto all the trees of the field." If we exercise what we learned from part IV (how to interpret allegoric symbols), we can apply what we learned in the following interpretative paraphrase: "Behold, Satan, a beautiful angel clothed in beautiful covering, an angel with high status. People and multitudes from every nation made him great, and the underworld set him up high with the multitudes running around about his idol and sent out all people to all the idols that were set for him." This is exactly what we see in the Muslim Hajj, which Muslims do yearly to have their sins forgiven by the right hand of Allah. They came from all over the world to the Ka'ba and roam round about it. In addition, Jeremiah 51:44 tells us, "I will punish Bel in Babylon, And I will bring out of his mouth what he has swallowed; and the nations will not stream to him anymore." The nations will not flock to Babylon and Bel, the Moon-god, will be ashamed in her. No longer will the nations flock to Mecca to worship Satan.[74]

All evidence indicates that the Black Stone in the Ka'ba is the image of Satan that 1.3 billion Muslims from all over the globe visit annually on a pilgrimage called the Hajj. Muslims are worshiping Satan when they think they are worshiping God. What a terrible tragedy!

THE LIBERAL / PROGRESSIVE ISLAMIC CONNECTION

The following was taken from a Matt Barber website that not only exposed Islam for what it is, but explains the "partners-in-crime" linkage between American Progressives and Islam:

> "Progressives" are crafty little buggers. One of their favorite sleights of hand is to disingenuously brand as "phobic" anyone with reasoned moral disapproval of their very unreasonable and immoral social deconstructionism.
>
> It works like this: Take any objective evil, say, homosexual sin. State its prefix, "homo." Just add "phobia," and voila! The person who holds to the millennia-old precepts of authentic biblical sexual morality is no longer a "Christian," but, rather, is magically transformed into that mythical creature called "The Homophobe."
>
> The same applies to so-called "Islamophobia." It's not an "illogical fear" if they really are trying to kill you. Islam is the "religion of peace" in the same way that rape is snuggling. A central tenet of Islam is to convert, enslave or kill the infidel. An infidel is anyone who is not Muslim or, depending on who's doing the killing, belongs to a different sect of Islam. Those who fall into that minority category tagged "moderate Muslim," are also infidels.
>
> "Moderate Muslim" is a contradiction in terms. It is intrinsically oxymoronic. Whereas "moderate" (read: liberal) "Christians," such as those belonging to the PCUSA, embrace certain apostasies that run directly counter to the biblical teachings of Christianity (which is the true "religion of peace"), "moderate Muslims," likewise, embrace an apostate version of Islam that runs directly counter to the clear teachings of the Quran.

Whereas devout followers of Jesus Christ, who is God incarnate, are characteristically peaceful; devout followers of that child-raping, woman-beheading "prophet" Muhammad, who was demon incarnate, are characteristically violent.

Islam is Christianity's photo-negative. While Christianity brings eternal life to those choosing to surrender to Jesus, who alone is "the Way, the Truth and the Life;" Islam brings eternal death to those who surrender to "Allah," who is "the best of deceivers" ("[A]nd Allah was deceptive, for Allah is the best of deceivers." [see Surah 3:54]).

It's worth mentioning here that the Bible similarly calls Satan a deceiver. Revelation 12:9, for instance, explains that he "deceives the whole world." Even though it is often claimed that Muslims, Christians and Jews "worship the same God," nothing could be further from the truth. Allah is not God. Allah *is* the deceiver, and insofar as Christianity, true Christianity, spreads peace, love and truth – Islam, true Islam, spreads violence, hate and deception. Allah is definitely real. He's just not God. Though he wanted to "ascend above the tops of the clouds" and "make [himself] like the Most High" (see Isaiah 14:14), Allah, most assuredly, is not God.

Which brings us to ISIS – Head-chopping, man-sodomizing, child-torturing, Jew-killing, Christian-sawing, women-enslaving ISIS. The Islamic State is not the exception to the rule; the Islamic state *is* the rule. ISIS is Islam and Islam is ISIS.

The aforementioned secular-"progressives" love Islam. While the mainstream media won't adequately cover it – it doesn't fit their narrative – you need only look to the new media to see that the Middle East runs red with the blood of Christian and Jewish martyrs. These are peaceful men, women and children, no different from you or me, being slaughtered by the tens-of-thousands at the wicked hands of the Islamic faithful.

And so the media busy themselves with Kim Kardashian and "hands up don't shoot!"

While there are exceptions, the left is overwhelmingly anti-Semitic, anti-Christian and pro-Muslim. Liberals and Islamists, such as those belonging to the American-Islamic terrorist group CAIR, as well as Obama's pals in the Muslim Brotherhood, have forged a bizarre and notably incongruous sociopolitical partnership I call the "Islamo-'progressive' axis of evil." The only explanation for this, as far as I can tell, is best illustrated by the maxim: "The enemy of my enemy is my friend."

The common enemy, of course, is likewise signified by an alliance. It consists of Christians and Jews worldwide. It, too, is built around a shared cause. But this cause, unlike that of the Islamo-progressive axis, intends freedom, not tyranny – representative democracy, not control. Most importantly, this Judeo-Christian cause is built upon the rock of truth given us by the God of Abraham, Isaac and Jacob. The God of the living, not the dead. The great "I Am."

The common enemy to both the Muslim and the "progressive" is truth. The common enemy is Christ.[75]

This chapter validates the conclusion of the previous chapter that showed statistically that the biblical Antichrist and the Muslim savior, the Mahdi, are one and the same and that the Muslim god, Allah, is the biblical Satan. It also exposes the evil modus operandi of Muslims and liberal / progressives to marginalize and silence their critics by making the truth bearers the ones that have a phobia problem when their accusers are actually the ones promoting false evil beliefs. Consequently, Islam's goal is to transform America into an Islamic state and abolish Christianity. The liberal / progressives share their goal of abolishing Christianity.

Next in Part 4 we identify how false secular foundations have been established.

Part 4

Establishment of false secular foundations

CHAPTER 14
Uniformitarianism and biological macro evolution

The bible speaks about good and bad foundations that represent truth and falsehood and wisdom and foolishness. The bible uses several metaphors to describe these in our world and our connection to truth and falsehoods or good and evil.

Matthew 7:21-27 states the words of Jesus concerning the foundation metaphor:

> [21] "Not everyone who says to Me, 'Lord, Lord,' shall enter the kingdom of heaven, but he who does the will of My Father in heaven. [22] Many will say to Me in that day, 'Lord, Lord, have we not prophesied in Your name, cast out demons in Your name, and done many wonders in Your name?' [23] And then I will declare to them, 'I never knew you; depart from Me, you who practice lawlessness!' [24] "Therefore whoever hears these sayings of Mine, and does them, I will liken him to a wise man who built his house on the rock: [25] and the rain descended, the floods came, and the winds blew and beat on that house; and it did not fall, for it was founded on the rock [foundation].

John 15:1-5 states the words of Jesus concerning the vine metaphor:
> "I am the true vine, and My Father is the vinedresser. [2] Every branch in Me that does not bear fruit He takes away; and every branch that bears fruit He prunes, that it may bear more fruit. [3] You are already clean because of the word which I have spoken to you. [4] Abide in Me, and I in you. As the branch cannot bear fruit of itself, unless it abides in the vine, neither can you, unless you abide in Me. [5] "I am the vine, you are the branches. He who abides in Me, and I in him, bears much fruit; for without Me you can do nothing.

In many other translations the word "gardener" is used rather than "vinedresser." This metaphor describes us as branches on a vine that represents Jesus and God. The implication is that the roots and the soil also represent God, the source of growth and everything good. When we are connected to the true vine we can and should bear good fruit.

Matthew 7:15-20 states the words of Jesus concerning the tree metaphor:
> [15] "Beware of false prophets, who come to you in sheep's clothing, but inwardly they are ravenous wolves. [16] You will know them by their fruits. Do men gather grapes from thornbushes or figs from thistles? [17] Even so, every good tree bears good fruit, but a bad tree bears bad fruit. [18] A good tree cannot bear bad fruit, nor can a bad tree bear

good fruit. [19] Every tree that does not bear good fruit is cut down and thrown into the fire. [20] Therefore by their fruits you will know them.

These texts with their three metaphors of "foundation", "vine" and "tree" help us to understand good and how it connects to God, Jesus and us. Similarly, the metaphors teach us the relationship between evil, Satan and us. One profound thing is that good or bad fruit does not just randomly appear in our world, it is supported by a foundation or a support system. The other profound concept is that false prophets described as ravenous wolves will pretend to be sheep (biblical Christians) for the obvious reason of subverting biblical Christianity.

What we have attempted to do is develop a theoretical framework or model of good and evil in our world based on biblical teaching that will help open our eyes to see a true perspective of good and evil just like a ruler can do when placed alongside an object to measure its length. This type of modeling is exactly what scientists do when they propose hypotheses and theories and verify them by examining empirical evidence. In this book, we expose those very things like false foundations that support evil and the subversion of biblical truth, the only true religion. The very fact that what the bible says about our world matches exactly what we see is another huge support for the truth of the bible and the fact that we can use it as a theoretical model of our world.

This entire concept of a framework or a theoretical model that explains our world and that empirical facts in our world verify the model when they fall in perfect sync with it, perhaps needs further explanation. Indiana Jones has a map and or documented clues that, if true, can lead to hidden treasure or the Holy Grail etc. That map and or documented clues are information that forms a framework or theoretical model that predicts things about our world. When that information actually leads to finding the artifact it means the empirical evidence supported the theoretical model. Although such a model is quite narrow in scope compared to considering the bible as a theoretical model that predicts many more things that we would expect to see in our world, it should help the reader understand this concept. This relationship between the model and empirical evidence is a two way street. If all the predictions appear to be true, not only does the empirical evidence basically prove the model, but the model can guide us on where to look for evidence. Later, we will look for evidence that evil philosophies and political positions need to be based upon false foundations to be accepted. Otherwise, without those accepted false foundations people would see that they are not consistent with the true foundations that are generally accepted and reject them. In addition, the model tells us that we should look for false teachers that according to the bible should be subverting the true biblical religion.

Adolf Hitler stated:
> "If you tell a big enough lie and tell it frequently enough, it will be believed."[76]

Wikipedia states:
> The Big Lie is a propaganda technique. The expression was coined by Adolf Hitler, when he dictated his 1925 book *Mein Kampf*, about the use of a lie so "colossal" that no one would believe that someone "could have the impudence to distort the truth so infamously." Hitler asserted the technique was used by Jews to unfairly blame Germany's loss in World War I on German Army officer Erich Ludendorff.[77]

The false foundations that have been established to support all the bad fruit in our world are based upon these types of big lies. As you know these lies are antithetical to Jesus' purpose documented below.

John 18:37 states Jesus' testimony to Pontus Pilate:
> [37] Pilate therefore said to Him, "Are You a king then?" Jesus answered, "You say rightly that I am a king. For this cause I was born, and for this cause I have come into the world, that I should bear witness to the truth. Everyone who is of the truth hears My voice."

In this chapter we will identify several of the false foundations that have replaced the previous foundations of truth that we held dear. These false foundations support additional false foundations and all the false beliefs that are embraced by our culture. Without them the bad fruit and plethora of lies would not be accepted. This results in us living in a cesspool of lies that are detrimental to us and society. The foundations of truth are those that are biblical. The false foundations that have been established are diametrically opposed to biblical principles.

Since we used the foundational metaphor and the vine and tree metaphors synonymously to mean support for a philosophy, belief or position on an issue, please consider them to be basically the same concept. The tree metaphor is ultimately the best way to envision the support structure, since it includes the source of God or Satan, us as the branches and the good or bad fruit that our beliefs, accepted philosophies and our political positions produce. The bible teaches that God is the source of the good tree and the good fruit. It also teaches that Satan ultimately is the source of the bad fruit, and the bad tree and his followers are the bad branches that support it. That means that Satan has to work through people, the branches, to accomplish his evil plans that result in the bad fruit.

Let's reiterate the Romans 1:18 text. It states:
> [18] For the wrath of God is revealed from heaven against all ungodliness and unrighteousness of men, who suppress the truth in unrighteousness,

This text explains that people have a conflict of interest against God, His plan and His righteousness. This somewhat explains why Satan does not have to be a super salesperson to deceive the world. However, people still need some sort of intellectual rationale that convinces them that they are believing in the truth rather than just admitting to themselves that they are believing lies. The Jewish Virtual Library website explains how Hitler used big lies that surprisingly were accepted since people couldn't believe that anybody could possibly tell such big lies. It states the following:

> All this was inspired by the principle - which is quite true in itself - that in the big lie there is always a certain force of credibility; because the broad masses of a nation are always more easily corrupted in the deeper strata of their emotional nature than consciously or voluntarily; and thus in the primitive simplicity of their minds they more readily fall victims to the big lie than the small lie, since they themselves often tell small lies in little matters but would be ashamed to resort to large-scale falsehoods. It would never come into their heads to fabricate colossal untruths, and they would not believe that others could have the impudence to distort the truth so infamously.[78]

We believe that Satan uses a similar ploy to get the masses to believe big foundational lies. Once he can establish those falsehoods he can (and he has) build a whole framework of lies based upon the false foundation he established.

SATAN'S FALSE FOUNDATIONS

Satan's big lie false foundations include the following:
1. Uniformitarianism
2. Biological Macroevolution
3. Relative truth vs. absolute truth
4. Goodness and perfectibility of man
5. Global warming
6. "The New Tolerance" and "Outrage Based Coerced Conscience"
7. Political correctness
8. Case Law
9. Separation of church and state

The establishment of these false foundations supports the framework of many additional false and evil beliefs and practices. Some of these are as follows:
1. Abortion
2. Fornication
3. Adultery
4. No-fault divorce
5. Pornography

6. Homosexuality
7. Homosexual marriage
8. Other self-serving cultural and political positions on issues

FALSE FOUNDATIONS OVERVIEW

The first five false foundations discredit and censor biblical truth. This case may not be as strong for global warming but it does conflict with Genesis 8:22 documented below:

[22] "While the earth remains, Seedtime and harvest, Cold and heat,
Winter and summer,
And day and night Shall not cease."

However, it primarily is bogus pseudoscience that is used by the UN and US progressive leaders to establish global governance and weaken the US.

The last four foundations subvert and or turn "upside down" traditional or historically established truths. By establishing these false foundations, Satan can win the masses by replacing truth with lies supported by these false foundations.

Uniformitarianism discredited the biblical teaching of the Noahic flood which supported a catastrophic mechanism of sedimentary layers. This opened the door for Darwinian macro-evolution. It discredited the creation narrative in Genesis 1 & 2. The belief in relative moral truth discredited all the many conceptual absolute truths that the bible teaches. The teaching that mankind was basically good and perfectible rather than wicked and having righteousness like filthy rags as the bible teaches in Jeremiah 17:9 and Isaiah 64:6 allowed Humanism to elevate man to godhood rather than being accountable to God. Global warming discredits God for His design of a stable earth suitable for mankind to have dominion over the earth and utilize the resources available to benefit mankind. In addition, it makes mankind the savior of the earth. These five big lies replaced the biblical foundation that supported all the good things in our culture and replaced them with a false foundation that supported all of the bad things in our culture.

"Political Correctness," "The New Tolerance," and "Separation of Church and State" false foundations censor, reframe or reverse the debate or the truth. Case Law provides a way of undercutting the Constitution by basing new laws on past cases rather than the Constitution itself. All that is needed is several corrupted cases to build a false foundation for bad laws.

In this chapter, we will only cover uniformitarianism and Darwinian macro-evolution. The other false foundations will be covered one at a time in the chapters that follow.

UNIFORMITARIANISM GEOLOGY

Both James Hutton and Charles Lyell are considered the fathers of uniformitarianism geology. Uniformitarianism geology is all that has been taught since shortly after the word geology was coined in 1778. Although catastrophism geology is alive and well amongst many geologists, currently the word geology connotes uniformitarianism.

James Hutton is credited with laying the foundation of uniformitarianism geology by questioning the then current belief that the sedimentary rock strata was laid down by Noah's worldwide flood. Hutton saw evidence of multiple deposition events and subsequent upheavals and igneous intrusions that revealed a long history of the earth. Although it would appear that much of that evidence would point to catastrophism, Hutton saw only uniformitarianism.

Forty-five years went by before Hutton's ideas really had a significant influence. At that time, Charles Lyell added a chronology of the rock layers called the geologic column and added age dates and names to the layers. So Hutton laid the conceptual foundation for uniformitarianism geology and Lyell built the structure of geology upon that foundation.

We need to ask whether this paradigm shift was a move toward truth or away from it. The Mount St. Helens eruption certainly has shown us that catastrophism is alive and well. The resulting depositions and canyon were formed very rapidly. We also saw how many tree trunks ended up floating vertically in a lake. This is similar to abundant poly-strata fossils seen across multiple sediment layers. Those poly-strata fossils traversing multiple rock layers have proven that layers were deposited rapidly. Also, we know that for fossils to be preserved, rapid burial is required. With only slow deposition, virtually no fossils would be preserved. Also, the sharp demarcation lines between layers testify to rapid deposition. Slow deposition would result in considerable erosion in the previous layers before new layers were added.

Also, Lyell's geologic column with its layers and age dates are a complete fabrication. Nowhere on earth can all the layers be found. The dates were arbitrary and the fossils are used to date the rocks and the rocks are used to date the fossils. This is a circular argument.

The scientific facts seen in the rocks scream catastrophism rather than uniformitarianism. This was the first of several false foundations that support today's politically correct post-modern atheistic secular humanism religion. The uniformitarianism concept, along with its mandatory accompanying old earth philosophy, provided the primary influence for Charles Darwin and his theory of evolution. Together these ideas have caused a paradigm shift from a Biblical creationist, young earth worldview to a humanistic, evolutionary old earth worldview.

DARWIN'S BIOLOGICAL THEORY OF EVOLUTION

Charles Robert Darwin (1809 – 1882) was an English naturalist whose revolutionary theory laid the foundation for both the modern theory of evolution and the principle of common descent by proposing natural selection as a mechanism. He published these theories in his 1859 the book, "The Origin of Species."

He introduced "natural selection" as a mechanism capable of evolving improved organisms and creating new organisms by inheriting traits that helped survival or were more compatible with a certain environment. In one sense natural selection is a tautology or circular argument. Natural selection theory predicts that the fittest organisms will produce the most offspring, and it defines the fittest organisms as the ones which produce the most organisms.

In spite of this, Darwin did get two things right. Natural selection actually does function and organisms do change. This change is referred to as microevolution. Natural selection does cause microevolution. Nobody disputes that. This is similar to dog breeding. Breeders have found that when breeding dogs, they never get cats. The primary difference is that dog breeding is intentional rather than natural or random. The difference between microevolution and macroevolution is that microevolution results from gene rearrangement or gene degradation whereas macroevolution, if it existed, would result from new genetic information. Nobody has ever gotten new information from a random process.

Since DNA had not been discovered until about 1950 Darwin didn't know anything about genes and the mechanism of heredity. Consequently, once those things were learned his theory was converted to what is called "neo-Darwinism." This theory would add DNA mutations as a driver of organism change in conjunction with natural selection.

Professor Michael Ruse refers to the fossil record as evidence of evolution. His argument is that if one assumes that the rocks were deposited over long ages of time, the order is roughly progressive. i.e. the small and presumably primitive near the bottom and the large and presumably modern near the top. He had to say "roughly" because there are many exceptions. Even one so called modern fossil imbedded with the so called primitive ones disproves evolution. There are many such anomalies.

The alternative to the theory of evolution and sedimentary rock layer formation at the same time is catastrophic deposition from Noah's flood. The order of deposition of fossils that would be expected from a flood would be the smallest at the bottom and the largest and higher life forms near the top. This is because the larger higher life forms have more ability to get to higher ground to escape a flood.

However, by far the most profound evidence against evolution is the fossil record that Ruse tries to use as evidence for evolution. Darwin's theory would predict that new kinds and species are formed slowly over long periods of time. Under this scenario, many of the fossils would be transitional fossils between species. With billions of total fossils, no transitional fossils have been found. If the theory of evolution were true, our museums would be full of transitional fossils. How can evolutionists ignore this elephant in the room?

The other thing that Michael Ruse and other evolutionists never point out is the difference between micro and macro evolution. Much evidence exists for what they call microevolution. Nobody is questioning its truthfulness. Macroevolution has no evidence supporting it. What evolutionists do is to present evidence for microevolution and then extrapolate across the barriers between kinds and species without distinguishing between them.

Ruse admits that evolutionists have presuppositions, or what I call a religious position. Ruse actually admitted this in a 1993 AAAS meeting in Boston:
> Those in academia especially should recognize, both historically and perhaps philosophically, certainly that the science side has certain metaphysical assumptions built into doing science, which—it may not be a good thing to admit in a court of law—but I do think that in honesty . . . we should recognize [this].[79]

There you have it! An evolutionist has admitted that the creation / evolution debate is actually religion vs. religion.

Other prominent evolutionists have stated things that refute evolution. The late Stephen Jay Gould stated concerning the evolutionary tree that:
> The extreme rarity of transitional forms in the fossil record persists as the trade secret of paleontology. The evolutionary trees that adorn our textbooks have data only at the tips and nodes of their branches; the rest is inference, however reasonable, not the evidence of fossils. . . . I wish in no way to impugn the potential validity of gradualism. I wish only to point out that it was never seen in the rocks.[80]

Gould also stated that the history of most fossil species includes two features particularly inconsistent with gradualism:
> (1) Stasis: Most species exhibit no directional change during their tenure on earth. They appear in the fossil record looking much the same as when they disappear; morphological change is usually limited and directionless.
> (2) Sudden Appearance: In any local area, a species does not arise gradually by the steady transformation of its ancestors; it appears all at once and fully formed.[81]

Dr. Richard Lewontin, a renowned Harvard geneticist stated:
> It is not that the methods and institutions of science somehow compel us to accept a material explanation of the phenomenal world, but on

the contrary, that we are forced by our a priori adherence to material cause to create an apparatus of investigation and a set of concepts that produce material explanations, no matter how mystifying to the uninitiated. Moreover that materialism is absolute for we cannot allow a divine foot in the door.[82]

Niles Eldridge and Stephen Jay Gould proposed a theory called Punctuated Equilibrium in 1972. The concept postulated that evolution took place with long periods of stasis (species not changing) and with speciation (evolution of a new species) occurring almost instantaneously or over a relatively short time period.

The concept also postulated that most evolution would take place in small isolated populations over relatively rapid geological time periods. By reducing the numerical size of the transitional population and the number of years for which it exists, Punctuated Equilibrium would greatly limit the number of expected fossilized organisms with transitional characteristics. The concept was proposed to find an alternative explanation for the absence of transitional fossils that otherwise are direct evidence for special creation. It is interesting that this theory would be supported by the same evidence as special creation.

ITEMS THAT EACH INDIVIDUALLY REFUTE EVOLUTION

Apparent design

Evolutionists have no trouble admitting that living organisms have apparent design. Richard Dawkins, a prominent evolutionist, wrote a book titled, "The Blind Watchmaker."[83] Just his title acknowledges apparent design.

Cambrian Explosion

The Cambrian explosion shows how life started with life fully developed. Nearly all the animal phyla appear in the rocks of this period, without a trace of the evolutionary ancestors that Darwin's theory requires.

Absence of transitional fossils

The absence of transitional fossils is completely incompatible with Darwin's theory of evolution. Darwin raised the question himself:

> Why then is not every geological formation and every stratum full of such intermediate links? Geology assuredly does not reveal any such finely-graduated organic chain; and this perhaps, is the most obvious and serious objection which can be urged against my theory. The explanation lies, as I believe, in the extreme imperfection of the geological record.[84]

In the 150 years since Darwin no transitional fossils have been found.

Existence of DNA

The function of DNA is to supply the design code that identifies all aspects of the body and do it in such a way that cells can use it as a template to generate all the proteins needed by each cell and form all the unique structures for different type of cells. The entire human genome consists of 23 DNA molecules called chromosomes. The pattern of nucleotides along the DNA molecule supply the information needed to specify a human being and the uniqueness for a specific human being. Scientists have found that the information is grouped along the molecule with areas between the groups that don't appear to have information. The groups of information are called genes. A human genome contains about 3,000,000,000 nucleotide pairs and about 20,000 gene groups.

Since James Watson and Francis Crick discovered DNA in 1953 the huge knowledge base that has been learned about DNA and how it functions within cells definitely has strong implications regarding the origins of life. Prior to discovering DNA and understanding the great complexity of the cell and how DNA functions within the cell, the cell was thought of as a simple blob of protoplasm by evolutionists. The amount of information in one strand of DNA is equivalent to the information in 10,000 floppy disks or the information in all the books in a good medical school library. In terms of information storage, DNA has been found to be light years ahead of even our high tech ability to store much information using minimal space or material.

Since DNA is basically the information library that specifies the design of an organism, and information cannot be generated without intelligence, the origin of life couldn't have developed by random forces. Also, natural selection cannot change DNA to bring about higher life forms since random changes cannot increase information, only rearrange and degrade the existing information.

Irreducibility complexity

Michael Behe wrote a book titled "Darwin's Black Box"[85] which introduced the concept of "irreducibility complexity." He used a mousetrap to explain how mechanical things like a mousetrap or a bacterial flagellum need all of their parts for the item to function. Behe explains how these type items or components that need all of their parts, cannot possibly evolve according to Darwin's theory. Prior to Behe, Professor Richard Goldschmidt of the University of California at Berkeley issued a famous challenge to neo-Darwinist's, listing a series of complex structures from Mammalian hair to hemoglobin that he thought could not have been produced by accumulation and selection of small mutations.[86]

Darwin even stated:

> If it could be demonstrated that any complex organ existed which could not possibly have been formed by numerous, successive, slight modifications, my theory would absolutely break down[87].

Consequently, all cells and components in a body that need all their components or chemicals are irreducibility complex and incompatible with Darwinian evolution.

Second Law of Thermodynamics (Law of Entropy)

Thermodynamics 2nd Law, or entropy, basically refutes evolution because the law states that everything in the universe tends to go from a more organized state where heat energy can be used effectively to a state less organized where available heat is less useful. Ultimately, the universe will die a heat death when all potential heat transfer has been transferred and the universe has reached equilibrium. We see this law at work in our daily lives with everything getting dirty, becoming unorganized and wearing out automatically. In biology we see organisms becoming extinct, but none being created.

Henry M. Morris and John D. Morris documented an insightful and comprehensive review of what the 2nd Law of Thermodynamics means to the evolutionary theory in their book series, "The Modern Creation Trilogy," Science and Creation, Volume 2. The following information is taken from that book: Modern Creation Trilogy: Science & Creation, Vol. 2, 'Evolution is not Even Possible,' Henry M. Morris & John D. Morris, (Green Forest AZ: Master Books, 1996), 131. Used with permission from the publisher.

> This entropy law applies in three different realms. These include 1) classical thermodynamics, 2) statistical thermodynamics, and 3) informational thermodynamics. Each of these corresponds to a different, but equivalent, concept of entropy."[88]

Morris stated that the statistical realm most directly applies to evolution. In addition Morris states:

> In this context, entropy can be expressed as a probability function related to the degree of disorder in a system. The more disordered (or disorganized) a system is, the more highly entropic it is, and the more probable it is. A highly organized system, alternatively, is highly improbable, and must be explained by something more than random processes.
>
> All real processes have an increase of entropy. The entropy also measures the randomness, or lack of organization of the system the greater the randomness, the greater the entropy.[89]

Note again how universal the Law of Entropy is for all real processes. Isaac Asimov defined this concept interestingly as follows:

Another way of stating the Second Law then is: "The universe is constantly getting more disorderly." Viewed that way, we can see the Second Law working all about us. We have to work hard to organize a room, but left to itself, it becomes a mess again very quickly and very easily. Even if we never enter the room, it becomes dusty and musty. We find it difficult to maintain houses, and machinery, and our own bodies in perfect working order. It is easy to let them deteriorate. All we have to do is nothing, and everything deteriorates, collapses, breaks down, wears out, all by itself – and that is what the Second Law is all about.[90]

Morris continues:
Remember that this tendency to move from order to disorder applies to all real processes. Real processes include biological and geological processes, as well as chemical and physical processes. The key question is: 'How does a real biological process, which goes from order to disorder, result in evolution, which goes from disorder to order?' Maybe the evolutionists can ultimately find an answer to this question, but at least they should not ignore it, or speculate their way around it, as most evolutionists do.

Such a question is particularly applicable when we are thinking of evolution as a growth process on the grand scale from particles to people. This represents an absolutely gigantic increase in organization and complexity, and consequently is clearly out of place altogether in the context of the Second Law![91]

No explanation for original life

Astrophysicist, Sir Fred Hoyle and his colleague Chandra Wickramasinghe argued that chance processes could not have formed the biochemical machinery of the cell, especially the enzymes. In their book, "Evolution from Space," they estimated the probability of forming a single enzyme of protein at random, in the rich ocean of amino acids, was no more than 10 to the 20th power. They then calculated the likelihood of forming by chance all of the more than 2000 enzymes used in the life forms on earth. This probability was calculated at one in 10 to the 40,000th power. A vivid analogy from Hoyle became a well-known cliché:
Belief in chemical evolution of the first cell from lifeless chemicals is equivalent to believing that a tornado could sweep through a junkyard and form a Boeing 747.[92]

George Wald, another prominent Evolutionist (a Harvard University biochemist and Nobel Laureate), wrote:
When it comes to the Origin of Life there are only two possibilities: creation or spontaneous generation. There is no third way. Spontaneous Generation was disproved one hundred years ago, but that leads

us to only one other conclusion, that of supernatural creation. We cannot accept that on philosophical grounds; therefore, we choose to believe the impossible: that life arose spontaneously by chance![93]

Consequently, random evolution cannot explain the origin of life.

Lack of positive mutations

A book titled "Genetic Entropy & the Mystery of the Genome" by Dr. J. C. Sanford identified that positive mutations are very rare. Natural selection is not selective on a specific gene. Even if one gene has a positive mutation, the other genes in its genome with negative mutations will have more weight on the survival effect of the genome. Dr. Sanford argues that our genome is devolving rather than evolving. His studies have identified that natural selection is not powerful enough to prevent the negative mutations in our genome from causing degradation of our DNA. Positive mutations are so rare that they are overpowered by negative mutations, preventing evolution and causing devolution.

Limits on natural selection

The book titled "The Edge of Evolution" by Michael Behe identifies the limit of natural selection acting upon mutations and determined that this limit prevents it from developing higher life forms. Behe compares his studies on malaria and their effect on Darwin's theory with the effect of the Michelson-Morley experiment on the theory of ether. Although the Michelson-Morley experiment didn't directly falsify the theory of ether, for all practical purposes it did.

Behe states:
> The intensive studies of malaria discussed in this book are the equivalent of a Michelson-Morley experiment for Darwinism. Darwinism implicitly entails the strong, broad, basic claim that, given enough chances, random mutation and natural selection can build the sorts of complex machinery we see in the cell. Intelligence implicitly entails an equally strong, broad, basic prediction, that random mutation cannot do so. Design denies not only that some specific piece of machinery (say, the bacterial flagellum) would be produced by random mutation, but that any complex, coherent molecular machinery would. Although random processes can account for small changes, there are real limits. Beyond those limits, design is required.
> Darwin and design hold opposite, firm expectations of what we should find when we examine a truly astronomical –a hundred billion billion– number of organisms. Up until recently, the magnitude of the problem precluded a definitive test. But now the results are in. Darwinism's most basic prediction is falsified.[94]

Behe says that the natural selection process cannot result in higher organisms and a tree of life as evolution claims. Design is necessary!

HOAXES

The other huge indictment against evolution is all the many frauds, hoaxes and misrepresentations that have been perpetrated on the public in an effort to sell the religion of evolution under the guise of science. Some of these include:
1. Piltdown Man
2. Archaeoraptor (Piltdown Bird):
3. Haeckel's embryos
4. Nebraska man
5. Peppered moths

Piltdown Man

The internet encyclopedia Wikipedia states:
> The "Piltdown Man" is a famous hoax consisting of fragments of a skull and jawbone collected in 1912 from a gravel pit at Piltdown, a village near Uckfield, East Sussex, in England. The fragments were thought by many experts of the day to be the fossilized remains of a hitherto unknown form of early human. The Latin name *Eoanthropus dawsoni* ("Dawson's dawn-man", after the collector Charles Dawson) was given to the specimen.
>
> The significance of the specimen remained the subject of controversy until it was exposed in 1953 as a forgery, consisting of the lower jawbone of an orangutan combined with the skull of a fully developed, modern man.
>
> The Piltdown hoax is perhaps the most famous archaeological hoax in history. It has been prominent for two reasons: the attention paid to the issue of human evolution, and the length of time (more than 40 years) that elapsed from its discovery to its full exposure as a forgery.[95]

Archaeoraptor (Piltdown Bird)

Charles Colson stated the following titled "The Archaeoraptor Fraud: This Bird Will Never Fly," Break Point Commentary # 000128 on 1/28/2000. Printed with permission.
> Most of us know National Geographic as the magazine we flip through at the doctor's office. Renowned for its stunning photography, National Geographic is one of the most highly esteemed periodicals in the world. That is, until last November's issue featured a discovery hailed as the best evidence to date for Darwin's so-called "missing link."

But what was supposed to be startling news has turned out to be yet one more example of the scientific community peddling fraud as scientific fact. The discovery was remarkable. Archaeologists in China had unearthed a fossil of a half-bird/half- dinosaur. This fossil was proclaimed to be irrefutable evidence of a transitional form between one species and another -- evidence that evolutionists have long sought but never found.

Then the truth came out. In reality, the Archaeoraptor fossil turned out to be the remains of two animals pieced together. While some call it an honest mistake, most now believe that it was actually an elaborate and deliberate hoax. But why, you may ask, is the scientific community so quick to embrace disreputable evidence? And why would an institution like National Geographic fail to take steps to confirm the reliability of such an amazing discovery?

The answer: They're desperate. You see, the lack of any evidence for transitional forms is one of Darwinism's dirty little secrets, and some scientists would do just about anything to keep it a secret - even to the point of fabricating evidence.[96]

Haeckel's embryos

Haeckel asserted that embryos from different species are similar even when adults look so different. He faked drawings of embryos to show that the embryos went through their past evolutionary stages before turning into their evolved progeny. Haeckel's faked embryo drawings were one of the greatest embarrassments for evolution. He was indicted for fraud, yet his fraudulent pictures persisted in our text books for another 50 years.

Darwinismrefuted.com documents the following regarding Haeckel's embryos:

> What used to be called the "recapitulation theory" has long been eliminated from scientific literature, but it is still being presented as a scientific reality by some evolutionist publications. The term "recapitulation" is a condensation of the dictum "ontogeny recapitulates phylogeny," put forward by the evolutionary biologist Ernst Haeckel at the end of the nineteenth century.
>
> This theory of Haeckel's postulates that living embryos re-experience the evolutionary process that their pseudo-ancestors underwent. He theorized that during its development in its mother's womb, the human embryo first displayed the characteristics of a fish, and then those of a reptile, and finally those of a human.
>
> It has since been proven that this theory is completely bogus. It is now known that the "gills" that supposedly appear in the early stages of the human embryo are in fact the initial phases of the middle-ear canal, parathyroid, and thymus. That part of the embryo that was lik-

ened to the "egg yolk pouch" turns out to be a pouch that produces blood for the infant. The part that was identified as a "tail" by Haeckel and his followers is in fact the backbone, which resembles a tail only because it takes shape before the legs do.

These are universally acknowledged facts in the scientific world, and are accepted even by evolutionists themselves. Two leading neo-Darwinists, George Gaylord Simpson and W. Beck have admitted:

> *Haeckel misstated the evolutionary principle involved. It is now firmly established that ontogeny does not repeat phylogeny.*[97]

Another interesting aspect of "recapitulation" was Ernst Haeckel himself, a faker who falsified his drawings in order to support the theory he advanced. Haeckel's forgeries purported to show that fish and human embryos resembled one another. When he was caught, the only defense he offered was that other evolutionists had committed similar offences:

> After this compromising confession of 'forgery' I should be obliged to consider myself condemned and annihilated if I had not the consolation of seeing side by side with me in the prisoner's dock hundreds of fellow - culprits, among them many of the most trusted observers and most esteemed biologists. The great majority of all the diagrams in the best biological textbooks, treatises and journals would incur in the same degree the charge of 'forgery,' for all of them are inexact, and are more or less doctored, schematized and constructed.[98]

Jonathan Wells stated:

> Haeckel's embryos seem to provide such powerful evidence for Darwin's theory that some version of them can be found in almost every modern textbook dealing with evolution. Yet biologists have known for over a century that Haeckel faked his drawings; vertebrate embryos never looked as similar as he made them out to be. Furthermore, the stage Haeckel labeled as "first" is actually midway through development; the similarities he exaggerated are preceded by striking differences in earlier stages of development. Although you may never know it from reading biology textbooks, Darwin's "strongest single class of facts" is a classic example of how evidence can be twisted to fit a theory.[99]

Nebraska man

In "Evolution: The Fossils Still Say No," Dr. Duane Gish documents the story of the Nebraska Man:

> In 1922 a tooth was discovered in western Nebraska which was declared by Henry Fairfield Osborn, one of the most eminent paleontologists of that day, and several other authorities, to combine the characteristics of a chimpanzee, *Pithecanthropus*, man.

Osborn and his colleagues could not decide whether the original owner of the tooth should be designated as an apelike man or a man like ape. He was given the designation Nebraska man *Hesperopithecus haroldcookii* and became known popularly as Nebraska Man.

An illustration of what this creature and his contemporaries supposedly looked like was published in the *Illustrated London News*.[100] In this illustration, *Hesperopithecus* looks remarkably similar to modern man, although brutish in appearance. In 1927 after further collecting and studies had been carried out, it was decided that *Hesperopithecus* was neither a man like ape nor an ape like man, but was an extinct peccary, or pig![101] This is a case in which a scientist made a man out of a pig, and a pig made a monkey out of the scientist![102]

The Nebraska Man's pig's tooth was presented as evidence at the 1920 Scopes trial and helped gain unjustified support for evolution.

Peppered moths

Dr. Duane Gish explains the peppered moth scenario that is used by evolutionists to explain the effects of natural selection. Although the explanation is a perfectly plausible result of natural selection, as explained later, it wasn't the correct explanation:

> Before the advent of the industrial revolution and resultant air pollution, the tree trunks in England were light-colored. The peppered moth rests on the tree trunks during the day, with wings outspread. The normal, or light-colored, is very inconspicuous against such a background. The melanic form, on the other hand, is easily detected under these circumstances. As a result, predators (birds) pick off a much higher percentage of the melanic form, and they thus remained a minor portion of the total population of peppered moths.
>
> This was the case in 1850 at about the time of the industrial revolution in England began. The tree trunks became progressively darker, however, and by 1895, ninety-five percent of these moths in the vicinity of Manchester were of the carbonaria, or melanic variety. This change had taken place because now the melanic form was inconspicuous against the blackened tree trunks, while the light-colored variant was easily detected when resting this background.[103]

Gish continues:

> Of greatest importance to our discussion, however, is the fact that no significant evolutionary change has occurred in these moths.[104]

In "Icons of Evolution" Dr. Jonathan Wells explains the misrepresentation that evolutionists have perpetrated on the public to make their story believable:

> Most introductory biology textbooks now illustrate this classical story of natural selection with photographs of the two varieties of peppered moth resting on light- and dark- colored tree trunks. What the text-

books don't explain, however, is that biologists have known since the 1980's that the classical story has some serious flaws. The most serious is that peppered moths in the wild don't even rest on tree trunks. The textbook photographs, it turns out, have been staged.[105]

They staged the photographs by pinning dead moths on the tree trunks.

OTHER EVIDENCE

Jonathan Wells stated:
> Besides all of these evidences against evolution and all the hoaxes, other evidences against evolution add to the case. One is the many, many missing links that have been found and promoted and subsequently exposed as false. Another is all the years of extensive work on the fruit fly to try to generate a superior fruit fly or a higher organism through radiation and other means to cause mutations. None of the flies were more fit than the original fly.[106]

Evolution is a false religion with absolutely no scientific evidence supporting it! It is part of the secular humanist's false foundation.

Genesis 2:4 states:
> This is the history of the heavens and the earth when they were created, in the day that the LORD God made the earth and the heavens, . .

Virtually no evidence exists that supports macroevolution. Much evidence does exist for extinction and devolution. Evolution is a religion that is diametrically opposed to biblical teaching and is probably the most fundamental false foundation that deceives a high percentage of our population.

Although we supplied much information above refuting evolution much more information is available on the subject. One book is "Stumbling blocks of evolution" by Chris Nitardy. He wrote a cute poem that is documented in Appendix D. Check it out!

Next we will cover the false foundation of relative truth vs. absolute truth.

CHAPTER 15
Relative truth vs. absolute truth

Once God is removed from the picture by a belief in random evolution we have a rationale that excuses us from following God's absolute moral code. If God doesn't exist, neither does His moral code. With our fallen nature and our history of falling away from God and his absolute commandments, we find it liberating to have a rationale that allows us to follow our own relative moral code and reject God's absolute moral code. I believe the psychologists call this rationalization.

Humanist John Dewey (1859-1952), co-author and signer of the Humanist Manifesto 1 (1933), declared:

> There is no God and there is no soul. Hence, there are no needs for the props of traditional religion. With dogma and creed excluded, then immutable truth is also dead and buried. There is no room for fixed, natural law or moral absolutes.[107]

Dewey also stated:

> It (modern philosophy) certainly exacts a surrender of all supernaturalism and fixed dogma and rigid institutionalism with which Christianity has been historically associated[108]

Those that advocate relative truth are primarily promoting moral relative truth. However, some actually carry the concept beyond moral concepts. It is hard to believe that anyone would believe such a concept since any debate on the merits of this type of relative truth would be a very short debate. Even the assertion of relative moral truth is a contradiction. For one to believe in relative moral truth you need to believe in one absolute truth. i.e. The existence of relative truth.

A discussion with a coworker was my first encounter with the concept of relative truth. He said to me "What I have come to believe is that we can't know anything for sure." The obvious question was (and still is) how can we know that for sure?

Some people believe that Einstein showed that everything is relative. Since everything includes the concept of truth, they conclude that Einstein showed that truth itself is relative. The fact is that Einstein never showed nor claimed to show any such thing. An article titled "It Didn't Start with Einstein" in *Time Magazine* claimed the following:

> Einstein himself often insisted that his theories had no relevance for anything except science. He called the hullabaloo surrounding his findings "psychopathological," and he disabused those who would misap-

ply his ideas. Asked what effect his theory would have on religion, he said: "None. Relativity is a purely scientific matter and has nothing to do with religion."[109]

The belief in relative truth serves as the false foundation for so many of the unbiblical, self-serving beliefs and conduct in today's culture. To reverse the culture we need expose the fallacy in the foundations that support the false beliefs.

CHAPTER 16
The false foundation of the basic goodness and perfectibility of man

BASIC GOODNESS AND PERFECTIBILITY OF MAN

With God, the Bible and absolute truth removed from our culture, our worldview defaults to a secular humanist worldview. With God out of the way, the secular humanist motto becomes the default absolute truth. That is "man is the measure of all things." Man makes the rules and decides the current morality.

It is amazing that in spite of what we see in the newspaper every day of man's inhumanity to man, secular humanists hold to the basic goodness and perfectibility of man. They believe that all the ills in our world are either caused by the environment or lack of education.

If man is basically good we would have to teach children how throw tantrums, how to whine and how to be selfish. The fact that they naturally know how to do all these things invalidates the basic goodness of man. Jeremiah 17:9 states:

> The heart is deceitful above all things, And desperately wicked; Who can know it?

Isaiah 64:6 states:

> But we are all like an unclean thing, And all our righteousnesses are like filthy rags;
> We all fade as a leaf, And our iniquities, like the wind, Have taken us away.

Belief in this false foundation acts as the foundation of many other false beliefs particularly in the political area.

Next we will cover the false foundation of Global warming.

CHAPTER 17
The false foundation of global warming

Dr. E Calvin Beisner makes the following statement concerning the science of global warming:

> Our examination of the science of global warming finds that global warming alarmism wrongly claims that recent temperature changes have been greater and more rapid than those of the past and therefore must be manmade, not natural. It exaggerates the influence of manmade greenhouse gases on global temperature and ignores or underestimates the influence of natural cycles. It mistakenly takes the output of computer climate models as evidence when it is only predictions based on hypotheses that must be tested by observation. It falsely claims overwhelming scientific consensus in favor of the hypothesis of dangerous manmade warming (ignoring tens of thousands of scientists who disagree) and then falsely claims that such consensus proves the hypothesis and justifies policies to fight it. It seeks to intimidate or demonize scientific skeptics rather than welcoming their work as of the very essence of scientific inquiry: putting hypotheses to the test rather than blindly embracing them.[110]

Dr. Beisner is stating that alarmist panic over what they claim to be manmade global warming is not valid or justified.

Natural News states the following:

> Practically everything you have been told by the mainstream scientific community and the media about the alleged detriments of greenhouse gases, and particularly carbon dioxide, appears to be false, according to new data compiled by NASA's Langley Research Center. As it turns out, all those atmospheric greenhouse gases that Al Gore and all the other global warming hoaxers have long claimed are overheating and destroying our planet are actually cooling it, based on the latest evidence.
>
> As reported by *Principia Scientific International* (PSI), Martin Mlynczak and his colleagues over at NASA tracked infrared emissions from the earth's upper atmosphere during and following a recent solar storm that took place between March 8-10, 2013. What they found was that the vast majority of energy released from the sun during this immense coronal mass ejection (CME) was reflected back up into space rather than deposited into earth's lower atmosphere.
>
> The result was an overall cooling effect that completely contradicts claims made by NASA's own climatology division that greenhouse gas-

es are a cause of global warming. As illustrated by data collected using *Sounding of the Atmosphere using Broadband Emission Radiometry* (SABER), both carbon dioxide (CO2) and nitric oxide (NO), which are abundant in the earth's upper atmosphere, greenhouse gases reflect heating energy rather than absorb it.[111]

One fact that has been mysteriously missing in the global warming debate is the fact that water vapor (another greenhouse gas) is at least twenty times more prevalent than carbon dioxide. That means the effect of carbon dioxide would be completely overshadowed by the water vapor. Also, there has been no warming during the last 15 years or more while the concentration of carbon dioxide in our atmosphere has continued to go up. Certainly the belief in global warming is a false foundation for the other evils identified by Dr. Beisner's quote below:

> And it bears fruit in unethical policy that would
> - destroy millions of jobs.
> - cost trillions of dollars in lost economic production.
> - slow, stop, or reverse economic growth.
> - reduce the standard of living for all but the elite few who are well positioned to benefit from laws that unfairly advantage them at the expense of most businesses and all consumers.
> - endanger liberty by putting vast new powers over private, social, and market life in the hands of national and international governments.
> - condemn the world's poor to generations of continued misery characterized by rampant disease and premature death.
>
> In return for all these sacrifices, what will the world get? At most a negligible, undetectable reduction in global average temperature a hundred years from now.[112]

Global warming is definitely a religion and a false foundation for the evils listed above by either Cap and Trade implementation or environmental taxation.

Next we will cover the false foundation of "The New Tolerance."

CHAPTER 18
The false foundation of The New Tolerance and Outrage Based Coerced Conscience

Another thing that has been turned on its head in our relativistic culture is to not view and debate issues as good and evil or true and false. When is the last time that you have heard any of those words on TV, newspaper or in any kind of debate? Our culture has reframed the argument so the debate is no longer between good and evil or true and false, but between the messengers who dare to identify something as evil or false and those that do not offend people by judging the goodness of things. This whole idea is supported by the concept of relative truth. If we have no absolute truth, then who are we to judge the goodness or badness of beliefs and behaviors etc.?

Traditionally, we knew what good and evil were and Christians tolerated evil even though it was not accepted, approved or certainly not celebrated. Today we censor debate on good vs. evil and switch the debate to demonize the messengers that are promoting truth and exposing evil. As the expression goes, "shoot the messenger of bad tidings." A book that coined the phrase and documents this issue is "The New Tolerance" by Josh McDowell.[113]

Just recently liberal progressives have added another level to their persecution of Christians with a biblical worldview. Now rather than just demonizing them, they are getting their coercive M.O. codified into law so they can actually prosecute people that do not embrace their unbiblical belief and lifestyle. Most everybody is familiar with bakers that are losing their businesses because they refused to bake a cake for a homosexual wedding or a photographer punished for not photographing a homosexual wedding. Also, a florist was punished for not providing flowers for a homosexual wedding and a pizza restaurant was also punished. This is taking "The New Tolerance" to a whole new level. Let's coin the name of this as "Outrage Based Coerced Conscience."

Today we not only censor debate on good vs. evil, we insist that all manner of evil, not only be tolerated, but be accepted, approved and celebrated. Romans 1:26-32 states the following:

> For this reason God gave them up to vile passions. For even their women exchanged the natural use for what is against nature. Likewise also the men, leaving the natural use of the woman, burned in their lust for one another, men with men committing what is shameful, and receiving in themselves the penalty of their error which was due. And even as they did not like to retain God in their knowledge, God gave

them over to a debased mind, to do those things which are not fitting; being filled with all unrighteousness, sexual immorality, wickedness, covetousness, maliciousness; full of envy, murder, strife, deceit, evil-mindedness; they are whisperers, backbiters, haters of God, violent, proud, boasters, inventors of evil things, disobedient to parents, undiscerning, untrustworthy, unloving, unforgiving, unmerciful; who, knowing the righteous judgment of God, that those who practice such things are deserving of death, not only do the same but also approve of those who practice them.

Although this passage places emphasis on homosexuality, it lists many other evil things. It goes on to state in the last sentence that not only those that practice those things are deserving of death, but also those who approve of those that practice them. This also implies the same for those of us that approve of the sin itself! Consequently, what our cultural is asking us to do is to essentially partake equally in their sin. We must put ourselves in the same boat. This concept laid out in verse 32, to my knowledge, is not well known to Christians and is virtually not taught by any ministers, yet is so relevant to what our position should be in our post-modern, politically correct world.

Again, this false foundation turns the truth upside down. The false foundations above support so many additional false beliefs in our culture.

Next we will cover the false foundation of Political Correctness.

CHAPTER 19
The false foundation of Political Correctness

Although most of us are very familiar with political correctness, we are not completely certain of what it really is or where it came from. An article titled "The Origins of Political Correctness" by Bill Lind on the Accuracy in Academia website answered both of those questions. Below are extensive excerpts from that article by Bill Lind copied with permission:

> If we look at it analytically, if we look at it historically, we quickly find out exactly what it is. Political Correctness is cultural Marxism. It is Marxism translated from economic into cultural terms. It is an effort that goes back not to the 1960s and the hippies and the peace movement, but back to World War I. If we compare the basic tenets of Political Correctness with classical Marxism the parallels are very obvious.
>
> First of all, both are totalitarian ideologies. The totalitarian nature of Political Correctness is revealed nowhere more clearly than on college campuses, many of which at this point are small ivy covered North Koreas, where the student or faculty member who dares to cross any of the lines set up by the gender feminist or the homosexual-rights activists, or the local black or Hispanic group, or any of the other sainted "victims" groups that PC revolves around, quickly find themselves in judicial trouble. Within the small legal system of the college, they face formal charges – some star-chamber proceeding – and punishment. That is a little look into the future that Political Correctness intends for the nation as a whole.
>
> Indeed, all ideologies are totalitarian because the essence of an ideology (I would note that conservatism correctly understood is not an ideology) is to take some philosophy and say on the basis of this philosophy certain things must be true – such as the whole of the history of our culture is the history of the oppression of women. Since reality contradicts that, reality must be forbidden. It must become forbidden to acknowledge the reality of our history. People must be forced to live a lie, and since people are naturally reluctant to live a lie, they naturally use their ears and eyes to look out and say, "Wait a minute. This isn't true. I can see it isn't true," the power of the state must be put behind the demand to live a lie. That is why ideology invariably creates a totalitarian state.
>
> Second, the cultural Marxism of Political Correctness, like economic Marxism, has a single factor explanation of history. Economic Marxism says that all of history is determined by ownership of means of production. Cultural Marxism, or Political Correctness, says that all history

is determined by power, by which groups defined in terms of race, sex, etc., have power over which other groups. Nothing else matters. All literature, indeed, is about that. Everything in the past is about that one thing.

Third, just as in classical economic Marxism certain groups, i.e. workers and peasants, are a priori good, and other groups, i.e., the bourgeoisie and capital owners, are evil. In the cultural Marxism of Political Correctness certain groups are good – feminist women, (only feminist women, non-feminist women are deemed not to exist) blacks, Hispanics, homosexuals. These groups are determined to be "victims," and therefore automatically good regardless of what any of them do. Similarly, white males are determined automatically to be evil, thereby becoming the equivalent of the bourgeoisie in economic Marxism.

Fourth, both economic and cultural Marxism rely on expropriation. When the classical Marxists, the communists, took over a country like Russia, they expropriated the bourgeoisie, they took away their property. Similarly, when the cultural Marxists take over a university campus, they expropriate through things like quotas for admissions. When a white student with superior qualifications is denied admittance to a college in favor of a black or Hispanic who isn't as well qualified, the white student is expropriated. And indeed, affirmative action, in our whole society today, is a system of expropriation. White owned companies don't get a contract because the contract is reserved for a company owned by, say, Hispanics or women. So expropriation is a principle tool for both forms of Marxism.

And finally, both have a method of analysis that automatically gives the answers they want. For the classical Marxist, it's Marxist economics. For the cultural Marxist, it's deconstruction. Deconstruction essentially takes any text, removes all meaning from it and re-inserts any meaning desired. So we find, for example, that all of Shakespeare is about the suppression of women, or the Bible is really about race and gender. All of these texts simply become grist for the mill, which proves that "all history is about which groups have power over which other groups." So the parallels are very evident between the classical Marxism that we're familiar with in the old Soviet Union and the cultural Marxism that we see today as Political Correctness.[114]

This explains very well what "political correctness" is. The same article explains where it came from and who promoted it.

> In 1923 in Germany, a think-tank is established that takes on the role of translating Marxism from economic into cultural terms that creates Political Correctness as we know it today, and essentially it has created the basis for it by the end of the 1930s...
>
> He endows an institute, associated with Frankfurt University, established in 1923, that was originally supposed to be known as the Insti-

tute for Marxism. But the people behind it decided at the beginning that it was not to their advantage to be openly identified as Marxist. The last thing Political Correctness wants is for people to figure out it's a form of Marxism. So instead they decide to name it the Institute for Social Research. . .

The initial work at the Institute was rather conventional, but in 1930 it acquired a new director named Max Horkheimer, and Horkheimer's views were very different. . .

Horkheimer's initial heresy is that he is very interested in Freud, and the key to making the translation of Marxism from economic into cultural terms is essentially that he combined it with Freudism. . .

What the Frankfurt School essentially does is draw on both Marx and Freud in the 1930s to create this theory called Critical Theory. The term is ingenious because you're tempted to ask, "What is the theory?" The theory is to criticize. The theory is that the way to bring down Western culture and the capitalist order is not to lay down an alternative. . .

What Critical Theory is about is simply criticizing. It calls for the most destructive criticism possible, in every possible way, designed to bring the current order down. . .

Fromm and Marcuse introduce an element which is central to Political Correctness, and that's the sexual element. And particularly Marcuse, who in his own writings calls for a society of "polymorphous perversity," that is his definition of the future of the world that they want to create. Marcuse in particular by the 1930s is writing some very extreme stuff on the need for sexual liberation, but this runs through the whole Institute. So do most of the themes we see in Political Correctness, again in the early 30s. In Fromm's view, masculinity and femininity were not reflections of 'essential' sexual differences, as the Romantics had thought. They were derived instead from differences in life functions, which were in part socially determined." Sex is a construct; sexual differences are a construct. . .

How does all of this stuff flood in here? How does it flood into our universities, and indeed into our lives today? The members of the Frankfurt School are Marxist, they are also, to a man, Jewish. In 1933 the Nazis came to power in Germany, and not surprisingly they shut down the Institute for Social Research. And its members fled. They fled to New York City, and the Institute was reestablished there in 1933 with help from Columbia University. And the members of the Institute, gradually through the 1930s, though many of them remained writing in German, shift their focus from Critical Theory about German society, destructive criticism about every aspect of that society, to Critical Theory directed toward American society. . .

These origins of Political Correctness would probably not mean too much to us today except for two subsequent events. The first was the student rebellion in the mid-1960s, which was driven largely by resistance to the draft and the Vietnam War. But the student rebels needed theory of some sort. They couldn't just get out there and say, "Hell no we won't go," they had to have some theoretical explanation behind it. Very few of them were interested in wading through Das Kapital. Classical, economic Marxism is not light, and most of the radicals of the 60s were not deep. Fortunately for them, and unfortunately for our country today, and not just in the university, Herbert Marcuse remained in America when the Frankfurt School relocated back to Frankfurt after the war. And whereas Mr. Adorno in Germany is appalled by the student rebellion when it breaks out there – when the student rebels come into Adorno's classroom, he calls the police and has them arrested – Herbert Marcuse, who remained here, saw the 60s student rebellion as the great chance. He saw the opportunity to take the work of the Frankfurt School and make it the theory of the New Left in the United States.

One of Marcuse's books was the key book. It virtually became the bible of the SDS and the student rebels of the 60s. That book was Eros and Civilization. Marcuse argues that under a capitalistic order (he downplays the Marxism very strongly here, it is subtitled, A Philosophical Inquiry into Freud, but the framework is Marxist), repression is the essence of that order and that gives us the person Freud describes – the person with all the hang-ups, the neuroses, because his sexual instincts are repressed. We can envision a future, if we can only destroy this existing oppressive order, in which we liberate eros, we liberate libido, in which we have a world of "polymorphous perversity," in which you can "do you own thing." And by the way, in that world there will no longer be work, only play. What a wonderful message for the radicals of the mid-60s! They're students, they're baby-boomers, and they've grown up never having to worry about anything except eventually having to get a job. And here is a guy writing in a way they can easily follow. He doesn't require them to read a lot of heavy Marxism and tells them everything they want to hear which is essentially, "Do your own thing," "If it feels good do it," and "You never have to go to work." By the way, Marcuse is also the man who creates the phrase, "Make love, not war." Coming back to the situation people face on campus, Marcuse defines "liberating tolerance" as intolerance for anything coming from the Right and tolerance for anything coming from the Left. Marcuse joined the Frankfurt School, in 1932 (if I remember right). So, all of this goes back to the 1930s.

In conclusion, America today is in the throes of the greatest and direst transformation in its history. We are becoming an ideological state, a country with an official state ideology enforced by the power of the state. In "hate crimes" we now have people serving jail sentences for political thoughts. And the Congress is now moving to expand that category ever further. Affirmative action is part of it. The terror against anyone who dissents from Political Correctness on campus is part of it. It's exactly what we have seen happen in Russia, in Germany, in Italy, in China, and now it's coming here. And we don't recognize it because we call it Political Correctness and laugh it off. My message today is that it's not funny, it's here, it's growing and it will eventually destroy, as it seeks to destroy, everything that we have ever defined as our freedom and our culture.[115]

Marx's primary goals were to dethrone God and to destroy capitalism. At least he knew that God and capitalism went together. Today, most of our churches don't seem to realize that they go together. Many think that the bible and socialism go together. The quotes from the article above did not bring the biblical position into the discussion as you might expect. However, all of Marx's and Freud's beliefs and all politically correct beliefs are in diametric opposition to biblical principles. The life styles of both Marx and Freud also were equally unbiblical as we will document in Chapter 24. All the deconstruction that Political Correctness is intended to accomplish is that of traditional and biblical principles. Again the significance of this diametric opposition is profound!

The next we will cover the false foundation of Case Law.

CHAPTER 20
The false foundation of Case Law

Wikipedia online dictionary states the following regarding Case Law:
> Case law is the set of existing rulings which made new interpretations of law and, therefore, can be cited as precedent. In most countries, including most European countries, the term is applied to any set of rulings on law which is guided by previous rulings, for example, previous decisions of a government agency. These interpretations are distinguished from statutory law which are the statutes and codes enacted by legislative bodies, and regulatory law which are regulations established by executive branch agencies. Trials and hearings that do not result in written decisions of a court of record do not create precedent for future court decisions. In some countries, such as the USA, the term is exclusively used for decisions from bodies discharging judicial functions, such as selected appellate courts and courts of first instance.[116]

At first glance it seems to make sense. However, the problem is that if for whatever reason a precedent is set that is contrary to established legislative law or Constitutional Law, all future judicial laws will be based upon the judicial precedent and ignores the legislative law or Constitutional Law. That is exactly what has happened below under separation of church and state and behavioral privacy laws.

Next we will cover separation of church and state.

CHAPTER 21
The false foundation of the separation of church and state

The following is an article I wrote for publication in a newspaper. Its title is "A False Foundation for "Dechristianizing" America:"

There is no limit to what lengths those opposed to Christianity are taking to expunge all Christian values, writings, symbols, music, speech and holidays from the public arena and now even from the private arena. Christianity is treated like a cancer or a deadly virus that must be removed. The most recent examples are "hate crimes" legislation against those who would express Biblical truths in a loving way and a court case to remove "IN GOD WE TRUST" from our currency.

The foundation for this rationale is the false "Separation of Church and State" argument. This argument does not represent the original use or intent of the metaphor, the direct meaning or the intent of the Constitution, nor does it represent the historical coercion and oppression that was the basis for the establishment clause and the free exercise clause of the Constitution. The facts and the truth are actually in 100 percent opposition to the argument being used to expunge Christianity from America.

Although the "Separation of Church and State" metaphor gives us a picture of a two-sided wall, the only implied meaning and use of the phrase by the judiciary, ACLU and the media has been to keep the church (Christian religion) out of the government and the public square. Certainly no attention has been given to the state interfering with the church. The concern has not been focused on a specific denominational church being connected to the state, but more broadly on censoring doctrinal Christianity.

Does the Implied Meaning Represent the Original Context?

On January 1, 1802 Thomas Jefferson wrote a letter to the Baptist Church in Danbury Connecticut in response to their previously communicated concern that contained the origin and source of the "Separation of Church and State" phrase. Their concern was that the federal government was going to intrude in their religion or in some way disturb their faith.

Jefferson wrote that "he was greatly impressed that the American people, through the First Amendment had, in effect, erected a 'wall of separation between the church and the state,' so the Baptists didn't need to fear that the federal government was going to intrude upon their religion or in any way disturb their faith."

Consequently, the implied meaning and use of the "Separation of Church and State" phrase not only does not represent its original source context, it is used in exactly the opposite way!

Does the Implied Meaning Represent the Constitution?

The verbiage where the Constitution relates to the "Separation of Church and State" issue is what is referred to as the "Establishment Clause" and the "Free Exercise Clause" in the First Amendment of the Constitution. The "Establishment Clause" states, "Congress shall make no law respecting an establishment of religion," The sentence continues with the "Free Exercise Clause" that states, "or prohibiting the free exercise thereof ... "

To ensure we understand what the framers of the Constitution meant by the "Establishment Clause" let's examine the three drafts prior to the final one. The three stated:

> 1. "Congress shall not make any law establishing any religious denomination."
> 2. "Congress shall make no law establishing any particular denomination."
> 3. "Congress shall make no law establishing any particular denomination in preference to another."[117]

From this, it is clear that the establishment clause was certainly not intended to restrict the doctrinal Christian religion in the public arena or in government. It is also clear that the doctrinal Christian religion was actually our state religion at the time the Constitution was framed. The Bible was used in schools and in government and Christian symbols were chiseled all over Washington D.C. The founder's only intention was to prevent Congress from passing any law that would make a specific denominational religion our state church!

Consequently, the implied meaning and use of the phrase "Separation of Church and State" does not at all represent what the Constitution stated or intended! The implied meaning is exactly opposite to what the facts show.

Does it represent the Concern of Historical Oppression?

In Europe, doctrinal Christians were oppressed by both Catholic and Protestant denominational Christian religions. The most recent and notable was the oppression that occurred when the denominational Anglican Church in England combined with King James I.

This historical concern matches perfectly with what the framers of the Constitution were trying to prevent in America when they wrote the Establishment Clause of the Constitution.

Consequently, the implied meaning, and the use of the "Separation of Church and State" phrase, does not represent the historical concern of oppression. Again, it is in 100 percent in opposition.

Conclusion

> The implied meaning and use of the "Separation of Church and State" phrase does not represent its original contextual meaning, the words or intent of the Establishment Clause of the Constitution or the European historical concern. It means just the opposite![118]

This false foundation was established by the U.S. Supreme Court. The phrase "Separation of Church and State" became a definitive part of Establishment Clause jurisprudence in *Everson v. Board of Education*, 330 U.S. 1 (1947). The 5-4 decision was handed down on February 10, 1947. The Court, through Justice Hugo Black, ruled that the state law was constitutionally permissible. Perhaps as important as the actual outcome, though, was the position that the entire Court adopted on the Establishment Clause. It reflected a broad interpretation of the Clause that was to guide the Court's decisions for decades to come. Other justices have pushed Black's concept even further. They have stated "The wall must be kept high and impregnable. We could not approve the slightest breach."

Some, including former Chief Justice William H. Rehnquist, have criticized *Everson* for its reliance on quotations and views from Thomas Jefferson, who had little to do with the framing of the U.S. Constitution or its Bill of Rights. Rehnquist's commentary stated:

> The metaphor of the wall of separation is bad history and worse law.[119]

Consequently, what Thomas Jefferson intended to be a wall that would just keep the government out of the church, Hugo Black established a jurisprudence precedent for a two sided wall that in practice would keep the church out of the state. What has been done is that true religion has been outlawed from the public square and replaced with the diametrically opposite false religion of Secular Humanism. In many subsequent cases, this precedent that effectively reversed the original intent of the metaphor has been used to outlaw the following in public schools:

1. Religious instruction
2. School prayer
3. Bible reading
4. Ten Commandments
5. Teaching creation science
6. Prayer at sports activities

Other religious prohibitions not directly related to schools include:

1. Nativity Scenes
2. Ten Commandments
3. Crosses
4. Bible verses
5. Christmas trees

The ACLU is using the Hugo Black precedent to try to get rid of everything Christian in the public square. The ACLU is using the courts to forcibly remove every vestige of Christian symbols from our society. Children have been punished for praying silently or reading the bible. Schools, governments, churches and others have basically been persecuted on this issue that has been completely built on a false foundation. David Limbaugh wrote a whole 352 page book titled "Persecution" documenting this great atrocity.[120]

Consequently, the Separation of Church and State scenario has been another example of a false foundation that has revised history and turned our culture from a Christian oriented culture to one that is 100% hostile to Christianity. Sadly, the Christian churches and many Christians have not objected and many actually support the Separation of Church and State concept! Those have been led to believe that the alternative to the Separation of Church and State is a theocracy.

What we need to do to combat all the evil beliefs that have been accepted by our society is not to attack each one, but attack the false foundations. Attacking each individual false belief is difficult since they are still supported by belief in the false foundation supporting them. In addition, it is less efficient to attack each one than taking them all down by destroying the false foundations that are supporting them. If we are addressing the bad fruit and not the tree trunk and the roots which support it, we are addressing things less foundational. Ken Ham promotes the concept that the false foundations have contaminated the soil where we plant the gospel seeds and consequently the seeds do not germinate well. Our priorities should be better placed so we are decontaminating the soil to help the gospel seeds to germinate. Satan also makes sure that we have misplaced priorities (see Chapter 8 Majoring in minors) for what is important and what is not.

Next in Part 5 we will cover the apostasy in the church as a reason evil has progressed so rapidly in America.

Part 5

Why haven't religions effectively resisted the evil progressing rapidly in America?

CHAPTER 22
Apostasy and heresy in Christian churches

The primary problem with our churches is that they are teaching and promoting doctrines of man rather than doctrines of God. The religious leaders in Jesus' time were the Pharisees. Jesus came down harder on them than anyone else. He accused them of writing many man made doctrines they expected to be followed religiously. Jesus also accused the leaders of hypocrisy since they didn't even follow their own rules and rituals that they created out of thin air.

When churches who previously followed the biblical doctrines of God, but have strayed away from this pure faith, it is called apostasy. However, when a particular Christian denomination or doctrinal religion teaches doctrines of man even though they are also teaching some biblical doctrines of God along with it, we consider that heresy. Almost all doctrinal religions or denominations teach some truth, but we should remember that Lucifer also mixed some truth with deception when he seduced Eve. Consequently, teaching some truth does not qualify a doctrinal religion or denomination as a good religion that we should follow! We need to identify those doctrines and beliefs being taught that are not biblical before giving them our blessing. This is how Jesus evaluated the seven churches in Revelation Chapter 2 & 3.

Apostasy and heresy in Christian churches today are Satan's most effective ways of preventing people from being saved and also from preventing our secular government from implementing biblical principles that maximize liberty and well-being while minimizing suffering and pain. This results directly from following rituals and doctrines of man, from denying the truth of scripture and by being co-opted by our secular culture or compromising with humanist philosophies.

Apostasy in Christian churches is not limited to a few denominations or churches. In fact, it is very difficult to find any denomination or church that has not succumbed to false teaching or been co-opted by our secular culture. We would like to primarily address heresy in the Catholic Church of Rome and apostasy in the Protestant realm.

Our purpose is not to offend anyone. However, if we have a choice between being silent about heresies and apostasies that result in people we love (everyone) rejecting the true gospel because of their misplaced faith in them or telling them the truth that may possibly offend them; our choice should be to warn people even at the risk of offending them. What other option do we have? Beyond this we view beliefs and personhood separately, unlike our politically correct culture. We certainly do not condemn people even if we condemn their false beliefs. See disclaimer at the beginning of this book. With that background, we will expose the heresies in the Catholic Church of Rome.

THE CATHOLIC CHURCH OF ROME

Worldwide there are 1.2 billion Catholics or $1/6^{th}$ of the world's population. In America there are about 65 million Catholics or about ¼ of America's population. If, in fact, the Roman Catholic Church is a heretical church and we do not signal the alarm, we are very negligent indeed. For Catholics and others that believe in the Catholic Church, please have the faith and fortitude to continue reading. Examine everything stated here against the bible and historical facts. The bible instructs us to do this for any and all religious beliefs. 2 Timothy 3:16 states:
> All Scripture is given by inspiration of God, and is profitable for doctrine, for reproof, for correction, for instruction in righteousness, . .

1 John 4:1 states:
> Beloved, do not believe every spirit, but test the spirits, whether they are of God; because many false prophets have gone out into the world.

Acts 17:11 states:
> These were more fair-minded than those in Thessalonica, in that they received the word with all readiness, and searched the Scriptures daily to find out whether these things were so.

Consequently, the scriptures teach us we that need to examine our doctrines and our beliefs and compare them with the teachings of scripture to know if what we are following is true or false doctrine.

Malachi 3:6 states:
> For I am the LORD, I do not change; . .

Matthew 5:18 states:
> For assuredly, I say to you, till heaven and earth pass away, one jot or one tittle will by no means pass from the law till all is fulfilled.

Revelation 22:18-19 states:
> For I testify to everyone who hears the words of the prophecy of this book: If anyone adds to these things, God will add to him the plagues that are written in this book; and if anyone takes away from the words of the book of this prophecy, God shall take away his part from the Book of Life, from the holy city, and from the things which are written in this book.

Consequently, any belief, doctrine or religious tradition that either conflicts with the bible, or religious edicts that keep changing, are not of God and are false and heretical. Even if the Catholic Church of Rome takes the biblical position on some beliefs, that does not mean that all their doctrines and beliefs are true and biblical. Indeed the Catholic Church's beliefs on some of the basic tenants of Christianity are biblical. These include the following: Deity of Christ, Godhead trinity, virgin birth, bodily resurrection and the return of Jesus to earth. We commend the Catholic Church for those biblical beliefs. However, whenever a church mixes truths with false doctrines and beliefs it is not commendable. It is heretical and apostate. I believe we can show that other beliefs and doctrines of the Catholic Church are not supported by biblical teaching and consequently are doctrines of men rather than doctrines of God. Before getting into the various areas where the Catholic Church adds to and conflicts with biblical teaching I need to acknowledge that basically all the information presented here comes from Mike Gendron, a former Catholic, and his website www.progospel.org. All the quotes of Mike Gendron are with permission. He tells his story on his website as follows:

> Twenty years ago, during Mike Gendron's last semester at seminary, he and his wife Jane began inviting Roman Catholics over to their home every Tuesday night to watch a Gospel video and answer questions. Within three months they witnessed 17 Catholics exchange their religion for a relationship with the Lord Jesus. They were even more excited when many of these friends came back on Wednesday nights to be discipled in the truth. There was no greater joy for the Gendrons than to see those who were dead in sin come alive in Christ and watch them grow in the grace and knowledge of our Lord.
> Upon graduation, Mike helped pastor a church and continued his own personal outreach and ministry to Roman Catholics. As the growing demands of this personal ministry increased, it became clear that such a ministry was greatly needed and would require all of his time. Mike and his wife Jane then officially began" Proclaiming the Gospel" Ministry and have been serving through it full time ever since.[121]

Mike Gendron wrote the following article on his website titled "Are Catholics Deceived?"

> Deception will always be exposed by Truth. Have you ever realized that you could be deceived and not even be aware of it? Those who are deceived will never know it unless they are confronted with the truth. Many go to their grave deceived about the most important issue we all face, and that is, locating the narrow road that leads to eternal life. Who are you trusting to show you the way and the truth to eternal life? What is your source for truth? Is it absolutely trustworthy? Will it protect you from the schemes and lies of the master deceiver? The prophet Jeremiah gave us wise counsel for choosing whom we should trust. He said if you trust in man you will be cursed liked a bush in the parched places of the desert. But if you trust in God you will be

blessed. You will be like a tree planted by water always bearing fruit, whose leaves are always green. No worries or fears will come upon you in a year of drought or when the heat comes (Jeremiah 17:5-8).

Who will you trust? Many people disregard Jeremiah's advice and put their trust in religious leaders. Catholics believe that the Pope and the Roman Catholic Church accurately teach what Jesus and His Word reveal. This can be a fatal mistake. Those who disregard the objective truth of the Bible and rely only on the subjective teachings of men leave themselves open to deception. We know God would never deceive anyone because He wants all people to be saved and come to a knowledge of the truth (I Timothy 2:4). He gave us His Word so we could know, understand and believe the truth (John 17:17).

Would the Pope have a person believe what is not true? Maybe not intentionally, but what if he was deceived by previous popes who were also deceived? How do we know if any of the pope's teachings or dogmas of the Roman Catholic Church are true? The only way we can be 100% sure is to do as the Bereans did --- check everything with the Scriptures (Acts 17:11). If the Apostle Paul's teaching had to be verified for its truthfulness, it stands to reason we must use the same standard for any religious leader. Unfortunately the elevation of tradition along with infallible teachings of popes to the same authority as Sacred Scripture has allowed deception to go unabated in the Roman Catholic Church. Popes and their teachings constantly change, whereas Jesus and His Word are constant and never change.

The Apostle Paul revealed the source of all deception, "The Spirit clearly says that in later times some will abandon the faith and follow deceiving spirits and things taught by demons" (1 Tim. 4:1). You may be familiar with some common deceptions taught by religious leaders today: heaven is a reward for those who live good lives...water baptism is necessary for salvation...purgatory purges and removes sin...the sacrifice of the Mass can turn away God's wrath on sinners...God's grace can be earned and purchased. Satan has used lies like these to become the greatest "soul winner" in human history. For two thousand years, the master deceiver has perverted the Gospel of salvation by grace. His ferocious wolves, disguised in sheep's clothing, preach counterfeit gospels that seduce people who are ignorant of God's word (Matt. 7:15). A counterfeit Christianity is Satan's ultimate weapon, so he can, one day be worshipped as Christ. His worldwide religious system is taking shape and unfortunately it includes many people in our churches today.[122]

Later in the same article Mike Gendron provides two tables as follows:
Jesus and His Word teach...
- You are saved by faith and not by works (Ephesians 2:8-9).

- All who rely on observing the law (commandments) are under a curse (Galatians 3:10).
- Salvation occurs at the moment you believe the Gospel (Ephesians 1:13).
- Jesus purifies sin (Hebrews 1:3).
- You can know for sure you are saved (1 John 5:13).
- The sacrifice of Jesus is finished (John 19:30).

The Pope and his church teach...
- You are saved by faith plus works.
- Obedience to the commandments is a condition for salvation.
- Salvation is a process from baptism through purgatory.
- Purgatory purifies sin.
- You are condemned if you claim to be saved.
- The sacrifice of Jesus continues in daily Mass.
- As you can see these two teachings directly oppose one another. You must make the choice as to which is true and which is deception. Your choice will determine your eternal destiny.[123]

Certainly, this shows the stark contrast of opposites. If one is true the other has to be false. If the teachings of the bible are true then the teachings of the Catholic Church are false. Before expanding on those specific false teachings, let's address the change in Roman Church traditions and compare that with what the bible has already stated regarding an unchanging God and unchanging scripture.

Again, Mike Gendron states in an article titled, "Catholic Traditions:"

"You nullify the Word of God by your traditions that you have handed down" (Mark 7:13)

Over the years many traditions have crept into the Roman Catholic Church, nullifying the Word of God and His saving grace. The following list shows a steady departure over the years from the pure Gospel of salvation. Each tradition goes directly against the truth of Scripture. Roman Catholics are required to believe all the doctrines of their church.[124]

Year	Tradition
431	Proclamation that infant baptism regenerates the soul.
500	The Mass instituted as re-sacrifice of Jesus for the remission of sin
593	Declaration that sin needs to be purged, established by Pope Gregory I
600	Prayers directed to Mary, dead saints, and angels.
786	Worship of cross, images, and relics authorized.
995	Canonization of dead people as saints initiated by Pope John XV.
1000	Attendance at Mass made mandatory under the penalty of mor-

	tal sin.
1079	Celibacy of priesthood, decreed by Pope Gregory VII.
1090	Rosary, repetitious praying with beads, invented by Peter the Hermit.
1184	The Inquisitions, instituted by the Council of Verona.
1190	The sale of Indulgences established to reduce time in Purgatory.
1215	Transubstantiation, proclaimed by Pope Innocent III.
1215	Confession of sin to priests, instituted by Pope Innocent III.
1229	Bible placed on Index of Forbidden Books in Toulouse.
1438	Purgatory elevated from doctrine to dogma by Council of Florence.
1545	Tradition claimed equal in authority with the Bible by the Council of Trent.
1546	Apocryphal Books declared canon by Council of Trent.
1854	Immaculate Conception of Mary, proclaimed by Pope Pius IX.
1870	Infallibility of the Pope, proclaimed by Vatican Council.
1922	Virgin Mary proclaimed co-redeemer with Jesus by Pope Benedict XV.
1950	Assumption of Virgin Mary into heaven, proclaimed by Pope Pius XII.

[125]

In addition to the evolution of these Catholic doctrines that are contrary to biblical teaching, Mike Gendron points out the individual proclamations are contrary to biblical teachings.

Individual false doctrines of the Catholic Church

Mike Gendron states the following in an article titled, "Hard Questions to Ask Good Catholics."

> Did you know those who distort the Gospel are condemned? This includes apostles, priests, popes, pastors or angels (apparitions of Mary) from heaven. The apostle Paul warned: "there are some who...want to distort the gospel of Christ. But even though we, or an angel from heaven, should preach to you a gospel contrary to that which we have preached to you, let him be accursed" (Gal. 1:7-8). Catholics need to be warned that their clergy is under divine condemnation for adding works and sacraments to God's Gospel (CCC, 1129).[126]

Priesthood

The following is from the same article titled "Hard Questions to Ask Good Catholics":

> Did you know that Jesus put an end to the ordained priesthood? God's Word reveals that the veil of the temple that separated the Holy of Holies from sinful man was torn open by God.
>
> Matthew 27:51 states:
>> Then, behold, the veil of the temple was torn in two from top to bottom; and the earth quaked, and the rocks were split, . .
>
> Man can now come directly to God through faith in the shed blood of the Savior.
>
> Romans 3:23- 26 States:
>> for all have sinned and fall short of the glory of God, being justified freely by His grace through the redemption that is in Christ Jesus, whom God set forth as a propitiation by His blood, through faith, to demonstrate His righteousness, because in His forbearance God had passed over the sins that were previously committed, to demonstrate at the present time His righteousness, that He might be just and the justifier of the one who has faith in Jesus.
>
> Priests are no longer needed to offer sacrifices for sin.
>
> Hebrews 10:18 states:
>> Now where there is remission of these, there is no longer an offering for sin.
>
> The only legitimate priesthood which remains on earth is the royal priesthood of all believers. They offer sacrifices of praise and thanksgiving for being called out of darkness into the marvelous light of the Son.
>
> 1 Pet. 2:9 states:
>> But you are a chosen generation, a royal priesthood, a holy nation, His own special people, that you may proclaim the praises of Him who called you out of darkness into His marvelous light; . . [127]

The Eucharist

Mike continues on the Eucharist:

> Do you really believe Catholic priests have the power to call the Lord Jesus down from heaven every day? According to Roman Catholic priest John O'Brien in his book Faith of Millions, "The priest...reaches up into the heavens, brings Christ down from His throne, and places Him upon our altar to be offered up again as the Victim for the sins of man...Christ, the eternal and omnipotent God, bows his head in humble obedience to the priest's command."
>
> Over 200,000 times each day, priests throughout the world believe they re-present Jesus on their altars as an offering for sins of the living and the dead (CCC, 1371-1374). Again Catholics ignore God's Word

which declares that Jesus "having been offered once to bear the sins of many, shall appear a second time for salvation not to bear sin" (Hebrews 9:28). The Bible also tells us how and when Jesus will appear. He will return the same way he left, immediately after the tribulation with power and great glory. Matthew 24:27-30 states:
> "Immediately after the tribulation of those days the sun will be darkened, and the moon will not give its light; the stars will fall from heaven, and the powers of the heavens will be shaken. Then the sign of the Son of Man will appear in heaven, and then all the tribes of the earth will mourn, and they will see the Son of Man coming on the clouds of heaven with power and great glory.

Acts 1:11 states:
> who also said, "Men of Galilee, why do you stand gazing up into heaven? This same Jesus, who was taken up from you into heaven, will so come in like manner as you saw Him go into heaven."

By the authority of God's Word we must conclude that the Eucharist is a false Christ that is deceiving millions.

Why do Catholic priests continue to offer Jesus as a sacrificial victim when He said "It is finished?" John 19:30 states:
> So when Jesus had received the sour wine, He said, "It is finished!" And bowing His head, He gave up His spirit.

God's Word says: Jesus appeared once and offered Himself once to bear sins. His offer- ing is not to be done again. Hebrews 9:25-28 states:
> not that He should offer Himself often, as the high priest enters the Most Holy Place every year with blood of another— He then would have had to suffer often since the foundation of the world; but now, once at the end of the ages, He has appeared to put away sin by the sacrifice of Himself. And as it is appointed for men to die once, but after this the judgment, so Christ was offered once to bear the sins of many. To those who eagerly wait for Him He will appear a second time, apart from sin, for salvation.

When Jesus "offered one sacrifice for sins for all time, [He] sat down at the right hand of God" (Heb. 10:12). Disregarding the infallible Word of God, Catholicism teaches: "the sacrifice of Christ and the sacrifice of the Eucharist are one single sacrifice. The vic- tim is one and the same. In this divine sacrifice, the same Christ who offered himself once…is contained and offered in an unbloody manner" (CCC, 1367).

Did you know Jesus has already obtained redemption for believers? Catholicism denies this by teaching: "The work of our redemption is carried on" every time the Eucharist is celebrated (CCC, 1405). God's Word declares: "He [Jesus] entered the holy place once for all, having obtained eternal redemption" (Heb. 9:12). "In Him we have redemption through His blood, the forgiveness of our trespasses, according to the riches of His grace" (Eph. 1:7).[128]

Transubstantiation

In an article titled, "John 6 and Transubstantiation" Mike Gendron stated the following:

> The Lord Jesus said, "Unless you eat the flesh of the Son of Man and drink His blood you have no life in you." Was Jesus speaking literally or figuratively? The Roman Catholic Church teaches His Words are literal. Their literal interpretation is the foundation for its doctrine of transubstantiation -- the "miraculous" changing of bread and wine into the living Christ, His body and blood, soul and divinity. Each Catholic priest is said to have the power to call Jesus down from heaven when he whispers over the wafer, "Hoc corpus meus est." Catholics believe they are actually eating and drinking the living body and blood of Jesus Christ when they consume the lifeless wafer. This is a vital and important requirement in their salvation and a doctrine they must believe and accept to remain a Catholic.
>
> If priests indeed have the power to change bread and wine into the body and blood of the glorified Christ, and if indeed consuming His body and blood is necessary for salvation, then the whole world must become Catholic to escape the wrath of God. On the other hand, if Jesus was speaking in figurative language then the Eucharist becomes the most blasphemous and deceptive hoax any religion could impose on its people. There is no middle ground.
>
> Catholics need to know that Jesus used figurative language when He spoke to the Jewish multitude in this sixth chapter of John. There are at least seven convincing reasons why this passage must be taken figuratively.
>
> Drinking Blood Forbidden:
> The Law of Moses strictly forbade Jews from drinking blood (Leviticus 17:10-14) A literal interpretation to drink blood would mean Jesus was teaching the Jews to disobey the Mosaic Law. This would have been enough cause for them to persecute Jesus. (See John 5:16)
> Biblical Disharmony:
> If John 6:53 is interpreted literally, it is in disharmony with the rest of the Bible. Eating the flesh and drinking the blood of Christ for eternal life adds another requirement to the Gospel of grace. Furthermore, it gives no hope of eternal life to any Christian who does not consume the body and blood of Christ. A literal translation of this verse would oppose hundreds of Scriptures that declare justification and salvation are by grace through faith alone in Christ.
> Unexplainable Dilemma:

Since the "eating and drinking" in verse 6:54 and the "believing" in verse 6:40 produce the same result - eternal life we have an unexplainable dilemma if both are taken literally. What if a person "believes" but does not "eat or drink"? Or what if a person "eats and drinks" but does not "believe?" This could happen any time a nonbeliever walked into a Catholic Church and received the Eucharist. Does this person have eternal life because he met one of the requirements but not the other? The only possible way to harmonize these two verses is to accept one verse as figurative and one as literal.

Eating and Drinking Can Be Figurative:

The Jews were familiar with the use of the figurative language of "eating and drinking" in the Old Testament to describe the appropriation of divine blessings to one's innermost being. It was God's way of providing spiritual nourishment for the soul. (See Jeremiah 15:16 and Ezekiel 2:8, 3:1)

Jesus Confirmed His Use of Figurative Language:

Jesus informed His disciples there were times when He spoke figuratively to impart spiritual truths. John 16:25 states:

> "These things I have spoken to you in figurative language; but the time is coming when I will no longer speak to you in figurative language, but I will tell you plainly about the Father.

He often used that type of language to describe Himself. The Gospel of John records seven figurative declarations Jesus made of Himself -- "the bread of life" (6:48), "the light of the world" (8:12), "the door" (10:9), "the good shepherd" (10:11), "the resurrection and the life" (11:25), "the way, the truth and the life" (14:6), and "the true vine" (15:1). He also referred to His body as the temple (2:19). When speaking to a mixed crowd of believers and unbelievers, Jesus used parables (figurative language) so that unbelievers could not understand the mysteries of heaven which were not granted to them (Mat. 13:10-17). The reason the multitude were seeking after Jesus was because they wanted more physical food. John 6:26 stated:

> Jesus answered them and said, "Most assuredly, I say to you, you seek Me, not because you saw the signs, but because you ate of the loaves and were filled.

Jesus was offering them spiritual food. John 6:32-33 states:

> Then Jesus said to them, "Most assuredly, I say to you, Moses did not give you the bread from heaven, but My Father gives you the true bread from heaven. For the bread of God is He who comes down from heaven and gives life to the world."

As believers partake of Jesus, He will abide in them (John 6:53). They will never hunger or thirst. Clearly this is in a figurative sense (John 6:35). As the good shepherd, He feeds His people knowledge and understanding of Himself (Jer. 3:15).

His Words Were Spiritual:

Jesus ended this teaching by revealing "the words I have spoken to you are spirit." John 6:63 states:

> It is the Spirit who gives life; the flesh profits nothing. The words that I speak to you are spirit, and they are life.

As with each of the seven miracles in John's Gospel, Jesus uses the miracle to convey a spiritual truth. Here Jesus has just multiplied the loaves and fish and uses a human analogy to teach the necessity of spiritual nourishment. This is consistent with His teaching on how we are to worship God. "God is Spirit and His worshippers must worship in spirit and in truth" (John 4:24). As we worship Christ He is present spiritually, not physically. In fact, Jesus can only be bodily present at one place at one time. His omnipresence refers only to His spirit. It is impossible for Christ to be bodily present in thousands of Catholic Churches around the world.

A Counterfeit Miracle:

There is no Biblical precedent where something supernatural occurred where the outward evidence indicated no miracle had taken place. (The wafer and wine look, taste and feel the same before and after the supposed miracle of transubstantiation). When Jesus changed water into wine, all the elements of water changed into the actual elements of wine.

Transubstantiation Conclusion

The 6th chapter of John took place three years before the Last Supper. If the Words of Christ were taken literally, why didn't people start gnawing on His flesh after this teaching? The ones who departed from Jesus were unbelievers (6:36) who had followed him to Capernaum for another free lunch (6:26). When Jesus offered Himself as "spiritual" food they were not interested (6:63). Those who ate of the spiritual food for eternal life were believers (6:40) and remained with Jesus. He had the words [not the flesh] of eternal life (6:68). Catholics need to know that when Jesus is received spiritually, one time in the heart, there is no need to receive him physically, over and over again in the stomach. Anyone who believes they are literally eating Jesus is absurd and cannibalistic.

At the Last Supper Jesus asked believers to remember Him until He comes again. Why do Catholics remember Him if they believe He has to come again in the Eucharist. "For I [Paul] received from the Lord that which I also delivered to you, that the Lord Jesus in the night in which He was betrayed took bread; and when He had given thanks, He broke it, and said, "This is My body, which is for you; do this in remembrance of Me." In the same way He took the cup also, after supper, saying, "This cup is the new covenant in My blood; do this, as often as you drink it, in remembrance of Me." For as often as you eat this bread and drink the cup, you proclaim the Lord's death until He comes" (1 Cor. 11:23-26). If transubstantiation were true and Jesus is indeed physically present, why would He ask us to remember Him. Furthermore, God does not dwell in Catholic tabernacles made with human hands (Acts 7:48).

The only way to receive Jesus is spiritually by faith. John 1:12-13 states:

> But as many as received Him, to them He gave the right to become children of God, to those who believe in His name: ^{13} who were born, not of blood, nor of the will of the flesh, nor of the will of man, but of God. [129]

Purgatory

Mike Gendron states the following in the "Hard Questions to Ask Good Catholics article:"

> Why do you call Jesus the Savior when you must save yourself? Catholicism teaches the sinner must "make satisfaction for" or "expiate" his sins. This satisfaction is also called "penance." (1459) "In this way they attained their own salvation and cooperated in saving their brothers" (1477). God's Word proclaims "There is salvation in no one else; for there is no other name under heaven given among men, by which we must be saved" (Acts 4:12).
>
> Why do you believe a place called Purgatory can purify your sins? God's Word says "when He [Jesus] had made purification of sins, He sat down at the right hand of the Majesty on high" (Hebrews 1:3). "He gave Himself for us to... purify for Himself a people for His own possession" (Titus 2:14). "The blood of Jesus...cleanses us from all sin" (1 John 1:7). These verses destroy the myth of Purgatory. Yet the Vatican continues to deceive Catholics by teaching they "must undergo purification [in Purgatory] to achieve the holiness necessary to enter the joy of heaven" (CCC, 1030). [130]

Mike Gendron documents the following in an article titled "Purgatory: Purifying Fire or Fatal Fable:"

> Catholics who believe a purifying fire will purge away their sins are deluded victims of a fatal fabrication. The invention of a place for purification of sins called Purgatory is one of the most seductive attractions of the Roman Catholic religion. Pastor John MacArthur of Grace Community Church described this deceptive hoax brilliantly. He said: "Purgatory is what makes the whole system work. Take out Purgatory and it's a hard sell to be a Catholic. Purgatory is the safety net, when you die, you don't go to hell. You go [to Purgatory] and get things sorted out and finally get to heaven if you've been a good Catholic. In the Catholic system you can never know you're going to heaven. You just

keep trying and trying...in a long journey toward perfection. Well, it's pretty discouraging. People in that system are guilt-ridden, fear-ridden and have no knowledge of whether or not they're going to get into the Kingdom. If there's no Purgatory, there's no safety net to catch me and give me some opportunity to get into heaven. It's a second chance, it's another chance after death" (from "The Pope and the Papacy").

The Origin of Purgatory:

There was no mention of Purgatory during the first two centuries of the church. However, when Roman Emperor Theodosius (379-395) decreed that Christianity was to be the official religion of the empire, thousands of pagans flooded into the Church and brought their pagan beliefs and traditions with them. One of those ancient pagan beliefs was a place of purification where souls went to make satisfaction for their sins.

The concept became much more widespread around 600 A.D. due to the fanaticism of Pope Gregory the Great. He developed the doctrine through visions and revelations of a Purgatorial fire. According to the Catholic Encyclopedia (CE), Pope Gregory said Catholics "will expiate their faults by purgatorial flames," and "the pain [is] more intolerable than anyone can suffer in this life." Centuries later, at the Council of Florence (1431), it was pronounced an infallible dogma. It was later reaffirmed by the Council of Trent (1564). The dogma is based largely on Catholic tradition from extra- biblical writings and oral history. "So deep was this belief ingrained in our common humanity that it was accepted by the Jews, and in at least a shadowy way by the pagans, long before the coming of Christianity" (CE). It seems incomprehensible that Rome would admit to using a pagan tradition for the defence of one of its most esteemed "Christian" doctrines.

The Deception of Purgatory:

Purgatory comes from the Latin word "purgare," which means to make clean or to purify. The Catholic Encyclopedia defines purgatory as "a place or condition of temporal punishment for those who, departing this life in God's grace, are not entirely free from venial faults, or have not fully paid the satisfaction due to their transgressions." They must be purified of these "venial" sins before they can be allowed into heaven. Here we see Catholicism perpetuating the seductive lie of Satan by declaring "you will not surely die" when you commit venial sins (Gen. 3:4). The Council of Trent dares to declare that "God does not always remit the whole punishment due to sin together with the guilt. God requires satisfaction and will punish sin...The sinner, failing to do penance in this life, may be punished in another world, and so not be cast off eternally from God." (Session 15, Can. XI). Those Catholic Bishops had the audacity to declare that the suffering and death of God's perfect man and man's perfect substitute was not sufficient to satisfy divine justice for sin.[131]

Indulgences

Mike Gendron states the following in an article titled "Purgatory: Purifying Fire or Fatal Fable."

> Over the centuries billions of dollars have been paid to Roman Catholic priests to obtain relief from imaginary sufferings in Purgatory's fire. The Catholic clergy has always taught that the period of suffering in Purgatory can be shortened by purchasing indulgences and novenas, buying Mass cards and providing gifts of money. When a Catholic dies, money is extracted from mourning loved ones to shorten the deceased's punishment in Purgatory. When my dear old dad passed away as a devout Catholic of 79 years, I was amazed at the hundreds of Mass cards purchased for him by well-meaning friends. We have heard of other Catholics who have willed their entire estates to their religion so that perpetual masses could be offered for them after they die. It is no wonder that the Catholic religion has become the richest institution in the world. The buying and selling of God's grace has been a very lucrative business for the Vatican.
> Another motivation for Rome to fabricate the heretical doctrine of Purgatory is its powerful effect on controlling people. Ultimately, the enslavement and subjugation of people is the goal of every false religion, and Purgatory does exactly that. The concept of a terrifying prison with a purging fire, governed by religious leaders, is a most brilliant invention. It holds people captive, not only in this life but also in the next life. Catholic clergy will not say how many years people have to suffer for their sins or how many Masses must be purchased before they can be released from the flames. This dreadful fear and uncertainty is the most ruthless form of religious bondage and deception![132]

Praying to Mary and the rosary

Mike Gendron states the following on this topic in the same article:
> Nowhere in the Bible do we see believers praying to anyone except God. Jesus taught us how to pray in the Sermon on the Mount. He instructed us to pray to the Father and not to use meaningless repetition. Mat. 6:7-13 states:
>> And when you pray, do not use vain repetitions as the heathen do. For they think that they will be heard for their many words.

> "Therefore do not be like them. For your Father knows the things you have need of before you ask Him. In this manner, therefore, pray:
> Our Father in heaven, Hallowed be Your name. Your kingdom come. Your will be done On earth as it is in heaven. Give us this day our daily bread. And forgive us our debts, As we forgive our debtors. And do not lead us into temptation, But deliver us from the evil one. For Yours is the kingdom and the power and the glory forever. Amen.

Yet Catholics are taught to pray the rosary which is made up of over 50 meaning- less and repetitious prayers to Mary.[133]

Salvation / Justification

The bible has many verses that explain that salvation is through faith in Jesus and God's plan of redemption. That plan includes God's Son becoming a mere human, living a sinless life, becoming a sacrifice for us while taking upon Himself all of our sins and being resurrected from the dead. All we need to do is recognize that we are sinners, repent of our sins and accept Jesus Christ's atonement for our sin. Works do nothing toward our salvation, but are evidence of our salvation. The following verses address this issue:

Ephesians 2:8-9 states:
> For by grace you have been saved through faith, and that not of yourselves; it is the gift of God, not of works, lest anyone should boast.

Galatians 2:16 states:
> knowing that a man is not justified by the works of the law but by faith in Jesus Christ, even we have believed in Christ Jesus, that we might be justified by faith in Christ and not by the works of the law; for by the works of the law no flesh shall be justified.

Romans 11:6 states:
> And if by grace, then it is no longer of works; otherwise grace is no longer grace. But if it is of works, it is no longer grace; otherwise work is no longer work.

Romans 3:27-28 states:
> Where is boasting then? It is excluded. By what law? Of works? No, but by the law of faith. Therefore we conclude that a man is justified by faith apart from the deeds of the law.

Matthew 23:5 applies to the Pharisees and us if we are Pharisaic:
> But all their works they do to be seen by men. They make their phylacteries broad and enlarge the borders of their garments.

Matthew 6:1-4 explains that the only works or giving that we will be given credit for in heaven are those that are done in secret:

"Take heed that you do not do your charitable deeds before men, to be seen by them. Otherwise you have no reward from your Father in heaven. Therefore, when you do a charitable deed, do not sound a trumpet before you as the hypocrites do in the synagogues and in the streets, that they may have glory from men. Assuredly, I say to you, they have their reward. But when you do a charitable deed, do not let your left hand know what your right hand is doing, that your charitable deed may be in secret; and your Father who sees in secret will Himself reward you openly.

In an article titled, "Justification" Mike Gendron writes the following table:[134]

Catholicism Teaches	Scripture Teaches
Justification is God's act of making man righteous by good works and obedience	Justification is God's act of declaring a sinner righteous by faith
Infused sanctifying grace through the sacraments makes the believer acceptable to God	Christ's imputed righteousness makes the believer acceptable to God
Justification is achieved by faith plus good works	Justification is received by faith alone
Justification is granted the sinner when he is actually made just	Justification enables God to see the sinner as if he were just
Justification can be increased by receiving more sacraments	Justification cannot increase since the ground is the perfect righteousness of Christ
Justification is affected by sin	Justification is a permanent verdict and is not affected by sin
Final justification is not determined until death	Justification comes at the moment of faith in Jesus Christ
The ground of justification is the righteousness of the person	The ground of justification is the righteousness of Jesus Christ
Sanctification and justification are similar	Justification precedes sanctification
Emphasis is on the sacraments	Emphasis is on God's verdict

Tradition vs Scripture

In an article titled, "Sola Scriptura" Mike Gendron writes the following:
The Bible gives overwhelming evidence as to why Scripture must always be our sole authority for faith. The Word of God is pure, perfect, inerrant, infallible, living, truth, light, holy, eternal, and forever settled

in heaven. It illuminates, cleanses, saves, frees, guides, converts, heals, quickens, judges, and sanctifies. It also brings conviction, gives knowledge, gives wisdom, produces faith, refutes error, searches the heart, equips for every good work, and is used as a weapon. The Word of God is exalted even above the very name of God. Have you read Psalm 138:2?

Compare this with tradition ... Jesus told the religious leaders of his day that their tradition was nullifying the very word of God. Yet the religious leaders of today continue to do the same and deceive their followers. Because of this we must take the exhortation of Peter seriously ... that is we ought to obey God rather than men.

For Christians, the Scriptures provide the only objective basis for authority while the indwelling Holy Spirit provides illumination, conviction and discernment. This dual authority, the Spirit of God working with the Word of God, is sufficient in all matters of faith and Christian living. Catholics, on the other hand, submit to a dual authority of tradition and Scripture, under the subjective interpretation of their church. The pope, speaking for the church, is said to be infallible in matters pertaining to faith and morals. You ask, "Where does it say that Scripture alone should be the authority for faith?" Is "Sola Scriptura," the battle cry of the Reformers, found in the Bible? There are at least nine biblical justifications for the authority of Scripture alone. [Indenting and numbering mine]

1. All Scripture is given by the inspiration of God and useful for reproof and correction of error (2 Timothy 3:16). Since Scripture is used to correct and reproof then it must be the authoritative standard by which everything else is judged for its truthfulness.
2. Jesus said, "Scripture cannot be broken" (John 10:34). The character of God is on the line. "God is not a man that He should lie ... and hath He spoken, and shall He not make it good (Numbers 23:19). Submitting to the authority of God's revealed word will guide us in His perfect will.
3. Christ used the authority of Scripture to rebuke Satan's attempt to deceive Him (Matthew 4:1-11). He gave prepositional statements to accurately convey the truth that Satan attempted to distort. Jesus was our perfect model for rebuking deception.
4. Jesus used the authority of Scriptures to rebuke false teachers (Matthew 22:29). The only way false teachers can be confronted and exposed is in the power of God's Word.
5. Repented sinners are saved by hearing and believing the Word (Ephesians 1:13-14). The integrity of the Gospel must be maintained and proclaimed for true conversions.

6. Jesus prayed for Christians to be sanctified (set apart) by the truth of His Word (John 17:17). Christians must separate themselves from apostate churches and false teachers. God uses division to show those in His approval (1 Cor. 11:19).
7. One must continually submit to the authority of Scripture to be a disciple of Christ (John 8:31). Those who follow the traditions and teachings of men are often led astray.
8. Christ rebuked the religious leaders for nullifying the Word of God with their tradition (Mark 7:13). Any tradition that nullifies the Scriptures must be exposed and renounced so others will not be deceived.
9. The Scriptures were written to all Christians, not to popes and Magisterium to be interpreted for lay people. Anytime we allow others to interpret God's word for us, we leave ourselves open to deception.

God foreknew the teachings and traditions of men would become corrupt and would lead many astray. In His wisdom, He left us with His Word, the only objective, absolute authority for truth, to lead us back to Him. It is pure, powerful, perfect, inerrant, infallible, living, holy, eternal, and forever settled in heaven. It illuminates, cleanses, frees, guides, converts, quickens, judges, sanctifies, brings conviction, gives wisdom, produces faith, and refutes error. Can you describe tradition in the same way God describes His word? Why would you want to add anything subjective to the objective standard God has given us?[135]

PROTESTANT CHURCH APOSTASIES

Unlike the Roman Catholic Church, the protestant denominations have a plethora of different beliefs. Although worldwide Catholic beliefs are more unified than those of protestant beliefs, the Roman Catholic Church has changed or evolved their beliefs over time as a result of papal edicts or Catholic council. However, fewer of these changes came from compromising with our humanistic, secular culture than protestant's, at least before Pope Francis came along. The change in the Catholic Church has been primarily driven for centuries by a desire to make the organization stronger, more powerful and richer. Much more recently, for about the last 50 years, many of the protestant churches, especially the mega churches, have succumbed to the same "it's all about the organization" marketing philosophy. This has relegated what should be the true mission of the church to a secondary status and suppressed the eternal value of the church to their parishioners and their communities. Today, many protestant churches have also changed by liberalizing their doctrine and by trying to avoid conflict with the culture. The liberalizing of their doctrine that has corrupted the traditional Christian beliefs held since the reformation has come about by skeptics that have discredited the truth of the bible. The compromising with the secular culture has been driven by a desire not to conflict with current scientific (perhaps pseudoscientific) and cultural beliefs. The other factor that has compromised their biblical beliefs is an ecumenical move toward unity with other denominations and even non-Christian religions. I believe this movement is directed toward a one-world religion. These three causes are probably responsible for all of the many unbiblical beliefs and new church movements in Christendom today. We will identify some of these apostasies (falling away) and heretical teachings (unbiblical beliefs). The causes of many of these apostasies and heretical teachings are not from a single cause and the influences of different factors overlap. Consequently, the classifications get blurred and the paragraph headings will not be as clean as desired or perhaps as expected by the reader.

Doctrinal apostasies

Unitarian

The Unitarian belief is a pluralistic, postmodern belief that absolute truth does not really exist. They believe one cannot take the bible seriously or literally. Consequently, they believe that all religions are basically the same and that all roads lead to God. Therefore evangelical or fundamentalist Christians are seen as narrow minded and judgmental. They reject the many, many places in scripture that state that all roads do not lead to God and heaven, but in fact, the bible teaches that there is only one way and the road to get there is very narrow. Author's comment – if we can interpret the bible any way we choose, why even be in the biblical or church business?

Liberal churches

Liberal church doctrines are basically watered down biblical doctrines. Specific doctrines that are the heart of the gospel have been rejected by liberal churches. Some of these include: Creation, the virgin birth, the trinity, the resurrection, the rapture, the millennial reign and the second coming. Authors comments – Again, if we can interpret the bible any way we chose, why even be in the biblical or church business.

Additional subversions from within

Another way to subvert Christianity is from within. Acts 20:29 states:
> For I know this, that after my departure savage wolves will come in among you, not sparing the flock.

2 Timothy 4:3-4 states:
> For the time will come when they will not endure sound doctrine, but according to their own desires, because they have itching ears, they will heap up for themselves teachers; and they will turn their ears away from the truth, and be turned aside to fables.

We know that Satan is at war with God and God's special creation, man. The Bible teaches that Satan's tactics are based upon what he is and what he represents. The following are three of his attributes that he uses to keep us from following God and His truths.

John 8:44 states:
> You are of your father the devil, and the desires of your father you want to do. He was a murderer from the beginning, and does not stand in the truth, because there is no truth in him. When he speaks a lie, he speaks from his own resources, for he is a liar and the father of it.

2 Corinthians 11:14 states:
> And no wonder! For Satan himself transforms himself into an angel of light.

Revelation 12:9 states:
> So the great dragon was cast out, that serpent of old, called the Devil and Satan, who deceives the whole world; he was cast to the earth, and his angels were cast out with him.

With these attributes and being at war with God and people that God created, we should expect that people would be deceived in many ways through lying and deceit. That is exactly what we see within our churches.

Since Constantine made the Christian Church the state church, denominational Christian churches have fallen into apostasy and have persecuted the true Biblical believers on many occasions. Consequently, we should not be surprised to see the church fall into apostasy in various ways.

What are some of the deceptions within the Christian Church? Jan Markell of Olive Tree Ministries covered some of these in her September-October 2009 Understanding the Times newsletter. She referred to:
> The Mystical Movement that includes Christian Yoga, contemplative prayer and walking the labyrinth.

This is basically New Age entering the church. The New Age religion will be covered separately in the next chapter as a false religion separate from Christianity.

The Emergent Church

Another heresy within the church is The Emergent Church. There are no absolutes in this belief. This movement tries to attract folks under 35. They rely on the senses, even smell, by using incense and candles.

The Mega Church or Seeker-Sensitive Movement

Another watered down movement is the Seeker-Sensitive Growth Movement. This movement avoids speaking of sin, hell or repentance that may chase people away. Leaders in this movement include Joel Osteen, Rick Warren and Bill Hybels. The church is treated like a business where what is being marketed is based upon what will stimulate church growth.

The Green Movement

Another movement that replaces the gospel is the Green Movement and concern for the environment. They are more concerned with saving the planet than saving souls. The current concern is global warming even though the planet has been cooling for more than fifteen years. This movement is connected with New Age and Gaia. Wikipedia defines it as follows:

> Earth-centered religion or nature worship is a system of religion based on the veneration of natural phenomena. It covers any religion that worships the earth, nature, or fertility gods and goddesses, such as the various forms of goddess worship or matriarchal religion. Also most Indian religions can be included in earth religion. Some find a connection between earth-worship and the Gaia hypothesis. Earth religions are also formulated to allow one to utilize the knowledge of preserving the earth.[136]

Ecumenism

Another movement is the push for ecumenical unity. However, rather than identifying truth and unifying around that, they find some common ground and compromise the remaining doctrines. The goal of the Jesuits is to reverse the Protestant reformation. Pope Francis is the first pope that is a Jesuit.

Kingdom Now or Dominion Theory

The last movement Jan Markel mentioned is the Kingdom Now or Dominion Theology. This teaching replaces the Biblical teaching of our world getting progressively more evil and violent with their teaching of a world where Christians convert the entire world and bring about the Kingdom of God on earth as a result. This movement believes in replacement theology. They believe that the

Jews lost their place in Bible prophecy because they crucified Jesus. They believe that all the future prophecies in Revelation have already taken place in about AD 70 and also that all the promises that were given to the Jews now apply to the church.

Apostasy from denominational leaders

Along with Satan's help, Denominational Christian churches have organizational hierarchies that have invariably corrupted the Biblical doctrines from the top down. This has happened to most protestant denominations. All this perfectly fits into the model that the Bible would predict and consequently confirms the truth of the Bible and strengthens our faith.

Matthew 7:13-15 states:
> Enter by the narrow gate; for wide is the gate and broad is the way that leads to destruction, and there are many who go in by it. Because narrow is the gate and difficult is the way which leads to life, and there are few who find it. Beware of false prophets, who come to you in sheep's clothing, but inwardly they are ravenous wolves.

SALVATION AND NEEDED BATTLE PLAN

The bible teaches that the battle between good and evil is manifest in each one of us and that without being born again and having a transformation of our minds we cannot overcome our carnal flesh since we are slaves to it. Some of the scriptures that support this truth are:

John 3:3-8 documents Jesus explaining to Nicodemus that he must be born again:
> Jesus answered and said to him, "Most assuredly, I say to you, unless one is born again, he cannot see the kingdom of God." Nicodemus said to Him, "How can a man be born when he is old? Can he enter a second time into his mother's womb and be born?" Jesus answered, "Most assuredly, I say to you, unless one is born of water and the Spirit, he cannot enter the kingdom of God. That which is born of the flesh is flesh, and that which is born of the Spirit is spirit. Do not marvel that I said to you, 'You must be born again.' The wind blows where it wishes, and you hear the sound of it, but cannot tell where it comes from and where it goes. So is everyone who is born of the Spirit."

Romans 6:16 explains that we are slaves to sin:
> Do you not know that to whom you present yourselves slaves to obey, you are that one's slaves whom you obey, whether of sin leading to death, or of obedience leading to righteousness?

Romans 12:1-2 explains that if we are born again we must have our minds transformed:

> I beseech you therefore, brethren, by the mercies of God, that you present your bodies a living sacrifice, holy, acceptable to God, which is your reasonable service. And do not be conformed to this world, but be transformed by the renewing of your mind, that you may prove what is that good and acceptable and perfect will of God.

The bible explains that we either serve God or Mammon. The Merriam-Webster Dictionary defines mammon as "material wealth having a debasing influence."

Matthew 6:24 states:

> "No one can serve two masters; for either he will hate the one and love the other, or else he will be loyal to the one and despise the other. You cannot serve God and mammon.

Galatians 5:16-23 states that we either walk in the spirit or walk in the flesh and the effects of each:

> I say then: Walk in the Spirit, and you shall not fulfill the lust of the flesh. For the flesh lusts against the Spirit, and the Spirit against the flesh; and these are contrary to one another, so that you do not do the things that you wish. But if you are led by the Spirit, you are not under the law. Now the works of the flesh are evident, which are: adultery, fornication, uncleanness, lewdness, idolatry, sorcery, hatred, contentions, jealousies, outbursts of wrath, selfish ambitions, dissensions, heresies, envy, murders, drunkenness, revelries, and the like; of which I tell you beforehand, just as I also told you in time past, that those who practice such things will not inherit the kingdom of God. But the fruit of the Spirit is love, joy, peace, longsuffering, kindness, goodness, faithfulness, gentleness, self-control. Against such there is no law.

Consequently, unless we get people to repent and accept God's redemption and become born again spiritually with a transformed mind, we cannot prevent them from being slaves to the flesh and to Satan. Even if we can get people to intellectually understand that God exists and that his plan is for our good individually as well as our society, without regeneration from within, we rationalize it away and stay in rebellion against God and slaves to Satan and our flesh. If all we do is fight against the culture by moralizing and being against homosexuality, abortion and the breakdown in the family there is another reason that we are not successful. To better explain this we want to transform the false foundation metaphor used in Chapter 14 to a tree metaphor. Here the foundations translate into the roots, trunk and main branches and the false beliefs supported by the false foundation translate to the fruit produced by the tree. Matthew 7:17-18 states:

> Even so, every good tree bears good fruit, but a bad tree bears bad fruit. A good tree cannot bear bad fruit, nor can a bad tree bear good fruit.

This adds to the above conclusion that we must be born again and have our minds transformed to bear good fruit. Otherwise we can only produce bad fruit. However, the main reason for quoting this verse is to establish the credibility of the tree metaphor. The additional problem is that moralizers and those exposing the cultural unbiblical position on homosexuality, abortion and the breakdown in the family are only trying to remove some of the bad fruit on the tree. There are two problems with this approach. The tree keeps producing more bad fruit faster that they can remove the bad fruit. The second problem is that all the false foundational "truths" that represent the roots and trunk are not challenged. Consequently, people's belief in those big lies is not shaken and their belief in those big foundational lies justifies the bad fruit since it was produced by what they believe is a good truthful tree. What is needed is to use truth to refute those foundational lies so people will not have them to support their false worldview. Our apostate churches are not doing that today! Many of them have actually brought in these false foundational lies. If those false foundational lies could be destroyed people would not be intellectually fulfilled by that false foundation and consequently, the alternative to choose between biblical truth and rebellion against God would be a very stark choice. People would recognize that they are choosing to rebel against God and consequently, many more would chose God and His redemptive plan.

Next we will cover the accepting of false religions.

CHAPTER 23
Accepting New Age and other false religions

We identified in Chapter 11 that Secular Humanism is in 100% diametric opposition to Christianity because it denies God, creation and everything Christian. However, other religions and religious teachings can also be diametrically opposed to Christianity. Opposition to the truth is not limited by only one dimension. There is no limit to how many false religious beliefs can exist that oppose Biblical Christianity.

Let's identify two other ways to subvert Christianity in addition to secular humanists denying that our monotheistic God exists. One way is to make everything God; then the personal God of the Bible doesn't exist and we can replace Him as God. This is exactly what the "New Age" or the "New Spirituality" does. The second way to deny the truth of biblical Christianity is through belief in false religions and false Gods. This is similar to what secular humanists do when they claim that "man is the measure of all things." They make man a god. However, our emphasis here is about other false religions that hold up and serve a different god which obviously replaces worship of the true God. First let's cover New Age that believes in Pantheism.

NEW AGE

New Age is a doctrinal religion as opposed to a denominational religion with church buildings and a budget. It does not deny the existence of God, but makes everything god including its followers. This religious type is pantheism. The religion was previously referred to as New Age. Now it is normally referred to as spirituality or the "New Spirituality." If they have a church leader or High Priestess it is Oprah Winfrey. Bookstore shelves are lined with books on self-help and spirituality. Its primary beliefs are in complete opposition to Christianity and blaspheme the gospel. The gurus that Oprah had on her shows redefine the following Biblical entities:

Entity	Christian Definition	New Age Definition
God	Personal God and creator	In everything including us
Morality	Man has a Sin nature & wicked heart	No sin, no morality
Death	Physical death and 2nd death for unsaved	Death is an illusion
Heaven	The saved will live with God forever	No heaven

| Conversion | Realization of sin and repentance | Become enlightened through spiritual experience and learn that you are god |

A book promoted by Oprah titled "The Secret" by Rhonda Byrne states:
> You are God in a physical body. You are spirit in the flesh. You are eternal life expressing itself as you. You are a cosmic being. You are all-powerful. You are all wisdom. The earth turns on its orbit for you. The oceans ebb and flow for you. The birds sing for you. The sun rises and sets for you. The stars come out for you. None of it can exist without you. No matter who you thought you were, now you know the truth of who you really are. You are the master of the universe. You are the heir of the kingdom. . And know you know the secret.[137]

Marianne Williamson the author of "A Return to Love" also promoted by Oprah teaches the following from a book by the late Helen Schucman titled "A Course in Miracles."
> My mind is part of God. I am very holy. There is nothing that my holiness cannot do. I am the light of the world. Salvation comes from my one self. Salvation of the world depends on me. I am the holy Son of God himself.[138]

All this is based upon the belief that we can be like God or even be God Himself. That is the same lie that the serpent told Eve in the Garden of Eden. Genesis 3:5 states:
> For God knows that in the day you eat of it your eyes will be opened,
> and you will be like God, knowing good and evil."

The New Age religion or what is better known now as spirituality is finding many followers both within Christianity and outside Christianity. This religion besides making believers out to be god, also is all about seeking a spiritual experience rather than belief in a doctrine from a theistic book like the Bible. I have trouble believing that people actually believe this stuff, but apparently our desire to be like God combined with our desire to avoid following God's moral law give Satan another way to deceive us and prevent us from following the truth and the God that created us.

The New Age religion has been subtly introduced into the Christian denominational churches for over fifty years. A recently published book titled "A Wonderful Deception," by Warren Smith lays out the history of Christian leaders that have been and are introducing the New Age spirituality into Christian churches. After reading Smith's book, I can see how some of the New Age teachings have been introduced into a church I attended. Smith states in the introduction of his book:

> I had already completed several chapters that describe how New Age sympathizers Norman Vincent Peale and Robert Schuller inspired and helped to create the Church Growth movement—a movement that subtly and not so subtly evolved from Peale's "Positive thinking" to Schuller's "Possibility thinking" to Rick Warren's "Purpose Driven" thinking.[139]

Smith in the introductory quote for the third chapter stated the following regarding the Occult source of Peale's New Age theology.

> Whatever may be the embarrassment caused by these striking similarities [between Norman Vincent Peale and New Age author Florence Scovel Shinn], it pales against the discomfiture that millions of mainline Christians, purporting to stand on orthodoxy and Scripture alone, have thus unwittingly embraced the Occult. So strong is its tacit foothold that it now may well be the primary faith of many in the churches.[140]

The subtlety of the New Age infiltration into Christian churches is based upon introducing only the parts of New Age that could be construed as Christian nice. Heretical concepts like sin don't exist or we are gods are avoided. Another way to introduce watered down or false teachings is by making sure not to offend parishioners by making the message "seeker sensitive." Rather than emphasizing negative things like sin emphasize positive things like self-esteem. The thought that God is in everything is subtly inserted into writings. Also, either Contemplative or Centering Prayer are introduced as methods of prayer. Smith includes a quote from Donald Walsch in Chapter 2.

> Rev. Robert Schuller, the American Christian minister who founded the famous Crystal Cathedral in Garden Grove, California, said twenty years ago in his book *Self-Esteem: The New Reformation* that what is needed is a second reformation within the church, to move it away from its message of fear and guilt, retribution, and damnation, and toward a theology of self-esteem.[141]

In Chapter 3 Smith quotes Schuller's answer when asked about the New Age:

> Well, I think it depends upon where you are working. I believe that the responsibility in this Age is to 'positive' religion. Now this probably doesn't have much bearing to you people, being Unity people, you're positive. But I talk a great deal to groups that are not positive . . . even to what we would call Fundamentalists who deal constantly with words like sin, salvation, repentance, guilt, that sort of thing.[142]

Contemplative prayer is the Christian version of New Age Transcendental Meditation. I have seen this also in a church I have attended. Smith stated:

> They too tout Nouwen and other mystics in their writings. Nouwen is a favorite of both Rick Warren and his wife, Kay. In Ray Yungen's book, *A Time of Departing*, which exposes the contemplative prayer move-

ment, Youngen documents the Warren's strong admiration for Nouwen as well as Warren's promotion of contemplative prayer teachers.[143]

The New Age or the New Spirituality that is based upon an experience rather than a set of doctrinal beliefs has become very popular both in the secular culture and within Christendom. It denies the personal God of the Bible and makes man and everything else God.

ISLAM

We covered the false religion of Islam in Chapters 12 & 13. We just want to emphasize here that Islam is not only a false religion with a false god, but its god is Satan himself that is in rebellion against God and resists God's plan in every way possible and actually is trying to prevent the completion of God's plan.

Other false religions

We are not going to cover other false religions because they are too numerous to cover.

Next we are going into Part 6 that asks the question: Why has evil progressed so rapidly in America?

Part 6

Why has evil progressed so rapidly in America?

CHAPTER 24
Stealth evils

Stealth evils are evils that are not perceived as evils. These are the most dangerous types of evil since they are not recognized as evil, they are not exposed or resisted and many times are actually supported by legitimatizing them and giving them financial support. Evils that are recognized as evils are mitigated by the light of truth shining on them, consequently they have difficulty thriving. The Merriam-Webster dictionary defines stealth as "a secret, quiet, and clever way of moving or behaving." This means that stealth evils operate under the radar and are undetected or unrecognized as evil.

Most stealth evils are stealth because they are created and designed to deceive like a conspiracy. Others are not necessarily designed to deceive but are supported by false foundations that legitimatize them so they can be promoted as good. Many things that were believed to be evil (and were evil) in the past now are still evil, but are not recognized as evil because of the cultural cover they get from the false foundations that are now accepted. However, many of these stealth evils are conspiracies including most of the false foundations. These were actually conceived and designed to deceive. Listed below are evils that include both types of stealth evils:

1. Uniformitarianism
2. Macro-evolution
3. Relative truth
4. Global warming
5. "The New Tolerance" and "Outrage Based Coercive Conscience"
6. Political correctness
7. Case Law
8. Separation of church and state
9. Marxism
10. Freudianism
11. Keynesianism
12. Affirmative action
13. Sexual liberation
14. Abortion
15. Social Justice

We have already exposed the false foundations as illegitimate in Part 4 and identified much of the false fruit that they support. The problem is that academia and our culture promote them as truth and recognizes them as good and legitimate. Here we will show that they are, in fact, considered legitimate and promoted as good. When it applies we will show that the stealth evils are meant to deceive and replace the current accepted biblical truth with its diametric opposite. Remember we established in Chapter 10 that diametric opposite worldview issues are significant in that when one represents good the other represents evil. They are covered individually below in order:

UNIFORMITARIANISM

The following quotes regarding James Hutton, the father of Uniformitarian geology, support that the philosophy was intended to replace the current biblical truth with its diametric opposite.

> In the late eighteenth century, when Hutton was carefully examining the rocks, it was generally believed that Earth had come into creation only around six thousand years earlier (on October 22, 4004 B.C., to be precise, according to the seventeenth century scholarly analysis of the Bible by Archbishop James Ussher of Ireland), and that fossils were the remains of animals that had perished during the Biblical flood.
> Hutton's theories amounted to a frontal attack on a popular contemporary school of thought called catastrophism: the belief that only natural catastrophes, such as the Great Flood, could account for the form and nature of a 6,000-year-old Earth. The great age of Earth was the first revolutionary concept to emerge from the new science of geology. [144]

Charles Lyell is the godfather of uniformitarian geology. He likewise was obsessed with disconnecting the currently accepted geological catastrophism belief that supported the Noahic flood story in the bible. See quotes below:

> Geology soon became his forte and as a member of the Geological Society, he took part in the lively debates in the 1820s about how to reconcile the biblical account of the Flood with geological findings. Lyell, as well as Roderick Murchison and George Poulett Scrope became an outspoken opponent of the diluvial position. [145]
> Lyell was obsessed with the implications of the evolutionary theory of J.B. Lamarck. In Lyell's view, if Lamarck was right then religion was a fable, Man was just a better beast, and the moral fabric of society would crumble to dust. [146]
> Lyell started his career studying under the catastrophist William Buckland at Oxford. But Lyell became disenchanted with Buckland when Buckland tried to link catastrophism to the Bible, looking for evidence that the most recent catastrophe had actually been Noah's flood. [147]

Consequently, a significant factor with both Hutton and Lyell rejecting the currently accepted belief in catastrophism that supported the Noahic flood and consequently the bible, was their desire to disconnect science from the biblical flood so the bible would be discredited.

MACROEVOLUTION

The quote below shows that evolutionists have presuppositions, or what I call a religious position. Ruse actually admitted this in a 1993 AAAS meeting in Boston:

> Those in academia especially should recognize, both historically and perhaps philosophically, certainly that the science side has certain metaphysical assumptions built into doing science, which—it may not be a good thing to admit in a court of law—but I do think that in honesty . . . we should recognize [this].[148]

There you have it! An evolutionist has admitted that the creation / evolution debate is actually religion vs. religion. This means that they are willing to corrupt science to uphold their religious position.

Dr. Richard Lewontin, a renowned Harvard geneticist stated:

> It is not that the methods and institutions of science somehow compel us to accept a material explanation of the phenomenal world, but on the contrary, that we are forced by our a priori adherence to material cause to create an apparatus of investigation and a set of concepts that produce material explanations, no matter how mystifying to the uninitiated. Moreover that materialism is absolute for we cannot allow a divine foot in the door.[149]

Dr. Lewontin certainly let the cat out of the bag when he admitted that their science is actually a religion that is diametrically opposed to God and the bible. He is admitting that he is willing to corrupt science to hide the link between the bible and real science.

George Wald, another prominent Evolutionist (a Harvard University biochemist and Nobel Laureate), wrote:

> When it comes to the Origin of Life there are only two possibilities: creation or spontaneous generation. There is no third way. Spontaneous Generation was disproved one hundred years ago, but that leads us to only one other conclusion, that of supernatural creation. We cannot accept that on philosophical grounds; therefore, we choose to believe the impossible: that life arose spontaneously by chance![150]

Consequently, random evolution cannot explain the origin of life and evolutionists would rather believe in something that has been disproven one hundred years ago than believe in biblical supernatural creation. Evolution is a false religion that like so many other lies has been foisted upon us. The false evolution religion is established as the only acceptable religion. Ben Stein's movie titled "Expelled: No Intelligence Allowed" clearly showed that any challenge to the evolutionary dogma is not allowed in academia and teachers and researchers that challenge the teachings typically get fired. Dr. Rex M. Rogers states the following about the film:

> This film asks the weighty question, "If we expel freedom in science, where will it end?" To find the answer, Stein travels to 12 countries on 4 continents, interviewing an impressive list of scholars in the sciences, theology, and philosophy. He asks them why "Big Science" makes no use of the hypothesis of God and why Intelligent Design discussions are suppressed. The answers he records are breathtaking in their political correctness, disdain for religion and religious people ("idiots," one scholar said), cavalier attitude toward debate, and fear of free speech.
>
> *Expelled* is not an advocacy flick for Intelligent Design. Rather, Stein probes why a scientific elite is systematically betraying one of America's founding principles: the freedom to create, explore, fail, overcome, inquire, debate.[151]

The stories of people that challenge evolution getting fired are numerous. I received another example on email today under the title of "Lawsuit Follows Christian's Firing from University." It quotes an article titled "California State University, Northridge will have a chance to answer in court how it has treated a Christian researcher whose findings contradict the theory of evolution." The quote below is reprinted with permission by The New American, "Cooking Climate Consensus Data: '97% of Scientists Affirm AGW' Debunked," written by William F. Jasper, June 5, 2013.

> In 2012, Mark Armitage – an electron microscope technician with the CSU-Northridge biology department – participated in a dinosaur dig in Montana, during which he unearthed a large triceratop's horn. He subsequently wrote a paper about it in which he estimated the age of the bone to be 4,000 years rather than the millions or billions attributed by evolutionists. (See related YouTube video)
>
> University officials questioned his motives and, after a discussion at the school, fired him – claiming his appointment of 38 months had been temporary, and that there was no longer funding for his position. OneNewsNow spoke with Brad Dacus, president of Pacific Justice Institute, which filed suit last week on behalf of Armitage for wrongful termination on the basis of religious discrimination.
>
> Dacus, Brad (PJI)"He was just examining a triceratop's bone that had soft tissue that seemed on its face to question the timeline that traditional evolutionists use for judging the development of creation and creatures," the attorney summarizes. "His supervisors in a very point blank way said that his religion has no place in science."

> In fact, according to court documents, one university official shouted at him: "We are not going to tolerate your religion in this department!"
> As PJI's Southern California office notes, it's apparent that attributes such as "diversity" and "intellectual curiosity" – often touted by academia – don't apply to those with a religious viewpoint.
> "True science welcomes all scientific evidence whether or not it supports religion," argues Dacus. "So what they're advocating is a very closed-minded censorship mentality which is a major disservice to true science and true academia."
> The PJI president is hopeful the case will send a message that true academia does not allow bigoted censorship and discrimination based on religious beliefs.[152]

Normal science is typically not embroiled in contention of diametric opposite beliefs. Also, it has been very beneficial to America and mankind. However, the science of origins has always been in diametric opposition to biblical teachings and real science and always will be until it has been rejected. In addition, origins science has not been beneficial to America and to the world like the rest of science. In fact as pointed out in "Expelled: No Intelligence Allowed," the belief in the theory of evolution has actually been very harmful in our world. The theory was the basis for the theory of eugenics that supported Hitler in his superior Arian race beliefs. It also supported Marx and Communism and the genocide of millions. Evolution has definitely been designed to discredit the biblical truth, replacing it with a false religion that is held up as truth, and support other stealth evils!

RELATIVE TRUTH

Once God is removed from the picture by a belief in random evolution we have a rationale that excuses us from following God's absolute moral code. If God doesn't exist, neither does His moral code. With our fallen nature and our history of falling away from God and his absolute commandments, we find it liberating to have a rationale that allows us to follow our own relative moral code and reject God's absolute moral code. I believe the psychologists call this rationalization.

Humanist John Dewey (1859-1952), co-author and signer of the Humanist Manifesto 1 (1933), declared:
> There is no God and there is no soul. Hence, there are no needs for the props of traditional religion. With dogma and creed excluded, then immutable truth is also dead and buried. There is no room for fixed, natural law or moral absolutes.[153]

Dewey also stated:
> It (modern philosophy) certainly exacts a surrender of all supernaturalism and fixed dogma and rigid institutionalism with which Christianity has been historically associated[154]

Those who advocate relative truth are primarily promoting moral relative truth. However, some actually carry the concept beyond moral concepts. It is hard to believe that anyone would believe such a concept since any debate on the merits of this type of relative truth would be a very short debate. Even the assertion of relative moral truth is a contradiction. For one to believe in relative moral truth you need to believe in one absolute truth. i.e. relative truth.

A discussion with a coworker was my first encounter with the concept of relative truth. He said to me "What I have come to believe is that we can't know anything for sure." The obvious question was (and still is) how can we know that for sure? This is pure deception to allow us to stretch liberty into license.

Again Romans 1:18 explains why this is done.
> [18] For the wrath of God is revealed from heaven against all ungodliness and unrighteousness of men, who suppress the truth in unrighteousness, . .

Wikipedia states:
> The Roman Catholic Church, especially under John Paul II and Pope Benedict XVI, has identified relativism as one of the most significant problems for faith and morals today. According to the Church and to some theologians, relativism, as a denial of absolute truth, leads to moral license and a denial of the possibility of sin and of God. Whether moral or epistemological, relativism constitutes a denial of the capacity of the human mind and reason to arrive at truth.[155]

Although I don't always agree with the Catholic Church, they nailed this one perfectly. It is obvious that relative truth is promoted as an intentional deception. Consequently, the establishment of relative truth belief was designed to discredit biblical moral truth and provide a foundation for license to be immoral and deny sin!

GLOBAL WARMING

E Calvin Beisner makes the following statement relating to the theology (religion) of global warming: It is quoted with permission.
> The world is in the grip of an idea: that burning fossil fuels to provide affordable, abundant energy is causing global warming that will be so dangerous that we must stop it by reducing our use of fossil fuels, no matter the cost. . .
>
> We believe that idea—we'll call it "global warming alarmism"—fails the tests of theology, science, and economics. It rests on poor theolo-

gy, with a worldview of the Earth and its climate system contrary to that taught in the Bible. It rests on poor science that confuses theory with observation, computer models with reality, and model results with evidence, all while ignoring the lessons of climate history. It rests on poor economics, failing to do reasonable cost/benefit analysis, ignoring or underestimating the costs of reducing fossil fuel use while exaggerating the benefits. And it bears fruit in unethical policy that would

- destroy millions of jobs.
- cost trillions of dollars in lost economic production.
- slow, stop, or reverse economic growth.
- reduce the standard of living for all but the elite few who are well positioned to benefit from laws that unfairly advantage them at the expense of most businesses and all consumers.
- endanger liberty by putting vast new powers over private, social, and market life in the hands of national and international governments.
- condemn the world's poor to generations of continued misery characterized by rampant disease and premature death.

In return for all these sacrifices, what will the world get? At most a negligible, undetectable reduction in global average temperature a hundred years from now.

Our examination of theology, worldview, and ethics finds that global warming alarmism wrongly views the Earth and its ecosystems as the fragile product of chance, not the robust, resilient, self-regulating, and self-correcting product of God's wise design and powerful sustaining. It rests on and promotes a view of human beings as threats to Earth's flourishing rather than the bearers of God's image, crowned with glory and honor, and given a mandate to act as stewards over the Earth—filling, subduing, and ruling it for God's glory and mankind's benefit. It either wrongly assumes that the environment can flourish only if humanity forfeits economic advance and prosperity or ignores economic impacts altogether. And in its rush to impose draconian reductions in greenhouse gas emissions, it ignores the destructive impact of that policy on the world's poor.[156]

The whole basis for the "global warming" philosophy and resulting effects of carrying it out are all diametrically opposed to biblical theology and God's desires for his people on earth. As we can see based upon the quotes below it is bald-faced lie that is designed to weaken America and the West while promoting a one world government through the UN.

The excerpt from this article below relates the global warming scheme to left wing politics (diametric opposite to biblical teaching) and UN goals.

"Consensus Drums" Aimed at Aiding UN Agenda

> However, the fact that the claims of the Cook/Skeptical Science survey have been exploded as bogus and the fact that the Cook/Skeptical Science team have been exposed as self-described "commies," "leftists," and "pinko/liberals" haven't stopped the MSM commentators from citing their fraudulent "research" as gospel. Incredibly, Prof. Eric Alterman of the left-wing *Nation* magazine cited the Cook survey in a June 4 posting on the left-wing ThinkProgress.org ("Think Again: Blame The News For The Public's Ignorance About The Climate") to condemn the mainstream media for not being sufficiently alarmist when it comes to global warming!
>
> Yes, we've only been marinating 24/7 for two decades in increasingly hysterical media predictions and pronouncements about the coming AGW apocalypse — and the American public still hasn't bought the false "consensus." However, with the United Nations Framework Convention on Climate Change (UNFCCC) now engaged in another conference in Bonn, Germany, and the UN's IPCC set to release a new series of reports, we can expect that the Cooked-up consensus results will be cited endlessly. Or, as Cook himself put it: "We beat the consensus drum often and regularly."[157]

Below is a testimonial from someone that we would expect to be an ardent supporter of global warming:

> Dr. Fritz Vahrenholt, a prominent Socialist and a father of Germany's environmental movement, has become another strong critic of the IPCC's alarmist global warming doctrine. His lack of trust began while serving as an expert reviewer for an IPCC renewable energy report as the renewable energy division head of Germany's second largest utility company. Upon discovering and pointing out numerous factual inaccuracies to IPCC officials, they simply brushed them aside. Stunned by this, he began to wonder if IPCC reports on climate change were similarly sloppy. After digging into the IPCC's climate report he was horrified to find similar incompetency and misrepresentations, including climate models that were fudged to produce exaggerated temperature increases. Dr. Vahrenholt concluded: "The facts need to be discussed sensibly and scientifically, without first deciding on the results." And although CO2 may have some warming influence, he believes that the sun plays a far greater role in the whole scheme of things.[158]

Dr. Vahrenholt reveals that the global warming alarmists are pushing a religious position since that is what is left when you remove the motivation for legitimate science.

Dr. Patrick Moore, a co-founder of Greenpeace, quit the activist environmental organization in 1986 after it strayed away from objective science and took a sharp turn to the political left and stated the following:

> When previously asked on Fox Business News who is responsible for promoting unwarranted fear and what their motives are, Moore said: "A powerful convergence of interests. Scientists seeking grant money, media seeking headlines, universities seeking huge grants from major institutions, foundations, environmental groups, politicians wanting to make it look like they are saving future generations. And all of these people have converged on this issue." Moore warns that, "The alarmism is driving us through scare tactics to adopt energy policies that are going to create a huge amount of energy poverty among the poor people. It's not good for people and it's not good for the environment. In a warmer world we can produce more food."[159]

Nobel Laureate physicist Dr. Ivar Giaever has referred to global warming ideology as:

> a "pseudoscience" that begins with an emotionally appealing hypothesis, and "then only looks for items which appear to support it," while ignoring ample contrary evidence.[160]

Pseudoscience means religion. In this case the religion is the diametric opposite of the biblical religion.

Emails that were exposed by a hacker and 5000 more recent emails show the religious / political nature of the United Nations Intergovernmental Panel on Climate Change (IPCC) organization pushing their climate change agenda. As James Taylor, senior fellow for environmental policy at the Heartland Institute, wrote in Forbes.com:

> A new batch of 5,000 emails among scientists central to the assertion that humans are causing a global warming crisis were anonymously released to the public yesterday, igniting a new firestorm of controversy nearly two years to the day after similar emails ignited the Climategate scandal.
>
> Three themes are emerging from the newly released emails: (1) prominent scientists central to the global warming debate are taking measures to conceal rather than disseminate underlying data and discussions; (2) these scientists view global warming as a political "cause" rather than a balanced scientific inquiry and (3) many of these scientists frankly admit to each other that much of the science is weak and dependent on deliberate manipulation of facts and data.
>
> Regarding scientific transparency, a defining characteristic of science is the open sharing of scientific data, theories and procedures so that independent parties, and especially skeptics of a particular theory or hypothesis, can replicate and validate asserted experiments or observations. Emails between Climategate scientists, however, show a con-

certed effort to hide rather than disseminate underlying evidence and procedures.

"I've been told that IPCC is above national FOI [Freedom of Information] Acts. One way to cover yourself and all those working in AR5 would be to delete all emails at the end of the process," writes Phil Jones, a scientist working with the United Nations Intergovernmental Panel on Climate Change (IPCC), in a newly released email.

"Any work we have done in the past is done on the back of the research grants we get – and has to be well hidden," Jones writes in another newly released email. "I've discussed this with the main funder (U.S. Dept. of Energy) in the past and they are happy about not releasing the original station data."

The original Climategate emails contained similar evidence of destroying information and data that the public would naturally assume would be available according to freedom of information principles. "Mike, can you delete any emails you may have had with Keith [Briffa] re AR4 [UN Intergovernmental Panel on Climate Change 4th Assessment]?" Jones wrote to Penn State University scientist Michael Mann in an email released in Climategate 1.0. "Keith will do likewise. ... We will be getting Caspar [Ammann] to do likewise. I see that CA [the Climate Audit Web site] claim they discovered the 1945 problem in the Nature paper!!"

The new emails also reveal the scientists' attempts to politicize the debate and advance predetermined outcomes.[161]

The whole global warming or climate change agenda is pseudoscientific and thus a religious and political agenda that is diametrically opposed to biblical principles. It is designed to deceive the world and particularly the United States so the UN will have control over sovereign nations, particularly the United States. If believed, it justifies the UN's ability to tax and have power over nation states and spread the United States wealth around the world and buy votes for our politicians. Certainly this is a conspiracy that would support many additional evils!

THE NEW TOLERANCE AND OUTRAGE BASED COERCED CONSCIENCE

Since these euphemisms and concepts are not familiar to most people, Lets repeat what was covered in Chapter 18.

> Another thing that has been turned on its head in our relativistic, politically correct culture is to neglect to view and debate issues as good and evil and true and false. When is the last time that you have heard any of those words on TV, newspaper or in any kind of debate? Our culture has reframed the argument so the debate is no longer between good and evil or true and false, but between the messengers

who dare to identify something as evil or false and those that do not offend people by judging the goodness of things. This whole idea is supported by the concept of relative truth. If we have no absolute truth, then who are we to judge the goodness or badness of beliefs and behaviors etc.?

Traditionally, we knew what good and evil were and Christians tolerated evil even though it was not accepted, approved or certainly not celebrated. Today we censor debate on good vs. evil and switch the debate to the evil of the messengers that are promoting truth and exposing evil. As the expression goes, "shoot the messenger of bad tidings."

A book that documents this issue is "The New Tolerance" by Josh McDowell.[162] Today's culture even goes beyond that. Today we not only censor debate on good vs evil, we insist that all manner of evil, not only be tolerated, but be accepted, approved and celebrated.

"The New Tolerance" in one sense is the "bad fruit" based upon foundations cited above, but also is a block in the false foundation that suppresses the truth by supporting censorship of truth and demonizes the messenger of truth. This is just another example of an evil that is in diametric oppositions to biblical principles. As the reader is well aware this "New Tolerance" is promoted widely in our culture with the debate being suppressed and the messenger demonized. What gives it legitimacy is the text below which is taken out of context and used for evil purposes. Matthew 7:1 states:

Judge not that you not be judged.

Two things are wrong with this unjustified conclusion. One is exposed in verses 2-5 that follow:

[2] For with what judgment you judge, you will be judged; and with the measure you use, it will be measured back to you. [3] And why do you look at the speck in your brother's eye, but do not consider the plank in your own eye? [4] Or how can you say to your brother, 'Let me remove the speck from your eye'; and look, a plank is in your own eye? [5] Hypocrite! First remove the plank from your own eye, and then you will see clearly to remove the speck from your brother's eye.

It is saying that we should not judge hypocritically. i.e. if we have the same problem, we are hypocritical to judge someone else with that problem. It says if we first remove the plank from our eye, then it is not only ok to judge our brother, but we should judge them or more correctly their beliefs and behaviors.

The other thing is that we should never judge people in respect to whether we think they are not as good as we are or condemn them for not having a proper relationship with God. Those are things we cannot be sure of. However, the bible does teach us that we should judge behavior, sin, philosophy and doctrine. 2 Timothy 3:16 states:

> [16] All Scripture is given by inspiration of God, and is profitable for doctrine, for reproof, for correction, for instruction in righteousness, . .

The New Tolerance and Outrage based Coerced Conscience philosophies are designed to reframe the argument or debate from a true debate where the pros and cons are objectively debated to censoring the actual debate while at the same time demonizing the messenger that is questioning something that he sees as wrong. Today our world accepts this evil reframing of the debate to the extent that laws can be passed that enforce this travesty of justice where the light is extinguished and one exposing evil is demonized and destroyed. This is definitely a stealth evil and a Satanic conspiracy!

POLITICAL CORRECTNESS

In Chapter 19 we learned what "Political Correctness" was and where it came from. Here we want to show that it is also stealth. First the fact that Political Correctness is actually cultural Marxism which has its roots in Communism is suppressed by giving a cute, misleading euphemism of "Political Correctness" for cover, shows it to be stealth. Second it is designed to criticize and deconstruct our traditional and biblical values that are our heritage without offering a superior alternative making it a stealth modus operandi. Thirdly, it acts as a false foundation to support much "bad fruit." All the fruits of political correctness are evil and diametrically opposed to biblical principles. If anything has been a conspiracy, it is political correctness.

CASE LAW

If it wasn't for the false foundation of Case law the false two sided "wall of separation" and the false "Separation of Church and State" legal stance could have never happened. The false foundation of Case Law breaks the link between subsequent laws and the Establishment Clause and other Constitutional teachings. Wikipedia defines Case Law as follows:

> In common law legal systems, a precedent or authority is a principle or rule established in a previous legal case that is either binding on or persuasive for a court or other tribunal when deciding subsequent cases with similar issues or facts. The general principle in common law legal systems is that similar cases should be decided so as to give similar and predictable outcomes, and the principle of precedent is the mechanism by which that goal is attained. Black's Law Dictionary defines "precedent" as a "rule of law established for the first time by a court for a particular type of case and thereafter referred to in decid-

ing similar cases." Common law precedent is a third kind of law, on equal footing with statutory law (statutes and codes enacted by legislative bodies), and regulatory law (regulations promulgated by executive branch agencies).[163]

The fact that Case Law is able to make a judicial law the precedent for future laws rather than the Constitution makes it a false foundation and makes it possible to support subsequent evil laws that are diametrically opposed to the constitution and biblical principles, gives these evil laws legitimacy.

SEPARATION OF CHURCH AND STATE

In Chapter 21 we learned that the current philosophy of Separation of Church and State did not represent the original contextual meaning of the metaphor, the words or intent of the Establishment Clause of the Constitution or the European historical concern. In each case it means the diametric opposite![164]

They took the opportunity to misuse the original inadvertent metaphor of "a wall of separation" that was intended to only use one side so that now it only represents the other side! They read two incorrect things into the Establishment Clause. One is that it only limited Congress on what they could do, not what people could do in the public square. Secondly, it assumed that the word religion meant a doctrinal religion like Christianity or Islam. The word religion really meant a denomination of the Christian religion, not total doctrinal or biblical Christianity. This can be seen from previous draft versions of the First Amendment. This quote excerpt is pulled from Chapter 21 and repeated below:

> To ensure we understand what the framers of the Constitution meant by the "Establishment Clause" let's examine the three drafts prior to the final one. The three stated: 1. "Congress shall not make any law establishing any religious denomination." 2. "Congress shall make no law establishing any particular denomination." 3. "Congress shall make no law establishing any particular denomination in preference to another."[165]

This false "Separation of Church and State" foundation was established by the U.S. Supreme Court and became a definitive part of Establishment Clause jurisprudence. Wikipedia explains how this happened:

> The 5-4 decision was handed down on February 10, 1947. The Court, through Justice Hugo Black, ruled that the state bill was constitutionally permissible because the reimbursements were offered to all students regardless of religion and because the payments were made to parents and not any religious institution. Perhaps as important as the actual outcome, though, was the interpretation given by the entire Court to the Establishment Clause. It reflected a broad interpretation

of the Clause that was to guide the Court's decisions for decades to come. Black's language was sweeping:
> "The 'establishment of religion' clause of the First Amendment means at least this: Neither a state nor the Federal Government can set up a church. Neither can pass laws which aid one religion, aid all religions or prefer one religion over another. Neither can force nor influence a person to go to or to remain away from church against his will or force him to profess a belief or disbelief in any religion. No person can be punished for entertaining or professing religious beliefs or disbeliefs, for church attendance or non-attendance. No tax in any amount, large or small, can be levied to support any religious activities or institutions, whatever they may be called, or whatever form they may adopt to teach or practice religion. Neither a state nor the Federal Government can, openly or secretly, participate in the affairs of any religious organizations or groups and vice versa. In the words of Jefferson, the clause against establishment of religion by law was intended to erect 'a wall of separation between Church and State.'" 330 U.S. 1, 15-16.[166]

Some, including former Chief Justice William H. Rehnquist, have criticized *Everson* for its reliance on quotations and views from Thomas Jefferson, who had little to do with the framing of the U.S. Constitution or its Bill of Rights. Rehnquist's commentary stated:
> The metaphor of the wall of separation is bad history and worse law.[167]

Consequently, besides broadening the Establishment Clauses from Christian denominations to Christianity itself, they denied that "religious secularism" or Secular Humanism were religions since no similar government funding restrictions were placed upon them. Fourteen years later the US Supreme court declared that "Secular Humanism" was a religion in Torcaso v. Watkins:
> The phrase "secular humanism" became prominent after it was used in the United States Supreme Court case *Torcaso v. Watkins*. In the 1961 decision, Justice Hugo Black commented in a footnote, "Among religions in this country which do not teach what would generally be considered a belief in the existence of God are Buddhism, Taoism, Ethical Culture, Secular Humanism, and others."[168]

The following is a great summary proving that Secular Humanism was and is a religion:
> John Dewey described Humanism as our "common faith." Julian Huxley called it "Religion without Revelation." The first Humanist Manifesto spoke openly of Humanism as a religion. Many other Humanists could be cited who have acknowledged that Humanism is a religion. In fact, claiming that Humanism was "the new religion" was trendy for at

least 100 years, perhaps beginning in 1875 with the publication of *The Religion of Humanity* by Octavius Brooks Frothingham (1822-1895), son of the distinguished Unitarian clergyman, Nathaniel Langdon Frothingham (1793-1870), pastor of the First Unitarian Church of Boston, 1815-1850. In the 1950's, Humanists sought and obtained tax-exempt status as religious organizations. Even the Supreme Court of the United States spoke in 1961 of Secular Humanism as a religion. It was a struggle to get atheism accepted as a religion, but it happened. From 1962-1980 this was not a controversial issue.

But then Christians began to challenge the "establishment of religion" which Secular Humanism in public schools represented. They used the same tactic Atheists had used to challenge prayer and Bible reading under the "Establishment Clause" of the First Amendment. Now the ACLU is involved. *Now* the question is controversial. Now Secular Humanists have completely reversed their strategy, and claim that Humanism is not at all religious, but is "scientific."[169]

We Christians and our religious leaders have allowed them to get away with it. We have allowed this huge false foundation and the evils it supports to undermine Christianity in the public square and academia. The truth has been turned on its head to justify promoting a philosophy that is in diametric opposition to biblical principles. The reader knows that this falsehood is well accepted in our society. Everyone thinks that separation of church and state is a good thing. Even pastors do not object to it. Consequently, the deception is certainly a stealth evil.

MARXISM AND KARL MARX

Brannon Howse tells the story of Karl Marx in his book "Grave Influence:"
As a young man, Marx was dismissed from several universities for his radical, revolutionary views. An atheist and a Secular Humanist, he wrote the "Communist Manifesto" with his friend Friedrich Engels. Marx did not believe in the spiritual world of life after death, only in the natural, material world. He valued people only for what they could do for the State. Is it any wonder, then, that the worldview of Marx—Communism—has been responsible for the murder of more than 100 million people?

Marx hated the free market and capitalism—and their roots in Protestant Reformation—perhaps because he was a lazy slob who wanted other people to take care of him. He lived largely off of his friend Friedrich Engels, who drew an income from the family business. How perversely ironic is that? Marx spread his hatred of capitalism while drawing his livelihood from the fruits of capitalism. Isn't that always the mode of operation for those who follow the economic philosophy of Communism, the most virulent form of socialism?

Marx was such a reprobate that out of his six children, three died of starvation while still infants, two others committed suicide, and only one lived to be an adult. The Marx family was often hounded by creditors. Yet, when Marx received a gift of 160 pounds (about $500), he neglected to pay his bills, his rent, or to buy food for his starving family. Rather, he went on a two month drinking binge with his intellectual buddies while his wife and infant children were evicted from their apartment. Marx, the parasite, also spent his wife's inheritances from her mother and uncle, causing his family to live on the edge of financial ruin for years.

Among the many infectious ideas Marx promoted was his hatred for the traditional family. Instead, he favored "a system of wives in common." Needless to say, Marx did not have a great marriage, and when his wife died, Marx didn't even attend her funeral. And not only was he a negligent husband and father, Marx was such an uncaring, arrogant bully that he had few friends. Even those that agreed with his teachings did not like him as a person. As a result, when he died, fewer than a dozen people attended his funeral.[170]

Clearly Marx's worldview was diametrically opposed to biblical principles. The effects of his beliefs were completely destructive to his family and to every country or leader that adopted his false philosophies. His false beliefs certainly laid a false foundation for much bad fruit including denigrating biblical Christianity, promoting eugenics and genocide. Marxism has been completely refuted from an economic standpoint. It certainly has also failed socially since it resulted in genocide in both Germany and the Soviet Union. In spite of those great shortcomings it still has not been condemned on moral grounds. It is still promoted in American academia and Marxism is basically synonymous with progressive ideology. We certainly showed that in our discussion on "Political Correctness." This evil philosophy is able to be promoted as good based upon allegedly being for the poor and disadvantaged just as it was for the Proletariat. The problem is that it takes power from the wealthy productive owners and gives it to the underclass to buy votes to keep the political class with the false philosophy in power. The end result is that the wealthy productive class is destroyed and the politicians become wealthy and powerful. Ultimately, the underclass is never better off but just used as a pawn to transfer the wealth from the productive class to the politicians. Marxism is definitely an evil stealth philosophy that should be condemned.

FREUDIANISM AND FREUD

Brannon Howse tells the story of Sigmund Freud in his book "Grave Influence:"

"To demolish religion with psychoanalytic weapons," Freud biographer Peter Gay reported, "had been on Freud's agenda for many years." Sigmund Freud, like Nietzsche who strongly influenced him, hated God and Christianity. In his own book, "The Future of an Illusion," Freud describes his absolutely negative attitude toward religion, in every form and dilution."

As Dr. Benjamin Wiker points out in "The Books That Screwed up the World:"

> We cannot forget Nietzsche's assumption that religion was an entirely human creation. Since Freud and Nietzsche, this may have done as much as anything to help form his presentation of religion in "The Future of an Illusion."[171]

With that viewpoint at the core of Freud's thinking, Wiker goes on to describe the psychoanalyst's resultant, perverted worldview:

> His rebellion took the form of baptizing as natural the most hideously unnatural sins, sins condemned by every society as the most unholy and unthinkable . . . Freud damned as unnatural the Christian-based morality of Western society.[172]

Freud himself points out several of these "unholy and unthinkable" inclinations: "Among these instinctual wishes are those of incest, cannibalism, and lust for killing." Freud believed that it is the people who reject a biblical worldview and follow their "natural" desires that are truly sane. As Dr. Wiker explains:

> He [Freud] claimed that psychological disorders were the result of the unnatural repression of our naturally unholy and anti-social desires, and that some people just couldn't handle the repression. . . Therefore, neurotics are the only sane people because they react to unnatural frustration by training to reclaim their original, natural, asocial and amoral state. The result: the anti-social psychopath who kills without conscience is the most natural of all. The interesting effect of Freud's proclamation that evil is natural was the seemingly untended consequence of making psychopathic insanity natural.[173]

Learning about Freud's bio almost takes your breath away. It is hard to believe that anyone would think his beliefs and philosophies are worth considering. His diametric opposition to what the bible teaches certainly tells us that he is on the dark side that includes Satan, Alinsky and all rebels. It is tragic that he has had so much influence in psychological academia and on our culture. Everything he believed and did was diametrically opposed to biblical principles. Consequently, his beliefs acted as a false foundation for how to help people with psychological problems. However, as the reader knows his philosophies are promoted and taught in our colleges. This makes them legitimate is the eyes of students and our culture. This makes Freudianism a stealth evil.

JOHN MAYNARD KEYNES

Brannon Howse tells the story of John Maynard Keynes in his book "Grave Influence."

> Like so many other losers on our list. Keynes was a blatant pervert. Zygmund Dobbs, who conducted research for the book "Keynes at Harvard," describes Keynes and his buddies this way:
>
>> Singing the Red Flag, the highborn sons of the British upper-class lay on the carpeted floor spinning out socialist schemes in homosexual intermissions . . . The attitude in such gatherings was anti-establishment. To them the older generation was horribly out of date, even superfluous. The capitalist system was declared obsolete and revolution was proclaimed as the only solution. Christianity was pronounced an enemy by force, and the worst sort of depravities were eulogized as 'that love that passed all understanding.' Chief of this ring of homosexual revolutionaries was John Maynard Keynes . . . Keynes was characterized by his male sweetheart, Lytton Strachey, as "a liberal and sodomite, an atheist and statistician." His particular depravity was sexual abuse of little boys.[174]

Similar to Sigmund Freud, John Maynard Keynes was against capitalism, against God and was sexually depraved. Consequently, his beliefs and his life were diametrically opposed to biblical principles. He established the false economic foundation that is being used to destroy our country today by burying us in debt. Under the guise of gigantic spending needed to relieve poverty and help the underclass, Keynesian economics is destroying our country through bankruptcy. The real reason for the spending is twofold. One to buy votes to keep progressives in power and secondly is to actually destroy America since that is necessary to set up a one world government and to justify destruction of what they believe is an evil empire. By definition, making evil legitimate is stealth.

AFFIRMATIVE ACTION

The political correctness quote from Chapter 19 revealed that Affirmative Action was part of Cultural Marxism or Political Correctness. The following is an excerpt from that quote:

> Fourth, both economic and cultural Marxism rely on expropriation. When the classical Marxists, the communists, took over a country like Russia, they expropriated the bourgeoisie, they took away their property. Similarly, when the cultural Marxists take over a university campus, they expropriate through things like quotas for admissions. When a white student with superior qualifications is denied admittance to a college in favor of a black or Hispanic who isn't as well qualified, the

white student is expropriated. And indeed, affirmative action, in our whole society today, is a system of expropriation. White owned companies don't get a contract because the contract is reserved for a company owned by, say, Hispanics or women. So expropriation is a principle tool for both forms of Marxism.

The bible has many quotes on not being partial. The following are repeated hear again from Chapter 10.

Leviticus 19:15 states:

[15] 'You shall do no injustice in judgment. You shall not be partial to the poor, nor honor the person of the mighty. In righteousness you shall judge your neighbor.

Deuteronomy 1:17 states:

[17] You shall not show partiality in judgment; you shall hear the small as well as the great; you shall not be afraid in any man's presence, for the judgment *is* God's. The case that is too hard for you, bring to me, and I will hear it.'

Job 34:19 states:

[19] Yet He is not partial to princes,
Nor does He regard the rich more than the poor;
For they are all the work of His hands.

Romans 2:11 states:

[11] For there is no partiality with God.

Consequently, Affirmative Action is in diametric opposition to biblical principles. It supports justification for partiality and a victimhood class. It is an evil deception that supports irresponsibility within the victimhood class. Since the "making America feel guilty" crowd makes this a moral philosophy, it is legitimized and consequently a stealth evil.

SEXUAL LIBERATION

The political correctness quote from Chapter 19 revealed that sexual liberation was a large part of Cultural Marxism or Political Correctness. Political Correctness supported the "sexual liberation" that was promoted and blossomed in the sixties. Below are excerpts from that quote from an article by Bill Lind:

Fromm and Marcuse introduce an element which is central to Political Correctness, and that's the sexual element. And particularly Marcuse, who in his own writings calls for a society of "polymorphous perversity," that is his definition of the future of the world that they want to create...

One of Marcuse's books was the key book. It virtually became the bible of the SDS and the student rebels of the 60s. That book was Eros and Civilization. Marcuse argues that under a capitalistic order (he downplays the Marxism very strongly here, it is subtitled, A Philosophical Inquiry into Freud, but the framework is Marxist), repression is the essence of that order and that gives us the person Freud describes – the person with all the hang-ups, the neuroses, because his sexual instincts are repressed. We can envision a future, if we can only destroy this existing oppressive order, in which we liberate eros, we liberate libido, in which we have a world of "polymorphous perversity," in which you can "do you own thing." And by the way, in that world there will no longer be work, only play.[175]

The bible addresses the seriousness of sexual sins in 1 Corinthians 6:18-19:

[18] Flee sexual immorality. Every sin that a man does is outside the body, but he who commits sexual immorality sins against his own body. [19] Or do you not know that your body is the temple of the Holy Spirit who is in you, whom you have from God, and you are not your own?

This establishes that cultural Marxism or political correctness promotes sexual liberation and irresponsibility. And we showed above that sexual liberation and irresponsibility represents Marx, Freud and Keynes character very well. We want to emphasize the relationship between a person's character and their philosophy is based upon what the bible states in Matthew 7:15-18:

[15] "Beware of false prophets, who come to you in sheep's clothing, but inwardly they are ravenous wolves. [16] You will know them by their fruits. Do men gather grapes from thornbushes or figs from thistles? [17] Even so, every good tree bears good fruit, but a bad tree bears bad fruit. [18] A good tree cannot bear bad fruit, nor can a bad tree bear good fruit.

We would expect to see an association between what an author's beliefs and morals are like and what his works are like. In these cases they are both very bad and very much alike.

Consequently, it would be fully expected that Satan would use sexual liberation as a major false foundation to support other evils that are diametrically opposed to biblical principles. The fact that sexual liberation has been considered the norm in our culture legitimized sexual liberation makes it a stealth evil.

ABORTION

R. Keith Martin documented a thorough history and insightful comments on abortion as follows:

Everybody knows that Roe V. Wade was the Supreme Court decision that ushered in legal abortion. But, few knew the details. Norma McCorvey was a young lady in Dallas who said she was raped and wanted permission to get an abortion. She was blocked in her attempt by District Attorney Henry B. Wade because abortions were illegal. Two feminist lawyers, Sarah Weddington and Linda Coffee, heard about the case and joined forces with Planned Parenthood and others hoping to change the law, and cash-in on the lucrative abortion business. McCorvey was given the pseudonym "Jane Roe" to hide her identity. The case first entered the Texas courts in 1969, but the Supreme Court ruling was not made until January 22, 1973. During this time the baby arrived alive, but this did not deter the pro-death cabal.

A few years after the ruling, McCorvey admitted she had not been raped. Then, after a few more years working in the baby killing business, she had an epiphany when she saw a woman killing their children simply because they were the wrong sex. She had routinely witnessed late term abortions which were supposedly illegal. She and the daughter that had been slated to be chemically fried in the womb became outspoken Pro-life advocates as they are to this day. Of course, Pandora's Box had been opened and the baby killing mills sprang up all over the country to meet the demand of the inconvenient consequences of our free-love society.

Abortion is the ultimate defining issue between conservatives and the "Darkside." It is truly a life and death matter. Real conservatives are 100% pro-life. So-called fiscal conservatives are not conservatives at all. But, they can't quite bring themselves to join the radical left which has become increasingly radicalized under Obama. The "Darkside" thirst for abortion has two components. One is the money. With an average of 4500 abortions per day at a typical fee of $700 means that about $11 billion made annually from the slaughter of children. The second component of abortion is the dehumanizing effect that humans killing their own young on an already sedated, relativistic society. Dehumanizing the masses until they resemble a herd of cattle, or a mindless mob, is a control technique used for thousands of years. Before the advent of the progressives in the 20th century, dehumanizing techniques were used to discipline armies and control captive populations. Once people inured to the killing of their own offspring, other atrocities offer few obstacles. The genocides of Hitler, Pol Pot, and Stalin show that once killing becomes the norm, the horror continues unabated and society self-destructs.

Abortion is simply one step in the progression of infanticide and euthanasia. This is indisputable. Infanticide is already practiced in the United States. When Obama was serving in the Illinois Senate he supported legislation to simply allow infants that survived abortion to be removed to a separate location and allowed to die a slow death. Could open, unlimited infanticide be far behind? Euthanasia is already practiced in Europe, Asia, and is legal in five of our states. It is included in Obamacare and don't dare believe otherwise. With the passage of Obamacare your tax dollars will now directly flow to Planned Parenthood. If you doubt that Obamacare will fund abortions with your tax dollars, or that "death panels" will decide who lives and who dies, then you need to lay this book down, and go and watch Oprah because you have not been watching and listening lately.[176]

If the false foundations listed above had not been laid and people still had faith in the bible and its principles, abortion could never have become legal. The bible has several commandments and principles that condemn abortion. The Ten Commandments given in Exodus 20:13 states that "You shall not murder." With modern science we know that life begins at conception and the baby has a different DNA than the mother. Consequently, we know that the baby is not really a part of the woman's body. So we know that when we intentionally abort a baby it is legal murder. Exodus 21:22-23 states:

> [22] "If men fight, and hurt a woman with child, so that she gives birth prematurely, yet no harm follows, he shall surely be punished accordingly as the woman's husband imposes on him; and he shall pay as the judges determine. [23] But if any harm follows, then you shall give life for life,

This text is not well known. It basically says that if an unborn baby is inadvertently killed through a careless physical blow to the mother, the person that was responsible should be put to death. If inadvertent killing of unborn baby deserves death, what about the intentional killing of an unborn baby? Matthew 18:6 states:

> [6] "Whoever causes one of these little ones who believe in Me to sin, it would be better for him if a millstone were hung around his neck, and he were drowned in the depth of the sea.

Jesus is telling how serious it is to cause children to sin. How much more serious would it be to cause one to be murdered. To refer to it as "a woman's right to choose" and never complete the sentence is an evil deception that again could only be considered after the validity of the bible has been destroyed by the many false foundations discussed above and in Part 4. That legitimizes abortion and makes it a stealth evil! Abortion is in diametric opposition to biblical principles.

SOCIAL JUSTICE

Although Social Justice is the last stealth evil on the list it is certainly not the least. We believe it to be the most lethal stealth evil of all and subverts the political, academic and religious realms. Friedrich P. Hayek agrees when he stated:

> The appeal to social justice has . . . by now become the most widely used and most effective argument in political discussion. Almost every claim for government action on behalf of particular groups is advanced in its name, and if it can be made to appear that a certain measure is demanded by social justice, opposition to it will rapidly weaken.[177]

It divides the ranks of biblical Christians that should be united on politics and thus takes what would be an overwhelming force for conservative biblical principles and places them instead on the progressive side that is diametrically opposed to biblical principles. The only reason this can happen is that Social Justice is presented as something that is good and allegedly biblical. The people claiming that it is biblical are not limited to Secular Humanists and progressives, but many ministers and Christian denominations and evangelical churches. Just as Political Correctness is a euphemism for Cultural Marxism, Social Justice is a euphemism for Socialism. If it is truly just, who could argue with Social Justice or that any other kind of justice is bad? We should examine if it is truly good based upon how well it has worked when implemented historically, ask if it is really just and ask if it is supported by the bible?

Since Social Justice is a euphemism for socialism its emphasis is on equal outcome rather than the philosophy of capitalism, equal opportunity. They are diametric opposites. Surprise, surprise! Another euphemism for Social Justice is Liberation Theology, meaning liberating the victims of poverty.

Historical record

Has any form of socialism worked well in the past? Marx's political answer to a wide gap in economic strength between the Bourgeoisie and the Proletariat was to justify eliminating the Bourgeoisie by confiscating their property and killing many of them and distributing their wealth to the Proletariat. To him that was justice. The question is was he telling the truth. Did it make the Proletariat wealthy like the Bourgeoisie? Absolutely not! They were no richer than they were before. The net result was that the new elite group were controlling the government and usurping the wealth of the country. How can it be justice when the wealth of a class was confiscated by force under the guise of helping the poor Proletariat with the end result being that the Proletariat was no better off and the liberators were the new Bourgeoisie? They just used the alleged plight of the Proletariat to promote themselves to the elite class. At least the Bourgeoisie earned what they got rather than stealing it.

We have a very similar thing going on here in America today with politicians gaining political power by claiming to have the answer to the economic problem of the underclass. Here in America this process is where wealth is stolen from those that are hardworking producers that generate wealth out of "thin air" and given to the economic underclass. The net result is that the underclass is even more trapped as an underclass and the politicians buy their power with other people's money, specifically the constituency in opposition to those in power. In addition, they prevent the pie from increasing in size while they are only interested is cutting up the pie allegedly more equitably. How can anybody think of that as justice?

America's first experiment with its consequences is documented below:

> George Santayana's aphorism, "Those who cannot remember the past are condemned to repeat it," should serve as a sober reminder that every generation is responsible for handing down the knowledge and wisdom attained by previous generations. Those who studied the revisionist-plundered history lessons in government schools may be surprised to learn America already experimented with socialism. Out of that failed experiment emerged our free-market, capitalist economic system.
>
> America's first experiment with socialism wasn't Lyndon Johnson's Great Society, nor was it Franklin Roosevelt's New Deal—although both made sweeping changes to the nation's underlying government structure and entrapped America in the bureaucratic quagmire of collectivism. No, America's very first experiment with redistribution of wealth occurred before America was officially a nation.
>
> In 1620, the Puritan Pilgrims arrived in the "desolate wilderness" of Plymouth, Massachusetts. Seeking escape from religious persecution in Europe, the Puritans risked their lives crossing the Atlantic to establish a new colony in the wilds of America. The Pilgrims decided that their new community would practice collectivism (socialism). All labor was communal, with men raising crops for all families, not just their own, and women engaged in domestic chores for their neighbors. . .
>
> The Pilgrims, a pious and decent people, discovered that even the best of men cannot thrive under socialism's incentive-crushing system. This experiment with socialism—probably its best chance for success amongst such selfless, righteous people—failed miserably. The Puritans discovered that government cannot deny man's inherent desire to work hard to provide for his own family and be rewarded when his labor exceeds his neighbor's.
>
> Having learned a valuable lesson about human nature, the Pilgrims established a new economic system that encouraged and rewarded personal initiative. Instead of a collectivist labor force, each family was given a plot of land on which to grow their own crops. Soon, each family was pulling its own weight. In fact, the harvest was so bountiful that the Pilgrims were able to trade with local Indians, and the colony prospered. Bradford reflected on the success of this capitalist approach to private labor:
>
>> They had very good success, for it made all hands very industrious, so as much more corn was planted than otherwise would have been. The women now went willingly into the field, and took

their little ones with them to set corn; which before would allege weakness and inability; whom to have compelled would have been thought great tyranny and oppression". By this time harvest was come, and instead of famine, now God gave them plenty, and the faces of things were changed, to the rejoicing of the hearts of many, for which they blessed God. Indeed, their bounty was so great, that they had enough to not only trade among themselves but also with the neighboring Indians in the forest.

Nowadays, the Puritans are maligned and disparaged by the politically correct for their religious devotion. But Americans should be thankful to these brave souls for not only bringing the concept of religious freedom across the Atlantic, but for surviving America's first experiment with socialism. The misery they experienced under socialism led to the free-market economy later established by their posterity.

The appeal of socialism is that it seems a benevolent form of government, where everyone works to help his fellow citizens. But, as the Puritans discovered, socialism denies man's innate incentive to work hard for his own family, not his neighbors. Capitalism, while not perfect, gives man the incentive he needs to work hard for his family and thereby help his entire community—not by force, but out of true generosity. If America fails to learn from the mistakes of our ancestors, we'll have forgotten the truth of Albert Einstein's famous aphorism: "Insanity: doing the same thing over and over again and expecting different results."[178]

The City of Detroit is the "poster child" for this liberal / progressive political philosophy just described above. It has kept the Democrats in power for more than fifty years and kept the underclass trapped as underclass regardless of how many billions of dollars that they confiscated and distributed to the economic underclass. It turned America's wealthiest city into a city that had to declare bankruptcy. Political corruption became rampant and the city now looks like a bombed out war zone. From any aspect the city became a "hell-hole." These examples expose the tragic unjust myth of Social Justice!

Biblical support

The bible has many teachings that refute social justice. The 10th Commandment in Exodus 20:17 states that:

> [17] "You shall not covet your neighbor's house; you shall not covet your neighbor's wife, nor his male servant, nor his female servant, nor his ox, nor his donkey, nor anything that is your neighbor's."

The politics of envy and covetousness that acts as the driving force for social justice is diametrically opposed to the 10th Commandment. Likewise the confiscation of tax dollars to redistribute to constituents is diametrically opposed to the 8th Commandment in Exodus 20:8:

> [15] "You shall not steal.

Matthew 26:11 states:

> [11] For you have the poor with you always, but Me you do not have always.

This statement by Jesus certainly implies that His primary mission was certainly not to eradicate poverty. The day after Jesus fed the five thousand he traveled to the other side of the Sea of Galilee. The crowds followed Him and asked Him a question. The question and His response is recorded in John 6:25-29:

> [25] And when they found Him on the other side of the sea, they said to Him, "Rabbi, when did You come here?" [26] Jesus answered them and said, "Most assuredly, I say to you, you seek Me, not because you saw the signs, but because you ate of the loaves and were filled. [27] Do not labor for the food which perishes, but for the food which endures to everlasting life, which the Son of Man will give you, because God the Father has set His seal on Him." [28] Then they said to Him, "What shall we do, that we may work the works of God?" [29] Jesus answered and said to them, "This is the work of God, that you believe in Him whom He sent."

Jesus again makes it clear that His primary mission is not to meet the physical needs of people. This time he was not going to feed the crowd again just because they were hungry. If that was His mission He certainly would have fed them again. His primary mission was to meet their spiritual needs. The next two texts confirm that Jesus was primarily concerned with spiritual needs not physical needs even when the physical need is staying alive. Matthew 10:28 states:

> [28] And do not fear those who kill the body but cannot kill the soul. But rather fear Him who is able to destroy both soul and body in hell.

Luke 13:1-5 states:

> There were present at that season some who told Him about the Galileans whose blood Pilate had mingled with their sacrifices. [2] And Jesus answered and said to them, "Do you suppose that these Galileans were worse sinners than all other Galileans, because they suffered such things? [3] I tell you, no; but unless you repent you will all likewise perish. [4] Or those eighteen on whom the tower in Siloam fell and killed them, do you think that they were worse sinners than all other men who dwelt in Jerusalem? [5] I tell you, no; but unless you repent you will all likewise perish."

Again Jesus was not as concerned about people dying unexpectedly and tragically, but about people repenting of their sin so their ultimate fate will not be to parish.

Matthew 25:14-30 tells the Parable of the Talents. The summary of the parable is stated in verses 28 & 29:

> ²⁸ Therefore take the talent from him, and give it to him who has ten talents. ²⁹ 'For to everyone who has, more will be given, and he will have abundance; but from him who does not have, even what he has will be taken away.

Jesus words are diametrically opposed to the liberal / progressive social justice doctrine. Jesus does not believe in equal outcome. Matthew 25:31-34 & 41 state the following:

> ³¹ "When the Son of Man comes in His glory, and all the holy[a] angels with Him, then He will sit on the throne of His glory. ³² All the nations will be gathered before Him, and He will separate them one from another, as a shepherd divides his sheep from the goats. ³³ And He will set the sheep on His right hand, but the goats on the left. ³⁴ Then the King will say to those on His right hand, 'Come, you blessed of My Father, inherit the kingdom prepared for you from the foundation of the world: . . .
>
> ⁴¹ "Then He will also say to those on the left hand, 'Depart from Me, you cursed, into the everlasting fire prepared for the devil and his angels:

The bible leaves no doubt that God does not believe in equal outcome! There is no question that the bible does speak much about helping the poor and being charitable. We certainly support everything the bible teaches on those subjects. The primary distinction between those admonitions and the application of Social Justice and equal outcome is that charity is always voluntary and Social Justice is always coerced. Doing "good" with someone else's money is actually doing harm.

Claims that the bible supports Social Justice

The proponents of Social Justice ignore all the biblical evidence documented above. They cite five scripture texts that they claim support Social Justice. E. Calvin Beisner addresses those false claims below in an article titled *Social Justice: How Good Intentions Undermine Justice and Gospel*, which I cite extensively below with permission:[179]

> DOES THE BIBLE REQUIRE WEALTH REDISTRIBUTION AND EQUALIZATION?
>
> Jesus and the Rich Young Ruler
>
> Some readers claim that the Bible requires equalization through wealth redistribution and reject the Bible's authority for that very reason. Libertarian economist Robert Higgs, for instance, in listing proponents of communism, wrote, "Jesus told his disciples to sell all that they owned and give the proceeds to the poor."[180] A little more care-

ful reading of Jesus' words and their context (Luke 18:18–30) reveals, however, that Jesus did not tell His disciples to do that. He was speaking to a particular man—the rich young ruler. The ruler was full of pride and confident that he'd fulfilled God's commandments from his youth up, though really he had broken the very first by making his riches his god. This man had a particular problem, and Jesus prescribed a particular cure, one targeted directly at the problem. The prescription didn't apply to everyone.

In the very next chapter (Luke 19:1–10) we read that Jesus encountered another person, Zacchaeus. The tax collector was detested by his neighbors for cooperating with the oppressive Romans, a man who implicitly admitted that he'd overcharged some of his countrymen on their taxes to enrich himself. Zacchaeus came to Jesus humbly, confessing his sin, and announced his willingness to repent by repaying anyone he'd wronged and then giving half of the remainder to the poor. How did Jesus respond? By saying, "Oh, no, Zacchaeus, you must give *all* you have to the poor"? No. He said, "Today salvation has come to this house"—not, by the way, because Zacchaeus had bought his way into Heaven but "because he, too, is a son of Abraham," i.e., his actions manifested his faith in God's covenant with Abraham (Romans 4:9–17, 24–29; 9:1–9).

Contrary to Higgs, then, Jesus didn't tell His disciples to sell all they had and give everything to the poor.

But there are others who claim the Bible requires equality through at least periodic redistribution of wealth. Unlike Higgs, they profess to accept the Bible's authority. They claim to find support for wealth redistribution and equalization from four teachings in Scripture.

The Sabbatical Year Law

The first Biblical teaching to which Progressives appeal is the Mosaic law's requirement regarding debts in the Sabbatical year: "At the end of every seven years you must cancel debts" (Deuteronomy 15:1, niv). That seems pretty clear. Or is it? Another translation puts it differently: "At the end of every seven years you shall *grant a release*" (esv). Do they mean the same thing? More important, what does the underlying Hebrew mean?

The Hebrew translated *cancel* by the niv and *grant a release* by the esv is the verb *'asah*, meaning "to make" or "do," followed by the noun *shemittah*, "**a letting drop** of exactions, a (temporary) **remitting**."[181] The word *temporary* interests us. Was the "release" or "remitting" or "letting drop" of debts a cancellation—permanent? Or was it a suspension—temporary? For the Progressives' application to be correct, it must be permanent.

The noun *shemittah* occurs only four times in the Old Testament (Deuteronomy 15:1–2, 9; 31:10), all connected with this law, so OT usage won't answer the question. However, the noun comes from the verb *shamat*, "let drop, fall."[182] Both noun and verb occur in the next verse: "And this is the manner of the release (*shemittah*): every creditor shall release (*shamat*) what he has lent to his neighbor. He shall not exact it of his neighbor, his brother, because the Lord's release (*shemittah*) has been proclaimed" (Deuteronomy 15:2).

The earliest OT use of *shamat* is in Exodus 23, again regarding the Sabbatical year. But here it describes what to do not with debts but with land: "For six years you shall sow your land and gather in its yield, but the seventh year you shall let it rest and lie fallow" (Exodus 23:10–11). Were the Hebrews to abandon a particular plot of ground forever after the Sabbatical year? No, they were to "release" it during that year but resume cultivating it the next. The requirements to release land and debts in the Sabbatical year were analogous to the requirement of rest on the weekly Sabbath (Exodus 23:12). Just as people, refreshed by a weekly Sabbath, would return to work after it, so land would be cultivated again, and debtors would resume their payments.[183]

Thus in every instance in which *shamat* and *shemittah* occur regarding the Sabbatical year, they must be understood in the sense of a temporary, not a permanent, release. Indeed, Deuteronomy 15:3, "Of a foreigner you may exact it, but whatever *of yours* is with your brother your hand shall release (*shamat*)," makes it clear that what the creditor had loaned remained his even during the Sabbatical year—he simply couldn't collect payments during that year.

In short, the Sabbatical year debt-release law required not permanent cancellation but a year-long suspension of payments so debtors could be refreshed by resting in the Sabbatical year, but creditors would still be repaid.

The Jubilee Year Law

The second Biblical teaching to which Progressives appeal to justify wealth redistribution and equalization is the Jubilee (Leviticus 25).

When God brought Israel into the Promised Land, He divided the land among the tribes, providing each family a plot over which it became steward and that it should hand down to its descendants. However, economic inequalities would develop due to differences in diligence, intelligence, physical ability, soil quality, water supply, oppression, or natural tragedies. Except when they resulted from oppression, however, these were not unjust. But to preserve family unity and possession of land, as well as to restrain any one person from squandering all his descendants' wealth by contracting debts he could not pay, God gave Israel the Jubilee regulations.

According to these regulations, land in ancient Israel should not be sold permanently, because God asserted a special ownership of it beyond what He asserts over the whole earth (Leviticus 25:23). It could, however, be "sold" temporarily, its price constituting a loan for a term not to exceed the years to the next Jubilee. The price was the value of the intervening harvests (presumably excluding those during Sabbatical years, when land was not to be worked) (Leviticus 25:13–16), "for it is the number of the crops that he is selling to you" (verse 16). Income the buyer (lender) earned from the land during the term of the loan would constitute repayment, entailing return of the land at the end since the loan would have been repaid. Also, if the seller (borrower) offered to repay the loan *before* its term ended, the buyer (lender) had to accept the offer—the price again calculated by the value of harvests in the intervening years (Leviticus 25:25–28). The land, in other words, would have functioned as collateral. Similar arrangements were made regarding houses (Leviticus 25:26–34) and labor (verses 39–54).

Careful examination of the Jubilee year's regulations disproves claims that it required any redistribution or equalization of wealth. The regulations did not cancel or forgive any debt but ensured repayment and then return of collateral. Also, the regulations notably said nothing of newly created wealth. If one farmer produced far more per acre than another or gained riches through industry or trade, the Jubilee regulations didn't require any redistribution of that wealth or any equality of outcome between him and his neighbors.

Sharing of Goods in the Jerusalem Church

Progressives may try to justify redistribution and equalization by appealing to the so-called "community of goods" practiced by the early Christians in Jerusalem. Acts 2:44–45 and 4:34–35 tell us believers "had all things in common" and "were selling their possessions and belongings and distributing the proceeds to all, as any had need." In this Christian community, "no one said that any of the things that belonged to him was his own, but they had everything in common."

One evangelical writer goes so far as to say that because of this "private property was an impossibility."[184] A liberation theologian comments that here Luke insists on "the universality of communism," adding, "If [people] wanted to be Christians, the condition was communism."[185]

But these claims ignore some important facts.

First, the giving was always voluntary, as another incident Luke records shows. When Ananias and Sapphira sold land and laid *part* of the price at Peter's feet but alleged that they had given *all* of it, Peter responded, "Ananias, why has Satan filled your heart to lie to the Holy Spirit and to keep back for yourself part of the proceeds of the land? While it remained unsold, did it not remain your own? And after it was sold, was it not at your disposal?" (Acts 5:3–4) Peter rebuked the couple—not for holding back their resources, but for lying.

Second, the selling and giving occurred periodically in response to specific needs, not all at once, as would have been required if redistribution and equalization were the goal. How do we know? Because Luke writes not that the Christians "sold their possessions and distributed the proceeds" but that they "were selling . . . and distributing." This translates Greek verbs in the imperfect tense, which denotes an action that began in the past *and continued*. People sold bits and pieces of their property from time to time, turning over the proceeds as need arose.

Third, Luke says "no one said that any of the things that belonged to him was his own." He does not say "everyone said that whatever belonged to anyone belonged to everyone." Luke's point is not about private property, protected by the Eighth Commandment—"Thou shalt not steal." Rather than abolishing private property, the Christians considered that what belonged to them (note the affirmation of ownership) was entrusted to them by God to serve their fellow Christians. When a Spanish speaker says, "*Mi casa es su casa*," he doesn't mean to deny title but to welcome you hospitably to his home. This was the Christians' attitude in Jerusalem—and it should be ours.

The Pauline Collections: "That There Might Be Equality"

The fourth Biblical teaching in question is what Paul writes of benevolence—the goal of the collections he took up from churches around the Mediterranean to relieve believers suffering famine in Jerusalem. The *New International Version* translates 2 Corinthians 8:13–14 thus: "Our desire is not that others might be relieved while you are hard pressed, but that there might be equality. At the present time your plenty will supply what they need, so that in turn their plenty will supply what you need. Then there will be equality."

If the other passages we've examined don't prove that Scripture requires economic equality, surely *this* one does! Indeed, Ronald J. Sider wrote that this passage "clearly shows that Paul enunciates the principle of economic equality among the people of God."[186]

Is this interpretation warranted? You decide. If Paul meant economic equality, then his saying "that ... your abundance at the present time should supply their need, so that their abundance may supply your need" would imply that the Corinthians should give materially to the believers in Jerusalem now *so that* when the positions were reversed those in Jerusalem could give to them. Is that consistent with Jesus' saying in Luke 6:27–35 that we should give with no expectation of receiving anything in return? Does it fit with the motives Paul said should underlie the giving—grace, joy, generosity, and love (2 Corinthians 8:1–9)?

What then did Paul mean? By writing "in the present time" and using verbs the tense of which implies instantaneous action, Paul emphasized the immediate effect of the Corinthians' giving—that their abundance would fill the Jerusalem saints' lack. In turn, the Jerusalem saints' abundance would fill the Corinthians' lack. There would be immediate and simultaneous equality. That is, Paul intended no hint that the Corinthians should give *now* so that their brothers and sisters in Jerusalem might give *later* so that *then* there might be equality. On the contrary, the instant the Corinthians gave, the Jerusalem saints' lack would be supplied out of the Corinthians' abundance, *and* the Corinthians' lack would be supplied out of the Jerusalem believers' abundance, *and* there would be equality.

But what was the Jerusalemites' abundance? And what was the Corinthians' lack? It seems at first as if the Corinthians have all the abundance and those in Jerusalem all the lack. Yet Paul insists that the Corinthians have both an abundance and a lack, *now*. Similarly, the saints in Jerusalem have both a lack and abundance, *now*. But at the moment the Corinthians give from their abundance to fill the Jerusalemites' lack, the Jerusalemites' abundance will meet the Corinthians' lack. How can that be?

The key is what Paul has observed among the Corinthians: a tendency to boast of a generosity they had not yet exercised. Paul wants them to prove the love of which they have boasted (verse 8). They had begun the collection a year before, but they had not finished it (verse 10). Now they need to complete it, so that their "readiness in desiring it may be matched by [their] completing it" (verse 11). "So give proof before the churches of your love and of our boasting about you," Paul tells them in conclusion (verse 24).

What the Corinthians lack is the fulfillment of their promise and desire to give generously; the moment they do so, their lack will be met, and so will be the financial lack of those in Jerusalem. What the saints in Jerusalem have in abundance is precisely their material lack—and the moment that is filled up by the Corinthians' giving, so will be the lack of those in Corinth.

And that will be the equality achieved—an equality in which a material lack becomes a material abundance and a spiritual lack becomes a spiritual abundance.[187]

The Bible Does Not Demand Wealth Redistribution or Equalization

Progressives most commonly appeal to the five passages reviewed above as proof that Christianity warrants redistribution or equalization of wealth. None does so. Yet many people still insist that the basic Biblical principle of justice does require redistribution. Does it?

Defining Justice Biblically

What do the Biblical words related to justice mean?[188] In the Old Testament, the key vocabulary falls into three groups: The first root "basically connotes conformity to an ethical or moral standard" defined by the nature and will of God and revealed in His law.[189] (The adjective form is *tsaddiq*, the nouns are *tsedaqah* and *tsedeq*, and the verb is *tsadeq*). The second root denotes "exercise [of] the processes of government,"[190] the root of which "basically connotes conformity to an ethical or moral standard" defined by the nature and will of God and revealed in His law.[191] (Here, the verb form is *shaphat* and the nouns are *shephet, shepot*, and *mishpat*). The third root "embodies the idea of government, in whatever realm, in all its aspects."[192] (The verb form is *din*, and the nouns are *din* and *dayyan*).

In the New Testament, the key vocabulary falls into two groups. The first root means "being in accordance with high standards of rectitude, *upright, just, fair*."[193] (Its noun forms are *dike⁻* and *dikaiosune⁻*, the adjective *dikaios*, and the verb *dikaioo⁻*). The second denotes "legal process of judgment" or "administration of what is right and fair, *right in the sense of justice/righteousness*."[194] (Its verb form is *krino⁻*, and the nouns are *krima* and *krisis*).

Careful study of these words throughout the Old and New Testaments leads me to summarize the Biblical concept of justice as *rendering impartially and proportionally to everyone his due in accord with the righteous standard of God's moral law.*[195]

Four Criteria of Justice

The Bible reveals four criteria of justice. First, justice requires *impartiality*, an equal application of all relevant rules to all people in all relevant situations. When Moses commissioned the judges of Israel, he charged them, "*Hear the cases* [*shaphat*, "judge"] *between your brethren, and judge* [*shaphat*] *righteously* [*tsedeq*] *between a man and his brother or the stranger who is with him. You shall not show partiality in judgment* [*mishpat*]; *you shall hear the small as well as the great; you shall not be afraid in any man's presence, for the judgment* [*mishpat*] *is God's*" (Deuteronomy 1:16–17). Just judgment, then, is always impartial.[196]

Second, justice requires *rendering to each his due*. Paul instructs believers to "render … to all their due" (Romans 13:7), and he puts this instruction in a discussion of justice or "judgment" (v. 2, "judgment" is *kríma*). Again, God is the chief exemplar: "… will He not render to each man according to his deeds?" (Proverbs 24:12; cf. Matthew 16:27; Romans 2:6; 1 Corinthians 3:8; Galatians 6:7–8). A key concept in justice, then, is that *something about the person being judged merits (or earns) the judgment*. Sometimes the "what is due" is determined by *who someone is*. Examples include governing authorities (Romans 13:1–7, 1 Peter 2:13–14); parents (Ephesians 6:1–3, Colossians 3:20,

Deuteronomy 5:16) and religious leaders (Hebrews 13:17, Acts 23:1–5). Sometimes, however, what is due is determined by *what someone does*. Elders are due double honor if they rule well (1 Timothy 5:17). The proud are due punishment (Psalm 94:2). Murderers deserve death (Genesis 9:6). The case laws of Exodus 21–22 detail what is due in crimes and torts against persons and property, all as matters of justice or judgment: "Now these are the *judgments* [*mishpat*] which you shall set before them" (Exodus 21:1).

Third, justice requires *proportionality*, symmetry between the initial acts, on the one hand, and the rewards or punishments, on the other. This principle appears in Scripture in two ways. First, proportionality distinguishes generally between violations of *property* and violations of *persons*. There are different kinds and degrees of punishment prescribed for the two (Leviticus 24:17–21). Second, proportionality distinguishes accidental harm, negligent harm, and intentional harm. For instance, if someone *accidentally* damages or destroys his neighbor's property, justice evens up the loss between them (Exodus 21:35). But if he might reasonably have foreseen and prevented the accident but did not, and so harms his neighbor *negligently*, he must bear the full loss alone and restore to his neighbor the full value of what was damaged or destroyed (Exodus 21:36; compare Exodus 22:6). And if he *intentionally* steals or destroys his neighbor's property, he must restore what is taken, plus some multiple of it, as punishment (Exodus 22:1). Similarly, *accidental* homicide deserves no punishment (Deuteronomy 19:4–6; Exodus 21:13); *negligent* homicide deserves death, but the heirs of the deceased (or possibly the judges) may permit a ransom (Exodus 21:29–30). However, the *intentional* murderer must be executed without pity (Deuteronomy 19:11–13; Exodus 21:14), no ransom being permitted (Numbers 35:31; see also Deuteronomy 25:1–3; Exodus 21:24–27; Leviticus 24:19–20; Luke 12:42–48).

Fourth, justice requires *conformity to the standard* set forth in God's law—summarized in the Ten Commandments but also in the many moral statutes, ordinances, and case laws that apply the Ten Commandments and make them more specific.

In this respect, justice (or righteousness) is closely akin to truthfulness and honesty. Thus, for instance, God commanded Israel, "You shall do no injustice in judgment, in measurement of length, weight, or volume. You shall have honest scales [literally, "scales of *righteousness*"] honest weights, an honest ephah, and an honest hin" (Leviticus 19:35–36; compare Deuteronomy 25:13–16). Measures of length, weight, and volume must be just, must accord with an unchanging standard. Differing weights and measures enabled buyers and sellers to defraud each other. Through the prophet Micah, God addressed these precise unjust trading practices when He said that His people must "do justly"

(Micah 6:8). How do we know? He went on to say, "Are there yet the treasures of wickedness in the house of the wicked, and the *short measure* that is an abomination? Shall I count pure those with the *wicked scales*, and with the bag of *deceitful weights*?" (Micah 6:10–11). Another means of injustice in trading was to dilute the purity of the goods (including gold or silver coin or bullion used as money) offered in trade, a practice God condemned and used as a metaphor for the wickedness of rebellious hearts (Isaiah 1:21–26; Ezekiel 22:17–22). Counterfeiting and inflationary monetary policy both violate this principle.

Justice and Rights

The four criteria of justice—impartiality, rendering what is due, proportionality, and conformity with the standard of God's law—imply that people have rights. These rights are implicit in the laws that are the standard of justice, most importantly the Ten Commandments. Consider those commandments with their obvious economic applications. The Fourth Commandment is "Remember the Sabbath day, to keep it holy. Six days you shall labor, and do all your work, but the seventh day is a Sabbath to the Lord your God. On it you shall not do any work, you, or your son, or your daughter, your male servant, or your female servant, or your livestock, or the sojourner who is within your gates …" This implies that people have a duty to rest one day in seven and therefore a right not to be forced to work every day. The Eighth, "You shall not steal," implies that people have a duty to respect others' property and a right not to have their property taken or harmed without just cause. The Ninth, "You shall not bear false witness," implies that people have a duty not to lie or to defame their neighbors and a right not to be lied to or defamed. And the Tenth, "You shall not covet," implies that people have a duty to respect whatever belongs to others and a right not to be envied or condemned for having what others don't.

Negative and Positive Rights

An important question is whether God's law, the standard of justice and the basis of rights, entails both *negative* rights—rights against harm—and *positive* rights—rights to certain benefits. Does my right not to be murdered, for example, mean I have a right to life? Does my right not to have my property stolen mean I have a right to food?

It's easy to let common usage confuse us. Of course I have a *right to life*. Nobody should murder me! We even have a whole political movement called the "right to life" movement—and I would be the last person on Earth to oppose that movement's goal of making abortion illegal except to save the life of the mother.

But consider this question: Does a murderer still have a right to life, or has he forfeited it? Since God's law says a murderer is to be executed

(Genesis 9:6; Exodus 21:12, 14; Romans 13:4), it follows that one's right to life is limited. It can be forfeited. Or consider another question: Does a person who refuses to work have a right to food? If the food is his property, undoubtedly he has a right to it, since the Eighth Commandment says, "You shall not steal." But what if he owns no food? Does he still have a right to food? What does Scripture say? "If anyone is not willing to work, let him not eat" (2 Thessalonians 3:10). Or yet another question: Does the owner of a luxury sailboat have a right to it? Well, yes; since we've already defined him as the *owner*, the Eighth Commandment entails that he has a right to it. But does he have a right for others to give it to him and maintain it for him? Now perhaps it becomes easier to see what we really mean by "right to it." We mean he has a right *not to have it stolen*.

That is what I think we really mean by "right to life" and "right to food," and indeed properly by any assertion of a "right to" anything. We have the right *against* having it taken or destroyed without just cause. My right to a good name means I have a right not to be defamed by false or injurious language—but it doesn't mean I have a right to be called honest if I'm a liar, or hard-working if I'm lazy. My right to a car means I have a right not to have my car stolen; it doesn't mean I have a right to any car without paying for it. My right to life means I have a right not to be murdered or assaulted, but it doesn't mean I have a right to have someone else ensure that all the conditions of my survival are met.

Properly understood, rights are not guarantees that something will be *provided for us* but guarantees that what is ours will not be unjustly *taken from us*. That is, properly speaking, rights are not *positive* but *negative*.

Why?

First, because there's no objective, universal, unchanging standard by which to determine how much of any given benefit everyone has a right to. Since justice requires impartiality, proportionality, and conformity to the standard of God's law, rights must be the same and unchanging for everyone. If everyone has a right to food, how many calories per day, and of what composition (meat, vegetables, grains, dairy products, fish) and quality does everyone have a right to? Does the 30-pound three-year-old have a right to the same food as the 200-pound thirty-year-old farm laborer? If everyone has a right to shelter, of what size and quality and in what location must it be? Is it even possible for two persons to have a right to shelter in the same location? But since, as every realtor knows, the fundamental rule of home value is "location, location, location," how can two people both have the same right to shelter if they can't both have it in the same spot?

> Second, this reasoning points toward another problem with positive rights. The assertion of positive rights necessarily entails the violation of negative rights, while the assertion of negative rights doesn't. If someone has a positive right to food but refuses to work for it, his "right" can be supplied only by taking food from someone else who has worked for it—i.e., from someone to whom it properly belongs. Such a "right" violates the Eighth Commandment. . . .
>
> Progressive social justice violates negative rights and Biblical criteria for justice in order to give positive rights as the government tries to mitigate such inequalities. To raise Charles's opportunities or outcomes relative to Elizabeth's, the government must treat Charles and Elizabeth differently—taking from her, in order to benefit him. That different treatment is precisely what is forbidden by the Biblical principle of impartiality. Taking from Elizabeth violates her right against unjust taking (i.e. theft) of her property.[197]

Consequently, we can clearly see that there is nothing just and nothing biblical about Social Justice. Again, it is diametrically opposed to what is just and biblical. Since "Social Justice" has been made legitimate by our culture, it is a stealth evil. For additional information on Social Justice order E. Calvin Beisner's 29 page book.[198]

We have shown that with all fifteen stealth evils listed that they indeed are stealth evils. Although each one is thought of as being a good thing, they are all supported by a foundation of lies and all have bad effects on society. They also are held up as good to satisfy individual selfish desires for escaping responsibility or gaining power or position. That is why we need to recognize them as evil and resist the promotion of them in our society.

Next we will look at the source of diametrically opposite worldviews and illegitimate control of America as a reason that evil has progressed so rapidly in America.

CHAPTER 25
Source of diametrically opposite worldviews and control of America

Starting in heaven, continuing in the Garden of Eden and since then the goal of Lucifer and later fallen man has been to control and rule mankind on earth so the leader(s) can become powerful, be recognized as god(s), and be worshiped. To accomplish this goal, they must rebel against the legitimate and just reign of God by discrediting and subverting truth, justice and liberty using the only bag of tricks that Satan and his followers have available. These include demonization, deception, lies, censorship, coercion, false accusations and pleasant sounding euphemisms. Satan also uses sexual perversion and self-destructive habits to entrap mankind and prevent them from accepting God's word and the truth. Since what they are doing is not truly legitimate or just (as in justice), it has to be done by a stealth modus operandi until they have the power and control in place to counter resistance to their evil plan. This stealth evil comes to a head at the end of the present age when Satan and his chosen protégé believe that they finally have the world under their control and evil grasp and consequently they no longer have to operate by stealth.

Near the end of the age, the bible speaks of the antichrist and the beast having dominion over the earth and being worshiped along with Satan who gave them his authority. Revelation 13:1-8 states:

> Then I stood on the sand of the sea. And I saw a beast rising up out of the sea, having seven heads and ten horns, and on his horns ten crowns, and on his heads a blasphemous name. [2] Now the beast which I saw was like a leopard, his feet were like the feet of a bear, and his mouth like the mouth of a lion. The dragon gave him his power, his throne, and great authority. [3] And I saw one of his heads as if it had been mortally wounded, and his deadly wound was healed. And all the world marveled and followed the beast. [4] So they worshiped the dragon who gave authority to the beast; and they worshiped the beast, saying, "Who is like the beast? Who is able to make war with him?" [5] And he was given a mouth speaking great things and blasphemies, and he was given authority to continue for forty-two months. [6] Then he opened his mouth in blasphemy against God, to blaspheme His name, His tabernacle, and those who dwell in heaven. [7] It was granted to him to make war with the saints and to overcome them. And authority was given him over every tribe, tongue, and nation. [8] All who dwell on the

earth will worship him, whose names have not been written in the Book of Life of the Lamb slain from the foundation of the world.

Lucifer couldn't use stealth in relationship to God since a God that knows everything can't be deceived or tricked. However, Satan must have used stealth to get a third of the angels to rebel against a legitimate and just God. However, to get mankind to unite with him and his evil, rebellious philosophy that is diametrically opposed to God, his character and justice, he has to operate by stealth, otherwise he would have few followers. This chapter is about exposing this evil goal for mankind and the modus operandi used to subvert mankind using evil stealth strategies and tactics.

It is not obvious or easy to understand why mankind appears to be in the center of the controversy we would think is just between God and Satan. In fact, it would be impossible to understand without studying what is revealed in the scriptures. However, it does becomes obvious and gives us insight that we are in the center of the controversy once we understand the scriptures.

First we are told that, unlike animals, man was created in the image of God. The bible teaches that things done to help people in need or conversely to injure or murder people is something that God sees as for or against Him. Jesus explained to those that will inherit God's kingdom, the reason why they were chosen. Jesus said in Matthew 25:35-40:

> [35] for I was hungry and you gave Me food; I was thirsty and you gave Me drink; I was a stranger and you took Me in; [36] I was naked and you clothed Me; I was sick and you visited Me; I was in prison and you came to Me.' [37] "Then the righteous will answer Him, saying, 'Lord, when did we see You hungry and feed You, or thirsty and give You drink? [38] When did we see You a stranger and take You in, or naked and clothe You? [39] Or when did we see You sick, or in prison, and come to You?' [40] And the King will answer and say to them, 'Assuredly, I say to you, inasmuch as you did it to one of the least of these My brethren, you did it to Me.'

This supports that we are so intertwined with God and His plan for us that when we do good things for people made in His image, we are doing those things to Jesus. The scriptures paint the same picture for those that do things against people, particularly against Christian believers. The story of Saul, who later became Paul the apostle to the Gentiles, is told in Acts 9:1-5:

> Then Saul, still breathing threats and murder against the disciples of the Lord, went to the high priest [2] and asked letters from him to the synagogues of Damascus, so that if he found any who were of the Way, whether men or women, he might bring them bound to Jerusalem. [3] As he journeyed he came near Damascus, and suddenly a light shone around him from heaven. [4] Then he fell to the ground, and heard a voice saying to him, "Saul, Saul, why are you persecuting Me?"

> ⁵ And he said, "Who are You, Lord?" Then the Lord said, "I am Jesus, whom you are persecuting. It is hard for you to kick against the goads."

Two more examples in scripture that show mankind is in the middle of the controversy between God and Satan is found in Job. The first story is in Chapter 1 verses 8-12:

> ⁸ Then the LORD said to Satan, "Have you considered My servant Job, that there is none like him on the earth, a blameless and upright man, one who fears God and shuns evil?" ⁹ So Satan answered the LORD and said, "Does Job fear God for nothing? ¹⁰ Have You not made a hedge around him, around his household, and around all that he has on every side? You have blessed the work of his hands, and his possessions have increased in the land. ¹¹ But now, stretch out Your hand and touch all that he has, and he will surely curse You to Your face!" ¹² And the LORD said to Satan, "Behold, all that he has is in your power; only do not lay a hand on his person." So Satan went out from the presence of the LORD.

It goes on to tell how Satan through raiders stole some of his animals and killed some of his servants and then fire from heaven burned up his sheep and servants and then all his children were killed in a house that collapsed from a sudden wind in verses 13-19. As a result Job did not sin or charge God with wrong (verses 20-22). A second encounter between God and Satan is told in Chapter 2:3-10 below:

> ³ Then the LORD said to Satan, "Have you considered My servant Job, that there is none like him on the earth, a blameless and upright man, one who fears God and shuns evil? And still he holds fast to his integrity, although you incited Me against him, to destroy him without cause." ⁴ So Satan answered the LORD and said, "Skin for skin! Yes, all that a man has he will give for his life. ⁵ But stretch out Your hand now, and touch his bone and his flesh, and he will surely curse You to Your face!" ⁶ And the LORD said to Satan, "Behold, he is in your hand, but spare his life." ⁷ So Satan went out from the presence of the LORD, and struck Job with painful boils from the sole of his foot to the crown of his head. ⁸ And he took for himself a potsherd with which to scrape himself while he sat in the midst of the ashes. ⁹ Then his wife said to him, "Do you still hold fast to your integrity? Curse God and die!" ¹⁰ But he said to her, "You speak as one of the foolish women speaks. Shall we indeed accept good from God, and shall we not accept adversity?" In all this Job did not sin with his lips.

These verses not only verify that man is in the center of the controversy between God and Satan but hint that there is a debate over the justice of God and mankind worshiping God. The battle over the justice of God and whether God or Satan deserves the worship of mankind started in heaven when Lucifer rebelled against God and continued in the Garden of Eden when mankind got in the center of the debate. In the Garden of Eden and ever since then Satan has strived to disrupt God's plan to have an intimate relationship with mankind. We mentioned in Chapter 1 the first prophecy in the bible that that predicted that a Messiah would come in the lineage of mankind to redeem fallen mankind. Some specific things that Satan has done to prevent God's plan from coming into fruition are included in the table below:

Satan's Action Taken	Desired Effect	Scripture Reverence
Tempted Eve and Adam to disobey the only thing that God required of them	That disobedience separated people from God going forward until Jesus sacrifice made provision to unite that relationship again. In addition, all creation was cursed causing both spiritual death and ultimately physical death and changing a perfect world into cursed world.	Genesis 3
Had Cane kill his brother Abel	Eliminate bloodline planned for the Messiah or to keep "the seed of woman" from coming into the world	Genesis 4:8 & 25
Corrupted mankind with offspring from fallen angels	To prevent mankind from following and worshiping God. Ultimately to grieve God and make Him sorry that He created mankind and corrupt any bloodline for the Messiah.	Genesis 6:1-6
The ultimate possibility of corrupting the "seed of woman" forced God to take drastic action to prevent Satan from defeating his ultimate plan for mankind. This resulted in the Worldwide	Destroy the evil that was destroying the relationship between God and mankind	Genesis 6:7

flood of Noah.		
*To corrupt mankind through urban global government, a one world occultist religion and an evil leader, Nimrod.	To get everybody to worship a false religion instead of worshiping God and establish a model for false religions. See paragraph heading below titled "Counterfeit mother / child system" that shows how what was established at Babel is the counterfeit model that infected the Gentile nations with a spiritual virus.	Genesis 10:8-12 & 11:1-9
**Abram (Abraham) and his progeny were called by God to represent Him on earth as light in a pagan Gentile world	God used Abraham's progeny to represent Him on earth and continue the bloodline to lead to the Messiah	Genesis 12:1-9, Chapters 15-17
After Joseph and his brothers died and a new Pharaoh arose to power he asked the midwives to kill all the baby boys because he was worried that the Israelites were getting too populous and strong. They wouldn't do it. So he made them slaves.	To prevent and destroy the bloodline of the Messiah and to weaken them and prevent them from entering the promise land, Israel.	Exodus 1:6-19
When the above plan failed, the Pharaoh commanded that every Hebrew boy born should be cast into the river.	Satan wanted to weaken God's chosen people and kill their future deliver, Moses.	Exodus 1:22
When Jesus the Messiah was born in Bethlehem and King Herod learned of it from the wise men	Satan knew the Old Testament prophecy that out of Bethlehem shall come a ruler that will	Matthew 2:1-18

he decreed that all male children two years old and younger should be killed in the area where Jesus was born.	shepherd my people, Israel. Satan tried to kill the promised Messiah, Jesus.	
Satan tempts Jesus at the start of His ministry and after he was in a weakened condition from fasting for 40 days. The third one was that Satan would give Jesus all the kingdoms of the world if He would just bow down and worship him.	If Jesus yielded Satan would have his victory since Jesus (God) would be worshipping Satan rather that Satan worshipping God	Matthew 4:1-11.
Satan guided the religious leaders to kill Jesus since His true religion was outshining their largely man-made religion.	When they crucified Jesus Satan thought he finally had destroyed God's plan; however, he didn't know that God can use evil to do His ultimate good. Rather than destroy God's plan Jesus' death and resurrection fulfilled it.	Narrative toward the end of each of the four gospels

***Counterfeit mother / child system:**

In addition to Nimrod's government becoming the model for global government, his wife, Semiramis, set up the model for the world's false religions. Marvin Rosenthal tells that story in his Zion's Fire "The War of the Ages" magazine and an article with the same title as follows:[199] Article is quoted with permission.

> The wife of Nimrod according to ancient tradition, was Semiramis. She became known as the "Queen of Heaven." The reason for the title becomes obvious in the next paragraph. It was her image, with a dove upon her head and wings outstretched like the horns of the moon which became the *sem* or sign of the defiance of God and banner of Babylonianism.
>
> Nimrod, after death, supposedly ascended to the heavens and united with the sun. Semiramis was said to have been miraculously impregnated by a sunbeam from her dead husband Nimrod. It was said that

the sunbeam carried Nimrod's sperm from the sun to his wife. And Semiramis, now known as the Queen of Heaven gave birth to a son and called him Tammuz. (This was a counter virgin birth.) Tammuz grew to manhood and while out hunting was killed by a wild boar. Semiramis, it was said, wept for her son for 40 days (the source of the observance of Lent), and he came to life again (a counterfeit resurrection). Tammuz because of his supposed, resurrection, was viewed as both the son of Nimrod and as Nimrod himself. This attempt to deify Tammuz as Nimrod should not surprise us. Jesus is the Son of God, but He is also God in the flesh. Nimrod is said to be the father of Tammuz and also Tammuz himself.

Thus began a counterfeit religious system which strove for the affections of men. A harlot – no – more than a harlot – Babylonianism became the mother of harlots. All of it centered on the worship of a counterfeit mother-son religious system. No wonder in the last book of the Bible this system is called "Mystery, Babylon the Great, the Mother of Harlots and Abominations of the Earth" (Revelation 17:5).

I feel confident in stating that all false religion, by whatever name it is called, has its origin in Babylon with Nimrod, his wife Semiramis, and their son Tammuz.[200]

The following table is presented as evidence of the above assertion:[201]

Mother	Son	Father
Semiramis	Tammuz	Nimrod
Mother	Son	Nation
Isis	Osiris	Egypt
Ishtar	Bacchus	Assyria
Isi	Iswara	India
Cybele	Deoius	Asia
Aphrodite	Eros	Greece
Venus	Cupid	Rome

The article goes on to state:

> The language, names, and countries change, but it is always the pagan mother and son. All false religions of every kind had their origin in Babylon. Semiramis is "the mother of harlots." She entices man away from the worship of the true and living God and into intimacy with false gods. It is spiritual adultery. Do not think for a moment that this is fanciful and outside the bounds of scripture.[202]

**God's action taken rather than Satan's

Consequently, we can see in biblical history that the battle between God and Satan has raged with the ultimate coming of the Messiah and His relationship with mankind at the center of the controversy. Now we will switch to more recent history including our country, America, and track the battle between a Godly worldview and Satan's diametrically opposite worldview. Michael S. Coffman, PhD. traces the history all the way back to Greece before Christ, but primarily during the last 230 years. These extensive quotes are quoted with permission. Dr. Coffman states:

> Progressivism now dominates almost every political, educational and judicial institution in America. Progressives are proud of their self-appointed superior intellect— to the point of arrogance. But where did it originate and why is it seemingly always associated with big government, strife and confrontation? To understand this, a brief discussion of the founding roots of America must be compared to the radically different roots of the progressive movement that is now threatening to destroy the greatest nation in the history of mankind. It is necessary because America's history, especially its founding principles, has been revised, even erased from the history books used in public schools.
>
> Although these two major worldviews can be traced back to Aristotle (384-322 B.C.) and Plato (428-347 B.C.), America is now engaged in a war between two philosophies that have been struggling for supremacy for the past 230 years; those of English philosopher John Locke and French philosopher Jean Jacques Rousseau.[203]

Dr. Coffman continues explaining how the philosophies of Locke and Rousseau relate to England and America and the rest of the world:

> America's Declaration of Independence and Constitution are rooted in the thoughts of John Locke (1632-1704), whose Two Treatises on Government (1689) provided a framework for England's Glorious Revolution of 1688 and the American Revolution of 1776. This political philosophy, with its basis in individual rights and individual sovereignty, has been under attack in America for nearly two centuries by the ideology of Jean-Jacques Rousseau (1712-1778) and his Social Contract (1762).
>
> The Social Contract focuses on an abstract "general will" of the people and forced state control.[204] Today the general will is called the "public good" and forms the heart of socialism and communism. It depends on a "statist" approach to government in which the all-powerful state is sovereign over the individual and all individual rights come from the state. It is the exact opposite of the form of government given to Americans by the Constitution. Tragically, it is also a history filled with unbelievable bloodshed and carnage.[205]

PROPERTY RIGHTS AND LIBERTY

The bible relates property with liberty in the sense that the bible supports property rights and supports liberty and justice. Corinthians 3:17 states: Now the Lord is the Spirit; and where the Spirit of the Lord is, there is liberty. Dr. Coffman describes how John Locke and Sir William Blackstone also relate property ownership with liberty and freedom below:

> All men are created with equal opportunity and no person has a right to suborn the rights of another by denying that person their natural rights— rights to what Locke terms "life, liberty and estate." These rights do not derive from government, according to Locke, but are God-given natural rights inherent to all men. Thus, these rights have existed before government. Sir William Blackstone (1723 -1780), who established the first law school and wrote the first legal dictionary, and others refined these ideas until Thomas Jefferson made them the cornerstone of the Declaration of Independence, which, Jefferson claimed, is based entirely on the "Laws of Nature and of Nature's God.". .
>
> If Locke, Blackstone and our Founders are right, then a nation must fail if it begins to deviate from God's law to man's law. I submit to the reader, isn't that exactly what is happening in Europe and the U.S. right now? As we shall see, we have abandoned God's law that gave us freedom and adopted man's law that is stripping away our once-guaranteed freedoms one by one; all justified in what seem to be good ideas.[206]

Dr. Coffman continues:

> Our nation is founded on the belief in God, regardless of all the convoluted efforts by the progressives to convince Americans otherwise. The belief in God primarily rested in Judeo-Christian beliefs. John Adams warned in a letter in 1798, nine years after the start of the French Revolution; . . .
>
>> Because we have no government, armed with power, capable of contending with human passions, unbridled by morality and religion. Avarice, ambition, revenge and licentiousness would break the strongest cords of our Constitution, as a whale goes through a net. Our Constitution was made only for a moral and religious people. It is wholly inadequate to the government of any other.[207] . . .
>
> Other letters by Adams at the time he wrote the above letter, strongly suggest he was referring to the horror of the French Revolution that wiped out Christianity in France. Adams claimed that without the moral framework of Christianity, society would devolve into the same morass as led to the French Revolution. Many other Founders and writers at the time were equally as adamant as John Adams. Tragically, his warning is now coming true even in America where citizen is pitted

against citizen and there is rioting in the streets. The foundation for the Declaration of Independence and Constitution is foreign to most progressive liberals and neocons. Like Rousseau, most progressives at best have only a "form of religion"[208] devoid of a living God acting in humanity's lives. If they don't believe in God, how can they accept that there is a God-given natural law that yields natural rights that no man can abridge? They can't. Progressive liberals believe man is the final arbiter of right and wrong. Therefore government is the grantor of civil rights as well as economic well-being. Progressive liberals call these positive rights. There is one fatal flaw, however. These rights are not unalienable. What the government giveth, the government can taketh away.[209]

Dr. Coffman goes on to discuss the purpose of government:
Locke then goes on to say the purpose of government is to join with others to "unite, for the mutual preservation of their lives, liberties and estate, which I call by the general name, property. The great and chief end, therefore, of men uniting into commonwealths, and putting themselves under government, is the preservation of their property."[210] . .

Conversely, progressives believe, as did Rousseau, property rights are evil and had to be controlled by the state. So, who is right and why are property rights so important?

In their book, Property Rights, constitutional attorneys Nancie and Roger Marzulla explain: "The Constitution places such a strong emphasis on protecting private property rights because the right to own and use property was historically understood to be critical to the maintenance of a free society."[211] The Marzullas continue by saying that property is more than just land. It includes buildings, contracts, money, retirement funds, savings accounts, machines and even ideas. "In short," say the Marzullas, "property is the fruit of one's labor. The ability to use, enjoy, and exclusively possess the fruits of one's own labor is the basis for a society in which individuals are free from oppression."[212] The U.S. Supreme Court agrees. In Lynch v Household Finance Corporation (1972), the Court ruled:

[T]he dichotomy between personal liberties and property rights is a false one. Property does not have rights. People have rights. The right to enjoy property without unlawful deprivation, no less than the right to speak or the right to travel, is in truth, a 'personal' right, whether the 'property' in question be a welfare check, a home, or a savings account. In fact, a fundamental interdependence exists between the personal right to liberty and the personal right in property. Neither could have meaning without the other.[213]

JEAN JACQUES ROUSSEAU WORLDVIEW

Dr. Coffman continues with his explanation of Rousseau's godless model of state control:

> IN CONTRAST TO THE LOCKE MODEL, various forms of the statist approach have dominated the governments of almost every nation for millennia. In more recent history Rousseau provided the foundational philosophy that spawned the incredibly bloody French Revolution as well as inspiring the writings of Immanuel Kant, Georg W. F. Hegel, Karl Marx[214] and many others. Rousseau also planted the seeds in America for the European model of socialism and Russian communism. It is based on government control of everything.
>
> Rousseau based much of his philosophy on the writings of Englishman Thomas Hobbes. Hobbes believed man was so greedy and selfish that the enlightened state should control all property and make a social contract to keep peace and order. Rousseau refined these ideas into a Social Contract that set the stage for the war of world views that is now occurring in America.
>
> Rousseau seeks to achieve equality of man through a vague socialist metaphysical concept called the "general will." To overcome the tension between individual interests and the community, Rousseau argues for the creation of the common good as embodied through an abstract, objective public will; a will that is supposedly free (but never is) from our subjective selves and personal interests.

Progressives try to convince us that Locke and Rousseau's philosophies were quite similar and equal in securing democracy and liberty. They are not. They are not even close. Rather, it is classic progressive revisionist history. Rousseau's ideas are in utter opposition to those of Locke.

> The key fundamental difference between Rousseau and Locke is the role that "participation" and "community" play in Rousseau's "general will." According to the Rousseau model, individuals give up their freedom for the good of all, not just for the protection of individuals as is the case for the Locke model. "The good of all" is today's "positive rights."
>
> "Positive rights" are rights granted by the government. Positive rights spell out what the government must do for the people as well as what the people can and cannot do. Positive rights were the basis of the Soviet Union's Constitution. History has not been kind to the actual practice of positive rights. Yet, progressives hold them up as the Holy Grail. As an example, positive rights include the right of every citizen to have a job, or if not, have the government provide them a base income. This is a government right to happiness. All rights are granted and con-

trolled by the government. Conversely the Locke/Constitutional model is based on negative rights or natural rights that limit what the government can do. The Locke model holds that everyone has a God given right to seek the best job they can find or create, free from government interference, a business in the pursuit of their happiness. It is imperfect because people are imperfect, but it is the best form of government in the history of mankind.

Rather than a government 'Of the People, By the People, and For the People,' described by Locke and enshrined in our Constitution, it is the enlightened state which determines the general will, or common good of the people. Progressives likewise place strict social control on private property to prevent the inequalities that they believe will lead to social division and private interest.

In the Social Contract, Rousseau acknowledges the great power of the state by admitting that raw force can bring consent to the general will; "That whoever refuses to obey the general will shall be constrained to do so by the whole body.... In this lies the key to the working of the political machine; this alone legitimizes civil undertakings."[215] (Italics added) In doing so, Rousseau states the individual is supposedly "forced to be free"[216] by the government from his own selfishness. That is exactly what we are seeing today being implemented by both progressive Democrats and Republicans in laws like Obamacare and the Endangered Species Act. The difference between the Locke and Rousseau model of governance is huge.[217]

These exact opposite worldview philosophies are compared in the table below and are similar to others exposed throughout this book and what has been seen throughout history. The Locke worldview is biblical and the Rousseau worldview is Satanic in origin. The table below was basically taken from Coffman's book.[218] Some rows were deleted because they weren't really political issues. Other rows were added when items included two political issues. A column was added to show a comparison with biblical teaching.

COMPARISON BETWEEN THE LOCK AND ROUSSEAU MODELS OF GOVERNMENT:

Locke	Rousseau	Difference
The individual is sovereign.	The government is sovereign.	Diametric Opposite
Unalienable individual rights form the basis of the U.S. Constitution and private property rights.	The "general will" (public good) as defined by the state (Nation).	Diametric Opposite
Focuses on self-government	All people supposedly share	Diametric Op-

where all men have equal opportunity.	equally (equal outcome) in the wealth called social justice today.	posite
Strongly limits the right of government to intervene in the lives of individuals.	Based on positive rights that are defined by the government.	Diametric Opposite
Administered by a minimum of government.	Administered by collectivist & ever-growing government.	Diametric Opposite
Power to make decisions primarily in the hands of the people thereby encouraging risk-taking.	Power to make most decisions primarily in the hands of government bureaucrats.	Diametric Opposite
The only laws needed are those to enforce the golden rule that no person can conduct activities that cause harm to another person or their property.	It is a breeding ground for government corruption and arbitrary enforcement of ever expanding regulations.	Diametric Opposite
Creativity to find new and better ways of doing things is encouraged by minimal regulatory structure.	Stifles creativity to find new and better ways to do things because there is no incentive. Considers capitalism and profits as wrong, even evil.	Diametric Opposite
Establishes and protects private property rights which allows the creation of needed capital and provides the only proven way to eliminate poverty.	Minimizes property rights to only those allowed by the state to reduce all risk. Places nature's perceived needs ahead of man's real needs.	Diametric Opposite
It is why capitalism works in America and doesn't within centrally controlled nations.	By controlling property rights there is little incentive to build a better widget.	Diametric Opposite
Encourages individual protection of asset value of privately owned property because of pride of ownership and the need to maintain environmental health for continued production or use.	Invokes the Law of the Commons where property is held in common by the state through deed or regulation. No one person, family or organization has a vested interest in protecting the property for the benefits it can pro-	Diametric Opposite

	vide.	
Depends on free markets with minimum of regulations to create incentives to maximize efficiencies of production through creativity and entrepreneurship.	Depends on controlled markets by government to achieve predetermined social and environmental goals based on precautionary principle which, in turn, stifles creativity and entrepreneurship.	Diametric Opposite

The reader can see that these two philosophies are diametric opposites. The Locke philosophy produces liberty and maximizes wealth. The Rousseau philosophy gives all rights to the state and hinders innovation and wealth creation.

THE RELIGIOUS CONNECTION

Just like Secular Humanism, evolutionism, environmentalism, Communism, Socialism, Marxism, Fascism, Nazism and atheism, Rousseau's philosophy is a religious secular religion as defined in Chapter 5 & 11. Like all other ism's listed above they are diametrically opposed to Locke's philosophy and biblical principles. Dr. Coffman explains Rousseau's religious thinking below:

> Because of the Church's corruption of power, Rousseau believed he must establish a civil religion in the place of Christianity. It would be a religion controlled by society with a profession of faith. It would allow leaders to invoke god in political speeches, quote religious texts, allow worship and establish cultural morality. In other words, as Paul warned in 2 Timothy 3: 1-5, Rousseau's civil religion would have "a form of godliness but denying its power."[219]
> Although Rousseau allowed that no one could be forced to adhere to this civil religion, the government "can banish from the State whoever does not believe them." Why? For being "anti-social, incapable of loving the laws and justice, and of sacrificing at need, his life to his duty." Rousseau concludes with this prophetic statement, "if he does not believe them [the civil religion tenants of faith], let him be *punished by death*: he has committed the worst of all crimes."[220] (Italics added). That's exactly what happened to thousands of priests when they were hacked, dismembered and guillotined in the French Revolution. Many churches were destroyed. Christianity was virtually wiped out during the Reign of Terror.
> That's not all. Rousseau attacked Locke's model in the name of the wholeness of man, arguing that focusing on self-interest, individual rights, and property divides man. Rousseau sees "man as a malleable

creature" to be molded by an "enlightened government." He "favors primitive man, the noble savage who lives in simple equality with his fellow man, with few needs, a limited appetite, over man in civilized society." That is exactly what the modern progressive environmentalist believes today.[221]

The removal of the existence of God from the lexicon of culture whether 200 years ago in France or right now in America allows a false foundation to be established that is in diametric opposition to biblical principles and results in tragic effects. We will end this part of the chapter with some final thoughts of Dr. Coffman relating to America and our current situation.

> This serves to point out yet another huge difference between Locke and Rousseau. Our Founders guided by Locke believed that virtue came from obedience to a righteous God, while Robespierre, as guided by Rousseau, believed virtue came from terror and brute force. It should not be forgotten that Rousseau's ideology also spawned fascism and communism, under which governments slaughtered in excess of 150 million of its people. Future chapters will document how this terror and raw force is beginning to be seen in America today.
>
> Rousseau has become known as the Father of the French Revolution.[222] Because modern progressive liberal philosophy is based in the same writings that resulted in incomprehensible atrocities, progressive liberals today are attempting to revise history to minimize or even eliminate Rousseau's contributions to the French Revolution as well as fascism and communism. . . .
>
> Can it happen in America? Progressive liberals will adamantly deny the possibility and throw up all kinds of smoke screens to obscure it. However, put aside their hubris and look at what they actually do. They bully, denigrate, and vilify all opposition to focus the population on hatred— hatred of the Republicans, vitriolic hatred of the Tea Party, hatred of Wall Street, deep hatred of capitalism, hatred of the rich, hatred of the U.S. Constitution, hatred of the United States itself, hatred of anyone who disagrees with them. They claim that they are the only real Americans, yet since when is hatred an American value? Since when does America stand for intolerance? Since when is Marxism, or even socialism the foundation of American economics? These are all anti-American characteristics.[223]

This concludes the discussion of how the Locke and Rousseau represented God's view and Satan's view respectively and how people can live under freedom with Locke's worldview, but end up living under tyranny with Rousseau's worldview. In the next chapter we want to cover how America is demonized from forces within our own country that want to destroy America.

However, before we go there let's continue with the big picture of the "War of the Ages" that we already covered between the Garden of Eden and the death and resurrection of Jesus. The Locke and Rousseau dichotomy discussed above covered some of the history between the cross and the present. To complete the big picture of the battle between God and Satan we should examine the wars against Israel since they became a nation and the prophesied nine end times wars covered in the bible that are still in the future and see how Satan has tried and is trying to destroy Israel and prevent God from fulfilling all the promises He made regarding Israel and the Jews. The Jewish Virtual Library website tells the story of all the wars since Israel became a nation. The story of those wars is paraphrased below.[224] Following the past wars is a prediction of future wars involving Israel. Most of this information was taken from two "Christ in Prophecy" programs titled as Wars of the End Times, Part 1 and Part 2 and paraphrased below the past wars. These are available on David Reagan's Lamblion.com website.

PAST WARS AGAINST ISRAEL

1948 War of Independence

Israel was attacked immediately when they became a nation on May 14, 1948. On May 15th 1948 Israel was attacked with the simultaneous, coordinated assault by five regular Arab armies from neighboring countries, with an overwhelming superiority of heavy equipment - armor, artillery and their air force. These countries included Lebanon, Syria, Iraq, Jordan and Egypt.

1956 Suez War

Egypt had maintained its state of belligerency with Israel after the armistice agreement was signed. The first manifestation of this was the closing of the Suez Canal to Israeli shipping. On August 9, 1949, the UN Mixed Armistice Commission upheld Israel's complaint that Egypt was illegally blocking the canal. UN negotiator Ralph Bunche declared: "There should be free movement for legitimate shipping and no vestiges of the wartime blockade should be allowed to remain, as they are inconsistent with both the letter and the spirit of the armistice agreements."

Although the Security Council, ordered Egypt to open the Canal to Israeli shipping on September 1, 1951. Egypt refused to comply. Muhammad Salah al-Din, The Egyptian Foreign Minister, declared the following in early 1954:

> The Arab people will not be embarrassed to declare: We shall not be satisfied except by the final obliteration of Israel from the map of the Middle East (Al-Misri, April 12, 1954).

SOURCE OF DIAMETRICALLY OPPOSITE WORLDVIEWS AND CONTROL OF AMERICA | 209

The story on the website changes focus to Egypt's historic animosity toward Israel. Egyptian President Gamal Abdel Nasser began importing arms from the Soviet Bloc in 1955 to build up his arsenal for war against Israel. He made the following announcement on August 31, 1955:

> Egypt has decided to dispatch her heroes, the disciples of Pharaoh and the sons of Islam and they will cleanse the land of Palestine....There will be no peace on Israel's border because we demand vengeance, and vengeance is Israel's death...

Abba Eban, Israeli Ambassador to the UN, explained the Egyptian provocations to the Security Council on October 30 with the statement below:

> During the six years during which this belligerency has operated in violation of the Armistice Agreement there have occurred 1,843 cases of armed robbery and theft, 1,339 cases of armed clashes with Egyptian armed forces, 435 cases of incursion from Egyptian controlled territory, 172 cases of sabotage perpetrated by Egyptian military units and fedayeen in Israel. As a result of these actions of Egyptian hostility within Israel, 364 Israelis were wounded and 101 killed. In 1956 alone, as a result of this aspect of Egyptian aggression, 28 Israelis were killed and 127 wounded.

Certainly, Satan was using Egypt to destroy Israel, "the apple of God's eye."

The 1967 Six Day War

Again, the Jewish Virtual Library tells the story of this war. The documentation below is paraphrased from that website:[225]

On Israel's Independence Day, May 15, Egyptian troops moved into the Sinai Peninsula and started amassing near the Israeli border. Three days later, Syrian troops were lined up for battle along the Golan Heights.

Nasser initially placed the UN Emergency Force (UNEF), as a buffer between Israeli and Egyptian forces after Israel's withdrawal from the Sinai. However, Egypt later withdrew the UN force without bringing the matter to the attention of the General Assembly (as his predecessor had promised). After the withdrawal of the UNEF on May 18, 1967 the Voice of the Arabs radio station proclaimed the following:

> As of today, there no longer exists an international emergency force to protect Israel. We shall exercise patience no more. We shall not complain any more to the UN about Israel. The sole method we shall apply against Israel is total war, which will result in the extermination of Zionist existence.

On May 20 the Syrian Defense Minister Hafez Assad stated the following enthusiastic damnation of Israel:

Our forces are now entirely ready not only to repulse the aggression, but to initiate the act of liberation itself, and to explode the Zionist presence in the Arab homeland. The Syrian army, with its finger on the trigger, is united....I, as a military man, believe that the time has come to enter into a battle of annihilation.

Nasser, speaking of Israel stated:

"Our basic objective will be the destruction of Israel. The Arab people want to fight,"

The following day on May 27 he stated:

"We will not accept any...coexistence with Israel...Today the issue is not the establishment of peace between the Arab states and Israel....The war with Israel is in effect since 1948."

On May 30th as soon as King Hussein of Jordan signed a defense pact with Egypt, Nasser announced:

The armies of Egypt, Jordan, Syria and Lebanon are poised on the borders of Israel...to face the challenge, while standing behind us are the armies of Iraq, Algeria, Kuwait, Sudan and the whole Arab nation. This act will astound the world. Today they will know that the Arabs are arranged for battle, the critical hour has arrived. We have reached the stage of serious action and not declarations.

Immediately, President Abdur Rahman Aref of Iraq joined the chorus of words:

The existence of Israel is an error which must be rectified. This is our opportunity to wipe out the ignominy which has been with us since 1948. Our goal is clear -- to wipe Israel off the map.

Iraq joined the military alliance with Egypt, Jordan and Syria on June 4. At this time the threatening words of the Arabs were matched by their mobilization. Israel was surrounded by 465,000 troops, more than 2,800 tanks and 800 aircraft. By then, Israeli forces had been on alert for three weeks. It was difficult for the country to remain fully mobilized indefinitely. Also it couldn't allow its sea lane through the Gulf of Aqaba to be interdicted. That is when Israel decided to do a preemptive attack against the Arab coalition. To "pull it off," Israel needed the element of surprise. If Israel would have waited for an Arab invasion, they would have had a potentially catastrophic disadvantage. Some of that potential disadvantage was removed suddenly when Prime Minister Eshkol gave the order to attack Egypt on June 5.

Israel was indeed alone. Their only hope was a brilliant war strategy designed by its military commanders. Except for just 12 fighter planes assigned to defend Israeli air space, the entire Israeli Air Force, took off at 7:14 a.m. with the intent of bombing Egyptian airfields while the Egyptian pilots were eating breakfast. Roughly 300 Egyptian aircraft were destroyed in less than 2 hours. Just a few hours later, Israeli fighter planes also attacked the Jordanian and Syrian air forces, as well as one airfield in Iraq. Nearly the entire Egyptian and Jordanian air forces, and half the Syrians', had been destroyed on the ground by the end of the first day.

The battle then moved into the ground war phase. Some of history's greatest tank battles were fought between Egyptian and Israeli armor in the scorching-hot conditions of the Sinai desert.

It didn't take Israel long to get the "upper hand" in the battles. After only six days of fighting, Israeli forces had advanced far enough to march on Cairo, Damascus, and Amman. By this time, the primary goals of capturing the Sinai and the Golan Heights had been accomplished. The Israeli political leaders had no desire to carry the fight into the Arab capitals. The rapid Israeli advance was alarming to the Soviet Union. As a result, they were threatening to intervene. Because of the Soviet threat, the U.S. Secretary of State, Dean Rusk, advised Israel "in the strongest possible terms" to accept an immediate cease-fire. Israel did that on June 10.

Once again all the Muslim, Arab neighbors of Israel plotted together to annihilate them. Satan again failed in his attempt to destroy Israel.

The 1967-1970 of War of Attrition against Israel

Again, the Jewish Virtual Library tells the story of this war. The documentation below is paraphrased from that website:[226]

Egypt began shelling Israeli positions near the Suez Canal as early as July 1, 1967. Egypt sank the Israeli destroyer *Eilat*, on October 21, 1967, killing 47 people. Egyptian artillery began to shell Israeli positions along the Suez Canal less than a year later.

Nasser was surprised that Israel could withstand a lengthy war of attrition. He believed Israel would be unable to endure the economic burden and thought the constant casualties would undermine Israeli morale. The War of Attrition was very bloody and lasted about three years. During that time, Israel lost 15 combat aircraft, with most being shot down by antiaircraft guns and missiles. The Israeli casualties included 1,424 soldiers and more than 100 civilian deaths. About 2,000 soldiers and 700 civilians were wounded.

Again, Satan used Egypt to attempt to destroy Israel.

The 1973 Yom Kippur War

Again, the Jewish Virtual Library tells the story of this war. The documentation below is paraphrased from that website:[227]

On October 6 the Israeli chief of staff, General David Elazar, initially recommended an immediate and complete mobilization of their military for a preemptive air strike. Unfortunately, he was overruled. However, basically immediately after the over-rule, a partial call-up of reserves was approved, but Prime Minister Golda Meir still would not allow Elazar to take military action. Meir updated the U.S. ambassador on the predicament and asked him to intervene so the Arabs could be restrained. Secretary of state, Henry Kissinger, subsequently warned Sadat and Syrian president Hafez Assad not to do anything precipitously. Likewise, he cautioned Meir not to start the shooting. Meir found herself in a "catch 22" position. She knew that the intelligence community wouldn't give her sufficient warning of an impending attack to adequately prepare the nation for war. However, she also knew that Israel's chances for victory and casualty reduction would be greatly enhanced by a preemptive strike and the rapid mobilization of the IDF (Israel Defense Forces). However, she was concerned that striking first, similar to what Israel had done in 1967, might enrage the United States sufficiently that Nixon would not support Israel in the war or have favorable policies toward Israel afterward. Consequently, she did not feel free to alienate the US which could result in Israel being isolated.

The article continues by explaining the circumstances surrounding the start of the war and how Israel won in spite of insurmountable odds under the title of "Unholy War":

> On October 6, 1973 Egypt and Syria launched a coordinated surprise attack against Israel. They chose to attack on Yom Kippur, the holiest day in the Jewish calendar (and during the Muslim holy month of Ramadan). A force equivalent to the total forces of NATO in Europe was mobilized on Israel's borders. Approximately 180 Israeli tanks faced an onslaught of 1,400 Syrian tanks on the Golan Heights. Along the Suez Canal, Even more lopsided, less than 500 Israeli defenders with only 3 tanks were attacked by 600,000 Egyptian soldiers including 2,000 tanks and 550 aircraft.
>
> As a minimum, nine Arab states and four non–Middle Eastern nations including Libya, Sudan, Algeria, and Morocco actively participated in the Egyptian-Syrian war effort. A few months before the attack, Iraq transferred a squadron of Hunter jets to Egypt. During the war, an Iraqi division of some 18,000 men and several hundred tanks was deployed to central Golan and participated in the October 16 attack against Israeli positions. As soon as 3 days after the start of the war Iraqi MiG fighter planes began operating over the Golan Heights.
>
> In addition to just committing men to battle, Saudi Arabia and Kuwait also supported the war financially. Saudi Arabia dispatched a brigade of approximately 3,000 troops to Syria, where it fought Israel to keep them from marching to Damascus. Libya violated Paris's ban on the

transfer of French-made weapons, by sending Mirage fighter planes to Egypt. In addition, other North African countries responded to Arab and Soviet requests to support the states that border Israel. One example is Algeria who sent three aircraft squadrons of fighters and bombers, an armored brigade, and 150 tanks into the battle. Another example is the 1,000 to 2,000 Tunisian soldiers that were positioned in proximity to the Nile Delta. Sudan stationed 3,500 troops in southern Egypt, and Morocco sent three brigades to the front lines, including 2,500 men to Syria.

The Syrian air defense forces used Lebanese radar units to protect themselves from Israel. In addition, Lebanon allowed Palestinian terrorists to shell Israeli civilian settlements from its territory. Palestinians fought on the Southern Front with the Egyptians and Kuwaitis in addition to their attacks from the North.

Again, the forces of evil plotted together to destroy Israel and almost accomplished their goal. America certainly did their part to prevent Israel from taking necessary preemptive action. God spared Israel again.

Additional wars fought against Israel

The following additional wars are also included in with Satan's attempt to destroy Israel, but we will not expand on the details:

1982-1985	The first Lebanon war
1987-1993	The first Intifada (Palestinian war)
2000-2004	The second Intifada
2006	The second Lebanon war (Hezbollah war)
2008-2009	Hamas
2012	Hamas rockets
2014	Hamas rockets

All of these wars and attacks are for the sole purpose of destroying Israel and the Jews. No other country has so many sworn enemies. From a humanitarian standpoint and from a standpoint of making the world a better place for everyone, Israel and the Jews should be given honors just as they have won Nobel prizes in areas of physics, chemistry, medicine, economics, literature and peace. Note the document showing the good things that Israel does and has done in Appendix C. The hate for Israel is of a supernatural source. There are so many evil countries on our planet, yet none of those is hated like Israel. Psalm 83:3-8 states:

> They have taken crafty counsel against Your people,
> And consulted together against Your sheltered ones.
> [4] They have said, "Come, and let us cut them off from being a nation,
> That the name of Israel may be remembered no more."
> [5] For they have consulted together with one consent;

They form a confederacy against You:
⁶ The tents of Edom and the Ishmaelites;
Moab and the Hagrites;
⁷ Gebal, Ammon, and Amalek;
Philistia with the inhabitants of Tyre;
⁸ Assyria also has joined with them;
They have helped the children of Lot.

The Bible predicts exactly what is happening, why it is happening and who the bad actors are.

FUTURE WARS AGAINST ISRAEL OR IN ISRAEL

David Reagan tells of eight future wars that will be against Israel including a final war that is fought for Israel by God in Israel in a Christ in Prophecy telecast.[228] In addition to these eight wars there is a ninth war that is fought against God after the 1000 year millennial reign of Christ when Satan is loosed again. This information is presented with permission. The wars will be listed individually with some comments on each.

The Psalm 83 war of Israeli extermination (1)

Israel will come under attack from all its bordering nations in this war in an attempt to exterminate Israel. The attacking countries include Lebanon, Syria, Jordan, Egypt and the Gaza Strip. Bill Salas believes that Israel will have an overwhelming victory and conquer much of the bordering territory and consequently will gain a large measure of peace. It is likely that the future destruction of Damascus prophesied in Isaiah 17:1 will likely happen during this war.

The Ezekiel 38 & 39 war of Gog and Magog (2)

After the bordering countries have been conquered in the Psalm 83 war the remaining Muslim countries in the Middle East will look to Russia to help them destroy Israel. These countries include Turkey, Iraq, Iran, Libya, Sudan and Ethiopia. Russia will be delighted to get involved. Ezekiel 38:11-12 describes their motive.

> ¹¹ You will say, 'I will go up against a land of unwalled villages; I will go to a peaceful people, who dwell safely, all of them dwelling without walls, and having neither bars nor gates'— ¹² to take plunder and to take booty, to stretch out your hand against the waste places *that are again* inhabited, and against a people gathered from the nations, who have acquired livestock and goods, who dwell in the midst of the land.

Verses 18-23 tell of the judgment against the invading armies as follows:

[18] "And it will come to pass at the same time, when Gog comes against the land of Israel," says the Lord GOD, "that My fury will show in My face. [19] For in My jealousy and in the fire of My wrath I have spoken: 'Surely in that day there shall be a great earthquake in the land of Israel, [20] so that the fish of the sea, the birds of the heavens, the beasts of the field, all creeping things that creep on the earth, and all men who are on the face of the earth shall shake at My presence. The mountains shall be thrown down, the steep places shall fall, and every wall shall fall to the ground.' [21] I will call for a sword against Gog throughout all My mountains," says the Lord GOD. "Every man's sword will be against his brother. [22] And I will bring him to judgment with pestilence and bloodshed; I will rain down on him, on his troops, and on the many peoples who are with him, flooding rain, great hailstones, fire, and brimstone. [23] Thus I will magnify Myself and sanctify Myself, and I will be known in the eyes of many nations. Then they shall know that I am the LORD.'"

The timing of this war "is up in the air," but Ron Rhodes in his book titled "Northern Storm Rising," makes a case that it will begin three and a half years before the tribulation. This is based upon the statement in Ezekiel 39:9 that states that the weapons of war will be burned for seven years after the war and Revelation 12:13-14 states that the Jews will be evicted from their land for three and a half years (the second half of the tribulation). Consequently, the war should start three and a half years before the tribulation. We don't state any of this dogmatically, but just for perspective and interest.

The conventional war of the tribulation in Revelation 6 (3)

David Reagan gives some insight into the seal judgements where one fourth of the world population (1.5 billion) die. He believes that beyond Europe which the antichrist would already control, the large Muslim countries, all of which are out of the Middle East, would not submit willingly to his authority. This would result in great carnage and is not atypical when a military leader is trying to conquer other countries.

The nuclear war of the tribulation in Revelation 8 & 9 (4)

Here the conventional war that the antichrist starts morphs into a nuclear war which the bible describes as trumpet judgments. This results in the deaths of one third of those that were left alive. That is another 1.5 billion people which means half of the original population are killed by the middle of the tribulation.

The bible has several hints that this carnage is caused by nuclear war. Revelation 8:7 states:

> ⁷ The first angel sounded: And hail and fire followed, mingled with blood, and they were thrown to the earth. And a third of the trees were burned up, and all green grass was burned up.

Another hint is found in Revelation 16:2 & 11 which state:
> ² So the first went and poured out his bowl upon the earth, and a foul and loathsome sore came upon the men who had the mark of the beast and those who worshiped his image. ¹¹ They blasphemed the God of heaven because of their pains and their sores, and did not repent of their deeds.

The war in the heavens in Revelation 12 (5)

This is a supernatural war that takes place in the middle of the tribulation and according to David Reagan it is probably prompted by Satan trying one last time to take over the Throne of God. Satan and his angels are opposed by Michael and his angels. Michael is pictured in the Hebrew Scriptures as an archangel and the Commander and Chief of God's armies and the protector of Israel. Michael and his angels will prevail in this war and Satan will be cast down to earth and his access to heaven will be cut off and in his rage Satan decides to destroy the Jewish people and this decision leads to the next war.

The war against the Jews and the saints in Revelation 12 (6)

The antichrist launches this war in the second half of the tribulation for the purpose of killing every Jew on the earth and their Christian defenders. David Reagan explains that Satan hates the Jews for the following reasons:

> They are God's chosen people
> Through them God gave the Scriptures
> Through them God gave the Messiah
> God has promised to save a remnant (bring to salvation)

This war will result in another holocaust during the second half of the tribulation (the Great Tribulation) because Satan, who hates the Jews with a passion, will possess the antichrist. His purpose will be to annihilate the Jews. It is not called the Great Tribulation because it will be worse that the first half, but because the persecution will focus on the Jews. The bible does teach that God will provide the Jews a place of escape. Revelation 12:13-16 states:

> ¹³ Now when the dragon saw that he had been cast to the earth, he persecuted the woman who gave birth to the male Child. ¹⁴ But the woman was given two wings of a great eagle, that she might fly into the wilderness to her place, where she is nourished for a time and times and half a time, from the presence of the serpent. ¹⁵ So the serpent spewed water out of his mouth like a flood after the woman, that he might cause her to be carried away by the flood. ¹⁶ But the earth

helped the woman, and the earth opened its mouth and swallowed up
the flood which the dragon had spewed out of his mouth.

However, this escape will not protect the majority of Jews since two thirds of the Jews will be killed.

Zechariah 13:8-9 states:

> ⁸ And it shall come to pass in all the land,"
> Says the LORD,
> "That two-thirds in it shall be cut off and die,
> But one–third shall be left in it:
> ⁹ I will bring the *one*–third through the fire,
> Will refine them as silver is refined,
> And test them as gold is tested.
> They will call on My name,
> And I will answer them.
> I will say, 'This is My people';
> And each one will say, 'The LORD is my God.'"

Consequently, God will use the Great Tribulation to ultimately bring a remnant of the Jews to understand that Jesus is the Messiah and be saved and become God's people again. Although the antichrist will be focused primarily upon annihilation of the Jews Revelation 12:17 indicates that he will also try to annihilate the Christians that are saved during the tribulation.

> ¹⁷ And the dragon was enraged with the woman, and he went to make war with the rest of her offspring, who keep the commandments of God and have the testimony of Jesus Christ.

The Middle East campaign of the antichrist in Daniel 11 (7)

With the antichrist preoccupied with attempting to annihilate the Jews many of the nations may see an opportunity to attack him. Verses 40-43 tells of an end time's military rebellion against the antichrist as follows:

> ⁴⁰ "At the time of the end the king of the South shall attack him; and the king of the North shall come against him like a whirlwind, with chariots, horsemen, and with many ships; and he shall enter the countries, overwhelm them, and pass through. ⁴¹ He shall also enter the Glorious Land, and many countries shall be overthrown; but these shall escape from his hand: Edom, Moab, and the prominent people of Ammon. ⁴² He shall stretch out his hand against the countries, and the land of Egypt shall not escape. ⁴³ He shall have power over the treasures of gold and silver, and over all the precious things of Egypt; also the Libyans and Ethiopians shall follow at his heels.

However, just when the antichrist thinks he has everything under control verse 44 tells us:

> ⁴⁴ But news from the east and the north shall trouble him; therefore he shall go out with great fury to destroy and annihilate many.

The antichrist then deploys his military in the Valley of Armageddon as described below in verse 45:

> ⁴⁵ And he shall plant the tents of his palace between the seas and the glorious holy mountain; yet he shall come to his end, and no one will help him.

The war described as the Middle East campaign of the antichrist in Daniel 11 is the precursor to the battle of Armageddon as described in verse 45 above.

The battle of Armageddon in Joel 3, Zechariah 14 & Revelation 19 (8)

What is commonly understood to be the battle of all battles where the blood will rise to the height of the horses bridles for 200 miles (Revelation 14:20) will really not be a battle at all. When the massive armies from both the North and East show up Jesus will set his feet on the Mount of Olives as stated in Zachariah 14:4:

> And in that day His feet will stand on the Mount of Olives,
> Which faces Jerusalem on the east.
> And the Mount of Olives shall be split in two,
> From east to west,
> *Making* a very large valley;
> Half of the mountain shall move toward the north
> And half of it toward the south

Revelation 19:15-21 tells the story of how Jesus will destroy the armies when He returns:

> ¹⁵ Now out of His mouth goes a sharp sword, that with it He should strike the nations. And He Himself will rule them with a rod of iron. He Himself treads the winepress of the fierceness and wrath of Almighty God. ¹⁶ And He has on His robe and on His thigh a name written:
> KING OF KINGS AND
> LORD OF LORDS.

The Beast and His Armies Defeated

> ¹⁷ Then I saw an angel standing in the sun; and he cried with a loud voice, saying to all the birds that fly in the midst of heaven, "Come and gather together for the supper of the great God, ¹⁸ that you may eat the flesh of kings, the flesh of captains, the flesh of mighty men, the flesh of horses and of those who sit on them, and the flesh of all people, free and slave, both small and great."
> ¹⁹ And I saw the beast, the kings of the earth, and their armies, gathered together to make war against Him who sat on the horse and against His army. ²⁰ Then the beast was captured, and with him the

false prophet who worked signs in his presence, by which he deceived those who received the mark of the beast and those who worshiped his image. These two were cast alive into the lake of fire burning with brimstone. [21] And the rest were killed with the sword which proceeded from the mouth of Him who sat on the horse. And all the birds were filled with their flesh.

The second Gog and Magog war (9)

After Jesus' return to earth (Christ's second coming) the curse will be removed from the earth and it will be changed to a more perfect state with Satan bound and prevented from tempting those living during the 1000 years. This is referred to as the millennial reign where God will rule with a rod of iron and with perfect justice. People living in the flesh would have long lifespans similar to before the flood. There is only "one fly in the ointment." Even though people will live in a perfect environment that does not make them good and perfectible like humanists believe we are today. The story is told in Revelation 20:7-10:

> [7] Now when the thousand years have expired, Satan will be released from his prison [8] and will go out to deceive the nations which are in the four corners of the earth, Gog and Magog, to gather them together to battle, whose number is as the sand of the sea. [9] They went up on the breadth of the earth and surrounded the camp of the saints and the beloved city. And fire came down from God out of heaven and devoured them. [10] The devil, who deceived them, was cast into the lake of fire and brimstone where the beast and the false prophet are. And they will be tormented day and night forever and ever.

This will forever settle the humanist assertion that people are good and perfectible. It will be clear that God and Jesus' atonement is the only solution to man's problem. To make that atonement personal we need to humble ourselves and repent of our sinful rebellion and accept the truth.

CONCLUSION

In this chapter we started with the big picture of the battle between God and Satan between the Garden of Eden and the cross. Then we covered the diametrically opposite philosophies or worldviews of Locke and Rousseau that represent that of God and Satan respectively. We showed how the battle between those two philosophies have represented the difference between good and evil in our world. Next we showed how that battle between good and evil has played out against Israel through wars against them since they became a nation in 1948. Finally, we recounted the biblical story of nine predicted future wars that continue that battle between God and Satan until it is temporarily ended after war number eight and permanently ended after war number nine.

Appendix E has a Symbolic Biblical History Diagram that captures symbolically the entire biblical history from Creation to Christ's return to earth known as His second coming and beyond.

Next we look at America and see how there are strong internal forces that want to destroy our country.

CHAPTER 26
Convincing us that America is evil and should be diminished and destroyed

Once America became a dominant power, criticism of America began. I believe it started because of America's economic and military power that was the envy of basically every other country that wanted the prestige of being viewed like America or at least not wanting to feel compelled to follow America's leadership. Envy and hatred towards America began with other countries that felt inferior when comparing themselves to America. Much of the rest of the world saw us as an imperial or colonial power that exploited them. Later, starting in the 1960's, many Americans themselves started seeing America as a Colonial power also. This concept of America as evil from within was obviously not strictly envy or a desire not to follow our leadership. Its resentment has a completely different source. The alleged justification for that resentment toward America from within and the refutation of that justification is the primary scope of this chapter. However, before we go there, let's expand on colonialism and the accusation of American colonialism from sources external to America. This ill feeling towards America whether from an external or internal source is referred to as "anti-colonialism" by D'Souza in his movie and book titled "America: Imagine a world without her."

> Anti-colonialism, as D'Souza defines it, is underwritten by a conviction that "colonialism is a system of piracy in which the wealth of the colonized countries is systematically stolen by the colonizers" and that at the present time the United States, originally a colony itself, is the chief neo-colonial power, continuing its flawed history of subjugating native Americans, Mexicans, Hawaii and the Philippines into the 21st century.[229]

America is actually referred to as a post-colonial power. In one sense this just means we came to power after colonial Europe. However, other countries and many Americans consider America a colonial power today. This situation is addressed on a blog below:

> Colonies are societies/countries who are ruled by a different society or country. Colonialism is used to describe the period of history when European countries controlled much of the rest of the world for the purposes of resources, trade and political advantage. These European countries had Empires. America began life as a British Colony and was part of The British Empire. Louisiana and Dixieland were a French colony.

> After independence, America was no longer a colony, so, simplistically you could say that it is a post-colonial society. We talk about post-colonial Africa and post-colonial India to describe countries which have thrown off their colonial masters.
>
> But America is more than that. America dominates the world, but generally speaking it does not have colonies. America has found a more advanced way to control other countries. Many people have talked about The American Empire, but unlike The British Empire it does not exist geographically. Most modern historians consider America's post-colonial empire is financial in nature. While it is obviously defended using military strength, its normal method of control is economic domination. America's 'colonies' are post-colonial in nature because they are not occupied by administrators and soldiers, they are occupied by businessmen and products.[230]

What we need to do is to determine if America is really an evil country that needs to be diminished and defeated based upon its leadership and governance against a backdrop of the kind of leadership and governance that has been typical historically and currently in our world. Are we really the bad guys? There are three types of colonial subjugation and control that we need to consider to answer that question. They are documented below:

1. That which imported large numbers of people, and pretty much wiped out the indigenous populations (Australia, North America).
2. That which imported a reasonable number of people, who then acted as a resident ruling class. (Rhodesia, South Africa).
3. That which imported a tiny number of people who cut deals with some of the local leaders, helped aid locals to entrench their own power bases, and then signed very one-sided trade deals (India).

I think we have to take the morality of each separately.[231]

Although if there is any justification to accuse America of being a colonial power it would be the first one or possibly an additional fourth one that could be added to the list; that of economic and military dominance compelling other countries to follow her lead. However, even though we didn't colonize other countries like Great Britain, Spain and France, we are seen by many in the same light since we were and are the dominant power in the West. Regarding America's takeover of the part of North America that is now America and wiping out the indigenous population, it is quite different than some of the colonial powers that exploited other countries for the purpose of enlarging their empire. The Pilgrims went to America to escape persecution and to find a new home for themselves, not to expand an empire.

Now let's turn to the extreme criticism of America from within. It seems that more and more we are hearing the mantra repeated ad nauseam that

America is evil, it's greedy, is a powerful bully, and an imperialist country that has colonized many countries and that needs to be reined-in to make the world a better place. We hear this mantra echoed in the halls of academia, by our own president in his speeches, by other politicians, and by the media. President Obama, rather than promoting America and its best interest, apologizes for America wherever he speaks around the world. Heritage.org has an article titled Barack Obama's top 10 apologies: "How the President has Humiliated a Superpower."[232] It listed Obama's top ten apologies. The essence of some of them are listed below:

- America Has Shown Arrogance
- We Have Not Been Perfect
- At Times We Sought to Dictate Our Terms
- Some Restoration of America's Standing in the World
- We Went off Course
- Sacrificing Your Values
- Our Own Darker Periods in Our History
- Potentially We've Made Some Mistakes
- Referring to Guantanamo – "A Rallying Cry for Our Enemies"

Obama's Pastor for 20 years stated:
Not God bless America, God damn America.

Although other countries and the UN criticize America, individuals living in rest of the world see America as the only country with great opportunity for individual freedom and justice as testified by the fact that multitudes want to immigrate to America to escape the tyranny and the lack of opportunity in their countries. When Dinesh D'Souza interviewed a border agent that has been serving 26 years for his book and movie titled, "America: Imagine a World Without Her," he learned that of the millions of Mexicans that have illegally crossed the border into America from Mexico, he has never seen even one American try to illegally cross from America into Mexico. Dinesh D'Souza stated his own testimony on how he feels about America as an immigrant at the beginning of his book:

> I love America. I chose this country. Like millions of immigrants I been blessed by my life in America. This country does something truly unique, it allows you to write the script of your own life.[233]

What about the fact that America prevented other powerful tyrannical countries from conquering the world in World War I and World War II. What about America rebuilding destroyed cities in Japan and Europe. What about America delivering Kuwait from its Iraqi invaders without asking for one drop of its oil? What about America saving the country of Iraq from the tyranny of Saddam Hussein without asking for a single drop of their oil? Are these the things that an evil country does?

This dichotomy seems like a paradox since America would have to be schizophrenic in order for both the accusations against America and the testimony of foreign immigrants that want to come here, to both be true. Something is obviously wrong here. If one of these is true the other has to be false. The significance of this is profound, just like the significance of the diametric opposites that have been identified already in this book. It is virtually impossible for the testimony of all the immigrants to be a sham and a deception. They really desire to come to America because they believe America is a much better place to live. This would mean that the story of America's alleged shame should be investigated to see if it is really true or just a deception to promote an ideology, religion or a worldview.

This is exactly what Dinesh D'Souza did in his documentary"," America: imagine a World without Her." He interviewed many of the most outspoken critics of America in the areas including the treatment of the Indians, alleged theft of the land that Mexico claims should be theirs, American slavery and American capitalism. After hearing the criticisms explained by D'Souza, for me, it seemed like it would be difficult to refute the indictments against America. He listened to all of the criticisms and then investigated to see if they were telling us the whole story. He did this by interviewing people directly involved or knowledgeable experts in various fields to establish accusations and the truth about them. In each case he determined that our critics are not telling the whole story. In fact the story they were telling was completely one-sided, self-serving and was based upon their personal ideology, religion or worldview.

Here we would like to give a broad summary of that story told in the documentary movie, America: Imagine a World without Her." To hear the total story I recommend that you buy the DVD or rent it. Here we only want to communicate the facts that the movie attempted to communicate. We do not want to communicate any artistry, sensationalism or humor etc. from the movie. However, the story is best told by quoting many of the information sources. D'Souza's eloquent words are almost impossible to explain without quoting them, so we took the liberty to quote much of what he said. To do otherwise would be to miss the profoundness of the story. Let's start with the criticisms.

GENERAL CRITICISMS

Some general criticism of America quoted by different critics in the movie were as follows:
- Thievery was central to the expansion of the American.
- America was founded on genocide and built on the back of slaves.

- American foreign policy has been aggressive and imperialist starting immediately after the revolutionary war.

D'Souza's comment to these criticisms was:

Incredible as it may seem there are people in America who want a world without America.

American Indians

D'Souza interviewed Charmaine Whiteface a Native American activist and a member of the great Sioux Nation whose ancestral land the Black Hills includes Mount Rushmore. Whiteface is a chief critic of America and one who feels she has been personally affected.

Charmaine Whiteface believed that Mount Rushmore is a horrible symbol of oppression to her and the entire Sioux Nation. She summarized her charges against America as follows:
- It's a symbol of genocide for our people
- The charge of genocide beginning with Columbus
- Enslaving 1500 Arawak Indians
- A disaster called the "trail of tears" where 1800 American Indians were forced to march 2000 miles leaving a third of them dead

These are the very serious charges against America by Charmaine Whiteface. Again, the question is are these charges true and are they the whole story?

Mexican border dispute

D'Souza interviewed Charles Trujillo, a professor of Chicano studies at the University of New Mexico. He's a leading representative of the movement trying to reclaim Mexico's lost land. His position and accusations against America are as follows:
- In 1845, Mexican territory covered most of Texas, New Mexico, Arizona and California.
- If America wouldn't have stolen what was once Mexican territory, the wealth of those areas in California, New Mexico, Arizona, Texas including the oil and minerals would have made Mexico a premier economic power.
- Trujillo claimed that finally Mexico is now becoming an economic power that it would have been much earlier.
- He calls those lands taken from Mexico the lost provinces.

After hearing Trujillo's position, D'Souza exclaimed:

> So to put it biblically you are in America but not of America.

D'Souza stated:

These are again serious charges that Professor Trujillo railed against America. The question is are they true and are they the whole story?

American slavery

The movie stated that:
"many black people do not see the American dreams as the white people do. They only experience the American nightmare."

D'Souza interviewed the African-American scholar Michael Eric Dyson at Georgetown University. Dyson had the following criticisms of America:

- We took Africans from their country to build our way of ease and kept them enslaved and living in fear.
- As a black person in America, I take it personally that part of the wretched history of this nation is that my foremothers and forefathers were not seen as fully human.
- America doesn't want to confront the vicious inequalities that it set loose in this nation absorbing things that are not yours, taking stuff that is not yours.
- We believe that thievery was a central element to the expansion of America and the establishment of the American way of life.

After hearing Dyson's criticism of America, D'Souza asked him about Obama's election and reelection;
"doesn't that say something about the end of racism?"

Dyson conceded that progress had been made but essentially wasn't enough to change his opinion.

D'Souza introduced Fredrick Douglass by stating:
Frederick Douglas was born a slave, but escaped to freedom and became a champion of the anti-slavery movement.

D'Souza presented some damaging points that Douglas made.

D'Souza recognized that Douglas presented some serious charges. They certainly have a large measure of truth in them. However, he asked if they are the whole story?

American imperialism

D'Souza interviewed MIT professor Noam Chomsky a leading critic of American imperialism and asked him if the United States has been a force for good or evil in the world? Chomsky made the following points:

- For the people we conquered like the Vietnamese, we killed a couple million of them.
- We are not a force for good.

- There is a good reason why most of the world regards the United States as a predatory colonial power.
- We overthrew the Democratic government of Guatemala in 1954, Iran in 1953, Cuba in 1961 Brazil, Chile, Uruguay, Argentina on through the world. It is not a pretty record.

D'Souza exclaimed!
> This is a pretty serious indictment of America. If this is true and the whole story we really need to be shamed and change our ways. We need to determine if this is the whole story.

SUMMARY OF THE AMERICAN INDICTMENT

D'Souza summarizes the indictment:
> These are the indictments against America. We stole the country from the Native Americans. We took half of Mexico in the Mexican war. We stole the labor of the African-Americans. And today our foreign policy and free-market systems are forms of theft. These indictments develop separately. Each has been around for a long time but now they come together in a single narrative of American shame. One professor pulled this narrative together his name is Howard Zinn.

D'Souza tried to capture Zinn's thoughts based on his way of telling history in his book, "The People's History of America." Zinn stated:
> I prefer to try to tell the story of the discovery of America from the viewpoint of the Arawak, of the Constitution from the standpoint of the slaves, of Andrew Jackson as seen by the Cherokees.

D'Souza summarizes the indictment again:
> This is the new story of American shame. Are our lives innocent on the surface, part of a ruthless engine of looting, exploitation and murder? It's a powerful critique, we can't just dismiss it with chance of liberty freedom and rah, rah, rah. The critics are raising the primary question of justice...

ARE WE GETTING A TWISTED PICTURE OF AMERICA?

Obama stated:
> Starting today we must pick ourselves up dust ourselves off and begin again the work of remaking America.

D'Souza stated:
> To remake America you have to unmake the America that is here now.

D'Souza comments on remaking America:
> Obama's remaking involves economic redistribution never before imagined. It's aimed at returning centuries of stolen goods. If our wealth

is stolen then we must give it back. So is America guilty as charged? It depends on whether the story of American shame is true or not.

D'Souza, being an immigrant himself, put the alleged American shame issue in perspective:

> I came from India to America 30 years ago. I know a world without her.
> When I hear young people on the campus repeat the Zinn narrative of American shame, I know they haven't been told the whole story.

D'Souza asked Ron Radosh a leading scholar of American radicalism and a contemporary of Howard Zinn, "is Howard Zinn a real historian?"

> No, Howard Zinn is not a real historian. He has constantly misstated the facts. More than misstatements, actually proven untruths and he doesn't care that it's inaccurate.

Howard Zinn states and admits the following:

> I come to history with sort of a very modest objective I wanted to change the world.

Ron Radosh stated:

> If you read his book, America is the single most oppressive nation in the world. America is intrinsically evil he wants us to understand how bad America is then we will join him creating a new social revolutionary movement.

D'Souza asked Radosh:

> If Howard Zinn gives us a twisted picture of America is there a more reliable source?

That is when the movie scene turns to:

Alexis de Tocqueville

D'Souza gives a monologue on De Tocqueville. Some excerpts from that monologue are described and quoted below:

Regarding Christianity:

> Tocqueville witnessed the importance of Christianity. He saw faith shaping not only people's inner life but also their political life. He wrote "religion must be regarded as the first of their political institutions.". . .

Regarding slavery and conquest:

> When Tocqueville saw slavery, when he saw the treatment of Native Americans he knew none of this was uniquely American. In fact, it was part of a universal conquest ethic. Most countries are founded in conquest. . .
> Conquest was how wealth was acquired not through entrepreneurship, invention or business. Historically, every culture has despised entrepreneurism merchants. . .

America is based on a different idea, the idea of acquiring wealth not by taking it from someone else. Instead wealth can be created through innovation, entrepreneurship and trade.

RESPONSE TO ZINN'S STORY OF AMERICAN SHAME

The American Indians – Theft of the land

D'Souza recites a monologue regarding America's story of shame. The following excerpts are from that monologue:

Regarding theft from Native Americans D'Souza pointed out that much of Zinn's blame was misdirected since his critique focuses on Columbus and the actions of the Spanish conquistadors. He points out that Columbus never even landed in America and the Spanish misadventures were 150 years before America. Consequently, Zinn blaming America for the sins of the Spanish, Portuguese, Britain and France is not justified.

Regarding the broken treaties:
> What about all the broken treaties since 1776. Well the very idea of a treaty is a departure from the conquest ethic. . . some restitution is due and some has been made, in the case of the Black Hills. American courts acknowledge the land was taken in violation of the Laramie Treaty of 1868. $1 billion fair market value of the land plus interest has been set aside, but the Sioux have rejected it. . . In the Late 1700's the Sioux took that land from the Cheyenne who earlier pushed out the Kiowa and the Arapahoe. . . The Native Americans, too, subscribe to the conquest ethic.

The Mexican border dispute – Theft of Mexican territory:

D'Souza asked the relevant questions and pursued the answer regarding the border dispute.
> Did America steal half of Mexico in the Mexican war? He asked Texas Sen. Ted Cruz what started the Mexican war.

Senator Ted Cruz stated:

Regarding background of hostilities:
> The Texans, who were part of Mexico at the time. General Santa Ana who was the dictator in Mexico began stripping away the rights of Texans and indeed they began to revolt to protect their freedom and independence and so the Texans fought a revolution just like our founding fathers in America did and won their independence from Mexico.

Regarding the war:

Texas joined the American union and its border dispute with Mexico precipitated the Mexican war. America won that war. As a result American troops were in Mexico City, we took all of Mexico and retired its debt and gave half the country back. The people who ended up on the American side of the border were made American citizens.

This makes it very clear that the United States is not guilty of theft of Mexican territory and far preferred as a place to live.

American Slavery – Theft of labor?

D'Souza admitted that the enslavement of African Americans was theft; theft of life and labor. Were the American founder's hypocrites in affirming that all men were created equal while approving a constitution that allows slavery to continue? This was debated by the Republican Abraham Lincoln and his Democratic Opponent.

Lincoln's opponent in a political speech voiced his opinion that If you support the ability of black folks to settle in states with white folks that you should vote for Lincoln.

Lincoln alternatively expounded on the equality of black and white men.

D'Souza stated:

> Lincoln recognized the founders could not have outlawed slavery and still have a union. No southern state would have joined such a union and slavery might have lasted a lot longer. Earlier in his career Frederick Douglass had called Lincoln the white man's president. . . But meeting Lincoln restored Douglass's faith in America. Douglass condemned that movement, he didn't want to leave America nor did he want to destroy America, he wanted to participate in America. He wanted to make this country his home.

American slavery – The big picture

D'Souza continues with a narrative that gives us the big picture of American slavery as it relates to the Founding Documents, black vs white culpability, universality and the uniqueness of abolition.

> For the first time in history a great war was fought to end slavery. 300,000 northern soldiers died in that war. They died to secure for the slaves a freedom that the slaves were not in a position to secure for themselves. Even the civil rights movement was not a break with the American founding.

The movie turned its attention to a feared black plantation owner named William Ellison Gates. Although he was born into slavery he was freed as a young man. He eventually owned 1000 acers of land and 60 slaves.

African American scholar Henry Louis Gates recounts the Ellison story and beyond:

> Gates and other scholars estimate that in the period before the Civil War there were approximately 3,500 free Blacks who owned more than 10,000 black slaves. In South Carolina and Louisiana Gates points out that the percentage of free Blacks who owned slaves was approximately the same as the percentage of whites who owned slaves.

D'Souza went on to summarize the slavery issue:

> These episodes illustrate the universality of the conquest ethic and the uniqueness of the American response to it. Slavery existed all over the world, Egyptians had slaves the Chinese had slaves the Africans had slaves American Indians had slaves long before Columbus and tragically slavery continues today in many countries. What is uniquely Western is the abolition of slavery and what's uniquely American is the fighting of a great war to end it. Zinn wants a narrative of American shame, that's why he leaves these stories out and that's why we have a moral obligation to put them back in.

Certainly the history of American slavery is not simply a white on black oppression and not uniquely American. What was unique is that America has unique founding documents that are not consistent with slavery, and that 350,000 white solders died to eliminate slavery and that America was unique by ending slavery.

American Imperialism – Theft of resources:

D'Souza asks asked himself the question:

> Did America get rich by simply stealing from other countries,...

D'Souza concluded that America did not get rich from stealing from other countries for the following reasons:

- We did not steal from the Vietnamese
- In Iraq we spent much money and then turned the oilfields over to the Iraqis
- In Afghanistan while bombing we delivered food rations to the Afghan civilians
- We rebuild Germany and Japan after World War II

D'Souza's comment was:

> Contrary to the Zinn narrative we're not the bad guys of the world. As Colin Powell said the only land that American asked for abroad is land to bury our dead.

American capitalism – Theft of the American dream:

Here D'Souza asks and answers the question, does capitalism rip off consumers? Did Steve Jobs rip people off when he created the iPhone and then charged a high price for it?

D'Souza stated:
> He created products that people didn't even know they wanted or needed, but once he made available they clambered for them and stood in line to buy them and freely spent their money for them. There is no rip off. Capitalism works not through coercion and conquest but through the consent of the consumer.

D'Souza questioned Jaqdish Bhaqwati a professor of economics at Columbia University about how many people have been lifted out of poverty in India as a result of capitalism in an interview?

Jaqdish Bhaqwati indicated the following:
- That over 200 million people have been pulled out of poverty
- About 400 to 500 million have been pulled out of poverty in China

He then stated:
> Capitalism, entrepreneurial capitalism is the most important moral case. So there's no reason for us to be apologetic. It's the other guys that should be apologetic because every bit of experience shows that they're the ones who really undermined the fortunes of the poor.

D'Souza turned the discussion to charity and who are the charitable and compassionate people in our country? He stated:
> And when it comes to helping the poor through charity you may be surprised at who cares the most. Meet Arthur Brooks, head of the American Enterprise Institute.

What Arthur Brooks stated in the movie and what this author has previously read in his book titled "Who Really Cares," is the following:
- That liberals that believe in big government charity and greater government wealth transfers, are the least likely to be charitable with their own money
- That conservatives that do not believe in big government charity are actually the most charitable with their own money
- Christian conservative people are the most charitable of all

POWER, POLITICS AND DECEPTION

D'Souza investigates, identifies and exposes the people and rationale behind the deception that tell the story that America is evil and needs to be destroyed when it has been, and still is, a huge force for good in our world! He states:

But now we turn to a political question. If America is a force for good, why are they trying to make us feel bad, who is behind this? The shaming of America is not accidental it is part of a strategy.

D'Souza plays part of a Saul Alinsky speech:
> This becomes a contest of power. Now power has always gone into two areas. Those who have money and those who have people. We have nothing but people. If an organizer doesn't have any idea what to do about it, he doesn't have any damn business being in there. Do I make myself clear?

D'Souza interviewed the scholar and author Stanley Kurtz who's done extensive research on Alinsky and asked him "who was Saul Alinsky?"

Kurtz response included the fact that Alinsky was a man of the very far left who wanted the United States to become a socialist nation and was willing to let that happen through the democratic process. Also he wanted to polarize people by encouraging the "have-nots" to be envious and resentful toward the "haves" while at the same time make the productive tax paying people feel guilty.

After considerable discussion with Kurtz, D'Souza's states his analysis:
> The American middle class is decent and wants to live up to its own ideals. Alinsky knew that if he could show a gap between people's lives and their ideals he could exploit their shame to gain power. Alinsky became the godfather in the art of using shame for political shakedown, but he needed an army of recruits to carry out the shakedown. And he knew where to look. The 1960s saw the birth of a new generation, alienated from its parents, alienated from America, right pickings for Alinsky, but first he had to straighten them out.

D'Souza Identifies Alinsky's "Rules for Radicals" book:
> Alinsky wrote an instruction manual for this new army of shakedown artists. In "Rules for Radicals" we discover that the mobster Frank Nettie was not Alinsky's only mentor.

As we identified in Chapter 1, Alinsky identifies himself with Lucifer as joint rebels against the legitimate establishment and desires to usurp their power.

Alinsky stated:
> You do what you can with what you have and clothe it in moral arguments.

D'Souza summarizes:
> Today Alinsky's influence can be seen across academia the media and government and his most famous disciple lives at 1600 Pennsylvania Ave.

Kurtz commented that Obama has not really leveled with Americans about his past. One prime example is his association with Saul Alinsky.

D'Souza conclusion:

Clearly Obama has mastered the Alinskyite strategy of deception. The movie confirmed that Obama has followed the Alinskyte modus operandi of deception. He has made many promises that he hasn't kept.

As the reader is familiar, they include:
- If you like your doctor, you can keep your doctor
- If you like your health insurance you can keep it
- Obamacare should save the typical family $2,500 per year
- He promised to make his administration open and transparent

As you know he didn't keep any of those promises! Kurtz also identified Hillary as an Alinsky disciple as well. He identified that while Hillary was still in high school, a Methodist minister introduced her to Alinsky's beliefs and writings.

Kurtz also explained how Hillary took and is taking Alinsky in a different direction. Alinsky wanted to subvert the government from the outside. Hillary came to the conclusion that the Alinsky organization could never truly transform America unless his philosophy could be inserted into the government. Consequently, Hillary wanted the radicals to be in the government and become the government.

Kurtz's comment:
> So I would say on ideology Hillary is closer to Obama than she is to Bill.

D'Souza's Comment:
> Hillary figured it out and now Obama is carrying it out.

D'Souza's final comments:
> The revolution was a struggle for the creation of America. The Civil War was the struggle for the preservation of America. World War II was the struggle for the protection of America. Our struggle is for the restoration of America. President Reagan once said "Ours is the only national anthem that ends with a question. Every generation must answer that question. Let us resolve to fight for America as if the outcome of the struggle depended on us alone. We cannot do anything less. This is our home."

CONCLUSION

The story that D'Souza tells in his book and his movie titled "America: Imagine a World without Her" is another example of diametrically opposite worldviews that confound the thinking of Americans regarding the moral underpinnings upon which it is based. The consequences of Americans having confused thinking is that they can be on the side of lies, deceit and evil with catastrophic consequences when they think they are promoting good. The deception and doing evil in the name of doing good is always based on some false political or religious ideology that promotes the interests of an individual or a specific group at the expense of the larger group. All this testifies to the tendency of man to seek power, money and prestige rather than making a better world for all people.

CHAPTER 27
America is beyond the tipping point

In Chapter 25 Locke's and Rousseau's philosophies were identified as diametrical opposites. In Chapter 2 of D' Souza's, "America: Imagine a World Without Her" book the observations of two Frenchmen were presented as somewhat opposites also. The observers were Alexis de Tocqueville and Michel Foucault. Although their views of America were based upon opposite worldviews, their observations were not in opposition nor were they similar because they were looking for completely different things. Tocqueville was looking for the secret to America's greatness regarding strength and goodness whereas Foucault was looking for a great place where liberty meant he wouldn't be restricted in his social and sexual desires. Foucault's thinking on social issues is similar to both progressive liberals and libertarians. I had dialog with an unnamed libertarian talk show host on this very topic. He stated "what people choose to consume or do within the confines of their own home is none of society's business, unless it directly (not potentially) harms someone." My response to him was as follows:

> This is the license part of liberty that you promote which is diametrically opposed to biblical principles. When you say "potential," you must be referring to one specific individual since certainly the harmful effects of the group stretching liberty into license can be proved statistically! You are giving credibility to and promoting Russian roulette, right? You are saying that since we are not sure that a specific individual will have adverse effects from him stretching liberty into license, perhaps no bullet in his chamber, that you see no problem with playing the game. What you are teaching is not a philosophy based upon rationale, but a religion. Not just any old religion, but one that is in diametric opposition to biblical Christianity.[234]

Consequently, Tocqueville was on an objective mission looking for honest answers and Foucault was looking for a sexual playground. Tocqueville found that the key to America's success as a country was liberty within biblical guidelines and Foucault found a wonderful country that allowed him to stretch liberty into license outside of biblical guidelines and not restrict his sexual pleasure and not condemn him or make him feel guilty. They both saw the real America. They observed America almost 200 years apart which explains the big difference they saw. In my view Tocqueville saw a host becoming strong and Foucault saw and participated in parasitic attack on the host that is destroying America.

Ron K. Martin wrote a book titled "It's Over." The Prologue starts out as follows: All quotes from his book are with permission.

> Allow me to be the first author to give you the ending at the beginning. Simply put, It's Over! By that I mean that the America of your father is gone forever. More importantly, your hopes and dreams for your children and their children shall remain just that, a dream. Your daily mundane routines and thoughts of 401K's, retirement, growing old together, Caribbean cruises and a cabin in the mountains are not in the cards. All that you have taken for granted since birth will change and disappear before your eyes. Happiness will turn to tragedy. If you survive, your life will be like the walking dead, a serf among many serfs.
>
> America is terminal and its demise is not the result of Al Gore's global warming or Michael Moore's phantom conspiracies. Neither is it Iran's nuke(s), Putin's reconstituted USSR or China rising. It's an "in house job" by people whose names you have come to know, but really don't know at all. For the past 100 years they have been called liberals, progressives, statists, communists, Nazis, fascists, socialists, leftists and most recently, Democrats. Regardless of how Webster defines each of these belief systems they all share the same dream: dismantling our 234 year old democratic republic and replacing it with a serfdom ruled by oligarchic elitists. For simplicity, I will combine all nine of these evils into one and simply call it the "Darkside," as in Star Wars. . .
>
> Fortunately for the "Darkside," most Americans are the products of 50 years of intentional numbing and dumbing down. Like a boiling frog, they are unaware of being slowly boiled to death. These Americans perceive that we are having a few problems lately, but so what, America has always bounced back, right?[235] . .

Martin continues:

> This book was written for those good Americans who have been working and living their lives, but have not had the time to read between the lines of a media that now does the bidding of the Darkside. I have tried to compress a year of diligent research into a few hundred pages to bring you up to speed on our grave danger and how we got here. After this book, I encourage you to read the writings of Friedrich von Hayek, Edmond Burk, Rudolph J. Rummel, Michelle Malkin, Rufus Choate, Mark Levin, Ann Coulter, Dore Gold, Brigitte Gabriel, and others like them. . .
>
> I have used the "fatal sequence" to take you through America's history from our colonial founding to today. Although the teaching of American exceptionalism to our children was sacrificed to political correctness long ago, it is still an axiom of truth. There has never been created by man a more perfect union of balanced opportunity, fair-

ness, freedom and faith. The more I study our founding fathers and their wisdom, the more I am amazed at their almost superhuman foresight and intellect. But even their knowledge of the ages could not prevent the eventual seepage of evil into our almost perfect system of governance. Simple, seemingly innocent acts of government charity actually start a democracy on the path to incremental progressivism which becomes socialism. Socialism always produces a single ruler that tastes the forbidden fruit of power. And as you will see later, power corrupts and absolute power corrupts absolutely.[236]

Martin explains the "fatal sequence" he referred to earlier in a section with that name. He identifies an 8 step sequence allegedly penned by Alexander Tyler, but was actually written by Henning Webb Prentis, Jr. in 1943 and modified it to a 10 step sequence 3 years later. Martin preferred to use the 10 step version for expansion and explanation in his book. He starts with Tyler's words:

> A democracy is always temporary in nature; it simply cannot exist as a permanent form of government. A democracy will continue to exist up until the time that the voters discover they can vote themselves generous gifts from the public treasury. From that moment on, the majority always vote for the candidates who promise the most benefits from the public treasury, with the result that every democracy will finally collapse due to loose fiscal policy which is always followed by a dictatorship. The average age of the world's civilizations from the beginning of history, has been about 200 years. During those 200 years, those nations always progressed through the following sequence:
> 1. From bondage to spiritual faith
> 2. From spiritual faith to great courage
> 3. From courage to liberty
> 4. From liberty to abundance
> 5. From abundance to complacency
> 6. From complacency to apathy
> 7. From apathy to dependence
> 8. From dependence back to bondage[237]

Most readers have seen this sequence somewhere as have I. Martin continues with and subsequently uses the expanded list that includes selfishness:
1. Bondage to spiritual faith
2. Spiritual faith to courage
3. Courage to freedom
4. Freedom to abundance
5. Abundance to selfishness
6. Selfishness to complacency
7. Complacency to apathy
8. Apathy to fear

9. Fear to dependence
10. Dependency to bondage[238]

In Europe, biblical Christians were in bondage and were persecuted by the denominational church and the government. This strengthened their spiritual faith and gave them the courage to not only endure persecution but to take the dangerous step of seeking and finding a new world to escape their bondage and persecution. Martin comments on those early years show how difficult the step from courage to freedom really was:

> At the conclusion of the French and Indian War (also called seven year's war) in 1763 the thirteen colonies were in bondage to the victor, England. Officially, the colonists were in subjugation, but really enjoyed more freedoms than existed in the mother country. Religious denomination, like ethnicity, language, and country of origin, was an important determinate of where the early colonists settled. Faith in a Christian God was the common thread that united the individual colonies and the glue that held the divergent peoples within each colony together. . .
>
> As it happened, our Christian-based religion was one of the important ingredients that gave the colonists the courage to weather the disease, starvation, and dangers of the frontier life, and perseverance to stay the course while suffering the increasing privations of the British Empire.
>
> Actually, the thirteen colonies were very, very slow to anger. It took about 150 years from the time the Pilgrims first settled in New England until the "shot heard around the world" was fired at Concord, Massachusetts on April 19, 1775. Of course that was just the beginning of the American Revolution. It would not really end until the Paris Peace Treaty was signed on September 3, 1783, even though Cornwallis had surrendered at Yorktown on October 19, 1781. Anyone that has not read and appreciated the all-or-nothing, life and death personal sacrifice of our known and unknown founders does not deserve to be called an American, or deserve to share in America's wealth and freedom. Few today realize that that George Washington and other patriots could count on only about one-third of the population for support. One-third was loyal to King George III of England, and the final third didn't give a damn who won or lost. . .
>
> So, after six years of combat and two more years of dickering in Paris, the 13 states won their independence from King George III. Now that the fighting was over, the farmers went back to farming and the rest took up where they had left off when they became soldiers. In September, 1786, five of the colonies met in Annapolis to discuss changes to the Articles of Confederation to improve commerce. It soon became apparent that they needed a more comprehensive agreement, so

work was begun at the Philadelphia Convention in mid-June to replace the Articles of Confederation with a Constitution. The new Constitution was completed on September 17, 1787, and in accordance with Article 13 of the Articles of Confederation, it had to be ratified by at least 9 of the 13 states. New Hampshire became the ninth state to ratify the document by a vote of 57 yeas to 47 nays on June 21, 1788. The new government began on March 4, 1789, and the electors voted George Washington to begin his first term as President on April 16, 1789 in the nation's capital of New York City.[239]

This is the point where American's went from bondage to spiritual faith and from spiritual faith to courage and from courage to freedom. Freedom was one of the main facilitators to wealth generation as verified in the article below:

> The United States, upon its founding, established the first experiment in near-complete economic freedom in world history. It has a constitutional guarantee to private property rights and a strong anti-tax sentiment. As a result, individuals were free to pursue their economic interests (i.e. start businesses, invent, etc.) without the burden of excessive taxation, regulation, coercion, or theft. The rule of law was upheld, which punished the use of force or fraud, which by and large, encouraged honest business practices and allowed for trade of property and labor in a market free from external coercion. This contrasted with the rest of the world for decades, where tyrants, despots, and even democratically elected governments would seize property, over-regulate, and block individual pursuit of profit for the purpose of political or financial gain of the governments. As a result of this freedom, American entrepreneurs invented the capacity to produce electricity cheaply, the assembly line, the airplane, etc. The jobs and wealth created by these and many other innovations remained in the United States. Freedom also allowed competition, which kept consumer prices low and quality of services high, compared to the rest of the world. This economic system, which was predicated on the natural and inalienable right to life, liberty, and pursuit of happiness, was formerly known as the "system of natural liberty", and is now known as capitalism.[240]

In "The Poverty of Nations" it states the following:

> In fact, the national economies of the world can be numerically arranged along a scale from "free" to "unfree." One such ranking has been published annually for the last eighteen years by the Heritage Foundation and The Wall Street Journal. The current volume is called 2012 Index of Economic Freedom.[241] In order to determine how free an economy is, each year the researchers score 179 countries according to ten factors grouped in four categories:

A. Rule of law
1. Property rights
2. Freedom from corruption
B. Limited government
3. Fiscal freedom
4. Government spending
C. Regulatory efficiency
5. Business freedom
6. Labor freedom
7. Monetary freedom
D. Open markets
8. Trade freedom
9. Investment freedom
10. Financial freedom[242]

These are the types of freedoms that are necessary for prosperity. Poverty is brought about by the absence or minimization of these factors. The article below describes the tremendous economic growth in America after World War II resulting from the above freedom factors.

> Periods of economic growth had been known in the past—the 1920s— and they would be known again in the future, as in the Reagan years. But never had there been anything quite like what happened in the 15 years after 1945. It was nothing less than a material transformation of American life that gathered momentum in the coming decades.
>
> In 1945, less than half of American households had a telephone. Making a long-distance call was a cumbersome business, requiring the help of an operator. By 1960, it was rare to find a household that didn't have a phone. And with the introduction of direct-dial long distance in 1965, the number of such calls rose from 3 million in 1940 to 26 million in 1970.
>
> On the eve of World War II, an electric washing machine was a rare luxury. In 1960, almost 75 percent of households had them. Twenty years later, 70 percent also had an electric dryer.
>
> In 1940, more than a fifth of Americans lived on farms; less than a third of those farms had electricity. A third of those farms had no indoor running water; a tenth had flush toilets. Barely half of all American households had a refrigerator, and 58 percent had no central heating. The typical workweek was 50 hours, with more than half the workforce earning a living through physically demanding labor such as farming, factory work, construction, and mining. With average life expectancy pegged at 63 years, it was common for a person to work until he lost his health.

In just 20 years the existence of an American home without electricity or indoor plumbing had gone from being a fact of life to a national scandal demanding federal action. National income rose from $78 million in 1940 to $409 million in 1960, and then quintupled to $2.3 billion in 1980. Life expectancy for American males rose to almost 70 by the time of John F. Kennedy's inauguration. A comfortable retirement with a private pension virtually became a human right; by 1980, 70 percent of all workers had one.

Even more remarkably, despite a steady expansion of government programs such as Social Security and the Pentagon and projects such as the Interstate Highway system, national debt between 1946 and 1960 rose by only 6 percent, even as GDP grew by 237 percent. Indeed, achieving an average annual GDP growth rate of 4.75 percent while running a budget surplus during 7 of those 14 years must have seemed a miracle to those who remembered the Great Depression. Today, in the shadow of the slowest economic recovery in modern history—with a growth rate at 1.5 percent—it looks like one, too. Understanding what triggered the Great American Transformation, and what didn't, might be a valuable guide to the future for the current resident of the White House and those who follow.[243]

Although American prosperity started much sooner, in the period of 1945 to 1960 and beyond America became very prosperous and also became a mighty military force making it uniquely the world superpower. Our debt compared with our GDP was minimal. We're still mainly a Christian nation that our founders initiated; however, more recently all that has changed dramatically. There is great concern that America is rapidly going from abundance on the "fatal sequence" list to selfishness, complacency, apathy, fear and dependency. The story of that catastrophic decent is documented below. D'Souza explains how he found the answer in Tom Brokaw's book, "The Greatest Generation:"

> As I read Brokaw's book, I asked myself: What made the "greatest generation" so great? The answer is twofold: the Depression and World War II. The virtues of that generation were the product of scarcity and war. Hardship and need forged the admirable qualities of courage, sacrifice, and solidarity. But the greatest generation failed in one important respect: it could not produce another great generation.[244]

He goes on to explain that the obvious answer is affluence that resulted in giving children everything they wanted. Consequently, they received everything on a "silver platter" and didn't have to struggle to give themselves the good life. This is exemplified when our children want everything and don't realize how hard it was to generate the money to have those things. They came to believe that their affluent situation is normal and they went looking for fulfillment beyond the work / benefit realm (something like moving up Maslow's pyramid). Because of this belief they didn't appreciate the Capitalistic engine that gave them the freedom and time to seek fulfillment beyond the historical struggle. They didn't connect capitalism to their freedoms and affluence and so they rejected it along with most of their parent's values. So D'Souza went on to explain that rather than appreciating what their parents went through they rebelled as explained:

> They regarded their parents as soulless conformists who lacked true openness and idealism. The 1960's was motivated by repudiation of the old way and the quest for a new way. "Liberation" now came to mean liberation from old values—from the spirit of 1776. This took many shapes and forms—drugs, religious experimentation, sexual promiscuity, even bra-burning, as well as protesting, looting, and rioting. Perhaps most repulsive was the heartless ingratitude and even meanness that young people showed their parents.[245]

Martin has the following comments on the complacency:

> It is my contention that the United States entered into a period of complacency around 1963 after enjoying 182 years of almost undisturbed abundance... Our complacency had no specific starting date. It was more like a cataract, slowly clouding our vision and blurring the very real dangers that we knew existed, but were not yet on our immediate horizon.
>
> Domestically, the generation fathered by the WWII vets had reached maturity. Their parents had sworn that their children would not suffer a depression or fight in a war like they had. They raised them according to Dr. Spock and spoiled them rotten. The intersection of Haight and Ashbury Streets in San Francisco became "Main Street" to the free loving flower children, and the only god they ever worshiped was at the altar of self-gratification. Madelyn Murray O'Hare was proof to them that there was no god looking over their shoulder to chastise their behavior...
>
> Dresses got shorter and sex was no longer sacred or requiring of love. Universities became the centers of descent rather than centers of learning. If complacency meant caring about nothing then this "beat" generation was in full blown complacency.[246]

Statistics in all the areas below clearly prove that America became apathetic and went downhill rapidly in the following areas since 1960:

1. Crime
    a. Murder
    b. Rape
    c. Theft
    d. Mass School shootings

        e. Other mass killings
        f. Terrorism
    2. Social morality norms
        a. Promiscuity
        b. Out of wedlock child births
        c. Venereal diseases
        d. Homosexuality
        e. Lying and cheating
    3. Debt
        a. Government
        b. Personal
    4. Traditional Family
        a. Divorce rate
        b. Single parent families
        c. Stress of feminism on marriage

Other factors that have led to the past and present descent of America are the following:

1. Teaching of macroevolution in school
2. Government driven revisionist history of America's founding
3. Outlawing prayer in public schools
4. Legalizing abortion
5. Dissolution on the family
    a. No-fault divorce
    b. Sexual promiscuity
    c. Feminism
    d. Homosexuality and other abnormal sexual orientations
    e. Government subsidizing single parent families
6. Government switching from protecting God-given negative rights to protecting imagined positive rights
7. Government switching from conservative Austrian economics to progressive Keynesian economics.

All these factors have unhitched America from a biblical worldview, the facts surrounding our founding and have put man and government on the throne instead of God. In addition this has corrupted institutions including the church, the family and government that God created and designed to benefit mankind. Our worldview philosophy has been inverted from the John Locke philosophy based upon truth and justice that was the foundation of our country to that of Jean Jacques Rousseau; one that is diametrically opposite. The formula for liberty and prosperity has now been turned on its head and the expected results will be the opposite of liberty and prosperity.

Our government switching from promoting negative rights to positive rights set us on a path to Socialism. This system holds the productive class hostage in the circle of corruption and strikes fear into anyone that is trying to run a business or support a family on their own earnings.

The switch from Austrian to Keynesian economics has turned our country from a wealthy country with surpluses to a country that has huge actual debts and much larger deficits based upon promised entitlements. Currently, America has the luxury of having its currency being the world's reserve currency. This puts our currency in demand by other countries. One factor that creates this demand is a past agreement that requires other countries to buy their oil in dollars. However, with our huge debt and irresponsible fiscal policies, other countries are no longer willing to buy our dollars and for the same reason are pushing to eliminate the dollar as the world reserve currency. If and when that happens it will be disastrous for America and we will have a huge reduction in our standard of living. I understand that beginning in October 2017 that the Chinese Yuan or Renminbi will be included in the basket of world reserve currencies by the IMF. This should signal the end of the US dollar as the primary world reserve currency. This should strike fear into the heart of every American and convince us to change course.

The evil philosophy that now governs us is locked into place by a circle of corruption where the ruling government promotes envy amongst the minions of poor by demonizing a smaller group of those that have worked hard to earn their money and to live within their means. This allows them to steal the money from those that have it and give it to those that want it by counting on the larger population's votes and thumbing their nose at those that sponsor their power and theft. Let's quote again the following by Professor Alexander Fraser Tyler who wrote this when the states were still colonies of Great Britain, explaining why democracies always fail.

> A democracy is always temporary in nature; it simply cannot exist as a permanent form of government. A democracy will continue to exist up until the time that voters discover that they can vote themselves generous gifts from the public treasury. From that moment on, the majority always votes for the candidates who promise the most benefits from the public treasury, with the result that every democracy will finally collapse due to loose fiscal policy, which is always followed by a dictatorship.[247]

Clearly we have gone from a wealthy nation to one that has squandered all of its wealth and now has enough debt that it can never be repaid without destructive hyperinflation. Our economy has stagnated and is about to go over a cliff.

America is already in a state of dependency and all that is left is for America to go into bondage. Not only are Americans dependent upon our own government, but America is dependent upon our creditors that have lent us our debt. All that is needed is a destructive natural disaster or man-made crisis that causes a financial panic. When the resources have dried up and cannot provide entitlements to all of us that are addicted to them we will have blood in the streets. At that time a politician and potential dictator will promise safety and food if we support him. That may be the end of our democracy. Alternatively, a military attack or a race war that the progressives are fomenting could panic Americans enough that they would accept strict government for a promise of safety that would calm their fears.

We need to look at all the things that have been done and are being done to weaken our country and make us ripe for some kind of dictatorial takeover. R. Keith Martin explains how enormous and difficult this task would be; however, he sees Obama as perfectly poised to accomplish this dastardly goal. His comments are documented below:

> Many conservatives are rerunning videos and recordings of Obama's speeches during the campaign, and showing us that he told us exactly what he was going to do to "fundamentally change" America. . .
>
> "Fundamentally" changing the most powerful empire ever to exist on a small planet is no small undertaking. Unraveling 234 years of layer upon layer of the footprints and legacies of seven generations of Americans preceding us won't be endured peacefully. Forcing unwanted and unwarranted degradation, hopelessness, and Godlessness on 50 million of our 310 million inhabitants will not come without resistance.
>
> Since childhood, Obama has been dreaming and postulating what seemed impossible a short few years ago; reclaiming the rightful throne of the black man from the white Satan, and punishing the progeny of those who held his race in bondage. From Hawaii to Indonesia, to California to New York, to Chicago to New York, and finally, back to Chicago again, he met new and ever angrier miscreants who stoked his racist hatred. He loved and felt at home in Chicago like no other place he had lived. Chicago was half black, one third brown, and the rest white. But, race was not the only attraction. There was a Democratic machine like no other in the United States. Obama ingratiated himself with Harold Washington's conglomeration of socialists, communists, Muslims, and aging radicals. In Chicago he slowly formulated the proper mix of persuasion, money, methodology, and religion to meld his radical ideas with the Cloward-Piven strategy and accomplish, in fact, what the 60's radicals could never quite get off the ground.

You should already know the basics of how Obama went from community organizer, to Illinois State Senate, to US Senate, to President in a whirlwind. He brought many of his closest mobsters with him, but has added many more as he and his fascist advisors verify their radical credentials. Obama now has most of his people in place, and a chronological plan for implementation for his takeover of America. He is still in the dismembering stage of his plan, and will not proceed to the re-assembling level for a while. Of course sometimes these two are, of necessity, simultaneous. Rest assured that revolution is coming. Obama and his radicals know that this may indeed be their first and last chanced to cause an upheaval that he, Alinsky, Ayers and the Cloward-Piven's crowd have been working on for 50 years. This cannot be just another Presidency that turned left like Clinton, only to turn right again under Bush. This must be the final battle, the one that sweeps away the evil capitalists and finally gives America back to the downtrodden, the disadvantaged, the non-participants in the American dream, especially the black victims of slavery.[248]

As mentioned above there are many things that have been done that have weakened America and many things are currently being done that continue to weaken America while at the same time many things are being done to consolidate the power of the federal government. All of these things are in diametric opposition to principles of our founders and in diametric opposition to biblical principles. America became the greatest country on earth by following the principles of the founders and the bible. America was not just a great economic and military power, but had moral power that made America the moral cop of our planet by trying to punish injustice while promoting justice. It might be good if we look at these things in light of what a President and the executive branch would do if it was trying to destroy America by establishing an all-powerful dictatorship while destroying freedom. I would think the following things would be done if one is trying to destroy America:

1. Add laws and controls that empower government and limit liberty
   a. Spy on individuals to coerce compliance
   b. Implement gun control laws
   c. Nationalize industries and businesses
   d. Nationalize healthcare
   e. Empower unions
   f. Control economy with Financial Regulatory Reform Agency
   g. Implement various forms of voter fraud
   h. Allow flooding our country with immigrants that vote to empower incumbent
   i. Fund your constituents and defund and harass your opponents

j. Promote socialism, communism or Islam
2. Weaken the economy
   a. Make spending skyrocket by Implementing Cloward-Piven strategy
   b. Implement high progressive income taxes on productive citizens
   c. Implement many and restrictive regulations on businesses
   d. Implement energy taxes like Cap and Trade based upon bogus science
   e. Restrict productive natural resource development like oil and gas
3. Get the country deep in debt
   a. High domestic spending
   b. High war spending
   c. Funding the UN and foreign aid
   d. Creating money out of thin air
4. Weaken the military
   a. Cut the budget
   b. No draft
   c. Cut manpower
   d. Reduce nuclear capability
   e. Weaken morals
      i. Allow known homosexuals
      ii. Allow Muslims
      iii. Implement inappropriate rules of engagement
5. Destabilize the country
   a. Form his own domestic military
   b. Foment racial tension
   c. Demonize those with money
   d. Open borders to allow criminals and terrorists access
   e. Neglect using our influence to prevent Iran from going nuclear
   f. Destabilize Muslim countries with strong secular dictators
   g. Not declaring the Muslim Brotherhood a terrorist organization
   h. Not seriously going after ISIS and the reestablishment of a Caliphate
6. Degrade the moral fabric
   a. Promote sexual promiscuity
   b. Incentivize single parent families

c. Promote no-fault divorce laws
   d. Promote abortion and euthanasia
   e. Promote homosexual lifestyles
   f. Promote homosexual marriage
   g. Promote alternative lifestyles
   h. Promote relativism and pragmatism as opposed to being principled
7. Disconnect people from the true God
   a. Rewrite our history to separate our success from our founders moral beliefs and their belief in God
   b. Promote pluralism where all religions are equal
   c. Promote the false "separation of church and state" dogma that only applies to Christianity
   d. Demonize Christians as terrorists
   e. Restrict free speech even within churches
8. Connect people to a false god
   a. Promote Secular Humanism (man is god and the measure of all things)
   b. Promote Islam

The following quote supports the outline above. The first is an entire article by Sylvia Thompson that is quoted below with permission.

Barack Obama is not seeking "legacy"

> To the many gullible souls out there who truly think that Barack Obama is "legacy building" in his all-out assault on America, I implore you to bow out of the conversation because you are not seeing clearly. The term *legacy* carries positive connotations of something bequeath that is to the receiver's benefit. Everything that Barack Obama does is calculated to destroy America, which he despises. This man no more cares about legacy than he fears being properly prosecuted by the white political leaders whose responsibility it is to remove him from office.
>
> I focus on white leaders, because whites are still in the majority and they fill the majority of political offices. If the majority of political operatives were of some other ethnicity, I would lodge my complaint against that group. Ethnicity is an issue only because Obama is half-black and he uses that fact to intimidate guilt-conflicted white people. Otherwise, he would have been impeached and likely in prison for treason by now.

Barack Obama's sole aim has been, since he first entered politics and continues as he winds down this presidency, the complete destruction of America as it was founded.

It is an insult to the intelligence of all Americans who must listen to elitist pundits on Fox news and elsewhere, and political drones in either party endeavor to make Obama's behavior fit a pattern of normalcy. Attributing his destructive policies to "legacy building" is either self-delusion on the part of the people who make that claim or cowardliness.

This is my take.

Obama's nuclear deal with Iran has nothing to do with legacy but rather to enable a Muslim nation to wage nuclear war with America and Israel – the two nations that he most despises. Does anyone wonder why Russians praise Vladimir Putin despite what the rest of the world might think of him? Putin cares about his country, that's why.

Obama despises the American military because traditionally it has been a mainstay of America's strength, and our strength infuriates him.

Imposition of a polluting homosexual, anti-Christian agenda upon the military ranks destroys unit cohesion and literally terrorizes male members with the prospect of sodomy rape. Such rapes have increased since the forcing of open homosexuality in the ranks, against the will of a majority of members I might add. Couple that with an infiltration of women, for whom all standards of strength must be reduced, and Obama attains his goal of emasculating and demoralizing the forces.

He could not care less about a legacy of making the forces more diverse. Besides, President Truman diversified the military as much as it should be when he integrated it. Obama's objective is its destruction.

Obama reopened relations with Cuba because Cuba is Communist. Legacy is not his concern here either, but rather to scuttle America's attempts to keep Communist influence out of the Americas. That Cuba has major issues with human rights does not matter. Like his Marxist African father before him, he despises the West and all that it represents.

Obama lawlessly declares open borders and amnesty for illegal aliens, because he wants to overrun America with third-world people who bring little more than dependency with them. This tactic not only does not ensure a legacy, but rather it guarantees the eventual conversion of America itself into third-world status, if it is allowed to continue.

Bill Clinton started the travesty of increasing the numbers of third-world immigrants at the expense of more culturally suited immigrants from European and European-influenced nations, but Obama has taken the trend to lawless, destructive extremes. He is fully aware that many of these invaders have no intention of assimilating.

It is only the outcry of a majority of Americans that holds back this hateful invasion scheme, and Donald Trump's entry onto the political scene to oppose that scheme is a saving grace for our nation.

These are but a few instances of behavior that display the loathsome character of Barack Hussein Obama. And he is allowed to roam freely through the American landscape poisoning and polluting as he goes, sure in the realization that no one will stop him because he is "black."

The day that we no longer have to hear the prattle about his "legacy building" will not be soon enough for me.

Many, many Americans are thoroughly fed up with Barack Obama and the spineless crop of political leaders who ignore his criminality. It is yet unknown whether Republicans will ever garner the backbone to become a true opposition party and hold him accountable. Promising signs are the House conservatives' getting rid of establishment types John Boehner and Kevin McCarthy as House Speaker and Speaker hopeful, respectively, and Donald Trump's entry into the 2016 presidential race with enough money and testicular fortitude to tell the Establishment and the Left where to shove it.

Should these positive trends not continue and the 2016 election cycle yield no movement to counter all the harm that Barack Obama has done to this nation, I think there will be massive disruption. Those folks in the National Rifle Association ads currently running on television seem very serious to me, and that is a good thing.[249]

This quote states explicitly the intended implication of all of Part 7, Where is America headed politically? Consequently, similar to all the diametric opposites we see between progressive positions and biblical ones, all the things that could be used to destroy America seem to be in perfect sync with what President Obama and progressives are doing. Now let's shift from our internal threat from Obama to the external threat from globalism.

GLOBALISM

The threat of the destruction of America does not only come from America's tyrannical leaders and citizens who hate the America that embraces Locke's philosophy, but from ambitious globalists that want to control and run the world. This threat from without is being implemented through the United Nations. Their Agenda 21 is the modus operandi playbook based upon justifying a world wide body to enforce environmental controls. The following is quoted from democratic website with permission based upon proper attribution:

> UN Agenda 21/Sustainable Development is the action plan implemented worldwide to inventory and control all land, all water, all min-

erals, all plants, all animals, all construction, all means of production, all energy, all education, all information, and all human beings in the world. INVENTORY AND CONTROL.----*Rosa Koire*[250]

The same website also does a great job of explaining Agenda 21 as follows:

Considering its policies are woven into all the General Plans of the cities and counties, it's important for people to know where these policies are coming from. While many people support the United Nations for its 'peacemaking' efforts, hardly anyone knows that they have very specific land use policies that they would like to see implemented in every city, county, state and nation. The specific plan is called United Nations Agenda 21 Sustainable Development, which has its basis in Communitarianism. By now, most Americans have heard of sustainable development but are largely unaware of Agenda 21.

In a nutshell, the plan calls for governments to take control of all land use and not leave any of the decision making in the hands of private property owners. It is assumed that people are not good stewards of their land and the government will do a better job if they are in control. Individual rights in general are to give way to the needs of communities as determined by the governing body. Moreover, people should be rounded up off the land and packed into human settlements, or islands of human habitation, close to employment centers and transportation. Another program, called the Wildlands Project spells out how most of the land is to be set aside for non-humans.

U.N. Agenda 21 cites the affluence of Americans as being a major problem which needs to be corrected. It calls for lowering the standard of living for Americans so that the people in poorer countries will have more, a redistribution of wealth. Although people around the world aspire to achieve the levels of prosperity we have in our country, and will risk their lives to get here, Americans are cast in a very negative light and need to be taken down to a condition closer to average in the world. Only then, they say, will there be social justice which is a cornerstone of the U.N. Agenda 21 plan.[251]

Glenn Beck stated the following on his website:

In so many words, the United Nations seeks to co-opt, via individual governments, and eventually, a "one-world government," privately held land under the auspices of ensuring its "sustainability." Worse still, the UN's Agenda 21 has even laid out plans for "depopulation" or rather, "population control." If it sounds like something out of George Orwell's 1984, that is because Agenda 21's tenets are eerily in line with the demented alternate reality Orwell himself had imagined while scribing the pages of his famed novel.[252]

It is obvious that what Obama is doing is in complete sync with the UN and Agenda 21. They want America to be a third world country. At that point they will be happy even though there will be no American prosperity to promote their agenda and no funds to buy the support of poor countries. However, they will no longer have a superior country to envy and will be the ones that can control and dictate illegitimately as opposed to America's legitimate and moral leadership.

Gary Kah wrote a recent article titled "Obama and the Pope" that is very enlightening regarding our convergence toward a one world government. However, first let's document a small thumbnail of his credentials that support his experience and knowledge that make him believable below:

> Gary Kah is the former Europe & Middle East Trade Specialist for the Indiana state government. While in that position he traveled extensively overseas working closely with the economic staff at American Embassies on trade-related projects. During that time, he learned of efforts underway to establish a one-world political/financial system. He also discovered there was a religious motivation connected with these endeavors...
>
> Gary has appeared on over one thousand radio and television talk shows and shares his message with audiences throughout the US as well as internationally.[253]

For much more on his credentials see http://www.garykah.org/GaryKah/Garys_Profile.html. His article on Obama and the Pope is quoted below with permission:

> This year has been a very active time for those in high places pursuing a new world order. Their agenda gained steady momentum throughout the spring and summer, with proponents hoping to use the 70th session of the UN General Assembly as a springboard to larger one-world events later this year and beyond. Two men, in particular, have appeared repeatedly on the global stage as strange bedfellows with a seemingly common vision. Francis, the first Pope to have come directly from the Jesuit Order, has been cooperating closely with President Barack Obama on numerous fronts which are shaping the emerging order. These areas of agreement include, but are not limited to, the following:
> - Pursuit of Mideast policies which are detrimental toward Israel
> - Promotion of the UN's climate change agenda
> - Support of LGBT rights and goals
>
> Make no mistake, this is a very wicked agenda. I personally believe that their alliance and joint goals are intentional. Both of these men are deceived and, whether they realize it or not, are being used to usher in the endtimes world order described in Revelation, chapters 13 and 14.[254]

Kah states the following concerning Obama and the Pope siding against Israel:

Late last summer we learned that France was preparing to introduce a resolution during this fall's session of the UN General Assembly which, if ratified, would give formal UN recognition to a Palestinian state — completely separate from Israel. Thus far, France has held back, possibly due to a concerted effort by Israel's Prime Minister Benjamin Netanyahu to dissuade France and the UN from making this move. However, both parties might still act on this measure in the near future. On the same note, in spite of Netanyahu's strong pleas, the UN raised the Palestinian flag this week at its New York headquarters, in essence siding with the Palestinian cause against Israel.

On October 1st, PM Netanyahu delivered a poignant speech before the UN General Assembly. In his passionate address he called on that global body to treat Israel with fairness, as his country's very existence is now being threatened. He pointed out that during the last year alone the United Nations has passed 20 resolutions condemning Israel, but only one against Syria — despite the thousands of executions being carried out there. (Excerpts of PM "Bibi" Netanyahu's speech may be reviewed at the end of this article.)

Unfortunately, Bibi's well-delivered speech probably won't change the UN's position on Israel. And it is highly unlikely that it will alter the positions of Pope Francis and Barack Obama either. The Pope, Obama, and the UN all share the same vision for global unification — an ultimate system of world government and religion that rules over, and possibly from, Jerusalem. A strong, sovereign, independent Israel is not part of the plan. It never has been. From their perspective, the Jewish state must be brought to its knees and forced into their new world order. (The same can be said of their plans for the United States.)

Obama and the Pope have publicly declared, on repeated occasions, their support for a "two-state solution" in which the Jewish state would have to return to its pre-1967 borders — the boundaries that existed prior to the "Six Day War" in which Israel was attacked by her neighbors. After winning that war, Israel rightfully kept the land it had gained as a defensive measure (a type of buffer) should future invasions occur. Given the current hostile atmosphere in the Middle East, Bibi Netanyahu would have to be out of his mind to surrender these strategic areas which are needed for Israel's defense.

Iran, which is allied with Syria and now Russia, has repeatedly called for the complete annihilation of Israel. Yet Obama, with the Pope's support, signed an agreement with that terrorist state which not only creates a legal pathway for Iran to build a nuclear bomb, but which obligates the United States to come to Iran's defense if it comes under attack. In other words, if Israel believes it has no choice but to attack Iran's nuclear facilities to prevent Iran from developing a bomb that it would use to destroy Israel, then the US would fight with Iran against Israel. This is huge! It represents a monumental shift in US Mideast policy. It's official: The United States, via its President, has betrayed Israel. Barack Obama favors an Islamic terrorist state over our longtime ally.

Obama successfully kept these and other important details from Congress until his agreement with Iran had been consummated. Conservatives who stand with Israel are outraged. But the agreement stands. Barring a miracle it will not be overturned.

It is also worth noting that Pope Francis supported Obama's pursuit before, during, and after the agreement was signed. Except for a few outspoken hosts on Fox News, some of whom are Catholic, there has been little mention elsewhere in the secular media about these matters. I credit these journalists for standing firm and not being afraid to confront Obama and the Pope on their dangerous decisions.

What are the consequences of Israel standing virtually alone? Its isolation will serve to further destabilize the Middle East by increasing the chances of a greater regional conflict. The Iran nuclear agreement almost assures that Israel will launch a pre-emptive strike. If it does, all the terrorist elements surrounding Israel will come against her — including Hamas, Hezbollah, Islamic Jihad, ISIS, Syria, Iran, etc. (The one thing these parties hold in common — besides their Islamic faith — is the goal of destroying Israel.). I personally believe such a crisis will be used to make the case for a new world order in the aftermath of massive destruction and loss of life. Israel would win the war, but the world would hate her for doing so and would do everything possible to work against her. The stage would be set for the Antichrist to introduce a world government claiming to bring lasting peace.[255]

Kah states the following concerning Obama and the Pope on Climate Change:

On September 23rd, Pope Francis arrived at the White House for a one-on-one closed-door meeting with Barack Obama. The details concerning what was actually discussed are sketchy at best. But we can be certain the subject matter included a variety of topics ranging from the Mideast situation to gay rights. Near the top of the list I believe was the subject of climate change; as both men have personal track records of being devoted to advancing this cause.

On September 24th, Francis made history by being the first Pope to address a joint session of the US Congress. One of his central themes, predictably, was climate change. Here are a few of his carefully worded remarks:

"Business is a noble vocation, directed to producing wealth and improving the world. It can be a fruitful source of prosperity for the area in which it operates, especially if it sees the creation of jobs as an essential part of its service to the common good" (Laudato Si', 129). This common good also includes the earth, a central theme of the encyclical which I recently wrote in order to "enter into dialogue with all people about our common home" (ibid., 3). "We need a conversation which includes everyone, since the environmental challenge we are undergoing, and its human roots, concern and affect us all" (ibid., 14). In Laudato Si', I call for a courageous and responsible effort to "redirect our steps" (ibid., 61), and to avert the most serious effects of the environmental deterioration caused by human activity. I am convinced that we can make a difference and I have no doubt that the United States — and this Congress — have an important role to play. Now is the time for courageous actions and strategies, aimed at implementing a "culture of care" (ibid., 231) and "an integrated approach to combating poverty, restoring dignity to the excluded, and at the same time protecting nature" (ibid., 139).

On the following day, September 25th, Pope Francis launched the UN's new sustainable development campaign, being the keynote speaker before the UN General Assembly. This was the official beginning of the UN's final push to ratify the International Climate Change Treaty. World leaders will convene in Paris, France from November 30 to December 11, at the invitation of the UN, for the specific purpose of signing this controversial treaty. Both the Pope and Obama have gone out of their way to promote and announce their support for the climate agenda and are expected to sign the treaty.

They have been quite a duo. Both men have been pushing the climate change agreement among the world's political figures, while the Pope has also been actively garnering the support of the world's religious leaders. Toward this end, Francis issued his potent encyclical (mentioned in his quote above) addressing the environment and climate change last summer. Another Vatican document, intended to set the stage for the Pope's encyclical, was released a few months earlier. It was titled "Climate Change and The Common Good" and was produced by the Pontifical Academy of Sciences and the Pontifical Academy of Social Sciences. Here are a few excerpts from that document which give us a glimpse into the Pope's strategy:

> Climate change is a global problem whose solution will depend on our stepping beyond national affiliations and coming together for the common good... Religious institutions can and should take the lead in bringing about that change in attitude towards Creation... The Catholic Church, working with the leadership of other religions, can now take a decisive role by mobilizing public opinion and public funds... Such a bold and humanitarian action by the world's religions acting in unison is certain to catalyze a public de-

bate over how we can integrate societal choices, as prioritized under [the] UN's sustainable development goals...

In order to create momentum for the support of the climate treaty, a number of interfaith religious gatherings are being planned between now and the UN's meeting in Paris. One such event designed to bring the world's religions together and serve as a catalyst for environmental action will be held on October 24th. Known as "Global Oneness Day," this massive worldwide celebration intends to usher in a New Age of world unity through the realization of "Oneness" — the deity of humanity and the interdependence of the universe. What is particularly disturbing about this undertaking is that many churches around the world will be participating in "Sunday Oneness Services," aligning themselves with this agenda. Christians are rapidly losing their discernment, being overwhelmed by the media's barrage of support for this treaty and church leaders' endorsement of the same.

So what is wrong with the Climate Change Treaty? Answer: Along with the underlying spiritual deception associated with this push — which is leading people to embrace earth-centered/pantheistic beliefs — the treaty itself happens to be the cornerstone for the one-world agenda. Few people are aware of the fact that if this treaty is ratified it will put in place the international legal framework and infrastructure for the United Nations to enforce the treaty at the national, state and local levels — in every country of the world. Through this agreement we will all be taking a giant step into a system of world government. What's more, this treaty has been cleverly crafted in such a way that it goes way beyond typical environmental matters to cover nearly every facet of our lives. For example, it addresses gender equality, ending hunger and poverty, reducing inequality within and among countries (this means income redistribution) and creating world peace, to mention just a few of its 17 points. In short, it uses every existing problem on our planet as a reason for needing a world government to solve it.

Investigative journalist Michael Snyder says it best:

> For those wishing to expand the scope of "global governance," sustainable development is the perfect umbrella because just about all human activity affects the environment in some way. The phrase, "for the good of the planet," can be used as an excuse to micromanage virtually every aspect of our lives... This [treaty] truly is a template for radically expanded "global governance."[256]

Do not be deceived, the UN's Climate Treaty is an intentional power grab; and unfortunately, a majority of the world's most visible political and religious figures — including Obama and the Pope — are fully on board.[257]

Kah states the following concerning Obama and the Pope concerning Homosexual Rights:

Along with cooperating on the Middle East and climate change, Pope Francis and Barack Obama are on the same page when it comes to most of the social and cultural issues of our day, including the gay agenda. It is no secret where Obama stands on this matter – especially after he lit up the White House with rainbow colors to celebrate the Supreme Court's ruling in favor of same-sex marriage. However the real "hero" on the international stage when it comes to LGBT rights has been Pope Francis.

Gay rights activist and rock legend, Elton John, described Pope Francis as his hero during his annual AIDS benefit concert in New York. John who is himself a homosexual, praised the Pope for pushing for the acceptance of homosexuality within the Catholic Church. John remarked, "It is formidable what he is trying to do against many, many people in the church... He is courageous and he is fearless, and that's what we need in the world today." He concluded, saying, "Make this man a saint now, OK?"[258]

Along with gaining the support of rock stars, Francis was named person of the year by the gay rights magazine, The Advocate, in December 2013 and appeared on the cover. He was also named Man of the Year in the Italian edition of Vanity Fair. The magazine wrote, "Francis is a miracle of humility in an era of vanity. His beacon of hope will bring more light than any advancement of science, because no drug has the power of love."[259]

Much of the liberal world's love affair with this Pope began with his now famous quote, "If someone is gay and seeks the Lord with good will, who am I to judge?" Ever since becoming the leader of the Catholic Church, Francis' statements of support for homosexuality have surprised and encouraged gay rights advocates.

Christians too were encouraged for a while, but for opposite reasons. During the Pope's recent visit to the US, many Evangelicals — naively wanting to believe that he was really on their side — celebrated when they learned that he briefly spoke with Kim Davis, the Kentucky clerk who has taken a stand against same-sex marriage. He also talked about "family" values in some of his speeches. However, the celebration was short-lived.

As it turned out, the Pope had cleverly "thrown a bone" to Conservatives by speaking with Ms. Davis, hoping it would get them off his back when it came to this issue. The fact of the matter is, only one non-political figure was granted an official audience with the Pope during his time in the US. It happened to be a former student of Pope Francis whom he has known for many years. The student's name is Yayo Grassi. He was interviewed by CNN on October 5th.

During the interview it was revealed that Grassi has had a same-sex partner for many years. Grassi mentioned that in a previous conversation when he asked the Pope about his homosexual relationship, the Pope responded by telling him that it is not a religious matter, but a civil matter.

All that the Pope has to do to side with God's moral law is to say that a legitimate marriage based on the Bible can only be between one man and one woman. He is refusing to do so. During his visit he spoke much about the family and family values, but he never defined his terms. I believe this was intentional so that the "modern" family would be included.

This Pope, predictably, is trying to be all things to all people. He is indeed a very astute politician. The polls reflect this fact. According to an ABC World News report (September 3rd), 66 percent of Americans have a favorable or very favorable view of Pope Francis. This survey was taken a few weeks before his visit to the United States. His numbers are almost certain to be even higher now, given all the attention surrounding his visit.

Have you noticed how the Pope was, and continues to be, hyped by the media? It's almost as if he can do no wrong. He is being portrayed as the chief spokesperson for the planet. If a conservative Christian leader presents an opposing view, he is ostracized by the same people. This should give us reason to pause and ask, "Why is this Pope — the supposed Christian leader of the world — admired and presented as virtually infallible by a secular media, while Bible-believing Evangelical leaders are treated with disdain and contempt by the same journalists?" Could it be because they all share the Pope's vision for a new world order and see true Christians and conservative Jews as standing in their way?

Isn't it interesting that Pope Francis and Barack Hussein Obama have become the world's most visible players when it comes to shaping the most important issues we face? From Mideast policy, to the environment, same-sex marriage, race relations, and interfaithism, these two men — with the backing of a litany of godless political advisers and promoters are pursuing their agenda for global unification with little resistance. Islam and every other false religion promoting anti-Christian principles is getting a free pass from the media. Meanwhile, public opinion is being intentionally mobilized against Christians and conservative Jews.

The hour is late. The persecution of saints is at the door in the Western world and is already well underway in the Mideast, Africa, and other parts of the world. May God help us to stand strong for Him![260]

It would appear that like Saul Alinsky, (as explained in Chapter 1) Obama, the Pope and progressives have a pact with the devil. In Part 7 we will cover "Where America is headed politically."

Part 7

―∞―

Where is America headed politically?

    Now that we have demonstrated in Part 6, Chapter 27 that President Barack Obama has done everything and is doing everything to destroy America as it has been and as our founders envisioned and established it, we need to ask where do we go from here? The next chapter covers the Democratic Party front runner Hillary Clinton and, as you will see from any of her personal characteristics or from what she would do to America; it is nothing but bad news. As is axiomatic with the Democratic, liberal, progressive party, they're are all about how to mobilize the underclass against the working class to keep themselves in perpetual political power. It is an illegitimate and corrupt game promoted with lies, deception, class warfare, demonization, coercion and censorship that makes the game seem legitimate to those in partnership in the diabolical scheme. The end result is that it unjustifiably enslaves and exploits the working class while making the dependent underclass lazy, dependent, unthankful and angry that they are not being given enough when in reality they are normally not deserving of largess any more than any other citizen.

    After documenting how terribly unfit Hillary Clinton is as a presidential candidate, we will discuss what kind of Republican candidate we need to represent American citizens and what is good and healthy for our country. This means we need to elect someone that is not selfish and self-serving. These characteristics are not only not found in any Democratic Party candidate, but are not found in establishment moderate Republicans either. This only leaves conservative candidates that don't identify themselves with the Washington establishment and big government to bring them and "their cronies" wealth and power.

That leaves Tea Party types including Christians that actual believe that freedom is a gift of God and believe in and demonstrate solid moral principles. Even amongst those best candidates there will be great pressure for them to compromise and conform to popular pragmatic cultural issues. What America needs is a clear choice between a pragmatic circle of corruption that I call parasitic politics (See letter to the editor in Appendix B) or a Christian Worldview. Although these principles never go out of date, the candidates discussed in Chapter 29 will go out of date rapidly as the nomination process progresses. The pressure from the media and our culture will do everything to see that a moderate Republican or a Democrat pretending to be a Republican is nominated. If so, once again we will not have a clear choice between good and evil in the general election.

America, we really need a clear choice between good and evil that gives us a chance of defeating evil. It is up to you. Choose sustainability and life that was the foundation of our country rather than a selfish temporary lust for money and power. As covered in Chapter 27, "America is beyond the tipping point," it may be too late to save our country with so many believing in a false narrative. Perhaps if we can't save our country we can save some people by helping them to know and accept the political truth and beyond that, personal salvation through Jesus Christ who is the truth!

CHAPTER 28
Hillary and the Clinton crime family

Now that we have documented that President Obama is doing exactly what a president would do if he was trying to destroy America, let's examine the current and past history of Hillary and Bill Clinton since Hillary is the Democrat front runner for president.

I find it stunning that Hillary Clinton is the leading Democratic Party candidate for president in light of both recent and historical shady and criminal actions by both Hillary and Bill. The June 2015 issue of Whistleblower Magazine was dedicated to this topic and had much historical information and testimonials exposing the Clintons for what they are; power hungry deceptive schemers that steamroll anyone that can potentially expose their criminal activity. They despise those of us who are proud citizens of the United States and just use us as pawns! Let's start at the beginning and move forward in time.

The movie "America: Imagine a world without her" had a scene with a Methodist minister introducing Hillary to the Saul Alinsky type of radicalism when she was still in High School. I believe that is where the story starts. Whistleblower magazine states the following under the paragraph heading of:

HILLARY'S RADICAL PAL, SAUL ALINSKY

> The exact nature and extent of Hillary's relationship with radical community organizer Saul Alinsky has long been the subject of speculation and intrigue. The interest has been largely fueled by her suppressed and later released 92-page senior thesis for Wellesley College offering an extensive, largely positive critique of Alinsky and his work.[261]

Just the fact that she suppressed her thesis give us pause and concern that she doesn't want her true beliefs to be widely understood. The article goes on to state:

> WND recently found that long after Alinsky's death in June 1972, a group Clinton co-chaired maintained a working relationship with Alinsky's main community organizing outfit, the Industrial Areas Foundation, or IFA.
>
> The partnership extended into the 1990's and yielded influence over the education policy of the Clinton presidency. Dick Morris, a former top political advisor to Bill Clinton both as governor of Arkansas and as president, told Whistleblower that education reform "is the key issue Hillary Clinton used to propel herself independently to the forefront of Arkansas politics during Bill's governorship."

> The revelation of how closely linked her efforts were back in the 80's - and have been since – to an Alinsky radical front group is deeply disturbing and expands our understanding of Hillary's fundamental radicalism and commitment to the new left of Saul Alinsky," Morris said.[262]

This explains why Hillary wanted to suppress her thesis since it exposed her radical beliefs that if known would have been political suicide. The article continues:

> Hillary was said to have met with Alinsky several times in 1968, when she was writing her thesis. In her most recent memoir, Hillary wrote that she rejected a job offer from Alinsky to instead attend law school. The Hillary-Alinsky relationship received more media attention last September, when the Washington Free Beacon uncovered direct correspondence between Clinton and Alinsky from the Alinsky's IAF. The correspondence dates to the summer of 1971, when the 23-year-old Clinton was living in Berkeley, California, and interning at the law firm Treuhaft, Walker and Burnstein. In a July 8, 1971, letter to Alinsky marked "personal," Hillary wrote: "Dear Saul, when is that new book [Rules for Radicals] coming out – or has it come and I somehow missed the fulfillment of Revelation?
> "I have just had my one thousandth conversation about Reveille [for Radicals] and need some new material to throw at people," she wrote, referring to a 1948 Alinsky treatise on community-organizing.
> The Free Beacon's Alana Goodman noted the letter documents Hillary and Alinsky had kept in touch since she entered Yale and that Alinsky even offered advice on campus activism.[263]

The article continues with Hillary explaining her thoughts and relationship with Alinsky:

> Hillary wrote that she missed their regular conversations and asked if Alinsky would be able to meet her the next time he was in California.
> "I am living in Berkeley and working in Oakland for the summer and would love to see you," she wrote. "Let me know if there is any chance of our getting together."[264]

CLINTON'S INNER-CIRCLE PEOPLE DYING

Vince Foster's 1993 death

It all started with Vince Foster's death in 1993. The Political Insider stated:
> In fact, 46 people who were close to the Clintons have died during their 3 decades of political power. That number should give us all pause. If Hillary Clinton was a Republican, that number would be the question asked by reporters every day.[265]

Whistleblower documented the following facts concerning Foster's death:

Vince Foster was deputy White House counsel and Hillary's friend and law partner who had connections to the Travelgate and Whitewater scandals. In 1993, Foster was found dead in a park with a fatal gunshot wound in his mouth. His suicide was the subject of much speculation and three official investigations.

Investigations by the U.S. Park Police, the Department of Justice, the FBI, Congress, and Independent Counsel Kenneth Starr concluded Fosters death was a suicide. However, one of Starr's key investigators challenged the official line, insisting the probe's result was predetermined, only a few plotters were required to engineer the result, the crime scene was altered and that major newspaper editors killed stories by reporters pursuing the truth. The Washington Post reported that federal investigators were not allowed to enter Foster's office after his death, but White House aides enter[ed] Foster's office shortly after his death, giving rise to speculation that the files were removed from his office.[266]

Additional evidence that Vince Foster's death was orchestrated by the Clinton's was documented in a 2005 book titled, "The Truth about Hillary: What She Knew, When She Knew It, And How Far She'll Go to Become President" by Edwin Klein. He supported Hillary's involvement in the effort to remove Foster's files by the following quotes: The night of [Foster's] death, Hillary launched one of the most shameful – and illegal – cover-ups of her entire career.

- She sent two of her most trusted White House loyalists – Maggie Williams, the First Lady's chief of staff, and Patsy Thomasson, who was in charge of White House administration – into Foster's office to retrieve embarrassing and incriminating documents relating to Whitewater and Hillary's other personal affairs. While White House Counsel Bernard Nussbaum barred investigators from entering Foster's office, Maggie Williams, Patsy Thomasson, and Craig Livingston, Hillary's director of White House security, removed armloads of files and loose-leaf binders.
- In addition, a White House staffer allegedly tampered with the titles of several memos and removed the First Lady's initials in an effort to erase her role in improper behavior.[267]

The Political Insider made this comment about Foster's death:

Foster knew the Clintons from his time at Rose Law Firm in Arkansas, and had intimate details of the Clinton's financial situation. Apparently, he made a phone call to Hillary Clinton just hours before his death. The person who found him never saw a gun.[268]

Deaths of others Clinton Associates

The Political Insider comments on several other prominent people associated with the Clintons that also died under mysterious circumstances:

> Also, you may not have heard of the Clinton's former lawyer Charles Ruff who died in 2000:
>> Charles Ruff was one of Clinton's attorneys during the impeachment trial and was known to have inside information on the White House email scandal as well. Original reports were that he died in an accident in his home although no details were given. Then the report changed to claim that he was found in his bedroom unconscious, then declared dead on arrival at the hospital. The authorities will provide no details other than the usual (and quite premature) assurances that there was no foul play involved.
>
> And don't forget James McDougal!
>> Jim McDougal was serving his 3-year sentence for bank fraud at the Fort Worth Federal Medical Center in Texas, a facility operated by the Federal Bureau of Prisons for inmates who need medical attention.
>>
>> Just prior to another round of testimony before Kenneth Starr's grand jury, and while the reporters who were covering that story were two hours away covering a standoff situation in Waco that just "went away," Jim McDougal suffered a heart attack while in solitary confinement. Left alone for too long, when Jim McDougal was taken out of solitary, instead of attempting to defibrillate his heart with equipment on hand at the facility, he was driven to John Peter Smith Hospital. Not the closest hospital to the Fort Worth Federal Medical Center, John Peter Smith Hospital is a welfare hospital, where (in the words of one local) ,"They let interns practice on deadbeats."
>>
>> NEW! The Fort Worth Star-Telegram acquired the official report of the McDougal death via a Freedom of Information Act request, and reported that doctors ignored McDougal's signs of imminent death.
>
> The Clinton body count is massive and growing. Hillary Clinton will stop at nothing to become President, and death seems to follow her everywhere she goes. It is time to learn the truth about these murders and expose the Clintons. Instead of the White House, it appears they both belong in prison.[269]

Whistleblower had the following comments on the Whitewater affair:
> The Whitewater investigation by independent counsel Kenneth Starr began in 1994 with accusations of impropriety against the Clintons and others concerning improper campaign contributions, political and financial favors and tax benefits. It's initial subject was a failed Arkan-

sas real-estate venture involving the Clintons in the 1980s that was linked to the collapse of Madison Guaranty Savings and Loan, a Little Rock savings bank run by the Clinton' Whitewater business partners.

Clinton friends James and Susan McDougal went to jail for fraud (James died while serving his sentence), as did former Arkansas Gov. Jim Tucker and municipal judges David Hale and Eugene Fitzhugh.

The probe eventually expanded to include the death of deputy White House counsel Vincent Foster, the dismissal of White House travel house employees, receipt by the White House of a number of FBI files and the issue of whether President Clinton lied or obstructed justice to hide an affair with White House intern Monica Lewinsky.[270]

FILEGATE: FBI FILES ON GOP ENEMIES

Whistleblower described the Clinton's role in "Filegate" as follows:
In "Filegate," the Clintons illegally obtained FBI files on perceived adversaries, most whom served in previous Republican administrations.

In an effort to discredit the women who charged President Clinton with sexual misconduct, personal files and papers were illegally obtained and released. The courts found under the Privacy Act, that the privacy of Linda Tripp and Kathleen Willy had been violated," a Judicial Watch report said, citing just a few of more than 900 relevant files.

Judicial Watch said Hillary had been linked "directly to the center" of the controversy.

The scandal was first detected by the House Government Reform and Oversight Committee, which investigated the Clinton's "Travelgate" caper. The committee found that the FBI files had been improperly accessed by Craig Livingstone, a former bar bouncer Hillary had hired to work in the White House Counsel's Office. However, Hillary called the whole affair a "completely honest bureaucratic snafu."[271]

HILLARY'S 'MUSLIM BROTHERHOOD PRINCESS'

Whistleblower stated the following about Hillary's close associate and confidant:
Huma Abedin, who served as Hillary's longtime deputy chief of staff and has worked with her for 20 years, has known ties to the Muslim Brotherhood – a group bent on "destroying Western civilization from within" – and other Islamic supremacists. As WND has exclusively reported, the Muslim Brotherhood and Islamic supremacists connections not only extend to Abedin's mother and father, who are deeply tied to al-Qaida fronts, but to Abedin herself.

A manifesto commissioned by the Saudi Arabian monarchy places the work of an institute that employed Abedin at the forefront of a grand plan to mobilize U.S. Muslim minorities to transform America into a

Saudi-style Islamic state, according to Arabic-language researcher Walid Shoebat.

Abedin was an assistant editor for a dozen years for the Journal of Muslim Minority Affairs for the Institute for Muslim Affairs. The institute – founded by her late father and currently directed by her mother – is backed by the Muslim World League, an Islamic organization in the Saudi holy city of Mecca that was founded by Muslim Brotherhood leaders. The 2002 Saudi manifesto shows that "Muslim Minority Affairs" – the mobilizing of Muslim communities in the U.S. to spread Islam instead of assimilating into the population – is a key strategy in an ongoing effort to establish Islamic rule in America and a global Shariah, or Islamic law, "in our modern times."

Abedin was also a member of the executive board of the Muslim Student Association, which was identified as a Muslim Brotherhood front group in a 1991 document introduced into evidence during the terror-financing trial of the Texas-based Holy Land Foundation.[272]

Michele Bachmann had the following comments about Huma Abedin:

"She is the chief aid for the -- to the Secretary of State, and we quoted from a document, and this has been well reported all across Arab media, that her father -- her late father who's now deceased was a part of the Muslim Brotherhood, Bachmann explained. She continued: Her brother was a part of the Muslim Brotherhood, and her mother was a part of what's called the Muslim Sisterhood. It would be, we have requirements to get a high level security clearance. One thing that the government looks at are your associations, and in particular your family associations. And this applies to everyone. It would be the same that is true with me. If my family members were associated with Hamas, a terrorist organization, that alone could be sufficient to disqualify me from getting a security clearance. So all we did is ask, did the federal government look into her family associations before she got a high level security clearance.[273]

CLINTONS TURN IRS INTO 'GESTAPO'

The quotes below are from the first topic on the list of topics in the article and probably the most serious and tyrannical thing a government can do:

Few federal agencies are more feared and loathed by Americans than the Internal Revenue Service – especially when corrupt presidents abuse the power of the IRS to harass and exact revenge on political enemies. As WND has reported, during Bill Clinton's terms in office, IRS audits were conducted against individuals and groups who caused problems for the administration.[274]

The article continues documenting groups targeted:

Several prominent groups found themselves facing IRS audits following their criticism of the president and his policies. Among the conservative groups targeted for audits were the Heritage Foundation, the National Rifle Association, Concerned Women of America, Citizens Against Government Waste, National Review, American Spectator (which was burglarized three times), the National Center for Public Policy, American Cause, Citizens for Honest Government, Progress and Freedom Foundation, David Horowitz's Center for Study of Popular Culture and the Western Journalism Center.[275]

The article continues documenting individuals targeted:

Individuals singled out for audits during the administration included Clinton paramours Gennifer Flowers and Liz Ward Gracen, sexual assault accusers Paula Jones and Juanita Broaddrick, fired White House Travel Office Director Billy Dale and attorney Kent Masterson Brown. Fox news' Bill O'Reilly an outspoken critic of both Bill and Hillary Clinton, said he was audited three times during the Clinton presidency.[276]

PARDONGATE

Whistleblower magazine documents unethical and immoral pardons that President Bill Clinton gave to connected people to enrich family members as follows:

Before Bill Clinton left the White House in 2001, he granted numerous controversial pardons – including to convicted tax evader Marc Rich, whose wife made significant contributions to Hillary's campaign and the Clinton's presidential library.

The Associated Press reported that Rich had been "indicted" by a U.S. federal grand jury on more than 50 counts of fraud, racketeering, trading with Iran during the U.S. Embassy hostage crisis and evading more than $48 million in income taxes – crimes that could have earned him more than 300 years in prison. Rich fled to Switzerland in 1983 after his indictment and remained on the FBI's Most Wanted List until President Clinton pardoned him.

Also, Hillary's brothers, Tony and Hugh Rodham, reportedly received large amounts of money from people who were pardoned by Bill Clinton. Hillary said she and Bill were unaware of the scheme.

Accuracy in Media reported: "Hugh Rodham, Hillary's brother, was taking money and promising access to help get pardons. Two such high profile cases were those of drug kingpin Carlos Vignali and convicted swindler Glenn Braswell. Rodham received hundreds of thousands of dollars from each, and they were both granted pardons. Rodham was quoted as telling a top White House aide that the pardon for Vignali was 'very important' to Hillary."[277]

EMAILGATE

Whistleblower documented the following facts about Hillary's private email server:

> In March 2015, WND reported that Hillary kept all her official correspondence as secretary of state, as well as her personal emails, on a private email server located in her home – instead of using the government-mandated process while serving in the high appointed position. Her email server was unsecured for months while she used it for government business, and she did not sign a standard agreement when she left office that promised that she had left government property behind.
>
> The Hill reported Hillary did not encrypt her private email service with a digital certificate for the first three months of her tenure as secretary of state. That was while she was traveling to China, Egypt, Israel, Japan and South Korea.[278]

Next the article goes on to explain the significance of Hillary's actions:

> Several present and former members of the U. S. intelligence committee said Hilary's private email server was a major security risk, and America, going forward, ought to assume enemies of the state all had access to it.
>
> "The name Clinton right on the email handle meant this was not a difficult find," said John Schindler, a former National Security Agency counterintelligence officer, Investors Business Daily reported.
>
> In April, J. Michael Waller – a longtime consultant to government entities ranging from secretary of defense to the U.S. Senate to the U.S. Marine Corps Warfighting Laboratory – told WND the Russians hack into the U.S. government and so does any foreign intelligence worth its salt, most likely through Hillary's private server. Waller said Hillary deserves prison time for insisting on an email system that clearly left the nation vulnerable to attack.[279]

In an article by Art Moore in Whistleblower magazine titled "I don't believe Hillary" he explains that a veteran newsman and Clinton admirer decries 'stupid,' 'seedy' scandals and serial lying while commenting on Hillary Clinton. The article states:

> Political journalist Ron Fournier has covered the Clintons for 30 years, since the time in Arkansas. He admits to admiring them and acknowledges Bill Clinton made my career. . .
>
> Now, as the senior political columnist and editorial director of National Journal, Fournier is getting considerable notice as a strong critic of the Clintons. . .
>
> Fournier said he doesn't believe Clinton [Hillary] "because a person's actions are more revealing than words: She kept her government

email on a secret server and, only under pressure from Congress, returned less than half of them to the State Department."[280]

BENGHAZI

An article in Whistleblower titled "Smoking Gun! Hillary Knew Benghazi Attack was Planned 10 Days in Advance" documents that "Defense memos revealed al-Qaida terrorists plans 'to kill as many Americans as possible.'" It goes on to state:

> Previously classified documents from the Department of Defense and the Department of State reveal that DOD almost immediately reported that the attack on the U.S. Consulate in Benghazi, Libya, was planned and carried out by al-Qaida and Muslim Brotherhood linked terrorists.
>
> A federal court ordered the government hand over to the D.C. watchdog Judicial Watch more than 100 pages of previously secret documents that showed then-Secretary of State Hillary Clinton and other senior Obama officials were given reports within hours of the Sept. 11, 2012 attack.
>
> In the memos, the DOD described details of a plan formulated 10 days in advance "to kill as many Americans as possible."
>
> The plans for attack had nothing to do with a provocative You Tube video by an obscure filmmaker, which the administration repeatedly blamed. Rather they had everything to do with terrorists from the "Brigades of the Captive Omar Abdul Rahman," the so-called "blind sheik."[281]

After the article identified Rahman as the one that is serving life in prison for his involvement in the 1993 World Trade Center bombing and other terrorist acts it tells the rest of the story as follows:

> The new documents also provide the first official confirmation that the U.S. government was aware of arms shipments from Benghazi to rebels trying to bring down the government of Bashar Assad in Syria.
>
> The documents also include an August 2012 analysis warning of the rise of ISIS and predicted failure of the Obama policy of regime change in Syria. Memos show the Obama administration knew about ISIS plans to establish a caliphate in Iraq and Syria several months before the November 2012 election.[282]

After explaining that it took two-and-a-half years after the attack for Judicial Watch to finally obtain the memos by suing in federal court the deceitful story continues as follows:

> The Obama administration says it was a coincidence that [the Benghazi attack] occurred on 9/11. In fact, their intelligence said it wasn't a coincidence, and in fact, specifically the attack occurred because it was 9/11," said Tom Fitton, president of Judicial Watch. . .

A Defense Department document from the Defense Intelligence Agency, or DIA, dated Sept. 12, 2012, the day after the Benghazi attack, details that the attack had been carefully planned by the BCOAR terrorist group "to kill as many Americans as possible."

The document was sent to Clinton, then-Defense Secretary Leon Panetta, the Joint Chiefs of Staff and the Obama White House National Security Council.[283]

CLINTON FOUNDATION FRAUD

An article titled "Analyst's Probe Implicates in Foundation Fraud" provides evidence of 'wanton transgressions' while she served as director. It goes on to explain the deceitful fraud and corruption as follows:

> Although Hillary Clinton was appointed to the board of directors of the Clinton Foundation after she had resigned as secretary of state, a Wall Street analyst and investor who has conducted a thorough investigation of the foundation's finances contends she is complicit in what he described as systematic fraud warranting a criminal investigation.
>
> After months of tedious investigation, Charles Ortel has concluded the foundation has filed financial and tax forms that were material misleading, incomplete and in error with the goal of enriching the Clintons and their close associates.
>
> Ortel alleges Hillary Clinton advanced an "inurement" scheme – enriching oneself through a nonprofit organization – in complicity with her husband by positioning various key associates within the Clinton Foundation structure while she served as U.S. senator from New York and subsequently as secretary of state under President Obama.[284]

After explaining that Hillary filed false and misleading financial and tax documents not only once, but for multiple years the article continues:

> Ortel previously found the Bill, Hillary, and Chelsea Clinton Foundation's explanation for why it was divided into three, legally separate tax-exempt organizations to be "misleading and false." Based upon his findings, a prominent lawyer and a top government watchdog in the nation's capital are calling for the Clinton Foundation to be shut down.
>
> In his first report, Ortel found what he characterizes as an elaborate system devised by the Clintons to enrich themselves through schemes such as skimming tens of millions of dollars from U.N. levies imposed on airline travelers...
>
> The evidence, Ortel believes, should prompt immediate state and federal criminal investigations and the shutting down of the Clinton Foundation from further fundraising while the investigations proceed.
>
> The foundation should be put in receivership and the board of directors replaced to prevent further defrauding of the charitable-giving population, he contends.

"Considering evidence already in the public domain in light of the New York and federal laws alone, acts by the Clintons Foundation while Mrs. Clinton served as director constitute multiple counts of financial reporting fraud and of fundraising fraud," Ortel maintains.[285]

That concludes the major Clinton scandals covered in Whistleblower magazine. However, below are listed additional scandals that we have not covered above:
1. Covering Bill's dirty deeds
2. Looting the White House
3. Chinagate: Sale of high-tech secrets
4. Travelgate: Always room for friends
5. 'Landing under sniper fire' in Bosnia
6. Hillary's 'missing' law firm billing records
7. Hillary's cash cows and 9,987 percent profit
8. Hillary laughs about defending a child rapist
9. Hill[ary] ca$hes in: Iranian fundraising
10. Peter Franklin Paul: Another Hillary friend goes to prison
11. Watergate: [Hillary] Fired for being a 'liar'
12. Gift-gate: Undisclosed gifts

FINAL COMMENTS AND CONCLUSION

Below are highlights from the initial article Whistleblower editor, David Kupelian, that summarize well the issue with Hillary Clinton. After telling an anecdote about watching Hillary on TV in an airport he explains:

> Within seconds, I realized Hillary was in the midst of delivering yet another carefully worked out, lawyer-parsed, completely outrageous, bald-faced lie.
> Looking directly into the camera – tight shot, her face filling most of the screen – there was Hillary Clinton, eyeball-to-eyeball with the world, flat-out lying with the confidence that comes only from years – nay, decades – of her and her husband getting away with a galaxy of scandals, lies, corruption, abuses and yes, crimes. . .
> A lifetime can sometimes be encapsulated into a single moment, and this particular airport moment has been replicated continuously throughout Hillary Clinton's political life. She is constantly "reinventing," "repositioning," "remaking," and "rebranding" herself – all amoral beltway euphemisms (like "misspoke" and "misremembered") for the familiar sociopathy that dominates the highest levels of today's Democratic Party.[286]

After explaining that Hillary is just the latest Democratic luminary in a surreal list of past presidents and candidates he continues:

> Barack Obama, a deceitful, America-hating, leftist radical; and now, Hillary Clinton, who iconic New York Times columnist and Presidential Medal of Freedom recipient William Safire correctly labeled "a congenital liar."
>
> Let's examine this business of getting one's way by lying, as Hillary Clinton (like Barack Obama) does almost as easily as breathing.
>
> To lie that easily, utterly without shame or embarrassment – something problematic for most people, since their conscience interferes – is the hallmark of a sociopath, someone apparently conscienceless, for whom *what he or she wants* is far more important than truth or well-being of others.
>
> Here's how famed Christian psychiatrist M. Scott Peck expressed it in his international bestseller, "People of the Lie":
>
>> All adults who are mentally healthy submit themselves one way or another to something higher than themselves, be it God or truth or love or some other ideal. They do what God wants them to do rather than what they would desire. "Thy will, not mine, be done," the God-submitted person says. They believe in what is true rather than what they would like to be true. ... Not so the evil, however. In the conflict between their guilt and their will, it is the guilt that must go and the will must win.[287]

After a discussion with a bomb-squad chief on an airplane regarding the secret service, Kupelian summarizes the personality and demeanor of Hillary:

> That Jekyll-Hyde split personality is precisely what author-journalist Ronald Kessler reports in his Hillary book, "First Family Detail," which quotes Secret Service agents as saying: "When she is in front of the lights, she turns it on, and when the lights are off and she is away from the lights, she a totally a different person. ... She's very angry and sarcastic and is very hard on her staff. ...She is a totally a different person behind the scenes than what you see when she is being interviewed.[288]

Kupelian states what people really think of Hillary besides her inside apologists as follows:

> Hillary is a thoroughly unlikable, mean-spirited, duplicitous, two-faced, foul-mouthed opportunist who desperately thinks she deserves to be president. No one left, right or center, has yet stepped forward to identify a single major accomplishment of hers, in her entire lifetime, that might even begin to qualify her to be elevated to the most important and most powerful position in the world.[289]

Based upon all the above evidence the beliefs, worldview, actions, behavior, deceptions, character and crimes of Hillary Clinton and that of her husband, Bill, are most undesirable for anyone in a leadership position let alone someone that is running for President of the United States! The American electorate seems almost oblivious to the important characteristics of a political leader and are drawn instead to popular figures that present themselves well in front of a camera. God help America!

CHAPTER 29
Conservative candidates

We documented in Chapter 10 that liberal / progressive positions are 100% diametrically opposed to biblical principles. Also throughout the book we have shown that those positions are self-serving, corrupt, freedom robbing, unsustainable and destructive to America. They are also socialistic or perhaps more technically fascist. The problem is that much of the Republican Party is quite similar to the Democratic Party rather than being the diametric opposite. However, the good news is that at least some of the Republican candidates have all their positions virtually in diametric opposition to the liberal / progressives. Those are the ones that will actually give us a clear choice between good and evil.

Scott Walker gave his speech in conjunction with announcing that he is officially running for the office of President of the United States. Although he has long ago dropped out of the race, his speech was remarkable in that on every topic his position is diametrically opposed to those of the Obama administration and are believed to be in sync with biblical principles. The positions taken include the following:

1. He fully supports our veterans
2. He emphasized the importance of our love for God and Country
3. He brings bold ideas from outside of Washington
4. He took on unions and won rather than pander to them
5. He reduced taxes on individuals, employers and property
6. He passed lawsuit reform to rein in lawyers
7. He passed regulatory reform that simplified regulations rather than making them more onerous
8. He defunded Planned Parenthood rather than funding it
9. He enacted pro-life legislation rather than pro-abortion
10. He enacted the castle doctrine legislations that protect people's right to defend their abode
11. He passed concealed carry legislation
12. He implemented voter ID requirements to vote in Wisconsin
13. He is for economic growth and citizen safety
14. He is for transferring power from the federal government to the states
15. He is for building the economy so everyone can live the American dream.
16. He is for protecting our children from Islamic terrorists

17. He believes when we need to fight we need to fight to win
18. He believes that we should take power away from special interest groups and return it to working Americans
19. He believes we should return control of schools to local taxpayers
20. He ended seniority and tenure in schools
21. He made teacher's pay and employment based upon merit
22. His policies made graduation rates, third grade reading scores and ACT scores go up
23. He recommends that we should move power and money out of Washington and send it back to our states and communities in key areas like Medicaid, transportation, workforce development and education.
24. As opposed to measuring success by how many people are dependent on the government, he measures success by how many people are no longer dependent on the government
25. He understands that true freedom and prosperity don't come from the mighty hand of the government, they come from empowering people to live their own lives and control their own destinies through the dignity that comes from work.
26. He enacted a program that says that adults who are able to work must be enrolled in one of our job training programs and pass a drug test before they can get a welfare check.
27. He is promoting strong families where both parents are involved in raising the children
28. He promotes freedom as a cornerstone of the American Dream.
29. He will promote policies that promote more jobs and higher wages
30. He promotes repealing "Obama Care"
31. He also promotes the need to rein in the federal government's out-of-control regulations that are like a wet blanket on the economy
32. He recommends putting in place an "all-of-the-above" energy policy that uses the abundance of what God has given us here in America and on this continent
33. He will support the Keystone pipeline
34. He trusts parents to make the right decision for their children
35. He will eliminate Common Core while implementing local high standards in schools
36. He understands the need to lower the burden on hard-working taxpayers to improve take-home pay
37. He supports lower tax levels that are competitive for job creators to bring jobs back from overseas to put more of our fellow Americans back to work

38. He believes in the Reagan doctrine that rebuilt our military, stood up for our friends, stood up to our enemies and – without apology – stood for American values: this led to one of the most peaceful times in modern American history
39. He knows that Iran is not a place we should be doing business and that Iran hasn't changed much since he and the other hostages were released on President Reagan's first day in office
40. He would terminate the bad deal with Iran on Day One, put in place crippling economic sanctions and convince our allies to do the same
41. Rather than focusing on climate change like Obama he would focus on the greatest threat to future generations, radical Islamic terrorism
42. He would lift the political restrictions on our military personnel in Iraq so they can help our Kurd and Sunni allies reclaim land taken by ISIS
43. As opposed to Obama's policy, he realizes that we need to acknowledge that Israel is our ally and start treating Israel like an ally. There should be absolutely no daylight between our two countries
44. He believes that we need to stop the aggression of Russia into sovereign nations like Ukraine
45. He believes we need to stop China's cyber-attacks, stop their territorial expansion into international waters and speak out about their abysmal human rights record
46. He believes in rebuilding the Defense budget at least to the levels recommended by Secretary Gates
47. He believes we need to honor our men and women in uniform by giving them the resources they need to keep us safe – and then give them the quality and timely healthcare they deserve when they return home
48. He believes that immigrants in the past didn't come here to become dependent on the government. The reason they came was because America is one of the few places left in the world where it doesn't matter what class you were born into or what your parents did for a living. In America, you can do and be anything you want. That is the kind of immigrants we want coming to America

As you can see all of Scott Walkers positions are in diametric opposition to Obama's and in line with biblical principles. These positions are exactly what the American public needs to be able to make a clear choice between good and evil, freedom and bondage. What the media always supports are moderate Republican candidates. They push the false narrative that a true conservative cannot win. That is a lie from the pit of Hell! Certainly, the moderate(ly) bad Republicans have not won recently.

We need to support true conservatives and particularly those that are willing to stand up against the Washington establishment's tyrannical policies, "Political Correctness," "The New Tolerance" and "Outrage Based Coerced Conscience."

The candidate that has recently spoke what he believed to be the truth on immigration issue and the Islamic issues in spite of knowing that he would be demonized by the politically correct media and liberals is Donald Trump. He has taken many conservative positions, but previously has never been a conservative. He has never been on my radar as a potential candidate, but has at least shown the attributes that are absolutely necessary to expose the evil policies that the liberal candidates promote. I have to give credit where credit is due. However, I cannot endorse him as a candidate because he is a narcissist like Obama and is the epitome of pragmatism rather than one that is principled. The main difference between Obama and Trump is that Trump actually loves America.

The other outspoken candidate that has consistently spoken up and stood up against Obama and even the Republican establishment is Ted Cruz. I believe he is the only one that has stated that the IRS should be abolished. His positions are completely based upon his personal principles and biblical principles, not public opinion or the establishment inertia. I certainly feel comfortable endorsing Ted Cruz.

The other candidates that appear to be running for the sole purpose of turning our country around and be the best candidates based upon diametric opposition to Obama's positions, in sync with biblical principles and being a strong political leader include Ben Carson, Carly Fiorina and Bobby Jindal. However, at this time they are no longer running. They are very principled candidates that should also be seriously considered.

The media, debates and perhaps the money will have a large effect on who comes out on top. However, what we need to do is to stay behind the candidate(s) that will expose all the false narratives and stand up and defend against the demonization being thrown at them while promoting liberty, opportunity, safety and biblical social values. Evangelicals need to understand which candidates support the biblical principles that their beliefs should support and they need to perform their biblical mandate by voting to promote "light" and expose evil.

Next in Part 8 we end the book with asking the question, "What can we do?" and then attempt to answer it.

Part 8

What can we do?

CHAPTER 30
To resist and defeat evil

The bible is clear that there is a war in progress and that we are in the center of that war.

Revelation 12:7-9 states:

> [7] And war broke out in heaven: Michael and his angels fought with the dragon; and the dragon and his angels fought, [8] but they did not prevail, nor was a place found for them in heaven any longer. [9] So the great dragon was cast out, that serpent of old, called the Devil and Satan, who deceives the whole world; he was cast to the earth, and his angels were cast out with him.

Verse 17 continues:

> [17] And the dragon was enraged with the woman, and he went to make war with the rest of her offspring, who keep the commandments of God and have the testimony of Jesus Christ.

Ephesians 6:12 States:

> [12] For we do not wrestle against flesh and blood, but against principalities, against powers, against the rulers of the darkness of this age, against spiritual hosts of wickedness in the heavenly places. [13] Therefore take up the whole armor of God, that you may be able to withstand in the evil day, and having done all, to stand.

2 Corinthians 10:3-5:

> [3] For though we walk in the flesh, we do not war according to the flesh. [4] For the weapons of our warfare are not carnal but mighty in God for pulling down strongholds, [5] casting down arguments and every high thing that exalts itself against the knowledge of God, bringing every thought into captivity to the obedience of Christ, . .

PERSONAL ACTIONS

The first thing we need to do is examine ourselves to see where we stand in the spiritual battle as summarized in the above scripture verses. In chapter 2 we discussed the fact that in this war there is no middle ground. Revelation 3:16 states:

> So then, because you are lukewarm, and neither cold nor hot, I will vomit you out of My mouth.

This confirms that we are either on the side of good or evil. However, just because we believe that we are on the side of good, God's side, doesn't mean that we are good and are destined for heaven based upon our goodness, church attendance, following tradition, doing sacraments or our giving to charity etc.

Although many of us have been brought up with Judeo-Christian values, and we try to follow them, that doesn't mean that we are saved and headed to heaven according to the bible. If those things would save us, Jesus wouldn't have had to die on the cross to save us, right?

The bible teaches that the only way to be saved is for us to realize our actual condition; that we are sinners and based on the justice of a holy God we deserve death. We need to accept Jesus' death as an atonement for us and that we cannot be saved by our own merits. Once we do, and by being sorry for our sins and repenting of them and accepting Jesus' atonement, then are we saved. Once we are saved, the Holy Spirit indwells our bodies (Ephesians 1:13) he transforms our mind (Romans 12:1-2) and leads us into all truth (John 14:16-17). The transforming of our mind changes our priorities and what we love. Before we are transformed, we live in the flesh and we tend to stretch liberty into license to satisfy our carnal passions, pleasures and lusts. When our desires and actions are contrary to what God's word condones we have a conflict of interest with our conscience. Consequently, we rationalize the evil that we think and do by accepting the false beliefs of the world while rejecting true biblical principles. This is what is meant in Romans 1:18 where it states:

> [18] For the wrath of God is revealed from heaven against all ungodliness and unrighteousness of men, who suppress the truth in unrighteousness, . .

Until or unless we become contrite and confess our sins and establish a personal relationship with Jesus, we have difficulty accepting or even recognizing the truth and certainly will not achieve our desired eternal destiny. The truth is such a precious commodity that we should value it highly. Although God also values it highly, He definitely does not force it upon us. When Jesus' disciples asked Him "Why do you speak to them in parables?" He stated the following in Matthew 13:11-13:

> "Because it has been given to you to know the mysteries of the kingdom of heaven, but to them it has not been given. [12] For whoever has, to him more will be given, and he will have abundance; but whoever does not have, even what he has will be taken away from him. [13] Therefore I speak to them in parables, because seeing they do not see, and hearing they do not hear, nor do they understand."

Consequently, until we allow God to transform us from our carnal state with primarily fleshly desires into a born again, new spiritual creation by establishing a relationship with Him we cannot align ourselves with or effectively promote truth because of our internal conflict with truth. Consequently, this must be the first step toward completely accepting truth and aligning with it or promoting it. Certainly a sales person cannot effectively sell a product that he does not really believe in. In the same way, until we really accept truth and completely align ourselves with it, we cannot help spread the truth even amongst our family and friends let alone in our corporate and public world.

The example of Saul Alinsky we used in Chapter 1 is the antithesis of a spiritually born again Christian. Alinsky is completely aligned with Lucifer (Satan) and is in complete rebellion against God.

TRUTHS NEEDED TO RESIST AND DEFEAT EVIL

The truths needed to resist and defeat evil are basically a summary of this book. However, let's summarize those things we must understand to effectively wage this spiritual battle.

1. Become spiritually born again and have your mind renewed by allowing the indwelling of the Holy Spirit to lead you into all truth
2. Understand the source of evil
3. Understand the attributes of evil
4. Understand the attributes of Satan and God
5. Understand concepts relating to evil
6. Understand how to recognize evil in our world based upon:
    a. The bible
    b. Modus Operandi
    c. Majoring in minors
    d. Effects
    e. Our conscience
7. Recognize that the war between good and evil can be seen in our political, cultural, secular realms and in various religions
8. Understand that the evil in our world has been supported by several false foundations that have been unjustifiably accepted by our society that include belief in:
    a. Uniformitarianism and biological macroevolution
    b. Relative truth
    c. Goodness and perfectibility of man
    d. Global warming
    e. The New Tolerance
    f. Political Correctness
    g. Case Law
    h. Separation of church and state
9. The failure of churches to promote the truth to offset the false foundations and bad fruit supported by the false foundations has allowed evil to flourish.
10. Recognize false religions

11. Understand that many of our evils are not obvious and even promoted as something good
12. Understand the false narrative that has been promoted that America historically has been evil
13. Understand how far America has been degraded in many aspects
14. Understand that President Obama is doing everything he can to destroy America as it was founded

APPLYING THESE TRUTHS TO EFFECTIVELY FIGHT THE BATTLE AGAINST EVIL

Once these truths are understood we are in a position to market these truths not only at the personal level but in the public square. The false foundations have been put in place through marketing using pseudoscience, evil philosophies, deception and through stealth modus operandi methods. I believe the primary failure has been Christian churches that have either been duped by pseudoscience and evil philosophies they accepted or have been too fearful of bucking cultural trends. Even more fundamental than these is the extensive apostasy on clear doctrinal issues. Even the evangelical churches that are teaching a biblical salvation message have failed to see and understand why the gospel has appeared to become irrelevant in the sense that it is no longer effective. They don't understand that when they have conceded that the false pseudoscientific and false cultural beliefs have trumped biblical principles, they have allowed the soil where the gospel seeds are to be planted to be contaminated to the extent that the seeds will no longer germinate. This analogy is based upon the parable of the sower in Matthew 13:3-23. Evangelical churches spend most of their efforts sowing the gospel seeds into soil that is incapable of germinating the gospel seeds. What needs to be done is for them to spend much more time cultivating the soil to make it receptive to the gospel seeds. Cultivating the soil includes exposing all the false foundations for what they are and their evil fruits as evil. That is where the effort needs to be expended. However, this effort is mostly nonexistent in our churches.

If marketing of the whole truth was done extensively in our churches where Christians contribute millions of dollars and get little in return, little other marketing would be needed. I do believe that in efforts going forward, the churches and pastors are the best place to market the truth. However, they need to understand the truth and have courage to speak to the culture rather than speaking within the culture. As Christians we need to support organizations that are speaking to the culture, particularly those that are also exposing all the false foundations. Unfortunately, these pastors and churches can be difficult to find. Otherwise we need to compel our pastors to understand and promote appropriate cultural issues through education and financial incentives. We need to redirect much of the money that is being spent on ineffective teaching and preaching.

Appendix A has some tools to appeal to pastors. Included is an appeal letter to pastors and religious leaders to become fully biblical with the help of an "Educational mission for spiritual and cultural awaking in America" document and a Biblical beliefs survey for pastors and churches to evaluate to what extent their cultural beliefs have corrupted their biblical beliefs.

Appendix B has a list of some recent letters to the editor that have been sent to newspapers in the last two years. Check them out. You may enjoy them.

Since we know that turning our churches around quickly is very difficult, we need to promote the truth through all possible grass roots methods. These include:
1. Promoting appropriate established books and DVD's etc. to our family, friends and pastors
2. Writing letters to the editor
3. Writing books
4. Write blogs
5. Having study groups
6. Letters to politicians
7. Letters to pastors
8. Start organizations to promote truth
9. Speak at meetings

This concludes our recommendations on what we can do to resist and defeat evil. It is time for you to get involved!

The next chapter documents strong evidence supporting the truth of the bible to give the reader a basis for believing everything presented in this book and as a basis for their personal salvation to secure their eternal destiny.

CHAPTER 31
Study to strengthen our confidence in the truth of God's existence and the bible

The most important supporting evidences for the truth of God's existence and the truth of the bible are fulfilled prophecy and the reliability of the scriptures based upon historic voracity and biblical internal consistency with itself and its external consistency with our world. Part of the internal consistency is what it tells us about itself.

FULFILLED PROPHECY

Biblical fulfilled prophecy is the most profound evidence of the truth of the Bible, the existence of God and the supernatural. The Bible is about one fourth prophecy. What does the Bible say about prophecy and the ability of God to know the future?

Isaiah 46:9-11 states:
> Remember the former things of old, For I am God, and there is no other; I am God, and there is none like Me, Declaring the end from the beginning, And from ancient times things that are not yet done, Saying, 'My counsel shall stand, And I will do all My pleasure,' Calling a bird of prey from the east, The man who executes My counsel, from a far country. Indeed I have spoken it; I will also bring it to pass. I have purposed it; I will also do it.

I Thessalonians 5:20 states, "Do not despise prophecies."

II Peter 1:19-21 states:
> And so we have the prophetic word confirmed, which you do well to heed as a light that shines in a dark place, until the day dawns and the morning star rises in your hearts; knowing this first, that no prophecy of Scripture is of any private interpretation, for prophecy never came by the will of man, but holy men of God spoke as they were moved by the Holy Spirit.

So the Bible states emphatically that Biblical prophecy is from God and will come to pass as predicted.

The Bible also addresses so-called prophets that prophesy and their prophecies do not come true. Deuteronomy 18:21-22 states that they are not God's prophets:
> And if you say in your heart, 'How shall we know the word which the LORD has not spoken?' when a prophet speaks in the name of the LORD, if the thing does not happen or come to pass, that is the thing

which the LORD has not spoken; the prophet has spoken it presumptuously; you shall not be afraid of him.

In Isaiah 41:21:23 God through Isaiah is mocking those that believe in idols rather than the true God:

Present your case," says the LORD. "Bring forth your strong reasons," says the King of Jacob. "Let them bring forth and show us what will happen; Let them show the former things, what they were, That we may consider them, And know the latter end of them; Or declare to us things to come. Show the things that are to come hereafter, That we may know that you are gods; Yes, do good or do evil, That we may be dismayed and see it together. Indeed you are nothing, And your work is nothing; He who chooses you is an abomination.

No religious book other than the Bible has any fulfilled prophecy. That is why God mocked the false idols and their false gods. They cannot predict the future! However, the Bible has many fulfilled prophecies.

Messianic Prophecies

Dr. David Reagan of Lamb and Lion Ministries has written a "Christ in Prophecy" study guide[290] that chronicles all the Messianic prophecies as well as other prophecies. Dr. Reagan states that the Bible has about 330 Messianic prophecies of which 108 or 109 of them are unique and every one of them fulfilled exactly as predicted. He tells how Dr. Peter Stoner has taken just 8 of the 109 fulfilled Messianic prophecies and calculated the probability of occurring in one individual. The chance of that happening by random chance is one chance in 10 to the 17th power.[291]

Dr. Stoner gave an example that shows us of how small a chance that is. If Texas were covered with silver dollars two feet deep and one marked dollar was randomly placed, a blindfolded person would have to pick the marked dollar on the first try.

That is only for 8 of the 109 prophecies being fulfilled. The chance of all of them being fulfilled like Jesus Christ fulfilled them is impossible on a chance basis. That is the point. Jesus was exactly who the Bible said He was. He was the Son of God incarnated into a man.

Many critics claim that prophecies had to have been written after the events took place because they deny the possibility of the supernatural.

However, scholars agree that all of the Old Testament books were written before Christ. Ra McLaughlin states the following in an article titled "Old Testament Dates of Composition in answer to a question of "When was the Old Testament written?":

The Old Testament was written over a long period of time, ranging from approximately the 15th century B.C. for some of the older books (e.g. Genesis, Exodus) to perhaps as late as the 4th century B.C. for the final forms of some of the most recent books (e.g. Ezra, Nehemiah, Chronicles. Because the Bible itself does not date its books, these dates are the results of scholarly dialogues and conclusions. The date range I have provided includes the most extreme (earliest and latest) dates generally attested by conservative scholars. Liberal scholars tend to set much later dates for many books (into the 2nd century B.C. for some). It is also likely that even the oldest books relied to some degree on prior written sources which have not been preserved through the ages.[292]

In the case of the birth, life, crucifixion and resurrection of Jesus many critics claim that Jesus knew of the prophecies and fulfilled them on purpose. That explanation is completely wishful thinking because Jesus could not have made many of them come true even if he wanted to.

How could he control the following Old Testament prophecies?

Prophecy	O.T. Prophecy Reference	N.T. Prophecy Fulfillment
Virgin conception	Isaiah 7:14	Matthew 1:22-23
Born in Bethlehem	Micah 5:2	Luke 2:4-11
Descendant of Abraham	Genesis 12:1-3	Matthew 1:1
Jewish rejection	Psalms 118:22	I Peter 2:7
Miracles	Isaiah 35:5-6	Matthew 9:35
Ascension	Psalms 68:18	Acts 1:9
Betrayed: 30 pieces of silver	Zechariah 11:12-13	Matthew 27:9-10
Crucified with thieves	Isaiah 53:12	Luke 23:33
Side would be pierced	Zechariah 12:10	John 19:34
Buried in rich man's tomb	Isaiah 53:9	Matthew 27:57-60
Lots cast for His garments	Psalms 22:18	John 19:23-24
Hands and feet pierced	Psalms 22:16	Luke 23:33
Betrayal money returned	Zechariah 11:13	Matthew 27:3-10
Gall and vinegar offered	Psalms 69:21	Matthew 27:34
No bones broken	Psalms 34:20	John 19:33-36
Daytime darkness at noon	Amos 8:9	Matthew 27:45
Betrayal money: bought field	Zechariah 11:13	Matthew 27:7
Scourged and spit upon	Isaiah 50:6	Mark 14:65
Resurrection	Psalms 16:8-10; 30:3	Luke 24:6, 31-34

This short list includes just 19 prophecies of the unique 108 or 109 that exist. Jesus had no control over any of these prophecies. The assertion of skeptics that Jesus simply made sure all the prophecies came true is impossible. The high specificity of the prophecies should be noted. These are not the vague type of prophecies like Nostradamus made. Each one can be and was readily validated. Also, it is interesting and revealing that each of the Old Testament prophecies has a text in the New Testament that verifies the fulfillment. It is also interesting that some of the prophecies from a natural standpoint had virtually no chance of being fulfilled. Crucifixion wasn't even used by the Romans as a form of execution until more than 700 years after the prediction. Who would predict a virgin birth or a resurrection from the dead!

The messianic prophecies alone should convince us that God exists, the supernatural exists and should give us great assurance that the Bible is true and reliable.

Jewish prophecies

Genesis 12:1-3 states:
> Now the LORD had said to Abram:
> "Get out of your country, From your family And from your father's house,
> To a land that I will show you. I will make you a great nation; I will bless you
> And make your name great; And you shall be a blessing. I will bless those who bless you, And I will curse him who curses you; And in you all the families of the earth shall be blessed."

This was an unconditional promise to Abraham. Abraham did what God requested and God kept His promise. Certainly God made a great nation from Abraham's seed. This includes both the Jews and the Arabs. Certainly Abraham's name is great. Also, since Jesus was in the lineage of Abraham, He certainly was correct when He said "And in you all the families of the earth shall be blessed." The other promise that "I will bless those who bless you, And I will curse him who curses you," has been fulfilled in many instances, but is still active and will continue to be fulfilled in the future. However, the majority of denominational Christendom are amillennial replacement theologists and do not believe that after Jesus Christ was crucified that those promises are still in effect since the Jews crucified Jesus. Not only is that belief contrary to scripture, but also since 1948 when Israel became a nation again, as the Bible predicted, was also contrary to recent history. If the promises to Israel are no longer in effect, how could that seemingly impossible event have come to pass!

Regarding blessing and curses, a book by William Koenig titled, "Eye to Eye: Facing the Consequences of Dividing Israel." The book documents how many, many catastrophes and events have happened to the United States within 24 hours of pressuring Israel to divide their land. The back cover of the book states:
What do these major record-setting events have in common?
- Nine of the ten costliest insurance events in U.S. history
- Six of the seven costliest hurricanes in U.S. history
- Three of the four largest tornado outbreaks in U.S. history
- Nine of the top ten natural disasters in U.S. History ranked by FEMA relief costs
- The two largest terrorism events in U.S. history

All of these major catastrophes transpired on the very same day or within 24 hours of U.S. presidents Bush, Clinton and Bush applying pressure on Israel to trade her land for promises of "peace and security," sponsoring major "land for peace" meetings, making major public statements pertaining to Israel's covenant land and / or calling for a Palestinian state.[293]

Zechariah 12:9 states:
> It shall be in that day that I will seek to destroy all the nations that come against Jerusalem.

We need to recognize that God is speaking to us when we see many tragedies occur in the US that correlate with our putting pressure on Israel to divide her land.

The Bible predicted that if the Jews would not observe His commandments that He would curse them as a nation. One thing He would do is to scatter them around the world.

Deuteronomy 28:64 states:
> Then the LORD will scatter you among all peoples, from one end of the earth to the other, and there you shall serve other gods, which neither you nor your fathers have known—wood and stone.

In 721 BC the Northern kingdom, ten tribes of Israel, was conquered and carried away by Assyria. II Kings 17:5-6 states:
> Now the king of Assyria went throughout all the land, and went up to Samaria and besieged it for three years. In the ninth year of Hoshea, the king of Assyria took Samaria and carried Israel away to Assyria, and placed them in Halah and by the Habor, the River of Gozan, and in the cities of the Medes.

An additional fulfillment of this prophecy came true when Jerusalem, Judah's two tribes, were conquered by Babylon in 587 BC (initial captives including Daniel in 605 BC) and the remainder hauled away to Babylon. II Kings 24:13-16 states:

> And he carried out from there all the treasures of the house of the LORD and the treasures of the king's house, and he cut in pieces all the articles of gold which Solomon king of Israel had made in the temple of the LORD, as the LORD had said. Also he carried into captivity all Jerusalem: all the captains and all the mighty men of valor, ten thousand captives, and all the craftsmen and smiths. None remained except the poorest people of the land. And he carried Jehoiachin captive to Babylon. The king's mother, the king's wives, his officers, and the mighty of the land he carried into captivity from Jerusalem to Babylon. All the valiant men, seven thousand, and craftsmen and smiths, one thousand, all who were strong and fit for war, these the king of Babylon brought captive to Babylon.

Next the Bible prophesied that the Jews would be in captivity for 70 years. Jeremiah 25:11-12 states:

> And this whole land shall be a desolation and an astonishment, and these nations shall serve the king of Babylon seventy years. 'Then it will come to pass, when seventy years are completed, that I will punish the king of Babylon and that nation, the land of the Chaldeans, for their iniquity,' says the LORD; 'and I will make it a perpetual desolation.

Also Jeremiah 29:10 states:

> For thus says the LORD: After seventy years are completed at Babylon, I will visit you and perform My good word toward you, and cause you to return to this place.

Both parts of this prophecy were fulfilled in 536 BC when Cyrus the Great of Persian conquered Babylon. Babylon was destroyed and the Jewish captives were set free. Although 605 minus 536 is only 69 years, the fact that the Jewish calendar had 360 days rather than 365 accounted for the one-year difference.

Consequently, the prophecy of seventy-year captivity was fulfilled exactly as predicted.

The next Jewish prophecy was given by Daniel in Daniel 9:24-27:

> Seventy weeks are determined For your people and for your holy city, To finish the transgression, To make an end of sins, To make reconciliation for iniquity, To bring in everlasting righteousness, To seal up vision and prophecy, And to anoint the Most Holy. " Know therefore and understand, That from the going forth of the command To restore and build Jerusalem Until Messiah the Prince, There shall be seven weeks and sixty-two weeks; The street shall be built again, and the wall, Even in troublesome times. " And after the sixty-two weeks Messiah shall be cut off, but not for Himself; And the people of the prince who is to come Shall destroy the city and the sanctuary. The end of it shall be with a flood, And till the end of the war desolations are determined. Then he shall confirm a covenant with many for one week; But in the

middle of the week He shall bring an end to sacrifice and offering. And on the wing of abominations shall be one who makes desolate, Even until the consummation, which is determined, Is poured out on the desolate."

This prophecy entails multiple separate prophecies, which include:
- Christ's death
- Fulfillment of multiple purposes of Christ's death
- The exact timing of Christ's death
- The future destruction of Jerusalem and the temple (what happened in 70 AD)
- The Antichrist of Revelation would destroy Jerusalem and the temple again during the great tribulation, just like the Romans did in 70 AD.

Christ's death was obviously fulfilled. Christian's understand the Biblical teachings on the purposes and accomplishments of Christ's death and resurrection. Jerusalem and the temple were certainly destroyed in 70 AD. However, the prophecy that predicts the exact timing of Christ's death, although well understood by many prophecy scholars, is not well understood by most Christians and those that need to appreciate the significance of this incredibly accurate prediction as important information to help us to accept the true Biblical worldview. The last prediction on the list is a prophecy of the future.

Only one prophecy was given in the Bible to restore and build Jerusalem. That prophecy was in Nehemiah 1-6:

> And it came to pass in the month of Nisan, in the twentieth year of King Artaxerxes, when wine was before him, that I took the wine and gave it to the king. Now I had never been sad in his presence before. Therefore the king said to me, "Why is your face sad, since you are not sick? This is nothing but sorrow of heart." So I became dreadfully afraid, and said to the king, "May the king live forever! Why should my face not be sad, when the city, the place of my fathers' tombs, lies waste, and its gates are burned with fire?" Then the king said to me, "What do you request?" So I prayed to the God of heaven. And I said to the king, "If it pleases the king, and if your servant has found favor in your sight, I ask that you send me to Judah, to the city of my fathers' tombs, that I may rebuild it." Then the king said to me (the queen also sitting beside him), "How long will your journey be? And when will you return?" So it pleased the king to send me; and I set him a time.

However, three other Biblical decrees were made regarding either the building of the temple or for things other than building something. The following table was taken from the Prophetic Technology website.[294]

Persian King	Decree Date	Decree to Rebuild	Biblical References
Cyrus	539-36 BC	Temple	2 Chron. 36:21-23 Ezra 1:1-4; 6:1-5
Darius	520-19 BC	Temple	Ezra 6:6-12
Artaxerxes to Ezra	March 8, 458 BC	None	Ezra 7:11-26
Artaxerxes to Nehemiah	March 14, 445 BC	Jerusalem	Neh. 2:1-6

The total prophecy of seventy weeks is divided into one part that is 7 and 62 weeks and the other part, the seventieth week. The first part is what the prophecy quotes for the interval of time between the decree and when the Messiah will be cut off. The reference to 62 weeks in addition to the 7 weeks that were included with it earlier. This is a total of 69 weeks. The prophecy used weeks as "weeks of years" so the 69 weeks is referring to 483 years.

The scholar Sir Robert Anderson has calculated the beginning and ending of this time interval and it fits the prophecy exactly. He used April 6, AD 32 as date Christ rode into Jerusalem on a donkey. He states:

> What then was the length of the period intervening between the issuing of the decree to rebuild Jerusalem and the public advent of "Messiah the Prince"—between the 14th March BC 445 and the 6th April AD 32? The interval contained exactly and to the very day 173,880 days, or seven times sixty-nine prophetic years of 360 days, the first sixty-nine weeks of Gabriel's prophecy.[295]

The next prophecy is the dispersion of the Jews throughout the nations and bringing them together again in the land of Israel. Ezekiel 36:19 states:

> So I scattered them among the nations, and they were dispersed throughout the countries; I judged them according to their ways and their deeds.

Ezekiel 36:24 states:

> For I will take you from among the nations, gather you out of all countries, and bring you into your own land.

Zephaniah 3:9 states:

> For then I will restore to the peoples a pure language, That they all may call on the name of the LORD, To serve Him with one accord.

Incredibly, all three of these prophecies have been fulfilled on May 14th 1948 when Israel became nation. Again, it is important that we grasp the profound significance of this event. The Jews (Judah) were scattered for 1878 years and Israel (the lost ten tribes) have been scattered for 2669 years before Israel became a nation again. Just the fact that the Jews have been able to keep their identity all those years is miraculous. No other peoples have done this.

The thoughts.com website states:

> The Hebrew language would be restored. (Zechariah 3:9) Remarkable, but today Hebrew is once again the official language of Israel. Ultimately, when Christ returns to set up his kingdom, all people will share one speech. Not only will one language be restored, as it was before Babel, (Genesis 11:1), but all people will call on the Lord with one accord[296]

Another prophecy relates to the land of Israel being desolate during their dispersion and then blooming like a rose after becoming a nation again.

Ezekiel 36:34-35 states:

> The desolate land shall be tilled instead of lying desolate in the sight of all who pass by. So they will say, 'This land that was desolate has become like the Garden of Eden; and the wasted, desolate, and ruined cities are now fortified and inhabited.

Mark Twain made this quote about Palestine in 1867:

> A desolate country whose soil is rich enough, but is given over wholly to weeds... a silent mournful expanse.... a desolation.... we never saw a human being on the whole route.... hardly a tree or shrub anywhere. Even the olive tree and the cactus, those fast friends of a worthless soil, had almost deserted the country.[297]

Today we all know how Israel has blossomed like a rose. Israel is supplying much produce to Europe.

Another type of prophecy is that Israel will have some level of security and will not be driven from their land once they returned to it from the great dispersion.

Jeremiah 23:3, 6 & 8 states:

> But I will gather the remnant of My flock out of all countries where I have driven them, and bring them back to their folds; and they shall be fruitful and increase.
> In His days Judah will be saved, And Israel will dwell safely; Now this is His name by which He will be called: THE LORD OUR RIGHTEOUSNESS.
> . . but, 'As the LORD lives who brought up and led the descendants of the house of Israel from the north country and from all the countries where I had driven them.' And they shall dwell in their own land.

It is a miraculous fact that modern Israel has been able to defend itself against its vastly superior armies and populations. The Arab countries had land areas that were 650 times the area of Israel. The Arab populations were 50 times higher. UnitedJerusalem.com documented the following about the 1948 war:

> The 1948 War of Independence:

On May 14th 1948 the State of Israel was proclaimed according to the UN partition plan (1947). Less than 24 hours later, the regular armies of Egypt, Trans-Jordan, Syria, Lebanon and Iraq invaded the country, forcing Israel to defend the sovereignty it had regained in its ancestral homeland. In what became known as Israel's War of Independence, the newly formed, poorly equipped Israel Defense Forces (IDF) repulsed the invaders in fierce intermittent fighting, which lasted some 15 months and claimed over 6,000 Israeli lives (nearly one percent of the country's Jewish population.[298]

Since then Israel has fought the 1967 Six-Day War, the 1973 Yom Kippur War and others. Although they have had no peace, they have survived and flourished while under constant oppression.

While on this subject, I would like to include two quotes. One from Charles Krauthammer and the other from Science.com regarding legitimatizing the Palestinian state issue:

> Israel is the very embodiment of Jewish continuity: It is the only nation on earth that inhabits the same land, bears the same name, speaks the same language, and worships the same God that it did 3,000 years ago. You dig the soil and you find pottery from Davidic times, coins from Bar Kokhba, and 2,000-year-old scrolls written in a script remarkably like the one that today advertises ice cream at the corner candy store.[299]

Israel Science and Technology website stated the following:

> It was only after the Jews re-inhabited their historic homeland of Judea and Samaria, that the myth of a Palestinian nation was created and marketed worldwide. Jews come from Judea, not Palestinians. There is no language known as Palestinian, or any Palestinian culture distinct from that of all the Arabs in the area. There has never been a land known as Palestine governed by Palestinians. Palestinians are Arabs indistinguishable from Arabs throughout the Middle East. The great majority of Arabs in greater Palestine and Israel share the same culture, language and religion.[300]

What we hear in the media about the Palestine issue over and over again is simply not true!

The following prophecy predicts that Jerusalem will eventually be recaptured by the Jews.

Luke 21:24 states:

> And they will fall by the edge of the sword, and be led away captive into all nations. And Jerusalem will be trampled by Gentiles until the times of the Gentiles are fulfilled.

This means that Jerusalem will once again be controlled by the Jews. That prophecy was fulfilled in June 1967.

If one looks at the history of the Jews since Israel became a nation the fact that it is still in existence is beyond comprehension.

The following prophecy predicts that the Jews will stay blind regarding Jesus being their Messiah until a specified time.

Romans 11:25-26 states:
> For I do not desire, brethren, that you should be ignorant of this mystery, lest you should be wise in your own opinion, that blindness in part has happened to Israel until the fullness of the Gentiles has come in. And so all Israel will be saved, as it is written: "The Deliverer will come out of Zion, And He will turn away ungodliness from Jacob;"

Although the number of Messianic Jews has increased in number, it is still only a small fraction of the population. Jews still do not recognize Jesus as their Messiah.

Just these Jewish prophecies should be sufficient for us to believe in God, the truth of the Bible and in Jesus and His plan of salvation.

Destruction of cities and empires

We already briefly mentioned the destruction of Babylon. However, there is more to the story that will help us to appreciate the improbability and uniqueness of the event. First of all King Belshazzar had a feast the night of the fall of Babylon. Daniel 5:22-28 states:
> But you his son, Belshazzar, have not humbled your heart, although you knew all this. And you have lifted yourself up against the Lord of heaven. They have brought the vessels of His house before you, and you and your lords, your wives and your concubines, have drunk wine from them. And you have praised the gods of silver and gold, bronze and iron, wood and stone, which do not see or hear or know; and the God who holds your breath in His hand and owns all your ways, you have not glorified. Then the fingers of the hand were sent from Him, and this writing was written. "And this is the inscription that was written: MENE, MENE, TEKEL, PHARSIN. This is the interpretation of each word. MENE: God has numbered your kingdom, and finished it; TEKEK: You have been weighed in the balances, and found wanting; PERES: Your kingdom has been divided, and given to the Medes and Persians."

Nothing about this event could have been associated with chance. The fact that they were drinking wine from vessels from Israel on that very night is not likely to be a coincidence. Certainly, the handwriting on the wall was supernatural. Also, the fact that Daniel was able to interpret the writing that the other wise men and astrologers could not interpret was also supernatural.

D. James Kennedy commented on the night that Babylon was conquered in "Why I believe." He identified that the walls surrounding Babylon were 200 feet thick and 87 feet high with 300 foot high towers extending way above the walls. He stated the following:

> It also could not be a coincidence that what was described above happened on that very day the Persians redirected the Euphrates River into a channel so the river going through Babylon was shallow enough for the soldiers to march right into the city. Other than the method used, the city was impregnable.[301]

Kennedy also identified another miraculous prophecy fulfillment concerning the destruction of the city of Tyre that included the fact that Tyre would never be rebuilt or ever be inhabited again. Under a paragraph heading of "Proclamation Against Tyre," Ezekiel 26:2-5 states:

> Son of man, because Tyre has said against Jerusalem, 'Aha! She is broken who was the gateway of the peoples; now she is turned over to me; I shall be filled; she is laid waste.' "Therefore thus says the Lord GOD: 'Behold, I am against you, O Tyre, and will cause many nations to come up against you, as the sea causes its waves to come up. And they shall destroy the walls of Tyre and break down her towers; I will also scrape her dust from her, and make her like the top of a rock. It shall be a place for spreading nets in the midst of the sea, for I have spoken,' says the Lord GOD; 'it shall become plunder for the nations.

Kennedy also described how Nebuchadnezzar, king of Babylon, attacked the city of Tyre. He explained how the inhabitants of Tyre resisted being conquered for thirteen years. Eventually, the city fell when the walls were breached. Nebuchadnezzar killed the inhabitants except for those who escaped. Those fortunate citizens that did escape did so by boating to an island about a half-mile from the mainland. This island became the new city of Tyre. Kennedy stated:

> At this point the prophecy was only partially fulfilled. Some critics claim that Ezekiel wrote this prophecy after the event transpired. However, that is not possible since Ezekiel was dead for 250 years before the rest of the prophecy was fulfilled. It would seem impossible that someone would come many years later and complete the prophecy, but that is exactly what happened.[302]

Kennedy described the history of Alexander the Great pursuing the Persian army along the Mediterranean coastline. He was attempting to nullify the power of the Persian navy before continuing to pursue the Persian army. His strategy was to conquer all the cities along the Mediterranean coastline first. None of the other cities really gave Alexander a fight. However, that was not the case for city of Tyre. He goes on to tell the story:

> When he commanded the city to surrender, the inhabitants laughed at him. However, Alexander the Great, being who he was, conceived of a

brilliant and unique plan to conquer Tyre. They would build a causeway across the Mediterranean Sea to the island of "new Tyre." The plan included the use of the materials in the walls of Tyre. Consequently, Alexander the Great was given the incentive to fulfill the prophecy by removing all the stones, timbers etc. and dumping them into the sea. History reveals that they scrapped the city down to the bedrock to get enough material to build the road to the island. Consequently, the place was prepared for the fishermen to spread their nets.[303]

Kennedy also tells the story of how a member of his church visited the city of Tyre. He took pictures that showed nets spread out on the flat rock that once had been the city of Tyre.

Frank Harber, in "Reasons for Believing" has a table that includes similar fulfilled prophesies for the following civilizations or cities: Sidon, Thebes, Egypt, Edom, Gaza, Philistia, Bethel, Nineveh, Samaria and Capernaum. The table includes the scripture location, type of judgment and fulfillment reference.[304]

This evidence of fulfilled prophecy in the Bible is overwhelming and far more than needed to convince anyone that the Bible is true when evaluated objectively without presupposition.

HISTORICAL VERACITY OF THE BIBLE

Reliable Documentation

This section covers three areas of verification and one area of preservation. One area of verification is that the Scriptures were documented in a timely fashion by eyewitnesses or those to whom God revealed prophesy or those who God appointed as editor of history like Moses, so that legend did not get a chance to contaminate the Scriptures with myth. A second area of verification is that those original scriptures were copied and passed down without significant errors that would change their meaning. The third area of verification is that the correct books were included into the Scripture. The last topic included is the remarkable preservation of the Scriptures under very destructive environments.

The information in this section is from Frank Harber's book "Reasons for Believing." Harber's book is very good on this topic and the reader should get a copy and read his entire book. Here we can only include small excerpts.

Verification

Because the Bible is an ancient book, some wonder if they are reading the original message and text of the Bible. Harber states:

> "The Bible is the most trustworthy document from all of antiquity. In standards of reliability, the Bible stands without any single peer."[305]

Harber starts with comments on the Old Testament:

> The original autographs of the Old Testament were written on papyrus. Papyrus deteriorates at a very rapid rate. Because of this, scribes were employed to copy the books of the Old Testament. These scribes believed the scriptures to be the word of God and went to great lengths to eliminate error. . . Prior to 1947 the oldest existing Old Testament copy was the Masoretic text that is dated about A.D. 900. In 1947 the Dead Sea Scrolls were found at Qumran. Many of the scrolls dated back to around 150 B.C. making them almost 1000 years older than the Masoretic text. The Dead Sea Scrolls read identical to the Masoretic Text. Both were identical to the Hebrew translations in our own Bibles. Only a small percentage of variation can be found, all of which can be attributed to variations in spelling.[306]

Harber continues with comments on the New Testament:

He first addresses the number of supporting copies:

> The reliability of the New Testament is also beyond question. More than 24,000 partial and complete copies of the New Testament are available today. No other document of antiquity can even come close to such large numbers. . . In addition to the New Testament manuscripts, there are over 86,000 quotations of the New Testament from the early church fathers. So thorough are these quotations that except for 11 verses of the New Testament all can be reconstructed from this material, which dates less than 200 years after the coming of Jesus.[307]

Next he addresses the short time span between the origin autographs and their copies:

> Not only are the New Testament documents superior because of their great numbers, but also because of the short time span that existed between the original autographs and their copies. . . All the books of the New Testament were probably written within 30 years of the death of Jesus. No book in antiquity can compare with the New Testament in the number of manuscripts or the short time interval between the originals and the copies.[308]

Harber includes a table of 15 different major works on antiquity showing how low the numbers of copies are compared with the New Testament and how much longer the time span is between the original and the copies. Get Harber's book and check it out.

Next Harber addresses the lack of textual corruption in the New Testament. He identified that only very slight differences have been found and that those differences do not affect doctrine of faith.

The Encyclopedia Britannica says:
> When the textual scholar has examined the manuscripts and the versions, he still has not exhausted the evidence for the New Testament text. The writings of the early Christian fathers often reflect the form of a text differing from that in one or another manuscript, their witness to the text, especially as it corroborates the readings that come from others sources, belongs to the testimony that textual critics must consult before forming their conclusions.

Next Harber addresses the general question concerning verification of canon. The important point is that a committee did not just arbitrarily select a group of books that would constitute the bible. The books selected were always considered scriptural. The Old Testament scriptures were developed over a period of more than 1000 years and were deemed authentic by God. These scriptures included Law, Prophets and Writings. The New Testament was written over a much shorter time span. The books about the life of Jesus included the four gospels. Paul's writings and the letters of the other apostle's filled out the remainder of the New Testament Canon. The Christian church accepted the Old Testament as well as the New Testament writings.

Next Harber addresses the miraculous preservation of the bible:

Overall summary of attacks on the bible:
> The Bible has been the most persecuted book in all of history. For 2,000 years every possible effort has been made to undermine the authority of the Bible. Attacked by emperors, popes, kings, and scholars, the Bible has endured attacks by intellectual, political, philosophical, scientific, and physical forces.[309]

Early specific attacks mentioned in Harber's book include:
- Arguments from Elsus, Prophyry, and Lucien
- By emperors that made it a capital offense to have a bible
- Roman emperor Diocletion who killed every family that had a bible
- Every confiscated bible was burned
- Thousands of Christians were slain
- Diocletion's attacks were so severe that he thought he brought an end to the bible
- Diocletion erected a column and inscribed the words "Extincto" and "Chrisianorum," which means, "The name of the Christians has been extinguished"

All these efforts to extinguish Christianity and the bible failed since Christianity became the official religion within ten years.

Anecdotal stories:

The book contained two anecdotal stories relating to the utter failure to extinguish Christianity and the bible. The first one is familiar to many. It is about Voltaire, the famous French philosopher who predicted that within 50 years the bible would be forgotten. God had different plans. Fifty years after Voltaire's death the Geneva Bible Society used Voltaire's home and printing presses to print bibles.

The other story was similar. Two hundred years ago, Thomas Paine wrote a book titled "The Age of Reason" that contained powerful reasons that he thought would dispose of the bible permanently. Since then his book has been relegated to antiquity and the bible remains the all-time best seller.

Harber's summary:
> How remarkable for a book which for centuries was pitted against the most intelligent and powerful forces in the world. During such dark times, only a persecuted and despised minority sought to uphold the Bible. No powerful army ever defended the Bible, but for every Bible destroyed, thousands have appeared. Like the three Hebrew men thrown into the fiery furnace, the Bible could not be burned out of existence. Out of the ashes arose the reproductive seeds of multiplication. Like a mythical Hydra with nine heads, each time one head was cut asunder, two more appeared. Every persecution brought against the Bible has resulted in the multiplication of the Scriptures. Throughout history, many times it seemed as though the Bible had been driven out of existence. Though the death bell rang, the corpse would not stay buried. The hammers of the Bible's critics have long since been worn out on the anvil of the Word of God.
>
> God himself promises the perseverance of His Word: "Heaven and earth will pass away, but My words will by no means pass away" (Matt. 24:35). Isaiah wrote over 2,500 years ago, "The grass withers, the flower fades, but the word of our God stands forever" (Isa. 40:8).[310]

SUMMARY

It is our fond hope and prayer that this chapter which supports the truth of scripture from different perspectives has strengthened your faith in the existence of God and the truth of the scriptures. We are not just trying to admonish people to have faith in faith. We hope that the concepts and facts presented in this book have helped you to understand that biblical teaching is in complete harmony with both science and what we observe around us in our world every day. With this understanding we are no longer confounded by an alleged discrepancy between science and biblical teaching and also, now have the strength to resist compromising with a culture that is diametrically opposed to biblical teaching and the truth. Finally, it is our hope and prayer that you have established a real relationship with God through Jesus Christ that will give you peace and strength in this life; and even more important is that your eternal destiny with God will be secured.

We all need to be exposing evil rather that promoting evil. With no "middle ground" we are either doing one or the other. Remember evil cannot flourish when it is exposed to the light of truth. Let your light shine and glorify God, your creator and sustainer!

APPENDIX A
Appeal to pastors

Included in Appendix A is an appeal letter to pastors and religious leaders, an educational mission statement to facilitate the spiritual and cultural awaking in America and a biblical beliefs survey for pastors, spiritual leaders and churches to reconcile their beliefs with biblical principles.

APPEAL LETTER TO PASTORS AND RELIGIOUS LEADERS

Dear Pastor or religious leader:

We would like you to join our initiative to reclaim America and the gospel by standing up and resisting the degradation of biblical principles and traditional American values. We have been silent for so long and haven't really publicly denounced the plethora of unbiblical, evil beliefs and philosophies that have taken over America. To join us in spirit and unity all that is required is to concur with the following:

1. America is in a severe spiritual decline based upon biblical principles.
2. The vigorous promotion of evil cultural and political positions by secularists has not been effectively countered by Christian churches.
3. My church or organization has been part of this failure by not publicly standing up and vigorously opposing evil cultural values and unbiblical political positions.
4. Misinterpreting Romans 13 and 1 Peter 2 as well as IRS government suppression should not be an excuse for not taking vigorous action.
5. Recognizing that several false beliefs and philosophies act as foundational building blocks that support the unbiblical cultural values and evil political positions that are accepted even within our churches. (See the educational mission page below):
6. Recognizing that the false foundations referenced above and listed below on the education mission page have been accepted in our culture and have made the soil where we plant seeds of the gospel infertile. This requires that we address the false foundations before we can expect our evangelical efforts to be successful.
7. Understanding that it is more effective to expose the false foundations than just exposing the bad fruit that is supported by the false foundations. (re-emphasizing #6 above)
8. Committing to publicly teach and preach how biblical principles relate to cultural values and political positions in a way that exposes

them as unbiblical and evil. See your legal rights at http://www.lc.org/media/9980/attachments/pastors_churches_and_politics4pg.pdf. The last paragraph on that website states: "In summary, while liberal groups seek to silence pastors and churches, I would encourage pastors to throw off their muzzle and pick up a megaphone. It's time pastors and churches became the moral conscience of the community."

Churches should unify around these truths for the spiritual and physical health of America.

Blessings,
William Nitardy

EDUCATIONAL MISSION FOR SPIRITUAL AND CULTURAL AWAKING IN AMERICA

Understanding the overall problem

To recognize that the basis for America's spiritual, economic, moral and cultural downward slide is a result of:
- Not believing that the bible is the inerrant word of God
- Taking God and biblical principles out of the public square. This has been accomplished by the false separation of church and state misnomer that is based upon a false religious humanism doctrine that has been masquerading as a secular entity.
- Lack of Christians, pastors and churches understanding the war between good and evil.
- Vigorous promotions of evil cultural and political positions by secularists (religious Secular Humanists).
- Nearly complete self-censorship of any public resistance to the encroachment of evil by Christians, pastors and churches.

Understanding the specific problem

We need to recognize the specific false foundations that have been built and accepted which support the evil in our culture, while Christians, pastors and churches acquiesced at every step. These false foundational blocks include:
- Biological macro-evolution (It's just a false religious belief that discredits the bible)
- Relative truth (It is easily logically disproven and discredits absolute biblical truth)

- The goodness and perfectibility of man (It discredits the bible and supports Humanism)
- Separation of Church and State (It illegitimately takes God, the bible and Christianity out of the public square and replaces it with the diametric opposite religion of Secular Humanism)
- Political correctness (It promotes Cultural Marxism, the diametric opposite of biblical Christianity)
- The "New Tolerance" (It censors the debate and vilifies the truth bearer messenger)
- The even newer "Outraged Based Coerced Conscience" (it codifies "The New Tolerance" into law)
- The above two bullet points restrict our freedom to act according to our conscience since that right is trumped by claims of discrimination by as few as one person (Here freedom is replaced by coercion to accept a lifestyle or behavior of a few that should not be condoned and is not biblical).

The proposed solution

The solution is to recognize that the following political issues are just the rotten fruit from a bad tree or a rotten structure supported by a false foundation:
- Abortion
- Gay rights / homosexual marriage
- Abandoning Israel
- Mistreatment of military personnel
- Economic collapse
- Releasing of terrorists
- Ignoring the constitution

We need to recognize the truth found in Matthew 7:17 that states that bad trees can only produce evil fruit and that a good tree can only produce good fruit. Consequently, our emphasis on only trying to expose the bad fruit as evil to "stem the tide," is an ineffective use of resources. Until we replace the bad tree or the false foundation, the "powers that be" will continue to produce more bad fruit. We need to attack the false foundations to expose them and invalidate them as legitimate foundations.

Relevant biblical texts

2 Chronicles 7:14
Matthew 7:15-20; 24-27

Isaiah 5:20
Ephesians 6:12

Partisanship and politics

Although we want to be non-partisan in respect to being inclusive of all people, parties and ideas, we have the bible as a standard measuring rod to determine the validity of ideas and political positions on issues. Consequently, we should be very partisan or principled in the positions we take on issues and carefully evaluate the positions of others or various political parties that we endorse. For those that don't totally accept the truth of the bible please read some of the referenced materials below and read Chapter 31:

The bible endorses the concept of liberty in many texts. However, It also explains how we can abuse liberty by taking it too far. 1 Peter 2:16 states:

> As free, yet not using liberty as a cloak for vice, but as bondservants of God.

D. James Kennedy called this stretching liberty into license. 2 Peter 2:19 explains about the type of political leaders that do not believe in biblical principles and liberty. It states:

> While they promise them liberty, they themselves are slaves of corruption; for by whom a person is overcome, by him also he is brought into bondage.

Dr. Wayne Grudem in his book titled "Politics According to the Bible," evaluated the liberal / progressive positions on sixty separate issues and found all of them either to be in direct opposition to the bible, in opposition to broad biblical principles or against established facts in the world. It is clear that what liberalism or progressivism have morphed into is diametrically opposed to the bible and known facts. That doesn't mean that Republican positions are necessarily biblical and always good for the populace since they are a liberal / conservative hybrid. However, true conservatism should be diametrically opposed to liberalism and be completely biblical. Unfortunately, most constituencies and politicians have a pragmatic worldview that is corrupt in that they want to benefit themselves, not our country and others and use tax money of their opposition constituency to finance their corruption. In politics, "social justice" needs a thorough evaluation based upon biblical principles (see Chapter 24) as does the "social gospel" within churches. See E. Calvin Beisner's 29 page book titled "Social Justice" available at http://ecalvinbeisner.com/.

Pastors and Christians must first understand the bible position on politics and then express that belief in the voting booth!

BIBLICAL BELIEFS SURVEY FOR PASTORS AND CHURCHES

Biblical credibility

Do you believe that the Bible is the inspired inherent word of God?
- ☐ Yes
- ☐ No

Biblical doctrine

Do you believe in the creation story in Genesis 1 & 2 is a factual narrative as opposed to just a symbolic story?
- ☐ Yes
- ☐ No

Do you believe the fall of man as described in Genesis 3 is a literal event as opposed to just a symbolic story?
- ☐ Yes
- ☐ No

Do you believe the curse as described in Genesis 3 is a literal event as opposed to just a symbolic story?
- ☐ Yes
- ☐ No

Do you believe the story of the world wide flood in Genesis 7 & 8 actually happened just as the Bible describes?
- ☐ Yes
- ☐ No

Do you believe in the virgin birth as described in Matthew 1 and Luke 1 & 2?
- ☐ Yes
- ☐ No

Do you believe that Jesus is coming again for the Church His bride?
- ☐ Yes
- ☐ No

Popular unbiblical doctrines

Do you believe that all roads lead to God?
- ☐ No
- ☐ Yes

Do you believe that the various churches should unify through ecumenicalism?
- ☐ No
- ☐ Yes

Do you believe that we should follow prominent church leaders even though those leaders do not have fully biblical beliefs?
- ☐ No
- ☐ Yes

Do you believe in replacement theology that holds that God's covenant is no longer with the Jews and that the prophecies and promises that God gave to the Jews are now for the church and that when the Bible refers to Israel it should be replaced with "the church" and when the Bible refers to Jerusalem it should be replaced with heaven?
- ☐ No
- ☐ Yes

Do you believe in preterism that holds that Christ returned to earth in AD 70 and that all end times prophecies were fulfilled at that time?
- ☐ No
- ☐ Yes

Do you believe in Centering Prayer and / or Contemplative Prayer (a Christian form of Transcendental Meditation that includes emptying your mind and repeating a mantra)?
- ☐ No
- ☐ Yes

Do you believe that Christian churches should be involved in Yoga?
- ☐ No
- ☐ Yes

Do you believe in pantheism (god is in everything but is not a personal God)?
- ☐ No
- ☐ Yes

Origin and environmental science

Do you believe in biological evolution (speciation came about by random evolution from a common ancestor)?
- ☐ No
- ☐ Yes

If yes, do you believe that God used random evolution to create everything?
- ☐ No
- ☐ Yes

Do you believe that man is destroying the earth's ecosystem by burning carbon based fuels that cause global warming and consequently catastrophic effects that justify drastic reductions in the use of fossil fuels?
- ☐ No
- ☐ Yes

Accepting cultural norms as replacements for biblical teachings:

Do you believe that sexual relations outside of marriage is a sin?
- ☐ Yes
- ☐ No

Do you believe that practicing homosexuality is a sin?
- ☐ Yes
- ☐ No

Do you believe that abortion is murder and requires a life for a life based upon Exodus 21:22-23 and the assumption that the intentional killing of an unborn baby is at least as serious a crime as killing the unborn baby inadvertently?
- ☐ Yes
- ☐ No

Do you believe that Christians should take politically correct positions on issues that our secular culture seems to demand?
- ☐ No
- ☐ Yes

Economic and social philosophy

Do you believe that the Biblical principles support capitalism and reject socialism?
- ☐ Yes
- ☐ No

Do you believe that the Biblical principles support Austrian economics and reject Keynesian economics?
- ☐ Yes
- ☐ No

Do you believe that biblical principles support personal and private charity only and not coerced public charity?
- ☐ Yes
- ☐ No

Do you believe that biblical principles support liberation theology that holds that an oppressed group is entitled to reparations as a vendetta against past oppression and that this would satisfy their need for group salvation?
- ☐ No
- ☐ Yes

Political Philosophy

Do you believe the current separation of church and state concept where Christianity should be treated like a deadly virus and expunge it from every aspect of public life?
- ☐ No
- ☐ Yes

Do you believe that government control over social institutions that God created like marriage, families, church, labor, community and the relationship between God and man is a good thing?
- ☐ No
- ☐ Yes

Do you believe that biblical principles support liberty for citizens and rejects coercive intrusive government?
- ☐ Yes
- ☐ No

Do you believe that biblical principles support nation states rather than global government?
- ☐ Yes
- ☐ No

End of test

To evaluate your percentage score against what the bible teaches, count the number of top box's checked and multiply that number by 100 and divide by the number of questions answered. If you checked yes for believing in evolution and then answered the subordinate question, divide by 30. Otherwise divide by 29. If you scored close to 100% your worldview is biblically based. Congratulations! Otherwise read this book, "Understanding the anatomy of evil" by William Nitardy to verify that your worldview is biblical.

APPENDIX B
Letters to the editor

The following list of letters to the editor is a selected segment of letters that have been submitted for publication at local newspapers in the last couple of years. Some have published and some have not.

The denial of good and evil   **February 27, 2016**

In the 50's and 60,s when TV was in its infancy, almost all the shows described reality with the good guys against the bad guys. In today's post-modern culture typically we do not distinguish between good guys and bad guys. If we do make a distinction, the bad guys have an excuse and are not responsible for their attitude, irresponsibility or behavior. Today, the only alleged bad guys are those that point out the evils that the real bad guys are perpetrating. The other sad juxtaposition is the fact that enduring principles that were once considered a virtue are now denigrated and pragmatism, the diametric opposite, is considered a virtue.

In the recent CNN debate Donald Trump argued that there are no bad guys in the Israeli / Palestinian conflict; a pragmatic solution is appropriate and justice and evil are irrelevant. Charles Krauthammer certainly didn't agree with Trump's false post-modern assessment with his quote that stated "Israel is using missile defense to protect its civilians and Hamas is using their civilians to protect their missiles."

The sad part is that a high percentage of Americans and particularly evangelical Christians support him and his narcissistic and pragmatic worldview that is the diametric opposite of biblical teaching. Following that worldview will result in catastrophic effects for America. Evangelical Christians and everyone else needs to support candidates that are principled and have a biblical worldview. Then and only then, will God bless America.

Replacing reality with fantasy and good with evil   **December 5, 2015**

Today our leaders are obfuscating the reality of violent Islamic extremism done in the name of their religion and equating it with past or present Christian or Jewish violence. This is complete insanity and any leader even hinting at that connection should be ridiculed, silenced and immediately removed from office and placed in an insane asylum.

The violent extremists are simply following the example of their prophet Mohamad, the history of their religion and believe in their (un)holy writings (the ones) that haven't been abrogated or superseded. Although they are extremists in regard to what we consider normal and ethical behavior, they certainly are not extremists as it relates to the fundamental teachings of their writings, what they claim their god wants and what Mohamad did.

Although we care greatly about Muslims and all humanity we must expose the false and evil ideology that they are committed to as detrimental to them and the rest of the world. Islam is diametric to biblical Christianity in regard to their doctrine, their god, their modus operandi and the effects of their religion. Alternatively, Islam's carnage is very similar to what was done in the name of Communism in the 20th Century. The Ideology of communism as well as socialism are also diametrically opposed to biblical doctrine.

One confirmation that Islam and Christianity are diametric opposites, with one evil and the other good, is that the Christian antichrist and the Muslim Mahdi have identical attributes in more than 40 characteristics! The Mahdi is considered the savior for Muslims while the antichrist is the destroyer of humanity in biblical Christianity until Christ's return when He destroys the antichrist and his hoards that have allegiance to him.

Choose wisely!

Terrorism and crime 101   **November 19, 2015**

Today, horrific terrorism and severe crime areas are tolerated in our country and abroad. "Lip service" is given by our leaders and the media that justifies and legitimatizes the horrific acts of murder, arson and barbarism. John Kerry legitimatizing Islamic terrorism is just a recent example of our tolerance toward and obfuscation of evil.

When doctors are trying to diagnose a disease they try to correlate the symptoms to that of known diseases. Another way of stating this is they profile the disease and once identified they choose a cure that is selective or discriminating in the sense that it targets the specific source or problem not every disease equally. It is simply lunacy to do otherwise.

However, in America with "political correctness" (cultural Marxism) on steroids rather that expose the specific group promoting and carrying out the evil, we consider them a victimhood group. This is lunacy!

We need to identify what groups, enclaves, political ideologies or religions are promoting and carrying out terrorism and neuter them by condemnation, disarming and either restricting rights, incarceration or deportation.

The answer is profile, profile and profile!

Today's enlightenment: Demonization of discussion   September 21, 2015

Today our culture demands demonization of any ideology or belief that runs contrary to the "Sacred Cows" of "Political Correctness." This includes censoring and punishing anyone that dares to express a different belief or has their actions guided by their conscience. We see this condemnation in the realms of

academia, politics and religion and is promoted by the media. We have elevated any offense or sleight against an individual, group or class as a high crime! These offenses certainly do not include intentional name-calling or demonization and are only done in an effort to promote truth and expose injustice by having a legitimate discussion. The response calls for censorship of the desired discussion and demonization and punishment of the offender. I believe this whole scenario could be labeled "Outrage Based Coerced Conscience." It identifies something that is very minor and makes it a major issue by responding with a major attack that actually destroys individual lives while apparently protecting a false narrative or ideology that would not hold up under scrutiny. We have absolutely no objective discussions on things that really matter like:
- Racism that cuts both ways
- The origin and basis for marriage
- Are Christians being discriminated against?
- Are Christians being annihilated in the middle-east? If so, by whom?
- What is the basis or ideology that supports radical Islamic extremism?
- Is there evidence that Obama is a Christian?
- Is there evidence that Obama is a Muslim?

Why can't we ask these questions without fear of repercussion?

Censorship, coercion, condemnation and criminalization   September 19, 2015

Certainly the censorship, coercion and condemnation syndrome that is prevalent in our culture and the media is a trifecta that is illegitimately preventing truth from being revealed and preventing evil from being exposed. The object of ridicule is defined by "political correctness" and the modus operandi of censorship and condemnation used has been identified by Josh McDowell in his book "The New Tolerance." More recently various hate laws have been codified to protect the alleged victims. This has resulted in devastating consequences for those that have been accused of the slightest of slights that didn't fully endorse the worldview of those offended. These "sacred cows" or victimhood classes protected by "political correctness" include women, blacks, gays and Muslims.

The most recent example of censorship, coercion and condemnation was when Donald Trump didn't condemn a person that asked what he was going to do about our Muslim problem including Obama being a Muslim. CNN stated the following:
> Donald Trump came under fire Friday morning for his handling of a question at a town hall about when the U.S. can "get rid" of Muslims, for failing to take issue with that premise and an assertion that President Barack Obama is Muslim.

Even Megyn Kelly condemned Trump for not immediately supporting the "politically correct" conventional wisdom that Islam is a legitimate religion of peace and is a victim of prejudice and should never be criticized. Alternatively, when Christians are compared to ISIS there is no outrage! Why do we want to censor a discussion on these subjects through coercion and condemnation if they can hold up to scrutiny? As for Obama, a book could be written on evidence that he completely aligns himself with Muslims and gives no indication that he is a Christian. Why can't we see through this "politically correct" hypocrisy?

Black lives matter August 28, 2015

Yes, black lives do matter, but is that really what the organization is about or is it just another misdirected euphemism? I am trying to think if I know anyone that believes that black lives don't matter. What group is it that doesn't think that black lives matter? Who are they are trying to expose and correct? Are they protesting Planned Parenthood that is the leading abortion provider that results in the killing about 680,000 black unborn babies each year? I don't think so! Are they targeting the black population that murders over 9,000 black people each year with a 93% black on black murder rate? No, I don't think so!

Are they recognizing the fact that black lives mattered to the 300,000 white, northern soldiers that died in the civil war to free the black slaves? No, I don't think so! Are they recognizing the bravery of the inner city police forces that are present to protect the law abiding black people? No, I don't think so!

Based upon this analysis, "Black Lives Matter" is just a euphemism to support an illegitimate cause; that of trying to gain power and respect through coercion rather than earning it.

My words speak louder than my actions July 17, 2015

When President Obama chided, CBS news' chief White House correspondent, Major Garrett, for his question: "Can you tell the country, sir, why you are content, with all the fanfare around this deal, to leave the conscience of this nation, the strength of this nation, unaccounted for in relationship to these four Americans?" he was saying to him and our country that we should understand that his words speak louder than his actions. That is exactly what he did to Mitt Romney during a debate question regarding Benghazi. He was indignant and demanded that we believe him and give him full respect, even when his words and actions are inconsistent.

We know that God's words and actions are always consistent because they stem from His character. We also know that the words of the Serpent, indwelled by Lucifer, in the Garden of Eden were intended to deceive and that is also consistent with his character (the father of lies). Saul Alinsky stated that he admired Lucifer, wanted to emulate him and would prefer to go to hell with him rather than go to heaven.

We also know that Obama as well as Hillary are students of Alinsky and their actions and allegiance are in sync with Alinsky and his "Rules for Radicals" book. That fully explains why his words that are always meant to deceive are always inconsistent with his actions and character. Lucifer's progeny all share his attributes.

Freedom from religion July 13, 2015

According to the atheists that had an angry letter of response published in the June/July issue, they want freedom from religion. There are two things that they don't understand. One is that our country's founding was based upon freedom of religion, not freedom from religion. The other is that they really don't want freedom from religion since atheism like humanism and Secular Humanism is a religion.

This assertion is supported by the dictionary definition of religion, by quotes of prominent humanist's and by 100 years of humanist's admissions in addition to the Supreme Court case *Torcaso v. Watkins*. In the 1961 decision, Justice Hugo Black commented in a footnote, "Among religions in this country which do not teach what would generally be considered a belief in the existence of God are Buddhism, Taoism, Ethical Culture, **Secular Humanism**, and others."

What they are objecting to is a bible based religion that is, not diametrically opposed to atheism by chance, but by their rebellion against God that mandates diametric opposition. They not only want freedom from America's founding religion, but don't want others to have freedom of their religion of choice. Three words explanation their position, hypocritical, coercive and wrong!

America: I have a question June 4, 2015

Here we go again! We are witnessing a repeated scenario in Baltimore that we previously experienced in Sanford, Ferguson and New York. One person gets killed resulting from an incident with the police and the police that are authorized to enforce the law are blamed and demonized. A lawless riot results that destroys property of innocent people and puts police and others in danger. The backlash is far more dangerous and destructive than the event being protested. The justification for the backlash is not just promoted by those protesting and rioting, but by Our President and Attorney General and State Governors and City Mayors.

WND reported that Mayor Rawlings-Blake said she instructed police "to do everything that they could to make sure that the protesters were able to exercise their right to free speech," which included giving "space" to those who "wished to destroy." By Monday evening, (after the rioting began in earnest) she walked back those statements, but it was too late.

The public mantra is that the blacks and inner city poor are innocent victims that have been oppressed by police and white people in general and that justifies their great anger and consequently their right to riot, destroy, loot and meme.

My question to America: is that really legitimate or is it the situation described below?

Police have a very difficult job enforcing the law in an area where crime is disproportionately high and people have no respect for authority or personal property of others. It puts police and the potential victim in unnecessary danger when people resist arrest. Statistically, some people are going to get hurt or killed in this situation. Out leaders which are actually in charge of police departments are enabling the anarchy and believe the mantra. They publically demonize the police and legitimize the justification of the lawless rioters. The bottom line is that they are delegitimizing and neutering the lawful authorities and giving power and legitimacy to anarchy and the lawless people.

America, we must choose between lawless anarchy and freedom!

Injustice in the name of justice   May 22, 2015

Although injustice in the name of justice by our government and their lapdog media is not limited to the racial and inner city issues like Ferguson and Baltimore, it is one of the most obvious examples. The most egregious other example would be where government authority is used against honest, respectful, law-abiding, hardworking citizens. An example of that is the IRS harassment of patriot and Tea Party organizations. In a complete juxtaposition, our government authorities are giving a pass to and justifying the behavior of dishonest, disrespectful, criminal rioters and non-working citizens and blaming the authorized police who are trying to keep a lid on this anarchical tinderbox. This injustice is promoted by our president, attorney general, a city mayor and a district attorney.

The officials and the anarchical citizenry are creating a false narrative that makes those that want to stretch liberty into license the victims and makes those responsible to restrain the anarchists, murderers, drug dealers and other criminals the evil perpetrators. When they are blaming the police they are straining at a gnat and ignoring the elephant in the room. Why are there no protesters to protest the burning of their city the day after the burning? Why are there no protesters concerned about the more than 100% increase in the murder rate after the police have been silenced and neutered by government officials?

This unjustified ridicule and neutering of the police is against a backdrop of ISIS murdering, torturing, raping and enslaving innocent Christians where an authorized police or military force would be the solution. In a similar way our government appears to be sympathetic with the evil criminal perpetrators by not taking any significant action to prevent the atrocities.

Promoting injustice and a false narrative will weaken and destroy our country.

Two religions are warring against Christianity   May 22, 2015

One is an evil ideology masquerading as a religion and the other is an evil religious ideology masquerading as a secular entity. The bible describes Satan as the one who is warring against God, His people and biblical principles. It states that Satan uses deception to lead people astray just like he did to Eve in the Garden of Eden. Islam identifies their god, Allah, as the great deceiver that leads people astray in verse 1 of chapter 1 in the Qur'an.

Walid Shoebat identified, in his book titled "God's War on Terror," that over 40 attributes of the Islamic savior, the Mahdi, documented in the Qur'an are identical or are similar to those of the Anti-Christ that are documented in the bible." This makes Islam aligned with the one rebelling and warring against God. Consequently Islam is against all Christians, the bible, everything good and life itself!

Humanism, Secular Humanism and progressivism all represent an evil ideology diametrically opposed to biblical Christianity that is also warring against religious freedom and biblical Christianity. Humanism declared itself to be a religion for over a 100 years. Secular Humanism was declared to be a religion by the SCOTUS, and defined as a religion by the dictionary. The original Humanist Manifesto published in 1933 was 100% diametrically opposed to biblical principles. The book "Politics According to the Bible" by Dr. Wayne Grudem identifies that 60 out of 60 progressive political positions are in opposition to biblical principles or known facts in our world.

Obama: Freedom Fighter or Radical Rebel   April 8, 2015

Everybody knows that a radical rebel to one group is a freedom fighter to another. It's just a question of which lens that you are looking through, right? Fortunately, that is not true if we believe in reality or the bible.

The bible teaches that God is the true moral authority based upon his creation of everything including the physical and spiritual realms, truth, justice, power and love. It also teaches that Lucifer rebelled against God's moral authority and wanted to be like God and control what God had created for his glory in kind of a deceptive immoral heist. He was a radical rebel that by definition was in complete opposition to God. Although he operates in the same realms he uses deceit rather than truth, opposes true justice and hates, demonizes and destroys rather than loves. The Qur'an Identifies Allah as the great deceiver and the one that leads people astray (3:54; 8:30 & 35:8). That is exactly what Lucifer does. Obama's speech and actions reveal that he is very anti-Christian and pro Muslim. That makes him a religious radical rebel against the Christian moral authority upon which America was founded.

In his book titled, "Rules for Radicles," Alinsky acknowledges Lucifer as the first radical to win his kingdom and identifies himself with Lucifer. The bible acknowledges that Lucifer is the prince of the power of the air. Alinsky saw himself as a freedom fighter, but was a communist radical rebel that wanted to undermine the moral authority of America and wrote a book that was an instruction manual on how to bring down America using subversive tactics.

D'Souza called the men that influenced Obama as his founding fathers. They include Bill Ayers, Jeremiah Wright and other communist mentors that were radical rebels.

Race to the bottom　　　　　　　　　　　　　　　　　　　　　　　March 6, 2015

Eric Holder just released the report on the racial incident in Ferguson that condemned the Ferguson Police Department for being racist while exonerating Officer Darren Wilson of unjustly shooting Michael Brown and of any racial motivation. What it didn't do was to apologize to Officer Wilson or condemn the black friends and supporters of Michael Brown that gave a unified false testimony and false hands-up symbolism, which along with the blessing of Obama, Holder and Sharpton, caused the riots and burning.

This type of racial response by Holder following the incident and in his report is not new, but an acceleration of the "'race' to the bottom" that he and Obama have fomented consistently.

The racist ideology that has afflicted our country is diametrically the opposite of our true race issue. The word "prejudice" means to pre-judge someone or some group without evidence. Based upon the dictionary, this only includes the case when no basis exists for an ill feeling or animosity. The problem is that the "word" has been widened to include and condemn those that have an obvious reason for an ill feeling. We need new words like "factjudice" for post-judged "prejudice" and "realotry" for post-judged "bigotry" when the feeling is based upon evidence and reality.

It has been obvious that Obama and Holder have demonstrated over and over an ill feeling towards whites that is based upon pre-judging or true prejudice and bigotry. To the contrary, the "factjudice" and "realotry" that many whites feel toward our black political leaders, rioters and those that see themselves in their supporter's image as completely innocent, always arrogant, disrespectful to people, the property of others and their authorities, and see themselves as victims of oppression, is based upon a mountain of facts and is justified.

The true equivocation between Jesus and Muhamad　　　　February 7, 2015

President Barak Obama tried to equivocate Christianity and Islam by linking "Christians to violence, and by claiming that atrocities such as the Inquisition and the Crusades were done 'in the name of Christ,'" during the National Prayer Breakfast.

Christian evangelist Franklin Graham on Thursday reminded President Obama, who discusses during one televised interview his "Muslim faith" but otherwise has stated being a Christian, that Jesus Christ came to earth to die for the guilty, while Islam's Muhammad killed the "innocent."

The true equivocation is not only revealed between how Jesus and Muhammad treated others, but by the diametric opposite doctrines revealed within the bible as opposed to the Quran or the Hadith.

One evidence of this equivocation is the forty plus similarities between the Mahdi, the Islamic savior, and the biblical antichrist identified in "God's War on Terror" by Shoebat and Richardson. The Quran itself describes Allah as the great deceiver in Surah 1:1, 3:54 & 8:30. Jesus is described as the way, the truth and the life in John 14:6. The Islamic doctrine teaches deception through Kitman and Taqiyya while the bible condemns lying and deception. The bible warns, "Woe to those who call evil good, and good evil; Who put darkness for light, and light for darkness" in Isaiah 5:20.

Turning truth and Justice on its head   **January 18, 2015**

The most recent attack on Christians who dare express their religious views in words or print is former Atlanta Fire Chief Kelvin Cochran who was fired from his job recently by the Atlanta mayor, Muhammad Kasim Reed, because of Cochran's Christian views on marriage.

The rationale for justifying this type of bigotry and persecution against Christians is not justified because false foundations are used to make good evil and evil good.

The initial false foundation is the "separation of church and state" (SOCAS) argument where biblical Christianity was to be kept completely out of the public square and government. This is based upon the following deceptions:

1. Thomas Jefferson's inadvertent use of a two sided wall metaphor opened the door for the judiciary to proclaim that the Christian religion should be kept out of government rather than Jefferson's assurance that the government would not interfere with the church.
2. The use of "Case Law" to codify a false foundation which was the opposite of Jefferson's concern and the Constitution.
3. The secular humanists who are pushing SOCAS claim they are not religious, but actually are a religion in diametric opposition to biblical Christianity. The evidence of their religion includes:

a. The dictionary definition
   b. The US Supreme Court determination
   c. Secular humanist leaders quotes
   d. 100 years of claiming to be a religion
4. The claim that moral truths are all relative, yet that claim they hold is an absolute truth
5. Codifying the "New Tolerance" where the person expressing a concern is vilified in the name of tolerating anything except Christianity while censoring the concern from debate.

The net result of all this is to nullify the constitution and its historical context and reframe evil as good and good as evil! The bible warns against this in Isaiah 5:20.

The a la Carte and disconnected gospel   January 11, 2015

Most Christians today pick and choose the parts of the bible that suit their fancy and disregard the rest. In the same way most churches focus only on a narrow portion of scripture and disregard much of the full council of God such as the creation narrative, prophecy, God's wrath and end times teaching.

In a similar way, most Christians and churches disconnect the truth of the bible from realities such as science, politics and social issues. If we are going to put our faith in the bible or use it at all, we should view it in the same way C.S. Lewis viewed who Jesus was. C.S. Lewis stated, "A man who was merely a man and said the sort of things Jesus said would not be a great moral teacher. He would either be a lunatic--on the level with a man who says he is a poached egg--or he would be the devil of hell. You must take your choice. Either this was, and is, the Son of God, or else a madman or something worse."

In the same way, we need to view the bible as having truth that applies to the realities in our world including science, politics and social issues. Disconnecting it from these realities within Christianity, basically disconnects Christianity from reality. It is completely understandable why non-Christians would want to do this, but for Christians to do this is a form of treason.

False narratives   January 9, 2015

The historical biblical account tells of a false narrative and how the serpent presented it to Eve in the Garden of Eden. It tells how believing and accepting this false narrative resulted in rebellion, curses being placed upon people and the environment, and was ultimately the cause of death. Today, not much has changed. The current promotion and acceptance of false narratives are primarily responsible for the evil in our world. In the Garden of Eden, this false narrative was accepted even though Eve knew God was her creator the source of truth. Today, all the false narratives are diametrically opposed to God's truth that has been revealed to us in the scriptures and are accepted in spite of this. That is no coincidence. It just shows that we are in rebellion against God.

Most of the false narratives today result from political or religious philosophies that are based upon a rebellion against God and his truth. These can be easily identified by the following characteristics:
- Opposition to the bible
- Promotion of special interests or classes of people
- Coercion and / or persecution
- Lies
- Theft
- Censorship and repression
- Self-serving

Compare various prominent political philosophies and religious beliefs and practices against this list to identify which are evil and based upon promoting a false narrative. Once you clearly see the evil, expose the false narrative. Evil cannot thrive when the light of truth exposes it.

They're digging in the wrong place December 1, 2014

Indiana Jones realized the Nazi's were digging in the wrong place based upon known facts in his possession. We too should know that the "mantra" espoused by President Obama, Eric Holder and the media that white racism and police profiling are the cause of high crime rates and rioting in black communities, is not supported by the known facts in our possession. Like the Nazi's the lies and the emotional frenzy created by the promotion of those lies is what is causing the angry anarchy in Ferguson and potentially across America.

Overt white racism is basically nonexistent in the public media while black racism is basically a certainty when we hear black "talking heads" on TV. Also, a large percentage of whites voted for a black president while 95% of blacks voted for one of their own race. Who are the real racists? If white racism is so prevalent, why are the only examples used to promote the "mantra" involve angry black criminal thugs with no respect for authority, the rule of law, whites, black businesses etc. If white police profiling was the cause of the high crimes rates in the black communities then crime levels in Detroit would have a normal level. We're digging in the wrong place!

Ferguson: An inside job November 28, 2014

The way the Ferguson riots have unfolded has all the fingerprints of an inside job. Although they had months to prepare, absolutely nothing was done to dissuade or hinder the rioters from taunting police, looting and burning. The authorities appeared powerless while the lawless mobs pillaged, plundered, burned cars and buildings with no consequences.

The timing of releasing the Grand Jury's verdict late in the afternoon, the absence of the National Guard, the police being huddled together and not challenging any actions of the lawless mob, the unavailability of Governor Nixon at the crucial time, the timing of the speech by the President during the lawlessness, Obama's lip service of restraint to rioters while telling them he supported them and their cause was just and that the police were the ones that really needed to be restrained, all made the situation look orchestrated.

The next night after "the horse was out of the barn" the National Guard troops showed up. The orchestrated and desired outcome, reinforced the false narrative that the anger of the demonstrators was justified and white people and particularly white police better be on guard and not restrict the black mobs from stealing, harassing, looting and burning.

Obama's worldview   **November 27, 2014**

The following are Obama's worldview beliefs, statements and values:
- America is not a Christian nation
- America is a large Muslim country with a large population of infidels
- The Islamic Brotherhood is primarily a secular organization
- The War on Terror is an Overseas Contingency Operation
- When Islamic terrorists murder Americans and yell Allah Akbar it is workplace violence
- When a newly converted Muslim beheads an American, it is not Islamic terror
- We will never be at war with Islam
- The Islamic State (ISIS) is not Islamic
- He calls ISIS, ISIL to signal his is approval for a larger (L)evant Caliphate that includes Israel
- He promotes parasitic politics, using tax money to buy votes
- He does everything possible to convert the private capitalist host, his source of wealth, into Swiss cheese
- He uses the Cloward-Piven strategy to bring economic ruin to America
- He uses Keynesian economics to ruin America through astronomical debt
- He sees America as a black country with white illegitimate interlopers
- He excuses black high crime rates including murder and blames it all on white police officers
- He excuses and justifies black bigotry, criminal acts, pillage and rioting
- Everything he does matches what a President wanting to destroy America would do

Progressives promote inverted incentives   January 26, 2014

In government, business or within the family it is important to have incentives that are consistent with the desired response as opposed to having inverted incentives. President Obama always promotes diametrically opposite incentives than what are desired. He has turned what should be a post-racial era into a potential race war.

While giving lip service to the rule of law, restraint and peace in Ferguson, Obama gave the rioters his support and sympathy to encourage them. To the police department which he should be supporting to prevent lawlessness, he gives them incentive not to engage and prevent lawlessness by promoting the false narrative that white cops always oppress innocent blacks. While stating that police are badly needed in black high crime areas he criticizes them for doing a very difficult job in those communities.

On immigration, Obama has done and is doing everything to reward people for breaking the law and encourage many others to cross our borders illegally. Australia doesn't have an immigration problem because they have the right incentive that disqualifies illegal immigrants from legal immigration.

On a plethora of parasitic entitlement programs the government spends money recruiting applicants to accept checks, food stamps, housing subsidies, cell phones etc. Although offering goodies to every parasite, no incentives are offered to the host that is supposed to generate the wealth to keep the circle of parasitic politics going. President Obama is not promoting what is right; but more what Jeremiah Wright is like.

Tortured logic   November 25, 2014

What just happened in Ferguson was tragic and completely unjustified, but not in the way that has been presented by Obama, Holder and the media. The initial narrative that was communicated and held up as truth at least until the grand jury made the evidence public. The narrative was that Officer Darren Wilson shot unarmed Michael Brown, an innocent young gentile boy, in cold blood and that represents the ongoing white racism against blacks particularly by racist white police officers. Now we know that the initial unrest and now the looting and burning in Ferguson was based upon false testimony that has been refuted by the facts. One of the false witnesses was Brown's best friend.

President Obama made a statement about the Grand Jury's verdict and unrest in Ferguson while the world was watching the looting and burning on a split screen. Although Obama gave some lip service to his support for a peaceful response by the black community and restraint by the police, his overall message was that the unrest was justified and that it is white racism by the white police that is the problem and is what needs to be addressed. All this while in the background the mob was going berserk against his admonition and the Dr.

Spock Police had so much restraint they did absolutely nothing to stop the lawlessness or arrest anybody. All this is a juxtaposition of who the good guys and the bad guys really are. Darren Brown should be given credit for his restraint in only killing Brown when he needed to defend himself. It is the false witnesses and the black mobs that need to be condemned and held responsible for their actions.

The president used the same tortured logic when stating the Islamic state is not Islamic.

The most "sacred cow" November 24, 2014

President Obama and progressives have various "sacred cows" that are above criticism, cannot not be questioned or even discussed. These "sacred cows" include things like homosexuality, abortion, feminism and Islam. However, the most "sacred cow" has to be racism, particular white on black racism. They do not consider black on white racism as racism. Consequently, when we see overt verbal racism on TV from Obama, Holder or the many black apologists, they imply it is just what we deserve as payback; not angry, arrogant racists that want to promote and establish reverse racism while proclaiming and establishing racism as the most "sacred cow." This is the height of hypocrisy.

I believe that some of the greatest Americans are non-European whites. These Americans are some of my favorite people. None of them promote the false mantra that it is white racism that keeps blacks as an underclass. If America is so bad for non European, non white immigrants, why do we have an immigration problem? Many of my favorite Americans have black skin. I am not sure that anybody is against black skin. I don't think that many white people are prejudice in the sense of the dictionary definition. i.e. an opinion made without adequate basis. How do you respect a group that insists on promoting a false narrative that divides out nation?

Rudy Giuliani just pointed out that the fact that 93% of blacks killed are killed by other blacks. He suggested that the black roving black mobs should address that issue rather than rioting when one of their own bad apples aggressively tries to assault an authority figure and gets killed or badly injured. This is un-American, unethical, unbiblical and totally wrong. The only antidote for a false nation narrative is the sunlight of truth!

Parasitic politics November 23, 2014

"Parasitic politics" means viewing politics exclusively through the lens of an allegedly victimized parasitic populace with no consideration of the host. The recent immigration action taken by Obama is just one example of "parasitic politics" perpetrated by Obama and the progressives. America's development as a very strong host was generated by a biblical worldview that promoted free enterprise and negative rights that guaranteed freedom from a strong central government that promotes positive rights and "parasitic politics." That strength is being used in a circle of corruption to keep progressives in power by bleeding the nation's wealth to buy illegitimate votes. We all should be well aware that a host will stay strong without parasites, but a parasite cannot exist without a host. We also should be aware that too many parasites will kill the host. The final result of "parasitic politics" is suicide not only for the host, but also for the parasites.

Progressives intentionally confuse private voluntary charity that is a "win / win" for both the giver and the recipient with coercive financial support for government defined victimhood groups that vote for their political sponsors. The former is a "win / win" and bonds both groups together with a common purpose. The later is a "lose / lose" and foments envy and divides the giver and receiver. The giver has no choice, is not thanked or felt appreciated. The recipient does not appreciate his gift and believes it is an entitlement. Contrary to progressives claim to be the charitable and compassionate ones, a book titled "Who Really Cares" by Arthur C. Brooks, documents that Conservatives and Christians are far more compassionate and charitable. The progressives are only good at buying their reputation and their power with others people's money, thus making their claim to virtue, illegitimate.

Two Politically Correct Evils: Coercion and Censorship   November 5, 2014

Two of the biggest evils in our world today are coercion and censorship. However, through the politically correct lens of progressive liberals, those evils are condoned, promoted and even codified into law to criminalize those they view as enemies of their perverse social agenda. With "political correctness" the discussion of the issue is censored so it never takes place and the person or organization trying to point out the hierocracy or evil is demonized.

Political correctness is only applied to progressive's "sacred cows," like abortion, homosexuality, feminism, and Islam. These "sacred cows" can do "no wrong." The common thread linking these "sacred cows" together is their diametric opposition to biblical Christianity.

Recently, these "sacred cows" have been turned into "sacred bulls" by codifying their "special interest" rights into law so the "sacred bulls" can attack and stomp on anyone that refuses to submit to their demands. One news source example is quoted below:

In May, Houston Mayor Annise Parker and two homosexual city council members rammed through a non-discrimination ordinance that gives special rights and protections to homosexuals and lesbians. The proposed "bathroom bill" ordinance passed despite vocal opposition by the Houston community, which was led by local churches and pastors. . .

The mayor is using intimidation, threats and bully tactics in an attempt to silence anyone who will not embrace her lesbian lifestyle.

Another example is documented below:

City officials told Donald Knapp that he and his wife Evelyn, both ordained ministers who run the Hitching Post Wedding Chapel, are required to perform such ceremonies or face months in jail and/or thousands of dollars in fines. The city claims its "non-discrimination" ordinance requires the Knapp's to perform same-sex wedding ceremonies. . . We have stretched our biblical, God- given liberty into license.

The icing on the cake October 10, 2014

When President Obama called ISIS, ISIL it was the ICING on the cake. The cake, unfortunately, is laced with many false and poisonous philosophies and beliefs that are designed to neuter if not destroy the America that was founded upon Christian biblical principles and the "golden rule." These diabolical philosophies are based upon an unjustified belief that America's strength and power is unjust and has been used unfairly to suppress other nations. Consequently, America needs to be weakened if not destroyed for the good of the world. President Obama is doing this by destroying our economy, decimating our military, destroying our moral fabric and sabotaging our best ally, Israel, while strengthening both our Communist and Islamic enemies.

We can see the strengthening of both Communist Russia and radical Islam. Contrary to our politically correct (cultural Marxism) apologists' contention, Islam has always been promoted by the sword and by terror from Mohammad himself until now and always will be until the whole world is Muslim. This is their modus operandi of using deceit (taqiyya) until they can rule with the sword as history and their own sanctioned religious writings have shown.

President Obama told us the truth when he said that he would "fundamentally change" America. His beliefs and actions are all consistent with what he was taught as a child and continued with his mentors like Frank Marshal Davis, Bill Ayers, Jeremiah Wright, Saul Alinsky and others. Certainly, he is a committed Muslim based upon both his own words and actions. Open the following link to see what was censored when Fox News was not allowed to show in it on the Hannity show at 9:00 PM on a specific Sunday http://www.youtube.com/watchpopup?v=tCAffMSWSzY#t=28 for proof of his self-avowed faith.

Back to the icing on the cake – Although public opinion forced Obama to decide on some strategy to counter the ISIS threat, his response was basically bluster for us to hear, but to his Islamic friends he announced everything he was not going to do and instead of calling the terrorist group ISIS, which represents a desired Caliphate in Iraq and Syria, he called it ISIL which represents a desired Caliphate over a larger area called "Levant" that includes Iraq, Syria, Cyprus, Israel, Jordan, Lebanon, Palestine and southern Turkey. Wow! America, we need to wake-up!

Progressive's MO: lying and demonizing   May 6, 2014

    This letter is in response to a letter titled "Making her case for Hillary Clinton in 2016" published on May 4th. The writer opens by making a bold-faced lie when stating the Benghazi attack "was proven to be a spontaneous attack." The truth, as has been recognized by all sides, is just the opposite. It was a planned attack. This puts the writer in Hitler's camp based upon Hitler's famous quote. "If you tell a big enough lie and tell it frequently enough, it will be believed." This makes the writer a Benghazi-Nazi.

    The letter continues mocking and ridiculing patriotic conservatives calling them "gasbags" ala Saul Alinsky. Rule # 5 in his book "Rules for Radicals" was, "Ridicule is man's most potent weapon." I believe that makes the writer an Alinsky-Nazi. With Alinsky dedicating his book to Lucifer, "the first radical known to man who rebelled against the establishment and did so effectively that he at least won his own kingdom." It is too bad Alinsky didn't tell the rest of the story that includes Lucifer's final destiny. That is exactly where we all will end up if we make lying and rebellion our Modus Operandi.

    Finally, the writer while denigrating male politicians, holds high a woman politician and states, "I, for one, will be more than proud to hear "Madam President!'" I believe that Rush Limbaugh would call the writer a femi-Nazi.

    Unless America recognizes the rapid path of destruction that the liberal / progressive ideology represents, America is doomed. Their utopia may be great in the short term for stretching liberty into license and enjoying the gluttony of a parasite feasting on its host, but there is no good or just ending. The host will die!

Lessons from Cliven Bundy   April 28, 2014

    Bundy made a big mistake when he used racial remarks to criticize liberal big government policies of entitlements that make people completely dependent and thus slaves of government. The politically correct firestorm reaction to any criticism of a "sacred cow" is a lesson we know well. The only response is to censor the critical factual message and demonize the messenger. One lesson we need to learn that normally escapes us is to understand this illegitimate evil Modus Operandi that reframes the argument such that it always avoids any discussion on the factual issue and makes the person pay dearly for daring to criticize a "sacred cow." "Sacred cow" groups are always identified as victims and are never responsible for any of our society's ills.

    Another lesson we need to learn is to understand how racial prejudice as an offence is elevated way above its rightful place on a scale of thought and motivational offences. One misunderstood element is that the word origin of "prejudice" is the word "prejudge," consequently the definition of "prejudice" only includes feelings that are not based upon reason or experience. When no critical discussion is allowed on the facts, even when the facts justify the criticism, the justified bad feelings toward the group are assumed to be unjustified. This makes a minimal justified offence become elevated to an unjustified prejudice, a higher offence. Note how low these are on the list below:

12. Conspiring to control the whole world
13. Systematic teaching hating a population
14. Conspire against a group
15. Hate toward a group by an individual
16. Conspire against an individual
17. Hate toward individual by an individual
18. Disregard for others rights
19. Demonization and denigration of others
20. Unjustified prejudice
21. Ambivalence toward others or "justified prejudice"

You thought we had trouble in River City **February 14, 2014**

Back in the era of the Music Man we had trouble, "Right here in River City.

Trouble with a capital "T" And that rhymes with "P" and that stands for pool!"

Now we still have trouble, but both the meaning of the acronyms and the kind of trouble have changed. Now, although we have "T" that stands for Tea Party and Truth we also have "P" and "L" that stand for Progressive Liberals and Perpetual Lies.

Now we have trouble right here in Washington D.C. with the acronym now standing for Destroying the Country!

Are Satanic forces destroying America? **January 27, 2014**

One threat is that followers of a Satanic (Sura 1:1, 3:54; 2 Cor. 11:14, John 8:44) religion of "piece" (beheadings and dismemberment - Sura 5:33, 8:12) are infiltrating our country, government and military with the ultimate goal of letting us chose between conversion and death (Sura 8:39). The other threat is the promotion and implementation of Saul Alinsky's and Lenin's communistic religion that has been dedicated to Lucifer, the original rebel, in Alinsky's "Rules for Radicals" book. These evil forces are infiltrating out country, revolutionizing our way of life, and rebelling against the biblical creator God to destroy everything that has made America, America, while at the same time censoring and demonizing everything biblical or moral. At least we can verify the source of this evil since it matches Satan's Modus Operandi which is diametrically opposite to God's.

Alinsky stated that there are eight levels of control that must be obtained before you are able to create a socialist state, with the first being the most important.

Healthcare – Control healthcare and you control the people

Poverty – Increase the Poverty level as high as possible, poor people are easier to control and will not fight back if you are providing everything for them to live.

Debt – Increase the debt to an unsustainable level. That way you are able to increase taxes, and this will produce more poverty.

Gun Control – Remove the ability to defend themselves from the Government. That way you are able to create a police state.

Welfare – Take control of every aspect of their lives (Food, Housing, and Income)

Education – Take control of what people read and listen to – take control of what children learn in school.

Religion – Remove the belief in God from the Government and schools

Class Warfare – Divide the people into the wealthy and the poor. This will cause more discontent and it will be easier to take (Tax) the wealthy with the support of the poor.

This is identical to what is being promoted and implemented in our country right now. It is also diametrically opposed to God's nature and biblical values. Most Christians and their pastors seem completely oblivious to these evils. Even those few that realize the true nature of the threats we face don't expose them because of political correctness and intimidation.

Embracing Islam and the Muslim Brotherhood　　　　　　　January 8, 2014

It is strange that Egypt, a largely Muslim nation, has recently classified the Muslim Brotherhood as a terrorist organization, yet America, a Christian nation, has embraced the Muslim Brotherhood and placed their operatives in key government positions. Obama gave the Muslim Brotherhood a special position at his first international speech in Cairo and bent over backwards when the Muslim Brotherhood took over Egypt to send them generous military aid. Then when the Egyptians rejected the Muslim Brotherhood and the Egyptian military took over, Obama cut off the aid. Then we have James Clapper, our Director of National Intelligence, stating that the Muslim Brotherhood is just a secular organization that is no concern to America.

"The document, *"An explanatory Memorandum On the General Strategic Goal for the Group In North America"* was seized by the U.S. government in 2004 and used in the 2008 Holy Land Foundation trial. The document states,

"The Iquan (Muslim Brotherhood) must understand their work in America is a kind of grand Jihad, in eliminating and destroying the Western Civilization from within and sabotaging its miserable house by their hands and the hands of the believers so that it is eliminated and god's religion is made victorious."

This all seems to be consistent with our president fawning over Islam in many speeches and actions while denigrating Christianity. This is exemplified at http://freedomoutpost.com/2013/09/contrast-barack-obamas-quotes-islam-quotes-christianity/ where Obama makes 20 statements promoting Islam and 20 statements denigrating Christianity.

When you add this to the real Islamic Jihad terror at Fort Hood that was classified as "workplace violence" by our government and Obama assigning NASA to promote the Islamic image in science, we can safely say, "Houston we have a problem!"

APPENDIX C
Why does the world hate Israel?

The document below was written by my Sunday school teacher Bob Barlow. It is quoted with permission.

There is an informative DVD available today entitled, **Israel Inside**, from which many of the facts of this article were derived and quoted. Israel and the Jewish people are in the news practically every day. When most people think of Israel, they think of war or religion. However, when one looks at Israel inside, a different picture appears – one of triumph of the human spirit. By the testimony of Israel's own citizens, they have a purpose: "**To find ways of helping other people and nations.**" That feeling of responsibility for the world directly contributes to Israel's accomplishments in the economic, technological and humanitarian arenas.

Education is one of the top priorities in Israel, and every Jewish child learns to read. Israelis are taught to think critically, outside the box. They are not afraid to fail, but use failures as stepping stones, not stumbling blocks. They are taught to take ideas and turn them into action. Israel sees part of their purpose to exist as helping other people. At a recent conference in Tel Aviv, this question was posed to all attendees: "What are you going to do to make the world a better place by the year 2020?"

Despite daily challenges ranging from limited resources to security needs, Israeli creativity and inventiveness help make the world a better place. Israel has made significant advancements in the fields of science, environment, medicine and technology, and has willingly and generously shared these developments with the rest of the world.

Family life is strong in Israel. Israeli families worship together, but they do not force their religious beliefs on any other people of the world. They respect the right of all peoples to worship as they please, and do nothing to hinder the practice of same. The Jewish people think of themselves as a united family. They are confident, thinking, caring for each other, and are resilient against adversity. They build very strong teams that are problem solvers, finding ways to turn adversity into advantage. They invent things. They tackle challenges that others say, "It can't be done."

The nations of the world are being kept in the dark concerning the benefit of this tiny nation in the Middle East. A few of the inventions and contributions of this nation, which are continually being shared with the rest of the world, include the following:

InSightec: Israeli technology has developed a non-invasive surgery that allows treating human beings without cutting the body. This technology allows the treatment of tumors within almost any part of the human body, as well as treating central nervous system diseases like Parkinson's and essential tremor.

ReWalk: An Israeli quadriplegic developed this wearable, robotic exoskeleton that provides powered hip and knee motion to enable individuals with Spinal Cord Injury (paraplegics) to stand upright and walk. For the first time, paralyzed people can walk!

Save A Child's Heart: Since its beginning in 1995, this Israeli organization has saved the lives of over 2500 infant children from 30 countries, more than half of which have been Palestinian children from Gaza and the West Bank. Open heart surgery is performed, at no charge, on infants born with congenital heart conditions.

Netafim: This Israeli company has developed the drip irrigation system which has turned a desert wilderness into a productive farmland. Today Israel is the leading exporter of fruit and vegetables in the world, and they are teaching this irrigation process to the third world, developing countries.

Desalinization: Israel is considered a pioneer in the area of water desalinization, converting salt sea water from the Mediterranean into fresh tap water. In addition, Israel now supplies fresh water to Jordan and the Palestinian Authority.

Technology R&D: Microsoft, Intel, Hewlett-Packard, and Google, have built research and development centers in Israel. Intel Israel remains the cutting edge leader in microprocessor technology development.

Kinect: A line of motion sensing input devices developed in Israel and purchased by Microsoft for Xbox 360 and Xbox One video game consoles and Windows PCs. This became the fastest-selling gaming device in history.

Time to Know: Redefining the way schools teach, Time To Know provides each student with a computer which uses adaptive lesson plans on each topic of the teacher's choosing. This enables each student to work at his or her own pace within the same classroom. The computers inform the teacher if a student is struggling, enabling the teacher to provide one-on-one support to individual students without interrupting the continuity of the curriculum for everyone else.

There is a phrase in Israel that is kept before the Jewish people: "Make the world a better place." **(Tikkam Olam)**

Israel chooses life. Israel simply wants to exist to make the world a better place. Israel is sharing their inventions and discoveries with other nations for the betterment of those citizens. Israel does not want the destruction or annihilation of any people or nation on this earth. Israel does not want to conquer, take over, suppress, or force into submission any nation or people on this earth.

Why, then, do the nations of the world hate Israel? Ask yourself that question. Don't pass it off as irrelevant. Has Israel benefitted the other countries of the world? Awarding of Nobel Prizes began in 1895 and have since included the areas of physics, chemistry, medicine, economics, literature and peace. Of all the individual awards given since the inception of the Nobel Prize organization, 194 of all the Nobel Prize recipients have been **Jews**, and they have been recipients in all six award areas. That is 23% of all the Nobel awards ever awarded. As of 2014, eleven Muslims had received Nobel awards, seven of which were for "peace."

Yet, today, Israel is the only nation that has been targeted for removal from the map of the world. Only an illiterate, ignorant, uneducated person, or a people who are kept in the dark by being told lies about Israel, never allowing them to see their tremendous benefits to their very own nations, would join the voice of "Death to Israel." Those who join that voice will show themselves to be fools, for the God of Israel has stated repeatedly that Israel will be His people forever and ever. And, they are still here, just as God said.

APPENDIX D
"From Slimy Goo, Came Me and You"

In the beginning was nothing; not a house or even a mouse
A universe without matter! What could be sadder?
Everything changed with one Big Bang; evolution produced its first Orangutan

Everything exists because nothing exploded; the very idea seems rather loaded
It's hard to fathom "Ameba to Man" – it's always been Darwin's game plan
From solid rock to four legged crock; now that's an intellectual stumbling block

Time & chance produced its first body part; it was simply the result of a huge cosmic fart
Imagine growing up in primordial soup; it must have felt somewhat like floating in poop
At times my great grandpa was known to be spunky, but come on man! Was he really a monkey?

"The Origin of Species" was Darwin's new book; his theory spread "by hook or by crook"
Richard Dawkin's "The God Delusion" – it's a major cause of so much confusion
Atheists cringe at the sound of "Design" – perhaps they are running from the God who's divine

They say natural selection can lead to perfection; I'd say it's based on wild speculation
Entropy states "Decay is the Way" – Uncle Sam says "public indoctrination" is here to stay
The fossil record is full of large gaps; the theory of evolution is on the verge of collapse

Science is exposing many hoaxes of evolution; could this be the start of a truth revolution
Courage is needed to put Darwin on trial; O Lord may it lead to Christian revival
Never forget that God is good; it's what the evolutionists have never understood
From "Stumbling Blocks of Evolution" by Chris Nitardy

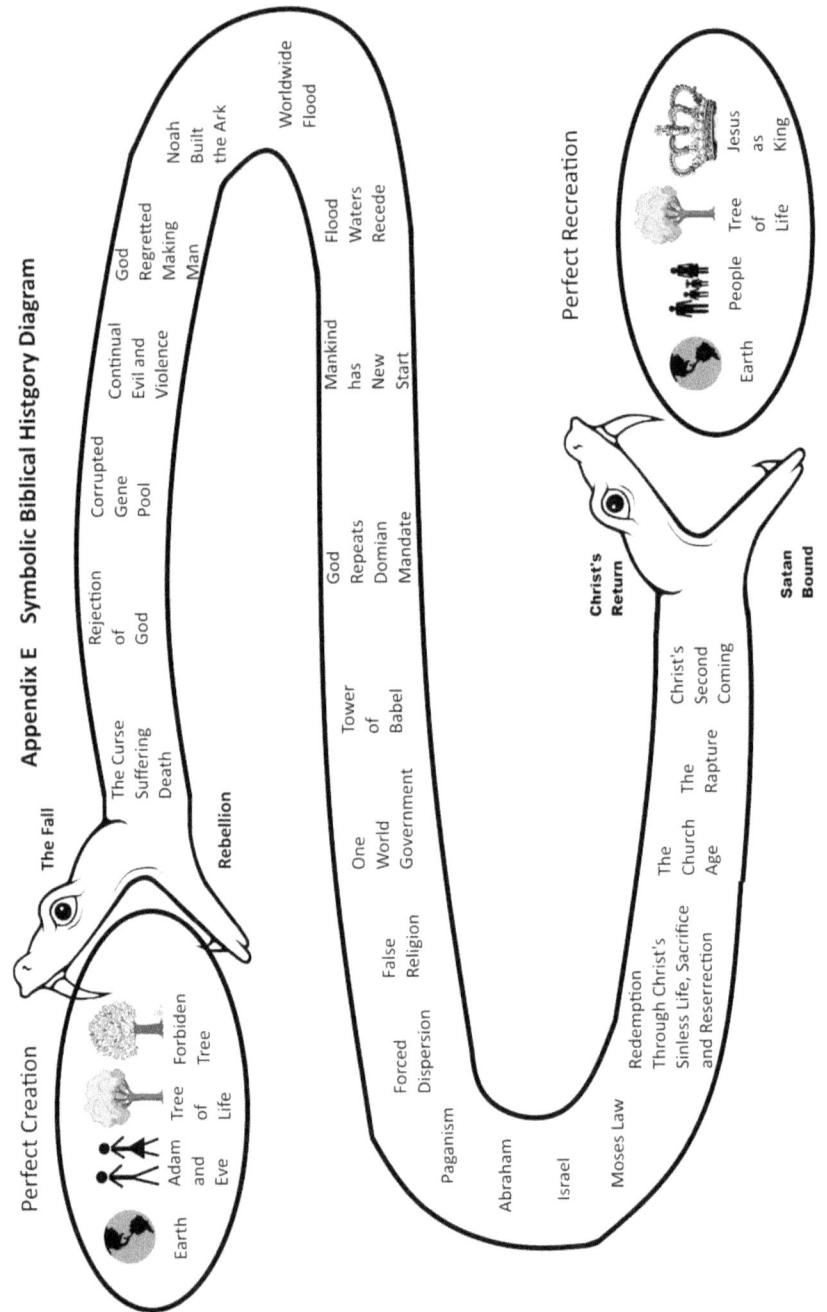

About the author

William (Bill) Nitardy has a degree in Chemical Engineering from the University of Minnesota and was employed at 3M Company for his entire career. Part of his needed knowledge for doing his job was understanding the science of statistics and probability. This knowledge has been beneficial in conceiving and presenting some of the concepts in this book.

His passion is truth and justice. He has been trying to write a book for a number of years relating to truth and justice without being satisfied with the books title, organization and content. Those three finally came together in "Understanding the Anatomy of Evil." In the meantime the writer has written many letters to the editor and had many published. All those that have been written in the last two years have been included in Appendix B.

His hope is that the concepts and thoughts presented in "Understanding the Anatomy of Evil" will help people to unify spiritual, cultural and political truth in their mind as well as evil in the same realms. It seems like we live in a sound bite world where the dots connecting individual beliefs and actions in the various realms are not normally connected to make the big picture visible. Without seeing truth and evil in the broad picture, evil is destined to prevail. His hope is that the dissemination and understanding of this book will expose evil and promote the truth to the glory of God and most importantly help secure people's proper eternal destiny.

Your feedback about the book is desired whether that feedback is positive or negative. Please send feedback to bookfeedback@usfamily.net

Endnotes

Introduction
[1] Dr. David Reagan, Christ in Prophecy, the Death of America, A Prophetic Manifesto, July 25, 2015, The Church Channel.
[2] Ibid.

Chapter 1
[3] Saul Alinsky, Rules for Radicals (Vintage) Initial quotes
[4] "Playboy Interview: Saul Alinsky," Playboy, March 1972. D'Souza, Dinesh (2014-06-02). America: Imagine a World without Her (Kindle Location 3811). Regnery Publishing. Kindle Edition.
[5] http://www.gotquestions.org/it-is-finished.html
[6] http://carm.org/it-is-finished

Chapter 2

Chapter 3
[7] Saul Alinsky, "Rules for Radicals"
[8] http://www.allaboutgod.com/attributes-of-god.htm

Chapter 4

Chapter 5
[9] The internet Merriam-Webster dictionary

Chapter 6

Chapter 7
[10] Charles Krauthammer, "Moral clarity in Gaza," The Washington Post, Published in the St. Paul Pioneer Press on July 19th or 20th, 2014.

Chapter 8

Chapter 9
[11] Archpriest Alexander Mileant, "The Action of Conscience in Man," Orthodox America, Issue 83, Vol. IX, No. 3, September, 1988, http://www.roca.org/OA/83/83b.htm

Chapter 10
[12] Wayne Grudem, Politics According to the Bible," Copyright © 2010, Used by permission of Zondervan, 2010, Introduction, p. 18, www.zondervan.com
[13] Ibid. p. 18
[14] Ibid. pp.18-19
[15] Ibid, pp. 8-10.

Chapter 11
[16] http://en.wikipedia.org/wiki/Secular_humanism
[17] http://en.wikipedia.org/wiki/Secular_humanism#Legal_mentions_in_the_United_States
[18] http://en.wikipedia.org/wiki/Secular_humanism#Legal_mentions_in_the_United_States
[19] http://dictionary.reference.com/browse/coup

[20] http://vftonline.org/Patriarchy/definitions/humanism_religion.htm
[21] http://quotes.liberty-tree.ca/quote/john_dunphy_quote_a71c>
[22] http://americanhumanist.org/Humanism/Humanist_Manifesto_I
[23] Ibid.
[24] Ibid.
[25] Ibid.
[26] Ibid.
[27] Ibid.
[28] Ibid.
[29] Ibid.
[30] Ibid.
[31] Ibid.
[32] Ibid.
[33] Ibid.
[34] Ibid.
[35] Ibid.
[36] Ibid.
[37] Ibid.
[38] Ibid.
[39] Ibid.
[40] Ibid.
[41] Ibid.
[42] Ibid.
[43] Ibid.
[44] Ibid.
[45] Ibid.

Chapter 12
Chapter 13

[46] Killer Angel, George Grant, Reformer Press: p. 104.
[47] Wikipedia, Johann Wolfgang Von Goese, Britannica, 2002 ed. CD-ROM.
[48] Islam: A challenge to Faith, Samuel M. Zwermer, F.R.G.S., New Y ork, 907, p. 112.
[49] In Search of Godn the Mother, Roller, p. 265.
[50] Maarten J. Vermaseren, Cybele and Attis, trans. A.M.H. Lemmers, Thames and Hudson, 1977 cited in Baring and Cashford, op. cit.
[51] Saint John of Damascus Against Heresies: The Fountain of Knowledge.
[52] Walid Shoebat and Joel Richardson, "God's War on Terror," 2nd Addition, 2010, p. 391-392.
[53] The Hastings' Encyclopedia of Religion and Ethics, volume I. p. 326.
[54] Arthur Jeffrey, ed., Islam: Mohammed and His Religion (1958), P.85.
[55] Ibid.
[56] Walid Shoebat and Joel Richardson, "God's War on Terror," 2nd Addition, 2010, p. 384-385.
[57] Dictionary of Deities and Demons in the Bible, p. 393.

[58] Islamic and Arabic Names Collection, Muslims Internet Dictionary.
[59] Clair Tisdall, The Original Sources of The Qur'an, Chapter II, page 13, also see Van Netton, Allah Divine Demonic, p. 94.
[60] Walid Shoebat and Joel Richardson, "God's War on Terror," 2nd edition, 2010, p. 386-387.
[61] W.H.T. Gairdner, The Reproach of Islam, (Foreign Mission Committee of the Church of Scotland, 1911) p.158.
[62] Karen Armstrong, Mohammad: A Biography of the Prophet (Harper Collins Books, 1993), p. 46.
[63] A. Guillaume, The Life of Mohammad, (Oxford University Press, 2001) p. 106.
[64] Ibid.
[65] At-Tabari Vol. 9, p. 157, note 1151.
[66] Sahih Bukhari, Volume 6, Book 60, Number 478.
[67] Walid Shoebat and Joel Richardson, "God's War on Terror," 2nd edition, 2010, p. 159-160.
[68] Saint John of Damascus (676-749) Against Heresies: The fountain of Knowledge.
[69] Histories 1:131.
[70] B. al-Kalbi, N.A. Faris 1952, pp. 14-15.
[71] Walid Shoebat and Joel Richardson, "God's War on Terror," 2nd edition, 2010, p. 388.
[72] Wikipedia, The Story of The Black Stone and Mohammad son of Abdullah.
[73] IslamOnline.net, Various aspects of Haj.
[74] Walid Shoebat and Joel Richardson, "God's War on Terror," 2nd edition, 2010, pp. 389-390.
[75] Matt Barber, "Muslim Goes Boom," December 12, 2014, http://www.wnd.com/2014/12/muslim-go-boom/

Chapter 14
[76] http://www.goodreads.com/quotes/553-if-you-tell-a-big-enough-lie-and-tell-it
[77] http://en.wikipedia.org/wiki/Big_Lie
[78] Yad Vashem - Adolf Hitler, *Mein Kampf*, Houghton Mifflin, New York: Hutchinson Publ. Ltd., London, 1969, Mitchell G. Bard, 7/15/2015, p. 134, http://www.jewishvirtuallibrary.org/jsource/Holocaust/kampf.html#2
[79] Thomas Woodward, 'The Roaring Nineties: David Takes on Goliath,' *Doubts About Darwin: A History of Intelligent Design*, (Grand Rapids, Mi, Baker Books, 2003), 77.
[80] Stephen Jay Gould, '*The Panda's Thumb* (New York: w. W. Norton, 1985). Or Stephen Jay Gould, *Natural History*, 86(5): 13 (1977).
[81] Stephen Jay Gould, "The Episodic Nature of Evolutionary Change," *The Panda's Thumb*, (New York: W. W. Norton, 1985), 182ff.
[82] Lewontin, Billions and Billions of Demons, The New York Review, January 9, 1997.
[83] Richard Dawkins, *The Blind Watchmaker* (New York: W. W. Norton, 1985).
[84] Darwin, Charles, *The Origin of Species* (1st edition) (New York: Avenel Books, Crown Publishers, 1979) p. 292
[85] Michael J. Behe, *Darwin's Black Box* (New York: Free Press, 1996).

[86] Thomas Woodward, 'The Matrix of Stories in Darwin on Trial,' *Doubts About Darwin: A History of Intelligent Design*, (Grand Rapids, Mi, Baker Books, 2003), 119.
[87] Charles Darwin, *The Origin of the Species* (New York: Bantam Books, 1859).
[88] Modern Creation Trilogy: Science & Creation, Vol. 2, 'Evolution is not Even Possible,' Henry M. Morris & John D. Morris, (Green Forest AZ: Master Books, 1996), p. 131. Used with permission from the publisher.
[89] Ibid., p. 133
[90] Ibid., P. 133
[91] Ibid., p. 133
[92] Thomas Woodward, 'Murmurs of Decent.' *Doubts About Darwin: A History of Intelligent Design*, (Grand Rapids, MI, Baker Books, 2003), p. 43.
[93] George Wald, "The Origin of Life," *Scientific American*, 191:48, May 1954.
[94] Michael J. Behe, 'All the World's a Stage,' *The Edge of Evolution* (New York: Free Press, 2007), 235.
[95] Piltdown Man – Wikipedia, the free encyclopedia, 29 August 2008, <
[96] From *BreakPoint*, January 28, 2000, reprinted with permission of Prison Fellowship, www.breakpoint.org.
[97] G.G. Simpson, W. Beck, "An introduction to biology," Harcort Brace and World, New York, 1965, p. 241, Darwinism Refuted.com, http://www.darwinismrefuted.com/embryology_04.html#319, August 29 2008.
[98] Keith S. Thomson, "Ontogeny and Phylogeny Recapitulated," *American Scientist*, vol. 76, May/June 1988, p. 273.
[99] Jonathan Wells, 'Haeckel's Embryos,' *Icons of Evolution*, (Washington D.C.: Regnery, 2000), p. 82-83.
[100] *Illustrated London News*, June 24 1922.
[101] W. K. Gregory, *Science* 66:579 (1927).
[102] Duane T. Gish, 'The Origin of Man,' *Evolution: The Fossils Still say No!* (El Cajon, CA: Institute for Creation Research, 1985), p. 327-328.
[103] Duane T. Gish, 'The Origin of Man,' *Evolution: The Fossils Still say No!* (El Cajon, CA: Institute for Creation Research, 1985), p. 31.
[104] Duane T. Gish, 'The Origin of Man,' *Evolution: The Fossils Still say No!* (El Cajon, CA: Institute for Creation Research, 1985), p. 31.
[105] Jonathan Wells, 'Peppered Moths,' *Icons of Evolution*, (Washington D.C.: Regnery, 2000), p. 138.
[106] Jonathan Wells, 'Four-Winged Fruit Flies,' *Icons of Evolution*, (Washington D.C.: Regnery, 2000), p. 177-193.

Chapter 15
[107] "Atheism Defined," Philosophies All About, < http://www.allaboutphilosophy.org/atheism.htm>.
[108] Thinkexit.com, John Dewey Quotes. < http://thinkexist.com/quotes/john_dewey/4.html>.
[109] David Greenburg, "It Didn't Start with Einstein," Slate, < http://slate.msn.com/id/74164/>, (February 3, 2000).

Chapter 16
Chapter 17
[110] Craig Vincent Mitchell, Roy W. Spencer, and G. Cornelis van Kooten, et al., *A Renewed Call to Truth, Prudence, and Protection of the Poor: An Evangelical Examination of the Theology, Science, and Economics of Global Warming* (Burke, VA: Cornwall Alliance, 2009). : http://www.cornwallalliance.org/docs/a-renewed-call-to-truth-prudence-and-protection-of-the-poor.pdf

[111] http://www.naturalnews.com/040448_solar_radiation_global_warming_debunked.html

[112] Craig Vincent Mitchell, Roy W. Spencer, and G. Cornelis van Kooten, et al., *A Renewed Call to Truth, Prudence, and Protection of the Poor: An Evangelical Examination of the Theology, Science, and Economics of Global Warming* (Burke, VA: Cornwall Alliance, 2009). : http://www.cornwallalliance.org/docs/a-renewed-call-to-truth-prudence-and-protection-of-the-poor.pdf

Chapter 18
[113] Josh McDowell & Bob Hostetler, *The New Tolerance*, (Carol Stream IL: Tyndale House, 1998).

Chapter 19
[114] Bill Lind, http://www.academia.org/the-origins-of-political-correctness/

[115] Ibid.

Chapter 20
[116] Wikipedia online dictionary

Chapter 21
[117] Brannon Howse, "One Nation Under Man," p. 47

[118] Bill Nitardy, "A false foundation for 'Dechristianizing' America," Accent, Faith and Religion section (Destin, Fl: The Destin Log, 2005), p. B11.

[119] William Rehnquist's dissent in the 1985 decision, *Wallace v. Jaffre*, Reprinted as a Special Supplement to *The Journal of the American Center for Law and Justice*, Virginia Beach, Va.

[120] David Limbaugh, *Persecution: How Liberals are Waging War Against Christianity* (Washington D. C.: Regnery, 2003).

Chapter 22
[121] Mike Gendron, http://www.pro-gospel.org/site/cpage.asp?sec_id=180014816&cpage_id=180064904

[122] Mike Gendron, http://www.pro-gospel.org/site/cpage.asp?cpage_id=180066646&sec_id=180014816

[123] Ibid.

[124] http://www.pro-gospel.org/site/cpage.asp?cpage_id=180066646&sec_id=180014816

[125] Ibid.

[126] Ibid.

[127] Ibid.

[128] Ibid.

[129] http://www.pro-gospel.org/site/cpage.asp?cpage_id=180066646&sec_id=180014816
[130] Ibid.
[131] Ibid.
[132] http://proclaimingthegospel.org/equip/articles/52-purgatory-purifying-fire-or-fatal-fable
[133] Ibid
[134] Ibid.
[135] http://proclaimingthegospel.org/equip/articles/60-sola-scriptura
[136] The Online Wikipedia

Chapter 23
[137] Rhonda Byrne, "A Return to Love," (New York, NY: Simon & Schuster Adult Publishing Group, 2006)
[138] Helen Schucman, A Course in Miracles," (Mill Valley, CA: Foundation for Inner Peace, 2007)
[139] Warren Smith, "A Wonderful Deception," (Silverton, Oregon: Lighthouse Trails Publishing, 2009), p.12.
[140] George D. Exoo and John Gregory Tweed, "Peale's Secret Source" (*Lutheran Quarterly: A Journal for the Evangelical Lutheran Church*, Vol. IX, No. 2, Summer 1995, Marquette University, Milwaukee, Wisconsin), sent by Pastor Larry DeBruyn, Franklin Baptist Church, New Palestine, Indiana.
[141] Neale Donald Walsch, *The New Revelations: A Conversation with God* (New York, NY: Atria Books, 2002), p. 281; Warren Smith, *Decieved on Purpose*, op. cit., pp 65-67.
[142] Dave Hunt and T.A. McMahon, *The Seduction of Christianity: Spiritual Discernment in The Last Days* (Eugene, OR: Harvest House, 1985), p. 153, citing Robert Schuller from his address at Unity Village; Unity tape.
[143] Warren Smith, "A Wonderful Deception," (Silverton, Oregon: Lighthouse Trails Publishing, 2009), pp. 62-63.

Chapter 24
[144] http://www.amnh.org/education/resources/rfl/web/essaybooks/earth/p_hutton.html
[145] http://www.victorianweb.org/science/lyell.html
[146] Ibid.
[147] http://evolution.berkeley.edu/evolibrary/article/history_12
[148] Thomas Woodward, 'The Roaring Nineties: David Takes on Goliath,' *Doubts About Darwin: A History of Intelligent Design*, (Grand Rapids, Mi, Baker Books, 2003), 77.
[149] Lewontin, Billions and Billions of Demons, The New York Review, January 9, 1997.
[150] George Wald, "The Origin of Life," *Scientific American*, 191:48, May 1954.
[151] http://www.dove.org/expelled-no-intelligence-allowed-why-ben-stein-says-no-lie-lives-forever/
[152] http://onenewsnow.com/legal-courts/2014/07/28/lawsuit-follows-christians-firing-from-university?utm_source=OneNewsNow&utm_medium=email&utm_term=16778823&utm_content=869855372660&utm_campaign=14817#.U9agzPp0xjo

[153] "Atheism Defined," Philosophies All About, <http://www.allaboutphilosophy.org/atheism.htm>.

[154] Thinkexit.com, John Dewey Quotes. <http://thinkexist.com/quotes/john_dewey/4.html>.

[155] http://en.wikipedia.org/wiki/Relativism

[156] Craig Vincent Mitchell, Roy W. Spencer, and G. Cornelis van Kooten, et al., *A Renewed Call to Truth, Prudence, and Protection of the Poor: An Evangelical Examination of the Theology, Science, and Economics of Global Warming* (Burke, VA: Cornwall Alliance, 2009). : http://www.cornwallalliance.org/docs/a-renewed-call-to-truth-prudence-and-protection-of-the-poor.pdf

[157] http://www.thenewamerican.com/tech/environment/item/15624-cooking-climate-consensus-data-97-of-scientists-affirm-agw-debunked.

[158] http://www.cfact.org/2014/03/18/top-scientists-debunk-climate-change-myths/

[159] Ibid.

[160] Ibid.

[161] http://www.forbes.com/sites/jamestaylor/2011/11/23/climategate-2-0-new-e-mails-rock-the-global-warming-debate/

[162] Josh McDowell & Bob Hostetler, *The New Tolerance*, (Carol Stream IL: Tyndale House, 1998).

[163] http://en.wikipedia.org/wiki/Precedent

[164] Bill Nitardy, "A false foundation for 'Dechristianizing' America," Accent, Faith and Religion section (Destin, Fl: The Destin Log, 2005), p. B11.

[165] Brannon Howse, "One Nation Under Man," p. 47

[166] http://en.wikipedia.org/wiki/Everson_v._Board_of_Education

[167] William Rehnquist's dissent in the 1985 decision, *Wallace v. Jaffre*, Reprinted as a Special Supplement to *The Journal of the American Center for Law and Justice*, Virginia Beach, Va.

[168] Musings on Secular Humanism and public education; response to the Humanist Manifesto, Psychiatry & the new world order, http://www.1prophetspeaks.com

[169] http://vftonline.org/Patriarchy/definitions/humanism_religion.htm

[170] Brannon Howse, "Grave Influence," p. 227-228.

[171] Benjamin Wiker, Ph.D., "10 Books that Screwed up the World," Regency Publishing, Washington DC, The future of Illusion, P. 167.

[172] Benjamin Wiker, Ph.D., "10 Books that Screwed up the World," Regency Publishing, Washington DC, The future of Illusion, P. 168.

[173] Brannon Howse, "Grave Influence," p. 299-300.

[174] Ibid., p. 250-251

[175] Bill Lind, http://www.academia.org/the-origins-of-political-correctness/

[176] R. Keith Martin, "It's Over," p. 25-26.

[177] Friedrich A. Hayek, *Law, Legislation and Liberty*, volume 2, *The Mirage of Social Justice* (University of Chicago Press, 1976), 65.

[178] http://townhall.com/columnists/meredithturney/2009/06/09/americas_first_experiment_with_socialism/page/full

[179] E. Calvin Beisner, *Social Justice: How Good Intentions Undermine Justice and Gospel*. Washington, D.C.: Family Research Council, Cornwall Alliance for the Stewardship of Creation, and Concerned Women for America, 2013. Accessed August 6, 2014. http://downloads.frc.org/EF/EF13E133.pdf.

[180] Robert Higgs, "Communism's Persistent Pull," *The Beacon Blog*, December 9, 2010, online December 11, 2010, at http://www.independent.org/blog/index.php?p=8826.

[181] Francis Brown, S. R. Driver, and Charles A. Briggs, eds., *A Hebrew and English Lexicon of the Old Testament* (Oxford: Clarendon Press, 1907, 1953, 1978), p. 1030; boldface and parentheses original.

[182] Ibid.

[183] The verb *shamat* appears elsewhere in the OT only five times (2 Samuel 6:6 [parallel to 1 Chronicles 13:9]; 2 Kings 9:33; Psalm 141:6; Jeremiah 17:4). In none is a permanent dropping implied, and in the last the context shows that it must be temporary.

[184] Arthur G. Gish, *Living in Christian Community* (Scottsdale, PA: Herald Press, 1979), 70.

[185] José Porfirio Miranda, *Communism in the Bible*, translated by Robert R. Barr (Maryknoll, NY: Orbis, 1982), 7.

[186] Ronald J. Sider, *Rich Christians in an Age of Hunger*, 2d ed. (Downers Grove, IL: InterVarsity Press, 1984), 96, 98.

[187] See R. C. H. Lenski, *The Interpretation of I and II Corinthians* (Minneapolis: Augsburg, 1963), 1145–1147.

[188] See Colin Brown, ed., *The New International Dictionary of New Testament Theology*, 3 volumes (Grand Rapids: Zondervan, 1967, 1969, 1971), 2:361–371 (on judgment), 3:347–352 (on right, worthy), and 3:352–377 (on righteousness, justification), and for studies particularly focusing on economic applications, see E. Calvin Beisner, "Justice and Poverty: Two Views Contrasted," *Transformation*, vol. 10, no. 1 (January/April 1993), 16–22, revised and reprinted in *Christianity and Economics in the Post-Cold War Era: The Oxford Declaration and Beyond*, edited by Herbert Schlossberg, Vinay Samuel, and Ronald J. Sider (Grand Rapids: Eerdmans, 1994), 57–80.

[189] Gleason Archer, R. Laird Harris, and Bruce Waltke, eds., *Theological Wordbook of the Old Testament* (reprint edition, Chicago: Moody Publishers, 2003), entry 1879.

[190] Archer, Harris, and Waltke, eds., *Theological Wordbook*, entry 2443.

[191] Archer, Harris, and Waltke, eds., *Theological Wordbook*, entry 1879.

[192] Archer, Harris, and Waltke, eds., *Theological Wordbook*, entry 426.

[193] Walter Bauer, *A Greek-English Lexicon of the New Testament and Other Early Christian Literature*, 2d ed., edited by William F. Arndt and F. Wilbur Gingrich (Chicago and London: University of Chicago Press, 1979), 195–198.

[194] Bauer, *Lexicon*, 450–453.

[195] Beisner, "Justice and Poverty," in *Christianity and Economics in the Post-Cold War Era*, 64.

[196] Compare Exodus 23:3, 6; Leviticus 19:15; Deuteronomy 16:19; Job 13:10; Proverbs 18:5; 24:23; 28:21; 1 Timothy 5:21; James 2:1–9; 3:17). God Himself is the chief exemplar of impartiality in judgment (Deuteronomy 10:17; 2 Chronicles 19:7; Job 13:8; Acts

10:34; Rom. 2:11; Ephesians 6:9; Colossians 3:25; 1 Peter 1:17), and He condemns all partiality in judgment or government (Psalm 82:2; Malachi 2:9).

[197] E. Calvin Beisner, *Social Justice: How Good Intentions Undermine Justice and Gospel*. Washington, D.C.: Family Research Council, Cornwall Alliance for the Stewardship of Creation, and Concerned Women for America, 2013. Accessed August 6, 2014. http://downloads.frc.org/EF/EF13E133.pdf.

[198] E. Calvin Beisner, Social Justice; Order at http://www.ecalvinbeisner.com/

Chapter 25

[199] Marvin J. Rosenthal, "The War of the Ages," Volume 26, No 2, May 2015, pp. 12-13.

[200] Ibid.

[201] Ibid.

[202] Ibid.

[203] Coffman, Michael (2012-06-01). Plundered, How Progressive Ideology is Destroying America (Kindle Locations 936-937). . Kindle Edition.

[204] Kenneth Weinstein. "Individual Rights v. The General Will: An historical perspective on John Locke & Jean-Jacques Rousseau and a look at how today's environmental movement is rapidly advancing one above the other." CFACT Briefing Paper #111 - Part A, August 2002. http:// www.cfact.org/ Issue Archive/ Limited% 20Government% 20Under%20Assault% 20Jean-Jacques% 20Rousseau% 20Versus% 20John% 20Locke.pdf

[205] Coffman, Michael (2012-06-01). Plundered, How Progressive Ideology is Destroying America (Kindle Locations 937-946). . Kindle Edition.

[206] Coffman, Michael (2012-06-01). Plundered, How Progressive Ideology is Destroying America (Kindle Locations 958-971). . Kindle Edition.

[207] Letter to the Officers of the First Brigade of the Third Division of the Militia of Massachusetts, 11 October 1798, In: Revolutionary Services and Civil Life of General William Hull (New York, 1848), Pp 265-6. http:// books.google.com/ books?id = E2kFAAAAQAAJ& dq = editions% 3AVsZcW99fWPgC& pg = PA265# v = onepage& q& f = false There are some differences in the version that appeared in The Works of John Adams (Boston, 1854), vol. 9, pp. 228-9, most notably the words "or gallantry" instead of "and licentiousness http:// books.google.com/ books?id = PZYKAQAAIAAJ& pg = PA228# v = onepage& q& f = false

[208] 2 Timothy 3: 1-9, especially verse 5. http:// www.biblegateway.com/ passage/? search = 2% 20tim% 203: 1-9& version = NKJV

[209] Coffman, Michael (2012-06-01). Plundered, How Progressive Ideology is Destroying America (Kindle Locations 971-995). . Kindle Edition.

[210] John Locke. Second Treatise Government. Chapter Fourteen, 1690. http:// libertyonline.hypermall.com/ Locke/ second/ second_frame.html. Coffman, Michael (2012-06-01). Plundered, How Progressive Ideology is Destroying America (Kindle Location 998). . Kindle Edition.

[211] Nancie and Roger Marzulla, Property Rights, Understanding Government Takings and Environmental Regulation. (Rockville, Maryland: Government Institutes, Inc., 1997), p. 2. Coffman, Michael (2012-06-01). Plundered, How Progressive Ideology is Destroying America (Kindle Location 998). . Kindle Edition.

[212] Ibid. Coffman, Michael (2012-06-01). Plundered, How Progressive Ideology is Destroying America (Kindle Location 998). . Kindle Edition.

[213] Lynch v. Household Finance Corporation, 405 U.S. 538, 92 S. Ct. 1113, March 23, 1972. http:// laws.findlaw.com/ us/ 405/ 538. Html. Coffman, Michael (2012-06-01). Plundered, How Progressive Ideology is Destroying America (Kindle Locations 998-1012). . Kindle Edition.

[214] Ken Weinstein. Individual Rights v. The General Will. CFACT, 2002, Briefing Paper 111. Coffman, Michael (2012-06-01). Plundered, How Progressive Ideology is Destroying America (Kindle Location 1034). . Kindle Edition.

[215] Jean-Jacques Rousseau. The Social Contract. Book I, 7-The Sovereign, Paragraph 8. 1762. http:// www.constitution.org/ jjr/ socon_01. Htm. Coffman, Michael (2012-06-01). Plundered, How Progressive Ideology is Destroying America (Kindle Location 1084). . Kindle Edition.

[216] Ibid.

[217] Coffman, Michael (2012-06-01). Plundered, How Progressive Ideology is Destroying America (Kindle Location 1029-1078). . Kindle Edition.

[218] Coffman, Michael (2012-06-01). Plundered, How Progressive Ideology is Destroying America (Kindle Location 1114). . Kindle Edition.

[219] New International Version. Coffman, Michael (2012-06-01). Plundered, How Progressive Ideology is Destroying America (Kindle Location 1176). . Kindle Edition.

[220] Jean-Jacques Rousseau. The Social Contract. Book 4, 8-Civil Religion, Paragraph 33. 1762. http:// www.constitution.org/ jjr/ socon_04. Htm. Coffman, Michael (2012-06-01). Plundered, How Progressive Ideology is Destroying America (Kindle Location 1193). . Kindle Edition.

[221] Ibid. Coffman, Michael (2012-06-01). Plundered, How Progressive Ideology is Destroying America (Kindle Location 1193). . Kindle Edition.

[222] Grace Denison. Jean Jacques Rousseau – —Father of the French Revolution. Reading Revolutions: Intellectual History, University of Maine, 2005-2006. http:// hua.umf.maine.edu/ Reading Revolutions/ Rousseau.html. Coffman, Michael (2012-06-01). Plundered, How Progressive Ideology is Destroying America (Kindle Location 1238). . Kindle Edition.

[223] Coffman, Michael (2012-06-01). Plundered, How Progressive Ideology is Destroying America (Kindle Location 1193). . Kindle Edition.

[224] https://www.jewishvirtuallibrary.org/jsource/History/Suez_War.html

[225] Ibid.

[226] Ibid.

[227] Ibid.

[228] David Reagan, Christ in Prophecy, "The Wars of the End Times." Part 2, http://christinprophecy.org/programs/sermon/

Chapter 26

[229] Stanly Fish, The New York Times, The Opinion Pages, Opinionator, "Obama's, D'Souza, and Anti-Colonialism," Aug. 27, 2012,

http://opinionator.blogs.nytimes.com/2012/08/27/obama-dsouza-and-anti-colonialism/?_php=true&_type=blogs&_r=0

[230] Desdamona | eNotes Newbie, Posted November 27, 2008, http://www.enotes.com/homework-help/how-can-we-discribe-usa-an-post-colonialism-49825

[231] Mark Harrison, Quora, "On the Whole, was Colonialism a good or bad thing,? http://www.quora.com/On-the-whole-was-colonialism-a-good-or-bad-thing

[232] Nile Gardiner, Ph.D. and Morgan Lorraine Roach, Obama's top 10 apologies: "How the president has humiliated a superpower," http://www.heritage.org/research/reports/2009/06/barack-obamas-top-10-apologies-how-the-president-has-humiliated-a-superpower.

[233] Dinesh D'Souza, "America: Imagine a World without Her," Movie, Lionsgate and D'Souza Entertainment, 2013.

Chapter 27

[234] Bill Nitardy, Aug. 14, 2014

[235] R. Keith Martin, :It's Over," 2010, p. 6.

[236] Ibid., p. 7-8.

[237] Ibid.

[238] Ibid.

[239] R. Keith Martin, "It's Over," p. 13-15.

[240] How did the USA become so wealthy, http://www.answers.com/Q/How_did_the_USA_become_so_wealthy

[241] Terry Miller, Kim R. Holmes, and Edwin Feulner, eds., 2012 Index of Economic Freedom (Washington, DC: Heritage Foundation/ New York: The Wall Street Journal, 2012) . The index is also available at www.heritage.org/ index/ default . Another excellent source on this topic is James Gwartney, Robert Lawson, and Joshua Hall, Economic Freedom of the World: 2012 Annual Report (Vancouver, BC : Fraser Institute, 2012). It is also available at www.freetheworld.org . Asmus, Barry; Grudem, Wayne (2013-08-31). The Poverty of Nations: A Sustainable Solution (p. 162). Crossway. Kindle Edition.

[242] Asmus, Barry; Grudem, Wayne (2013-08-31). The Poverty of Nations: A Sustainable Solution (pp. 135-136). Crossway. Kindle Edition.

[243] Arther Herman, "How America got Rich," http://www.commentarymagazine.com/article/how-america-got-rich/

[244] D'Souza, Dinesh (2014-06-02). America: Imagine a World without Her (Kindle Locations 1021-1037). Regnery Publishing. Kindle Edition.

[245] Ibid

[246] R. Keith Martin, "It's Over," 2010, p. 21-22

[247] Alexander Fraser Tyler

[248] R. Keith Martin, "It's Over," p. 340-341.

[249] Sylvia Thompson, Renew America, October 26, 2015, http://www.renewamerica.com/columns/sthompson/151026

[250] Rosa Koire, http://www.democratsagainstunagenda21.com/

[251] Ibid.

[252] http://www.theblaze.com/stories/2012/11/19/what-is-agenda-21-after-watching-this-you-may-not-want-to-know/
[253] http://www.garykah.org/GaryKah/Index.html
[254] Ibid.
[255] Ibid.
[256] "Planetary Sustainable Development and the Vatican," Michael Snyder, Hope for the World Update, Summer 2015.
[257] http://www.garykah.org/GaryKah/Index.html
[258] "Rock Star says Pope Francis is 'My Hero'," Pastor Hal Mayer, Prophetic Intelligence Briefing, September 2, 2015.
[259] Ibid.
[260] http://www.garykah.org/GaryKah/Obama%26thePope.html

Chapter 28
[261] "Hillary's 22 Biggest Scandals," Whistleblower, June 2015, p. 17.
[262] Ibid, p. 17
[263] Ibid, p. 17-18
[264] Ibid, p. 18
[265] "Another Clinton Associate Found Dead, Bill and Hillary's Body-Count Increases," The Political Insider, http://www.thepoliticalinsider.com/another-clinton-associate-found-dead-bill-hillarys-body-count-increases/
[266] "Hillary's 22 Biggest Scandals," Whistleblower, June 2015, p. 13.
[267] Ibid, p. 13
[268] "Another Clinton Associate Found Dead, Bill and Hillary's Body-Count Increases," The Political Insider, http://www.thepoliticalinsider.com/another-clinton-associate-found-dead-bill-hillarys-body-count-increases/
[269] Ibid.
[270] "Hillary's 22 Biggest Scandals," Whistleblower, June 2015, p. 15.
[271] Ibid, p. 12
[272] Ibid, p. 12-13.
[273] Jonathon M. Seidl, "Bachmann Hits Back at Critics Regarding Her Letter About Muslim Brotherhood and Its U.S. Tentacles," July 19, 2012, http://www.theblaze.com/stories/2012/07/19/bachmann-hits-back-at-mccain-critics-regarding-her-letter-about-muslim-brotherhood-and-its-u-s-tentacles/
[274] "Hillary's 22 Biggest Scandals," Whistleblower, June 2015, p. 11.
[275] Ibid.
[276] Ibid, p. 11
[277] Ibid, p. 16
[278] Ibid, p. 13-14
[279] Ibid, p. 14
[280] Ibid, p. 8
[281] Ibid, Leo Hohmann, p. 22-23.
[282] Ibid, p. 23.
[283] Ibid, p. 23-24.

[284] Ibid, Jerome R. Corsi, p. 34.
[285] Ibid, p. 34-35
[286] Ibid, David Kupelian, p. 4.
[287] Ibid, David Kupelian, p. 4
[288] Ibid, p. 5.
[289] Ibid, p. 5.

Chapter 29
Chapter 30
[290] Dr. David Reagan, *Christ in Prophecy Study Guide*, (McKinney, TX: Lamb and Lion Ministries, 200X).
[291] Peter W. Stoner, *Science Speaks*. (Chicago: Moody Press, 1963), p. 100-107.
[292] Ra McLaughlin, Third Millennium, Old Testament of Composition, http://www.thirdmill.org/answers/answer.asp/file/99963.qna/category/ot/page/questions/site/iiim, September 9, 2008.
[293] William Keonig, *Eye to Eye: Facing the Consequences of Dividing Israel* (Alexandria, VA: About Him, 2004).
[294] Propethic Technology, http://www.harvardhouse.com/prophetictech/new/linear.htm, September 9, 2008.
[295] Israel in Prophecy, August 6, 2008, http://www.thoughts.com/journeyman/blog/israel-in-prophesy-133905/, September 9, 2008.
[296] thoughts.com
[297] http://www.jewishvirtuallibrary.org/jsource/Quote/TwainJews.html
[298] UnitedJerusalem.com, *Israel Wars, Maps & History*, <http://www.unitedjerusalem.com/HISTORICAL_PERSPECTIVES/Israel_Wars_Maps_History/israel_wars_maps_history.asp#anchor1_map1947>, September 10, 2008.
[299] Quote from Charles Krauthammer – The Weekly Standard, May 11, 1998, http://zoadc.org/2011/12/14/a-brief-history-of-israel-and-the-jewish-people/
[300] http://www.science.co.il/History-Palestine.php
[301] D. James Kennedy, "Why I believe in the Bible," *Why I Believe*, (Nashville: Word Publishing, 1999), p. 4-7, http://www.harpercollinschristian.com/
[302] Ibid.
[303] Ibid.
[304] Frank Harber, "The Bible is True," *Reasons for Believing*, (Green Forest, AZ: New Leaf Press, 1998), p. 56.
[305] Ibid., p. 66.
[306] Ibid., P. 66-67.
[307] Ibid., P. 67.
[308] Ibid., P. 67-68.
[309] Ibid., P. 81.
[310] Ibid., p. 83.

www.ingramcontent.com/pod-product-compliance
Lightning Source LLC
LaVergne TN
LVHW021049050725
815432LV00035B/405